JOURNALISM IN AMERICA
An Introduction to the News Media

Journalism in America

★★★★★★★★★★★★★★★★★★★★★★★★★★★★★★★

An Introduction to the News Media

★★★★★★★★★★★★★★★★★★★★★★★★★★★★★★★

THOMAS ELLIOTT BERRY

West Chester State College

West Chester, Pennsylvania

COMMUNICATION ARTS BOOKS

HASTINGS HOUSE, PUBLISHERS · New York 10016

LIBRARY OF CONGRESS CATALOGING IN PUBLICATION DATA

Berry, Thomas Elliott.   Journalism in America.

  (Communication arts books)
  Bibliography: p.
  Includes index.
  1. Journalism. 2. Journalism—United States.
I. Title.
PN4775.B45   070.4′0973   76-6565
ISBN 0-8038-3712-7
ISBN 0-8038-3713-5 pbk.

11024

Published simultaneously in Canada by
Saunders of Toronto Ltd., Don Mills, Ontario

Designed by Al Lichtenberg
Printed in the United States of America

Contents

Preface   ix

1. JOURNALISM—AN OVERVIEW   **1**
The Role and Influence of the Media—The Media and Mass
Culture—The Value of the Media—Recent Developments in
Journalism

**2. RECENT ISSUES IN THE FIELD OF
MASS COMMUNICATIONS**   **7**
Freedom of Expression—Radio and Television—The Mass Au-
dience—Prestige—Defamation and Privacy—The Future of the
Newspaper

3. THE NEWS STORY   **26**
What is News?—Finding the News—The Writing and Structure
of the Newspaper News Story—Style of the News Story—
Rewriting—Treatment of News; Slanting and Coloring—Cut
Lines—"The Journalistic Style"—Interpretative Reporting—
Examples for Discussion

4. INTERVIEWING   70
Requisities for Successful Interviewing—Kinds of Interviews; Qualities and Problems—Note Taking

5. THE NEWSPAPER FEATURE STORY   83
What is the Feature Story?—Abilities Needed for Feature Writing—Sources of the Feature Story—The Lead in the Feature Story—Examples for Discussion

6. PICTURES IN NEWSPAPERS   106
The Photographer—Pictures in the Newspaper Operation—Qualities of Effective Photographs—Picture Improvement—Some Representative Pictures—Sources of Pictures

7. NEWSPAPER COPY EDITING   132
Printing the Modern Newspaper—Photocomposition—The Copy Editor Handles the Story—Headlines—Other Work of the Copy Desk—Type

8. MAKE-UP   168
Make-Up as an Art—Principles and Patterns of Make-Up—Balanced Make-Up—Unbalanced Make-Up—Using Make-Up Patterns—Other Guiding Points—Examples of Make-Up

9. EDITORIAL POLICY   190
What is Editorial Policy?—Conditions Affecting Editorial Policy—Finances—Responsibilities of the Press—The Tone of the Paper—Demands of the Readers—Political Outlook—Business Considerations—Religious Considerations—Ethnic and Social Considerations—Patriotic Considerations—Personal and Group Considerations—Whims of the Editor—Sectionalism—Taboo Subjects—The Publisher's Role in the Community—Crusades—Effect of Editorial Policy on the Editorial and the Column

10. THE EDITORIAL   212
What is the Editorial?—Writing the Editorial—Classification of Editorials—Guiding Points for Editorial Writing

11. THE COLUMN   232
Sources of Material for the Column—Attracting Readers to the Column—The Style of the Column

12. THE SCHOOL PAPER   246

Basics for the School or College Paper—Operation of the School Paper—Problems of the School Paper—The School Paper and the Underground Press—Recent Changes in Coverage—Advisers' Problems and Responsibilities—Sources of News—The Column and the Editorial

13. WRITING FOR RADIO AND TELEVISION   271

Radio: the Background—Television: the Background—Basic Principles of Writing—News—Specialized Newscasts—Difference between Radio and Television Newscasts—Editorials—Program Continuities—The Commentary—Sustaining Announcements—Miscellaneous Writing

14. WRITING FOR MAGAZINES   302

What "Magazine" Means—Who Writes What Magazines Publish?—Changes in the Magazine Field—Qualities Affecting Salability of Material—Literary Forms in Magazine Writing—The Writing Process—Selling Material—Kinds of Magazines

Appendix I The Stylebook   339
Appendix II Reading Proofs   352
Appendix III A Glossary   355
Appendix IV The Basic Professional Library for the Journalist   367
Index   371

Preface

This book is intended as a basic text for the introductory or the survey course in journalism. Its purpose is to give a broad picture of the most important phases of the journalist's work and to treat the main types of writing and editing associated with journalistic endeavors. Every attempt has been made to arrange the material in a clear and logical order so that the reader can locate information readily. Thus the book should serve both as a text and as a handbook.

The main focus is on the concerns of the working newsperson in the various fields of journalism. As a starting point, the book discusses the manner in which news is handled in the print media. Thereafter it considers the principal adjustments to be expected for electronic-media journalism.

The material in the opening chapters is especially important as a prelude to understanding the far-reaching influences exerted by and upon American journalism. As the reader progresses through the later "working" chapters, he should attempt to relate this basic material to all that he studies. Further, he should try to discern the patterns that journalism follows as a "fourth estate" and as a major element in our national life.

Although the reader will probably gain most from a study of the chapters in sequence, such a procedure need not be followed. Individual class needs may well dictate another arrangement. The author strongly suggests, however, that the material on the news story be covered before any later chapter is studied.

In writing this book, the author has gone directly to the world of mass communications. He has drawn on his own experience as a full-time, professional newspaperman on one of America's largest dailies, on his free-lance work for several other large dailies and magazines, and on his study of the mass communications industry. In addition, he has drawn on the advice and assistance of some of America's leading journalists. To all this, he has added his experiences as a college teacher of journalism.

For assistance in one or more of the major phases of this work, the author expresses his genuine gratitude to the many newspapermen and electronic media personnel who gave so freely of their time and counsel; to Timothy A. Berry who made every photograph in the book not credited to an individual newspaper; to Sam Berry, Jr., journalist and public relations expert, whose advice proved especially helpful in several chapters; to Willis L. Parker of San Francisco, editor and publishing specialist, who made many valuable suggestions regarding changes and innovations; and to Professor William R. Landrum who, as always, lent generously of his time and expertise to discussions of the manuscript.

T.E.B.

West Chester, Pennsylvania   May, 1976

★ **1** ★ The Role and Influence of the
Media
The Media and Mass Culture
The Value of the Media
Recent Developments
in Journalism

Journalism—An Overview

Like many other common terms, "journalism" resists any attempt at a concise, unassailable definition. The reason is that over the past half century a series of sudden and powerful influences have altered the whole institution of journalism, thereby invalidating the older and simpler definitions. Where once journalism could be defined rather clearly in terms of the newspaper and its supporting activities, the word can now be explained only within the context of mass communications.

This statement, however, raises another problem in definition: "What is mass communications?"

In some quarters, this expression is used to designate any process by which a person or a group communicates with the masses—any published, broadcast, telecast, filmed, or sound-track material, plus such assorted practices as skywriting, bumper stickers, and sound trucks. In other quarters, the expression is extended to include the copying-machine industry, the distribution of handbills through the mail, billboard advertising, and all similar endeavors.

However, the phrase "mass communications" can usefully be restricted to a much more limited area, specifically to four chief media—the newspaper, the magazine, radio, and television. These media are then labeled the "media of mass communications," the "forces of mass communications," and the "vehi-

cles of mass communications.'' This restricted usage of ''mass communications'' is currently being popularized by the four media themselves.

A further subdivision is also useful in thinking of these four media. The
newspaper and the magazine are often termed the ''print media'' while radio
and television are called the ''electronic media.'' These terms give rise to the
phrases ''print journalism'' and ''electronic-media journalism.'' In the electronic media, ''journalism'' encompasses news programs, feature programs,
documentaries, and other offerings aimed at satisfying for the listener or the
viewer the same interests which impel him to read the newspaper.

THE ROLE AND INFLUENCE OF THE MEDIA

The pivotal role of the four media of mass communications in our society
can be revealed by the estimate that approximately 98% of our population rely
solely on the media of mass communications for 95% of their information
regarding the activities of their own and other nations' governments.[1] These
media, therefore, provide the data upon which the majority of citizens reach
their conclusions regarding major domestic and foreign affairs. Also, the interpretations which the media give this information naturally bear strongly on
the nature of the conclusion. Still further, and more subtly, many of the philosophical concepts and opinions that arise with day-to-day living are derived,
often without the public realizing from the writers, speakers, and other personalities met in the media of mass communications. The newspaper columnist,
the TV commentator, the entertainer, and even the obscure announcer on the
local radio station undoubtedly influence many conclusions regarding social
conduct, educational theory, environmental control, and similar subjects.

To present the impact of the media from a statistical viewpoint, some
basic figures are revealing. Currently there are approximately 2100 daily and
Sunday newspapers in the United States with a combined circulation of more
than 114 million. There are an estimated 9755 publications broadly classifiable
as magazines and a total of 6500 radio and 519 network-affiliated television stations, plus an estimated 3000 independent, educational, and cable TV stations.[2]
All these, quite clearly, constitute a strong voice in our daily lives.

THE MEDIA AND MASS CULTURE

When we comprehend the role of the major media in our lives, we can understand the media's relationship to an entity of fundamental concern to the

[1] This estimate is undoubtedly sound because only a small portion of our citizenry has the opportunity to attend lectures, visit distant places, read the latest books, and engage in the other activities that can provide direct, reliable, and prompt information on domestic and foreign government
movements.

[2] The source for the newspaper figures is the January 1975 edition of Standard Rate & Data
Service publications. The source for the magazine and electronic media figures is the 1975 editions
of the N. W. Ayer directories.

sociologist—the mass culture. This phrase designates, broadly speaking, the cultural climate which envelops the great majority of citizens at any given time; it is the dominant cultural atmosphere of a specific society at a specific period. Reflections of the mass culture are evident on every hand—in the articles sold in department stores, the dress worn in various settings, the topics discussed in the public conveyance, and the over-all deportment of people on all social occasions.

Although the mass culture emerges from a host of unperceived sources, it draws heavily on the body of thoughts, concepts, ideas, entertainment, and data disseminated by the media. The mass culture, therefore, thrives in great part on a cultural fare prepared and served by the media; that is, the mass culture results, to some degree, from the material which the media choose to present to their audiences.

In any discussion of the mass media and the mass culture, however, a reservation must be noted: the media reflect the mass culture as much as they influence it. Hence the total situation is one of interaction. The media provide cultural and informational material of their choosing, but they still work within the confines of audience demands.

The media, therefore, are very much like the large department stores which must stock merchandise that they know will sell.

When we understand this interaction of the mass culture and the mass media, we can see that criticisms of the media often ignore the culture's influence.

THE VALUE OF THE MEDIA

Because of their deep and pervasive influence, the media are brought under a never-ending scrutiny—in places low and high. On the one hand, they are praised for their contributions to society. Television is cited for its ability to take the viewer to the mid-Pacific splashdown of the returning astronauts, to the inauguration of the President of the United States, to the scene of a raging flood, or to a World Series game. Radio is praised for its ability to inform the listener of "late-breaking developments" as he drives his car or putters about his home. The newspaper is praised for its thoughtful editorial opinions, its exposures of corruption in high place, its excellent feature stories. The magazine is praised for its fine pictorial essays, its interesting articles, and its timely and valuable discussions.

Yet in the main, the media are more often criticized adversely. Most frequently, they are upbraided for their influence on mass thought and their role in shaping the values of the very young.

Government leaders, for instance, are likely to score the media for swaying public opinion on important issues. They argue that for the media to have such power is dangerous—especially when, as they see matters, that power is flagrantly abused. Consequently some have advocated a degree of control on the media—all in the name of "national welfare." Meanwhile, well-intentioned persons and organizations voice concern over the ill-effects on the nation's youth of the "violence" and "negative news" presented by both the print and the electronic media.

Against these viewpoints, one of the most important but troublesome issues in a democratic society must be weighed: the issue of freedom of expression.

Clearly, easy answers are not available to any question as complex as freedom of expression. Opposing views are so involved and so often clouded that caution, thoroughness, and expertise are required to construct a foundation for discussion.

Yet despite the almost overwhelming nature of the subject, the student of mass communications must wrestle with this problem. He must know the best opinions in the field, and he must weigh and consider for himself. Only then will he have an opinion worthy of respect.[3]

RECENT DEVELOPMENTS IN JOURNALISM

The history of the four media of mass communications in the United States has been one of competition against and influence on one another.

Until the early 1920s, when only the newspaper and the magazine occupied the field, the competition was slight because these two media tended to cater to specific interests within society. Thus the newspaper concentrated on relating "news" while the magazine treated appealing or pertinent topics, both old and new, in interpretative or reflective discussions. So clearly was the province of each medium delineated that the competition was, at best, rather distant.

However, when radio sets suddenly cropped up by the thousands in the early '20s the newspaper was forced to change its focus.

As is shown in Chapter 13, radio seized from the newspaper the ability to be "first with the news." Hence the newspaper, now deprived of its monopoly on news-as-it-breaks, was forced to rely more on the in-depth coverage found in the magazine.

With this development, a process of "bumping" began. As radio bumped the newspaper from its first-with-the-news perch, the newspaper began to bump the magazine from its role of interpreter of leading current questions, thus forcing the magazine to fight for its life by finding new and striking treatments and approaches. Then, with the appearance of television in the late 1940s, a more severe and eventful bumping began.

Television, armed with the ability to bring on-the-spot news and high-quality documentaries right into the home, created an almost overwhelming competition. Not only could it give a pictorial treatment of news-in-the-making and other timely topics; it could also interpret the material simultaneously through authoritative comment and visual aids (maps, charts, and the like). Hence it made heavy inroads into the provinces of the newspaper, the maga-

[3] Freedom of expression is treated more extensively in Chapter 2 and in other places throughout this book. It is mentioned here only as part of the overview of journalism in America.

zine, and the radio, eventually becoming a force of gigantic magnitude in American life.

The total influence of each medium on the others is a vast and challenging study. Some of the major influences have been cited above. Yet there are many less well known examples of this influence.

As is well known in the newspaper world, television advertising has influenced newspaper advertising; and as is demonstrated in Chapter 8, magazine make-up has influenced newspaper make-up. Meanwhile, television has borrowed some newspaper practices and terminology. Thus TV newscasters are likely to use visual devices that resemble newspaper headlines—while they proclaim themselves as "columnists of the air" or "editorial voices of this station." More important, perhaps, television and the magazine have influenced the newspaper by forcing it to become a more visual enterprise: the old newspaper, filled with columns of black type, has been prodded into using more pictures and finding more appealing layouts.

In addition to the many changes prompted by intermedium competition and influence, rather sharp changes have occurred in the working personnel of each medium—the newspaperman, the magazine staffer, the radio performer, and the television personality. Perhaps the one word which best describes these changes is "maturity." These professions have undergone a growing process which has made their people, generally speaking, more finely honed, more highly refined practitioners of their calling.

This maturing process has given more of the professional—and hence less of the craft—aura to the individuals themselves. The old-time newspaper reporter, for instance, slouching about the city room and the local police station with his shirt collar open and his rumpled suit hanging like a bag from his protuberant corpus, has been replaced by a more methodical, better educated, higher-minded person. Similarly, the radio announcer of the early years, with his glib line of patter and his frequently inane ad lib remarks, has gone; his more finished successor speaks better, conducts himself on a more elevated level, and he displays an over-all polish. The same kind of improvement is manifest in the television announcer and the magazine writer. In short, mass-communication personnel have acquired the atmosphere and the *savoir faire* of the professional.

EXERCISES

In the latest year for which figures are available:

1. How many newspapers were published in the United States? How many are dailies? How many are weeklies? How many publish Sunday or weekend editions?

2. How many magazines were published in the United States? How does the list break down among weeklies? monthlies? other publication intervals? How many are Sunday or week-end newspaper inserts?
3. How many radio broadcasting stations were operating in the United States?
4. How many television stations were operating in the United States?
5. How do the latest figures you can find compare with those given at the opening of this chapter?
6. Examine carefully the several publications of Standard Rate & Data Service and write a descriptive paragraph for any four.
7. Follow the same procedure for the N. W. Ayer Directory of Publications.
8. In May 1975, The *Fresno Bee* case attracted national attention among news-media personnel and the populace generally. This case centered about the old story of reporters, backed by their editor, refusing to divulge in court the source of a news story. The judge then held all in contempt of court and threatened them with jail terms.

   Review the facts of the case as presented in wire-service stories and comment intelligently on the whole matter.

FOR FURTHER READING

Blanchard, Robert O. *Congress and the News Media*. New York: Hastings House, Publishers, 1974.

Emery, Edwin. *Press and America*. Englewood Cliffs: Prentice-Hall, 1972.

Gordon, George N. *Communications and Media: Constructing a Cross-Discipline*. New York: Hastings House, Publishers, 1974.

Hynds, Ernest C. *American Newspapers in the 1970's*. New York: Hastings House, Publishers, 1975.

McQuill, Dennis. *Toward a Sociology of Mass Communication*. London, England: Collier-International, Inc., 1969.

Minor, Dale. *The Information War*. New York: Hawthorn Books, 1970.

Pember, Don R. *Mass Media in America*. Palo Alto: Science Research Associates, 1974.

Schramm, Wilbur, and Donald F. Roberts, eds. *Process and Effects of Mass Communications*. Urbana: University of Illinois Press, 1971.

Stanley, Robert H., and Charles S. Steinberg. *The Media Environment: Mass Communications in American Society*. New York: Hastings House, Publishers, 1976.

Steinberg, Charles S. *The Communicative Arts: An Introduction to the Mass Media*. New York: Hastings House, Publishers, 1970.

Talese, Gay. *The Kingdom and the Power*. New York: World Publishing Co., 1969.

★ **2** ★

Freedom of Expression
Radio and Television
The Mass Audience
Prestige
Defamation and Privacy
The Future of the Newspaper

Recent Issues in the Field of Mass Communications

The field of mass communications, like every other complex institution, changes constantly. Influences are always at work altering—sometimes gently, sometimes severely—the basic character of the entire field; and issues are constantly arising that force the media into new courses of action. Therefore, to understand the media at any given moment, a study of these influences and issues becomes necessary.

On some occasions, the matters can be isolated and examined easily—as when television in the late 1940s began to compete seriously with the other media. On other occasions, however, the forces may be so subtle as almost to escape detection—as when the newspapers learned belatedly in the late 1950s that readers were shunning the old society page.

In the following pages, six important facets of the present situation are presented. These are the subjects which must be examined as a prelude to understanding the current movements within the field. All have two elements in common: they are more complex than first notice reveals, and they are extremely challenging. Therefore, any student of mass communications must reflect carefully upon them.

7

FREEDOM OF EXPRESSION

Most Americans think that freedom of expression is a concept long since woven firmly into our national fabric, that the First Amendment and the many related court cases have settled once and for all the right of newspapers and other media to speak without restraint. They realize, of course, that war and similar conditions may curtail this freedom temporarily; but on the whole, they tend to regard the media's right to freedom of expression as an accepted commonplace of our way of life.

Unfortunately, however, our history shows that freedom of expression has been assaulted in every period, including our own, because some powerful person or group has called for a restriction. The person may be a high government figure, such as a President of the United States, who wants limitations imposed in the name of national welfare. The group may be an organization like the American Bar Association which wants curtailments in the name of a fair trial for persons accused. Yet whatever the source, the call for restriction has usually been strong and insistent.

The controversies arising over the attempts of outside forces to limit the media's freedom on speech have led to many spirited and significant confrontations during the present century. A discussion of the most important follows.

The first notable instance occurred in 1908 when the Federal government, at the insistence of President Theodore Roosevelt, had Joseph Pulitzer and his top editors of the *New York World* indicted in a District of Columbia court for criminal libel. The action resulted from the *World's* disclosure of the means by which this government had secured the right to build the Panama Canal. The case eventually was carried to the Supreme Court, where the judges agreed unanimously that since only documentary evidence had been printed, the *World* was in no sense guilty. This decision, as others before it, re-established the right of the press to print the truth.

Slightly less than a decade later—specifically on June 15, 1917—trouble erupted again when Congress passed the Espionage Act. This legislation set up a system of fines and imprisonments for anyone who "shall wilfully cause or attempt to cause . . . disloyalty . . . or shall wilfully obstruct recruiting" into the armed forces of the nation. Publications guilty of breaking this law also were to be denied the use of the mails.

Then, on October 6, 1917, came the Trading with the Enemy Act which required that all messages sent abroad be censored and that any publication printing material in a foreign language file a sworn translation with the local postmaster. Further restrictions were imposed with the Sedition Act of May 16, 1918, which provided heavy fines and imprisonment for writing or publishing "any disloyal, profane, scurrilous, or abusive language about the form of government of the United States, or the Constitution, military or naval forces, flag, or the uniform of the army or navy of the United States." It also forbade the use of language that would tend to bring upon the things mentioned "contempt, scorn, contumely, or disrepute."

The language of these laws was so broad and sweeping that trouble between government and the newspapers was inevitable. Yet the trouble came not, as one would expect, with the Department of Justice, which is the law-enforcing agency of the nation; the trouble came, rather, with the Post Office Department, which set itself up as censor of all publications using the mails. During the first year of the Espionage Act, 75 papers ran afoul of the Post Office Department, the more fortunate of which were allowed further use of the mails only after promising to print no more discussion of war questions. Since appeals to the courts made no headway, the Post Office became a powerful control on the press.

When World War I ended, the newspapers' troubles faded away. Yet this was really no victory for freedom of expression. It was, instead, a case of a contest being suspended because one contestant, the Post Office, saw nothing more to fight over.

Freedom of expression did not become a serious problem again until a clash between President and press occurred with the passage of the National Recovery Act (1933) during the first term of Franklin D. Roosevelt. Under the terms of the act, every industry was to draw up a "voluntary" code regulating hours of work, wages, and similar considerations. Inserted in the act, however, was a provision giving the President the right to revoke the license of any newspaper which violated the code. Because this provision clearly gave the President a potentially strong control over every newspaper, the American Newspaper Publishers Association, in drawing up the code, insisted on a statement guaranteeing the traditional freedom of expression based on the First Amendment. And because the Association continued to demand the written statement despite Roosevelt's oral assurances, Roosevelt became so angered that strained relations ensued.

This clash and later eruption of ill-feeling caused the press to be definitely uneasy during the tenure of this same President, Franklin D. Roosevelt. To this day, no one has shown conclusively how long Roosevelt wanted to remain President or how much power he really desired. But the fact does stand that he disliked intensely to be crossed; he was a man who resented opposition in practically any form. At first his relations with the press were extremely cordial, but as time passed his temper rose. He was especially caustic at election time, referring to the fact that most newspapers in the nation were opposed to his winning. He also resented the power of the press in helping to defeat some of his major domestic plans, such as the enlarging of the Supreme Court. Consequently, the press was wary of his opposition because his power was so all-encompassing. One major newspaper chain even went so far as to run nation-wide full-page advertisements on the subject of freedom of the press. However, the newspaper successfully rode out this contest, as it did so many others, by holding steadfastly to its right to move in its traditional patterns.

The next serious attempt to restrict the media in their work was a condition that slowly gained momentum throughout 1954, 1955, and 1956, finally coming to a showdown in 1957. This was the situation wherein powerful figures in the Federal government began to close off news sources in the name of "national security." Several high-ranking figures in the Federal departments decided completely on their own that certain news sources were to be controlled, and they issued orders accordingly. The most famous of all such instances was the refusal of the State Department to grant newspapermen visas to visit Red China. The newspapermen contended that since the United States was not at war with China they had the right to visas, especially since they were going as journalists rather than as tourists. The Secretary of State, John Foster Dulles, contended that his department was acting in the best interests of the nation in refusing the visas. Although the most prominent organizations of editors, publishers, and other newspapermen passed formal resolutions condemning the action of the State Department, President Eisenhower would not reverse the ruling of his Secretary of State.

The difficulties between government and press continued during the Kennedy and Johnson administrations—although no really serious confrontations occurred—despite efforts by the two Presidents to lessen the contention. The problems stemmed, of course, from the old situation: A President does not like unfavorable criticism of his administration; he wants to determine how news is to be released and treated; and he seems to feel that the press should be an arm rather than a critic of his administration. As clashes between the press and the Kennedy administration occurred, the term "managed news" arose to describe the administration's handling of news. This term and the condition behind it continued into the Johnson administration, where an even more important situation arose. The newspaper and electronic-media reporters, finding that administration personnel were sometimes distorting facts or withholding information, openly challenged the veracity of that administration by discussing its "credibility gap."

The relationship between the Federal government and the press was calm for only a relatively short time after President Richard M. Nixon succeeded President Johnson. Before the end of the first year, the journalistic media, especially the newspapers, were displaying widespread hostility toward the Nixon administration because of remarks made by then Vice President Spiro T. Agnew who, in a series of speeches, accused both television and the newspaper of "monopolistic practices." Agnew argued that news portrayal was "one-sided" and "unfair;" hence some corrective measures were needed. Meanwhile, he denied any intention of "censoring" or "muzzling" the news media. In fact, as might be expected, he praised the "press on the whole."

President Nixon, when questioned about his Vice President's view, hastened to emphasize that Agnew was always free to speak as an individual. This kind of disclaimer, obviously, impressed only the most naive. Throughout the episode, however, the blunt and derisive comments of newspaper editors indicated small fear of Agnew's or the administration's displeasure.

A matter far more serious than the Agnew accusations and their ramifications suddenly surfaced in June 1971 when a legal battle of far-reaching significance occurred between the newspapers and the Federal government.

On Sunday, June 13, the regular edition of the *New York Times* appeared with a seemingly routine headline over a lengthy story: VIETNAM ARCHIVE PENTAGON STUDY TRACES 3 DECADES OF GROWING U.S. INVOLVEMENT.

But when official Washington examined the story, it found material that was far from routine; it found verbatim statements from "secret" documents on file in the Pentagon. The problem was intensified when other newspapers—notably the *Washington Post* and the *Boston Globe*—shortly thereafter printed additional excerpts from the same source, accompanied by editorial judgments and running comments. The material had been supplied, later evidence showed, by more than one person; but the ultimate source had been Daniel Ellsberg, a researcher for the Rand Corporation, a firm employed to assist in a highly confidential government study of the Vietnam War. Ellsberg, after publicly admitting that he had made and distributed photographic reproduction of the documents, was indicted in Federal court in Los Angeles for illegal possession of government material and related offenses.[1]

In an attempt to prevent further disclosure by the *New York Times* and other newspapers, the Federal government established a precedent. It created a historical first by petitioning the courts to impose a prepublication restraint on newspapers. Specifically, it asked the courts to prohibit the *New York Times* and the other papers involved from printing any material extracted from the documents. The government's argument was that national security and the common good were under threat.

Beneath this main issue, however, lay other highly important questions: Should the Federal government ever have the right to control publication of material already in the possession of the newspaper? Should the Federal government be permitted without restriction to label material "secret," thereby denying the public knowledge of it? If the government were to win this issue, would it be well on the road to suppressing news in general?

The suit against the *New York Times,* the first to enter the legal arena, moved rapidly upward through the courts in New York where each successive judge saw the issue as one to be settled eventually by the Supreme Court. Meanwhile, newspapers and other interested parties throughout the nation also wanted a decision from the high court as a firm guideline.

Upon being petitioned to review the case, the Supreme Court decided by the narrow margin of five to four,[2] to do so. After agreeing to hear the case, however, the court moved with an almost unprecedented speed, and on June 30 announced its verdict. By a vote of six to three, it upheld the right of the *New York Times* (and thus the other papers involved as well as all papers) to print and comment on the documents as it saw fit.

Although each of the nine justices wrote separate opinions, clear lines of

---

[1] On May 11, 1973, Federal District Judge W. M. Byrne, Jr. dismissed all charges against Ellsberg and his fellow defendant, A. J. Russo. Byrne cited "improper government conduct shielded so long from public view" as his reason.

[2] Notice that the five-to-four vote was on a decision to consider the case. The later six-to-three vote was on the merits of the case.

reasoning were observable. The majority held that the First Amendment to the Constitution precluded any right of the government to invoke prior restraint on the newspaper—even though three in this majority of six stressed the significance of an inherent threat to national security. Meanwhile, the three opinions upholding the government stressed the dangers of publishing secret government documents. Of further importance, six of the nine opinions contained open or implied conclusions that the whole issue needed further refinement—in a more relaxed and deliberate atmosphere.

Aside from the legal aspects of the case, however, a result of great import became apparent: the published material proved indisputably that in some instances the government had employed a flimsy defense of national security to deny significant information to the public, that in other instances the government had misled the public, and that in still other instances the government had disseminated information that was patently untrue. All this, obviously, cast some doubts on the credibility of presidents and other high government figures—as well as underscoring the necessity of a free press to serve as a check on government officials in general.

Before the dust created by the Pentagon Papers litigation had a chance to settle, the contest between the Federal government and the agencies of mass communication took still another turn when Dr. Frank Stanton, then president of the Columbia Broadcasting System, was called before the Commerce Committee of the House of Representatives on July 5, 1971, to explain the means by which his network procured the information for the important TV documentary, "The Selling of the Pentagon"—a film which exposed the propaganda and news-manufacturing devices of the Department of Defense.

In the course of the session, Committee Chairman Harley O. Staggers (D., West Virginia) and several of his colleagues demanded that Stanton surrender unedited films, outtakes, scripts, recordings, and other material used in making the now much discussed documentary. Stanton "respectfully declined" to relinquish the material, explaining his stand: "There can be no doubt in anyone's mind that the First Amendment would bar this subpoena if directed at the editing of a newspaper report, a book or a magazine article. If broadcasters must comply with such subpoenas, broadcast journalism can never perform the independent and robust role in preserving those freedoms which the Constitution intended for American journalism."

The Committee, startled and angry, voted 25–13 to request the full House to pursue a contempt of Congress citation against CBS and Dr. Stanton. The House, however, mindful of the strong public reaction to the documentary, let the measure die in the labyrinth of committees, rules, procedures, and cloakroom understandings which characterize that body. Thus the electronic media, like the newspaper in the instance of the Pentagon papers, won a rather important skirmish.

An important sidelight on the many legal and other discussions of the Pentagon papers and the television documentary, "The Selling of the Pentagon," was the strong popular endorsement of the philosophy that underlies two synonymous phrases: the "fourth estate" and the "fourth branch of government." This philosophy holds that journalism serves as a window for the public to maintain a watch over the three branches of government—the legislative, the judicial, and the executive—thereby becoming a fourth element in a clearly desirable system of checks and balances.

Because these phrases were used widely and approvingly throughout the nation, the necessity of a free press in a democracy was further impressed upon the public consciousness. (This statement does not imply unqualified public approval of the media and their manner of operation.)

All the preceding discussion regarding the Pentagon papers and "The Selling of the Pentagon" might suggest that government and press had reached a state of truce, however uneasy. They had not. In 1972, trouble between the government and the media broke out anew. This time it resulted from a journalist's insistence on withholding information regarding the source of his story in the face of a judge's order to do so.

The situation moved to center stage when the Supreme Court agreed to consider cases involving four reporters charged with contempt of court for refusal to divulge information which they considered confidential. Of the four, the spotlight fell most prominently on Earl Caldwell, a reporter for the *New York Times,* who would not testify about facts obtained in confidence from the Black Panther Party. Ruling five to four, the Supreme Court on June 29, 1972, declared that journalists do not have a right—as they have contended—under the First Amendment to decline to answer certain questions regarding news sources.

The defiance by the media and the accompanying support of such organizations as the ACLU (American Civil Liberties Union), however, seem to have had little effect on most of our high courts. The Supreme Court, for example, issued a far less noticed but more portentous decision than its ruling in the Caldwell case when in October, 1973, it refused to hear the appeal of Larry Dickinson of the *State-Times* and Gibbs Adams of the *Morning Advocate,* both Louisiana newspapermen, who had been adjudged guilty of contempt of court and fined $300 each for publishing an account of a public hearing. The presiding judge in the case, Federal District Judge E. Gordon West, had ordered journalists covering the case not to write about it; and the Supreme Court, in effect, upheld this order. The very serious implication of this decision, of course, is that any judge may forbid any journalist to inform the public about a specific case before the courts; or carried to an extreme, the public could be denied all knowledge of court cases until the case is over.

As of this writing, more than 20 prominent newsmen have been in jail, have been threatened with jail, or are free pending appeals because of their refusals to reveal sources and other data which they believe must be kept confidential. In addition, many more journalists have announced that they will choose prison terms rather than compliance. Meanwhile, legislators and others are striving to draft laws to protect newsmen whose functions are threatened by the courts. Appropriately, the laws are termed "shield laws."

The great problem in drafting such a law is twofold: (1) how to construct a law that can withstand the test of constitutionality; (2) how to draft a law applicable only to newsmen.

These questions are not likely to be answered easily. Any shield law, for example, that will protect newsmen from contempt-of-court citations will run counter to present laws that require all citizens to give full, truthful statements when on the stand.[3] Then, too, if newsmen are to be given the right to withhold information on the grounds that they are essential to a properly informed public, why not extend this law to authors of certain kinds of books, to scholars doing research, to commentators of any kind (for instance, small time lecturers), and to any other person claiming to be a source of information needed by the public?

By June 1, 1975, the House Judiciary Subcommittee had more than 50 proposed shield-law bills under consideration, but none seemed worthy of reporting to the full House. In March 1973, the then chairman of the subcommittee, Representative Robert Kastenmeier, had declared, "The odds favor our coming out with some kind of recommended legislation." Yet as this is written, no such recommendation has been made—or appears likely to be made.

RADIO AND TELEVISION

In the twentieth century two new media of mass communication have appeared on the American scene to create a strong influence on the entire course of journalism; they are radio and television.

Radio emerged in the 1920s. The first commercial broadcasting station was constructed in East Pittsburgh, Pennsylvania, in January 1921; and soon there were thousands throughout the land. From their inception, the great majority of stations relied heavily on newscasts to attract listeners.

With the advent of radio, newspaper coverage and treatment of news were forced into radically different patterns. Heretofore, the newspaper designed its basic character on its ability to "break" spot news. It employed the eight-column streamer, the black headline, and the late-flash box to give readers the first inkling of all that was "new"; and it strained to emphasize recency in every news item. Radio, however, was now invoking an unbeatable time advantage for scooping the newspaper. With its numerous news programs, its use of headlines at frequent intervals, and its practice of interrupting regularly scheduled programs to broadcast important flashes, radio was seizing from newspapers the great advantage of being "first with the news." Hence many persons began to depend on radio receivers—in the home, the business office, the waiting room, and the car—for election returns, major court decisions, and similar material that could be broadcast within minutes of its coming off the news wires.

[3] Newsmen argue that some few people—such as the psychiatrist and the priest in the confessional—are already given this protection. Hence, why not newsmen also?

As radio gained a position of dominance, the newspaper strove to offset radio's time advantage by resorting to in-depth coverage of news and to a heavier use of discussive features (columns, opinion polls, letters to the editor, and the like) not adaptable to radio broadcast. In these ways, the newspaper attempted to capitalize on the advantages of the printed page, to counter the time advantage of radio by presenting more extensive, more varied, and more multifaceted treatment of news. Thus the emergence of radio was instrumental in changing both the nature of the newspaper and the general movement of journalism.

Television became an important force in American life in the late 1940s, immediately after World War II ended. Almost overnight, television sets moved into homes throughout the nation. And like radio, television presented immediate competition with the newspaper. Moreover, its competition was both visual and auditory.

Television has always provided both on-the-spot news and background material of strong appeal. The television viewer, for example, can witness the actual funeral of the important person; and he can see on his screen—either during or soon after the event itself—neighborhood disturbances, conflagrations, and similar scenes. Obviously, coverage of this type lies beyond the ability of the newspaper.

As they did against radio, newspapers have striven to withstand the competition of television by fighting on the battleground where they hold an advantage. Thus the newspapers now print more pictures than formerly and have increased their use of in-depth discussion. Meanwhile, they have sought to impress on the reader, subtly and overtly, the fact that the newspaper provides something of a permanent record, whereas the television program gives only a once-around exposure controlled by a director and a camera crew.

At present, the competition of newspapers and television has placed the two media in something of a complementary rather than a competitive situation. This is clearly evident, for instance, in sports events. No enthusiastic baseball fan relies exclusively on either the newspaper or television for an account of a World Series game; he relies on both. He watches the game on television. Then he turns to his newspaper for a summary of the game, interesting pictures, and authoritative comment and discussion.

The impact of television on the newspaper's coverage of general news can be summarized rather clearly. Where news is important enough to merit extensive television coverage, the newspaper makes a pronounced attempt to enlarge upon and interpret the facts. Where the event does not merit major television coverage, the newspaper presents the news in pre-television patterns.

THE MASS AUDIENCE

As the present-day media attempt to fulfill their traditional roles in society, they need to respond to pronounced changes that are occurring in the entity called the "mass audience."

The people served by the media today are quite different from those of a short time ago. Hence the media must adjust their offerings or suffer grave consequences. But to make the proper adjustments, the media must first know more about these new readers, listeners, and viewers—and therein lies a host of perplexing questions.

Because handling these questions demands a professional competence, the media have turned to sociologists and other behavioral scientists for answers. They want to identify, for example, the conditions within the mass audience that explain the fading appeal of the Sunday paper for so many readers; they want to know why so many magazines suddenly begin to limp; and they want answers to numerous other questions.

Although the professionals have offered many vague or challengeable explanations, they have also provided some valuable insights into the mass audience of the moment.

The present mass audience has a far wider range of interests than our citizens of the 1940s and 1950s. Many more people travel to distant places—thanks to the chartered air trips. Many more people are financially able to pursue hobbies and pastimes once beyond their reach—thanks to a more equitable distribution of income. And many more people have a closer touch with other cultures—thanks to travel, education, and television.

More important, our way of living, our "life style," has undergone a metamorphosis. Families are no longer welded into the tight little units of the past. The big Sunday dinner, the frequent entertaining of relatives, and the practice of congregating in the living room night after night are lessening or disappearing. Individual family members now tend to belong to separate organizations, to socialize apart from their families, and to move in worlds of their own choosing. Furthermore, everyone has more leisure time to follow his own life style or to indulge himself as he pleases.

These changes have made explaining our total society an almost overwhelming task. Where our citizenry could once be divided nicely into large blocks and examined in terms of representative persons or groups, such is no longer the case. Society is now widely fragmented. Because many, many small groups—with diverse and as yet unanalyzed interests and outlooks—have replaced the large blocks, many leading sociologists now question the existence of anything approaching a "mass audience." Moreover, these same sociologists see, in many instances, continuing changes within these small groups. Therefore, even if every group could be isolated and analyzed, the results would be valid for only a short period.

The impact of these changes can be especially important for a field like advertising which is the economic life blood of the media. Because of shifts within the mass audience, advertisers are no longer asking *"How many* people are we reaching?"* but *"Who* are the people we are reaching?"

As a consequence, advertisers are often dropping apparently successful print-media campaigns or highly popular television programs. A cosmetic firm, for instance, was recently overwhelmed by responses to a newspaper ad campaign that offered a free travel guide book. But it had to scuttle the campaign because the ads were reaching the wrong people; most of the respondees were beyond sixty, an age when few people use cosmetics. Similarly, a country TV show had to be dropped, despite its great audience appeal, because the viewers were non-buying—middle-aged and older, and therefore in little need of merchandise.

Advertisers have also forced the national magazines into regional advertising. For example, a local bank ad may appear in only those copies of a national magazine that are distributed in the bank's area, say the Chicago hinterland, or California.

The changes in the mass audience have also forced marked changes in the content of the metropolitan newspaper. The large daily is now striving to provide something for everybody with its improved suburban sections, its numerous stuff-ins, and its wider range of feature material. Meanwhile, radio has adopted new talk shows, interviews, and other novel programming. And even television, which is accused constantly of being absolute master of its own domain, keeps a sensitive ear to the ground for soundings on our multi-faceted society.

Throughout all, the enormity of the task of satisfying the demands of a widely fragmented society is apparent. The media, therefore, can only do their best—and hope.

PRESTIGE

Prestige is one of the really grave problems in the mass communications field at present, primarily for the newspaper and television. Both of these media, the soundest evidence indicates, are fighting for something comparable to personal dignity.

The plight of the newspaper can be shown by citing one fact. In the fall of 1973, a Harris Poll reported that less than 30 percent (specifically 29.8) of our population accept at face value the statements found in newspapers. This finding was substantiated across the next two years by individual newspaper and professional organization investigations. In essence, readers distrust the newspaper because they suspect a "distortion of facts" and a generally nebulous type of "bias." Many authorities in the field call this whole situation a "confidence gap."

In conducting the survey, the investigators found that many citizens mentioned the Watergate story as an argument for their stand. This story, it seems, earned widespread praise for the ingenuity and industry of the two *Washington Post* reporters who unearthed the facts; but it also drew the fire of irate citizens who charged the newspapers and other media with irresponsibility in the treatment of the President. Because this story has so often been linked to public respect for the newspaper, further discussion is in order.

Without doubt, a segment of the press did display irresponsibility in handling this story. *Time,* for instance, employed an uncharacteristic display of emotion, half-truth, and innuendo in treating the whole episode. In the summer of 1973, long before the pertinent facts were established or any tight definition of "impeachment" had been developed, this magazine blasted the President unceasingly and called editorially for his resignation. Meanwhile, many news-papers were resorting, like *Time,* to a slanting and an editing that resembled the yellow journalism of the turn of the century.

This kind of reporting, however, did not bother the public alone; editors and columnists everywhere chided the press for its antics. For instance, in March 1974, Joseph Kraft, never a Nixon fan, wrote a strong article deploring the newspaper treatment of the President and recommending that the "traditional inhibitions on reporting" be applied—or in other words, that more responsi-bility be invoked. He was followed shortly by Harry Reasoner, one of America's foremost TV commentators, who scored *Time* heavily for "below the belt journalism," and by Managing Editor Howard Simons of the *Washington Post,* who cautioned newsmen about "shark frenzy" or the "tendency to attack a bleeding body in water." [4]

Although writers like James Reston (*New York Times*) argued that the news media did not create the Watergate story—that instead the President's ad-ministration did—neither Reston nor any other writer was able to defend the unsound interpretations, the presentation of opinion as fact, and the accusatory headlines found in so many papers.

Widespread resentment toward the media because of their treatment of the President was softened somewhat when the truth eventually surfaced—that is, when the fact became known that the President had ordered the case covered up.

Nonetheless, many citizens still resented the irresponsibility of a large seg-ment of the media in accusing and demanding a resignation before they had the evidence. These citizens, in short, felt that the media, like such politically minded Senators as Hubert Humphrey (Minn.) and Richard Schweiker (Pa.), were both unfair and negatively motivated.[5]

Clearly, no one can say finally what impact Watergate or any other story may have had. Yet throughout all, the indisputable fact stands that the prestige of the newspaper at this time was very low.

And what about television's prestige? A large share of the adverse attitude squares with the old accusation that television offers only violence, crime, un-savory subjects, and trivia to a public deserving of better things—the idea, in

---

[4] Public reaction against the treatment of the President was not directed only at the print media. CBS newsman Dan Rather, for example, aroused considerable public ire by a treatment of President Nixon that was at times hostile and rude. In addition, Rather was accused by numerous writers of "showboating" instead of remaining objective.

[5] The concern of newspaper editors over the matter of prestige can be appreciated by noting this fact: at its annual meeting in Washington, D.C. on April 17, 1975, the American Society of Newspaper Editors had a panel discussion on the subject, "Why Readers Hate Us—And What We Can Do About It?"

brief, that television is truly a "boob tube," or worse still, a dangerously negative force in society.

A typical disparagement is cited by Jeffrey Schrank in an article on the controversy that surrounds television: [6]

Count 'em. Every hour, according to a recent study, TV serves up an average of 7.29 brutal scenes. By the age of 14, a child has witnessed the mauling of 18,000 fellow human beings.

What's the message all this mayhem conveys to viewers? Here's one view: "Violence is an (acceptable) way of solving problems," says Dr. Albert E. Siegel, a professor of psychiatry at Stanford University School of Medicine.

When criticism of TV programming reached a crescendo in 1971, D. Thomas Miller, President of CBS Television Stations Division, came vigorously to the medium's defense. After citing statistics to prove the wholesome nature of programs in general, he took society itself to task; [7]

Unfortunately, people have a tendency to tell you what *should* be on television—not what they would actually be willing to watch themselves.

To television stations, the matter of prestige has a special significance. They must ever beware the power of the Federal Communications Commission, an organization that has shown itself to be acutely sensitive to political pressures. After all, the stations do want to continue, and to do so they must have an FCC license.

Public distrust of the newspaper during this period was also encouraged by an old conclusion rooted deep in the thought processes of society: the newspaper holds an insurmountable advantage over the ordinary citizen. The man-in-the-street knows that he can resort to the libel suit when the newspaper prints flagrant untruths, but he sees no way to combat the newspaper's little innuendoes and twists of expression that ridicule or cut him down. He expresses his resentment with such statements as "You can't fight city hall" and "You're never going to lick them, so why try?"

Unquestionably, there is a basis in fact for this conclusion. For example, many newspapers pursue a letters-to-the-editor policy similar to that of the Philadelphia *Evening Bulletin*. This paper, despite its ethical procedures in other departments, allows letter writers to make flagrantly personal attacks on other letter writers—however sound the first letter writer's statements may be. The *Bulletin* employs this practice especially when the first letter criticizes an article

---

[6] Geoffrey Schrank, "Boob Tube or Bright Light," *Senior Scholastic,* V. 106, p. 7, April 10, 1975.

[7] D. Thomas Miller, "Television, the Only Truly Mass Medium Remaining Today: Its Role in Our Society." Columbia Broadcasting System, Inc., 1971. All rights reserved. Reprinted by permission of the Department of Communication Arts, College of Agriculture and Life Sciences, Cornell University.

in its paper. The attack by the second letter writer is often factually wrong, thoroughly illogical, and even vituperative. But for the paper, the letter accomplishes the purpose of telling the first writer: "Criticize our paper, will you!" Risking this treatment, only a thick-skinned person will write to criticize the newspaper's stories, and thus the paper forestalls a large amount of justifiable criticism. Meanwhile, the paper can trumpet sanctimoniously that its letters-to-the-editor column is a forum for free, open expression of opinion.

DEFAMATION AND PRIVACY

For the people who select and prepare the material distributed by the media of mass communications, the possibility of a defamation suit, usually called a libel suit, is a serious consideration. They realize that many newspapers and magazines have faced such suits, and they know that while radio and TV media seldom find themselves in defamation litigation, the possibility is always there.

Further, these people realize that some very large judgments have been awarded. They know, for instance, that in 1963 radio and television performer John Henry Faulk was awarded $1,250,000 plus $1,000,000 compensatory damages for remarks published in a "News Supplement" by Aware, Inc.[8] They also know that in 1964 University of Georgia Athletic Director Wally Butts was awarded $3,000,000 plus $60,000 compensatory damages for an article in the *Saturday Evening Post* that alleged he had helped to fix a football game.[9]

Because the field of defamation is ever-changing, it must always be examined in the light of current conditions. Any examination, naturally, must begin with a definition.

Broadly speaking, *libel,* is an attempt to defame by writing, printing, pictures, images, or any other means that appeals to the vision of the beholder. That is, if one person or group attempts to bring another into disrepute by means of published material that can be seen, he commits libel.[10] If he attempts to bring on the disrepute by uttering the material orally (as by radio), he commits *slander*. Either libel or slander is *defamation,* and either can be costly to the journalist, his employer, or both. Thus fine distinctions (and there are important ones) may not matter greatly in practice.

The first difficulty in adjudging libel arises in deciding when one person has defamed another. Frequently a hair's breadth separates the libelous material from the nonlibelous.

Libel is also difficult to adjudge because words, especially slang and

---

[8] The court later reduced the first amount to $100,000 and the second to $50,000. But the award remained largely uncollectable because of the inability of Aware, Inc. to pay.

[9] The court later reduced the first amount to $400,000.

[10] For a discussion of libel as it touches on copy editing, see Chapter 7. For some remarks about libel and pictures, see Chapter 6.

idioms, have such a variety of meanings. A Pennsylvania woman, for example, sued a newspaper because it had referred to a social occasion in her home as a "hot party." She contended the adjective "hot" possessed an immoral implication; the newspaper contended that the word connotes "loud, hilarious, boisterous," as used, for instance, in the old song, "There'll be a hot time in the old town tonight." The court eventually agreed with the newspaper.

Another problem exists because of the sharp variance of libel laws from state to state. To see the variety in these laws, one need only make a cursory examination of them throughout the United States. In some states, a newspaper is guilty of libel when it invades, however lightly, the "privacy" of a citizen. In some other states, a libelous action has been committed when the newspaper prints an obituary of a living man; makes light of an individual's deformities; or calls someone a "liar," a "gambler," a "deadbeat," or any other name of a disparaging nature.

Further difficulty with state laws arises because of the vagueness of their language. A representative situation is that of the Penal Law of New York, which defines libel in these terms:

A malicious publication, in writing, printing, pictures, effigy, sign or otherwise than by mere speech, which exposes any living person, or the memory of any person deceased, to hatred, contempt, ridicule or obloquy, or which causes, or tends to cause any person to be shunned or avoided, or which has a tendency to injure any person, corporation or association of persons, in his or their business or occupation, is a libel.

Obviously, interpreting this statute is difficult because of the breadth of the language and the problem of interpreting such words as "malicious," "contempt," and "shunned."

Also important in any discussion of libel is the fact that most present-day newspapers knowingly print potentially libelous statements. They do so because, otherwise, they would have a very dull paper. Consequently, some of the best stories in the paper would run a chance of being adjudged libelous if examined in court. But the newspaper, in its attempt to present interesting material, is willing to take the risk. It also prints potentially libelous material because many of the people libeled are not in a position to sue the paper, or because the paper can often make a small out-of-court settlement if the probable outcome appears dark. The wisdom of the newspaper's course is evidenced by the small number of cases won by the plaintiffs as compared with the abundance of material which is potentially libelous.

A final thought concerning libel is, in one sense, the most important of all. It concerns the case of the *New York Times Company v. Sullivan,* finally settled by the Supreme Court in 1964 (376 U.S. 254).

The case began when L. B. Sullivan, Commissioner of Public Affairs of the City of Montgomery, Alabama, sued the *New York Times* over the contents of a full-page ad carried by that paper on March 29, 1960. The ad derided the state of Alabama, the Montgomery County Police Commissioner, and assorted other persons. In the ad were several factual errors of a rather minor sort.

When an Alabama court awarded Sullivan $500,000 damages against the *New York Times* and four clergyman, the newspaper naturally carried its appeal all the way to the Supreme Court. In reversing the Alabama court, the Supreme Court invoked a line of reasoning with portentous implications for the field of libel. The reasoning is: Public discussion and public debate are needed in a democratic society. Some of the remarks made therein are certain to be derogatory and/or factually unsound. But this is an unfortunate concomitant of the necessary debate. Therefore a public official cannot recover for libel unless he can prove wilful intention to malign—because his very presence and acts engender the type of debate that may lead to erroneous statements.

Three years later (1967) the Supreme Court extended this law to cover "public figures." These are people who attract widespread public attention— for instance, a person involved in widely discussed litigation with the government becomes a public figure. Then in 1971, the Supreme Court extended this law still further to cover cases involving "public interest."

The matter of public interest, however, was nullified by the Supreme Court on June 25, 1974, when it reversed District Court Judge Bernard M. Decker in the case of Elmer Gertz against the John Birch Society publication, *American Opinion*. In this case, the Court ruled that Gertz and other private citizens need not meet the requirements demanded of public officials and public figures—even though the case may involve public interest. Hence they need not be forced to prove a wilful intention to malign; they need only prove that they were harmed. (*Gertz v. Welch*, 418 U.S. 323).

These decisions have affected the question of libel in two important ways: (1) they have given the media a legal basis for treating the public official and the public figure in a manner different from that accorded the nonpublic personality; (2) they have shaken the old guideline that the media must always be able to prove every statement true or be exposed to financial or other penalty.

Meanwhile, these decisions leave some questions open to factual dispute: "Who is a public official?" "Who is a public figure?"

"Can one separate their public from their private lives?"

Translated into specifics: Is the obscure candidate for tax collector in a rural town a public figure? May a medium make statements about his private life that it may not make of other people's private life? When does the obscure citizen become a public figure? Therefore, what statements can be made of him as a public figure?

THE FUTURE OF THE NEWSPAPER

Because of the changes within the field of mass communications, some well-informed people are predicting a dark future for the newspaper. They contend that the newspaper, in its present form, cannot withstand the competition of the other media—especially television—and therefore will soon be reduced to the status of a second-rate force. In its place they see television newscasts, cable TV, teletype machines in the home, and even screens upon which news will be flashed as the viewer may choose.

On the basis of available facts, these predictions are distinctly premature. Though the competition of radio and television has already made itself felt, the newspaper has clearly survived. In addition, each of the media—radio, television, the magazine, and the newspaper—serve specific needs. Hence each has a specific place in the scheme of things.

As for teletype machines in the home, the expense of initial installation, the cost of maintenance, and the effort involved in searching through reams of copy to find the desired material certainly make the whole enterprise questionable. Similarly, screens in the home for controlled distribution of news would also be an expensive undertaking—scarcely to be compared to the price of the newspaper. In contrast, the newspaper enjoys the specific advantages cited constantly by its advocates. It presents a permanent record; it can be scanned, read, and reread as the individual may choose; and it can be perused comfortably in a variety of physical situations.

Even more important in the view of newspaper publishers: the newspaper presents a collection of diverse and interesting reading for a large segment of the middle class. This group enjoys reading—especially about contemporary subjects and problems—but it has easier access to newspapers than to opinion magazines and similar publications. Therefore, it turns to newspaper columnists, editorials, feature stories, and specialized material (accounts of medical research, theater reviews, round-ups of opinions on pressing problems) for its leisure-time reading. For this group, there is simply no available substitute for the newspaper.

Naturally, only a reckless thinker would speak confidently of future changes—such as the possibility of an inexpensive method of printing the newspaper via teletype right in the subscriber's home. But basing any sound conclusion on the present situation and the foreseeable future, the newspaper as it now exists is firmly embedded in the American way of life.

This particular statement can be substantiated by some rather impressive statistics. According to figures compiled by the Standard Rate and Data Service, more than 100 million Americans read a newspaper every day—while daily newspaper circulation stands at an all-time high of 62 million.

However, a qualification must be placed on the expression "the newspaper as it now exists," for the reason that the number of high-circulation newspapers in the United States is decreasing even though the nation's population is growing. The decrease is largely the result of mergers. When newspapers merge, they are no longer "as they existed" before—no matter why they merge. The competition between them ends and—usually and more important—so does the presentation of differing viewpoints, a presentation needed in a democratic society. This situation characterizes the "one-newspaper city"—a term that unfortunately applies to the vast majority of United States cities.

The expression can be reworded, for many cities, to "one-medium city," for the newspaper often owns the radio or television station that serves its city.

In fact, most large newspapers own radio or television stations. And even though the owners argue that the papers and the broadcasting stations are independent units, the fact of their having the same ownership creates the probability of offering the same viewpoint on public affairs. Indeed, in some instances the Federal government has prosecuted antitrust actions to make newspapers divest themselves of radio and television stations.

EXERCISES

1. Discuss some recent experience of media people—print media or electronic media—in protecting sources of their news from courtroom questioning.
2. From the most recent Yearbook of Standard Rate and Data Service, obtain the figures for the total circulation and readership of newspapers in the United States. Do these reflect increasing monopoly in the newspaper business? Do they show increasing or declining ownership of newspapers and broadcast stations by the same owners?
3. What cities in your state have two or more newspapers? If you are in a state-boundary area, where two or more states share a major business area, how many communities in this area have two or more newspapers? Are they chain-owned papers or independent? Do newspapers own broadcast stations or are they owned by broadcasting companies? Has your community—or the state or Federal government—made any effort to separate the ownership of broadcast stations from the ownership of newspapers?
4. In May 1975, Senator William Proxmire (Wisconsin) suggested a reconsideration of the "Fairness Doctrine" that is one of the chief tests in FCC investigations of radio and TV stations' dissemination of news material and viewpoints in general. Examine the newspaper and magazine comments of the time on Senator Proxmire's ideas and pass a careful judgment on the whole situation.
5. For a period of at least one month, make an analysis of the "Letters to the Editor" section of your newspaper. Discuss the readers' complaints against the selection and handling of news. Answer especially: What complaints arise most often? How sound are these complaints? How often is the newspaper clearly in error?
6. Using your home town or your community as a microcosm of a large segment of the American populace, discuss how you would improve television offerings to lure more viewers and to contribute generally to the uplift of society.

7. Select any libel suit of the past year and discuss its merits as objectively as you possibly can.
8. Write a thoughtful explanation of the United States citizen's right to privacy from the activities of the media.

FOR FURTHER READING

Barnouw, Eric. *A Tower of Babel*. New York: Oxford University Press, 1966.

Barnouw, Eric. *The Golden Web*. New York: Oxford University Press, 1968.

Barnouw, Eric. *The Image Empire*. New York: Oxford University Press, 1970.

Blanchard, Robert C. *Congress and the News Media*. New York: Hastings House, Publishers, 1972.

Devol, Kenneth S. *Mass Media and the Supreme Court: The Legacy of the Warren Years,* Revised Edition. New York: Hastings House, Publishers, 1976.

Emery, Edwin. *The Press and America: An Interpretative History of the Mass Media*. Englewood Cliffs: Prentice-Hall, 1972.

Gallup, George. *The Sophisticated Poll-Watcher's Guide*. Princeton: Princeton Opinion Press, 1972.

Hynds, Ernest C. *American Newspapers in the 1970's*. New York: Hastings House, Publishers, 1975.

Johnson, Nicholas. *How to Talk Back to Your Television Set*. New York: Bantam, 1970.

Kobre, Sidney. *Development of American Journalism*. Dubuque: Wm. C. Brown, 1969.

Merrill, John C. *The Imperative of Freedom: A Philosophy of Journalistic Autonomy*. New York: Hastings House, Publishers, 1974.

Merrill, John C., and Ralph D. Barney. *Ethics and the Press: Readings in Mass Media Morality*. New York: Hastings House, Publishers, 1975.

Rosenberg, Bernard, and David M. White. *Mass Culture Revisited*. New York: Van Nostrand Reinhold, 1971.

Steinberg, Charles S., ed. *Broadcasting: The Critical Challenges*. New York: Hastings House, Publishers, 1972.

★ **3** ★

What Is News?
Finding the News
    The Reporter
    Sources of News
The Writing and Structure of the
    Newspaper News Story
        The Lead in the News Story
        The Body in the News Story
Style of the News Story
    Conciseness
    Clarity
    Forceful Expression
    Factual Accuracy
    Dictional Don't's
Rewriting
Treatment of News—Slanting and
    Coloring
Cut Lines
"The Journalistic Style"
Interpretative Reporting
Examples for Discussion

The News Story

WHAT IS NEWS?

In any discussion of the news story, the first step should be to define "news." This, however, is a baffling task, for although many definitions have been advanced, few have gained even limited acceptance. Consequently, most newspapermen make no attempt to define; they simply come to recognize news by association—by learning the situations that provide news. An all-inclusive definition is impossible because news is a relative matter, varying sharply (1) from one paper to another, (2) from one time to another, and (3) from one locality to another.

How the idea of "news" varies from one paper to another can be made clear by placing the tabloid against the conservative daily. In the tabloid are many stories that never appear in the conservative paper—such as accounts of family squabbles, gossip about semifamous personalities, or maudlin descriptions of obscure people and their personal troubles. Conversely, the conservative daily carries many stories generally ignored by the tabloid—such as detailed analyses of the stock market, discussions of lectures at nearby colleges, or interviews with visiting scientists. These differences demonstrate clearly that news for one paper is not news for the other.

How "news" varies from one time to another can be seen by checking the stories in some one newspaper for an extended period. On days when newsworthy items are scarce—as on a Saturday in August when most papers must scratch furiously for local news—a routine neighborhood banquet becomes news. On days when newsworthy items are more numerous—like the morning after a national election when most papers have more stories than they can handle—a similar banquet doesn't merit even a short. Time thus makes the difference between news and no news.

How "news" varies from one place to another is evident from a comparison of the stories in a rural paper with those in a metropolitan daily. In the rural area, a small house fire is news. In the metropolitan area, a dozen similar fires are ignored. In the rural area, the purchase of a new police car may get a page-one spot. In the metropolitan area, such routine purchases possess no appeal as news. Locality, therefore, makes a difference in the existence of news in these and similar instances.

Further evidence of the varying nature of news is seen in the manner in which several papers may handle the same story. While they agree that a given set of facts provides news, they may disagree on kind of news, facts to be omitted, and angles to be stressed. For example, the tabloid, the conservative daily, and the neighborhood weekly generally differ widely in their treatment of automobile accidents in which children are killed. The tabloid often plays up the sentimental side, using one or more gory pictures. The conservative daily most often confines itself briefly to the main facts, using pictures of the traditional pattern. The neighborhood weekly generally handles the story from a strictly local angle, interpolating the maximum in local interest (names of residents involved even slightly, playmates' reactions, schools attended, and the like). Thus, the story provides a different type of news for each paper.

Despite these insurmountable obstacles to establishing an all-inclusive definition, journalists are in fairly common agreement that the following five qualities characterize news stories.

First, *news is any printable story which, in the opinion of the editor, will interest the readers of his paper* (or the audience of his broadcast). A story is "printable" [1] if it meets the editorial policy standards of the particular paper; a story will interest readers if (1) it concerns them directly or (2) it makes interesting reading.

The most common stories that concern readers directly are accounts of government actions (tax increases, new laws, appointments); advances in science (cures for disease, new inventions, experiments); and economic analyses (employment studies, price-level explanations, stock-market predictions). The stories that are news because they make interesting reading run a wide gamut. They tell of the President's Christmas purchases, county fairs, changes in clothing fashions, freak auto accidents, or indeed anything that the editor believes newsworthy. How deeply the editor thinks the reader will be interested largely determines the "play" that the story receives.

[1] See Chapter 9 for a discussion of editorial policy.

Second, *news is always completely true,* or it is at least a set of facts that have been presented to the reporter as truth. It is the story of something that has actually happened or it is a statement that has been made. In relating news, therefore, the newsteller may not resort to conjecture or supposition; he is limited to the cold facts of the story, told without emotion, prejudice, or personal opinion. Hence the story must have the atmosphere of veracity that characterizes the scientist's account of his experiment. Any deviation from this restriction is termed "editorializing," a fault that most newspeople view as serious.[2]

Third, *news has a quality of recency about it.* It is the story of something that has just happened or something being told for the first time. In short, it is a story that possesses the appeal of freshly discovered material. The successful newspaper or newscast, therefore, must carry the latest newsworthy items in places ranging from the police court to the conference rooms of the United Nations. And it must put out its accounts as soon after the actual occurrences as possible. The old statement, "as out of date as yesterday's newspaper," is still a reliable indication of the emphasis placed on recency.

Fourth, *news has an element of proximity about it.* People, generally speaking, are most interested in events that are near them in space, time, and general background. This statement means that people are usually most interested in stories from their own city, state, and nation; in stories of or close to the present time; and in stories related to their racial, social, cultural, or national background. The element of proximity thus places a heavy emphasis on stories of local interest, current events, and activities of racial, religious, and national groups.

Fifth, *news must have some element of the unusual about it.* Although some few stories, such as routine announcements from public officials (the President's proclamation regarding Thanksgiving), can have little of the unusual, the good editor always wants stories that get outside the commonplace. The unusual aspect brightens the newspaper page or the radio or television newscast. Its importance is to be seen in the old saw, "If a dog bites a man, it's not news; but if a man bites a dog, it is news."

In any consideration of these five qualities that characterize "news," two cautions are important. The first is that there can be no "chemistry" of the news story because newspapers do not emphasize the qualities uniformly. The *Christian Science Monitor,* for instance, concerns itself almost exclusively with national and international news; the New York *Daily News,* a tabloid, leans most heavily on sensational stories of New Yorkers; the *St. Louis Post-Dispatch* strives to cover a wide field of interests. In each case, therefore, there is a different emphasis on the qualities that characterize news. Comparable differences are found in newscasts.

The second caution is that many news purveyors, chiefly newspapers but also some broadcasters, are currently incorporating an important concept into their definition of news: they see controversy as an ingredient in many news

---

[2] This statement cannot be applied strictly to interpretative reporting. The reason is explained later in this chapter under "Interpretative Reporting."

stories. Those who cultivate this concept contend that numerous events heretofore treated briefly or impersonally—or bypassed entirely—possess a vein of controversy that contributes substantially toward making the story "news" in the true sense of the term. For instance, in stories of urban protest, suits against the government, and educational reform, the real story emanates from the controversy involved—not from the settled facts of the situation. Therefore, controversy is part of the news itself and must be accepted and developed in the writing of a story.

This "news-is-controversy" philosophy is not a new approach so much as it is an updating of an old practice. In days past, many newspapers really employed this philosophy as they crusaded for specific causes to which they committed themselves. These papers worked for changes in government policies, for improved consumer protection, for better sanitation, and for similar reforms; and in so doing, they interpreted carefully the controversial aspect of all stories related to the cause. Hence when discussing, for instance, a proposed law that touched their special interest, they singled out the controversial aspects for interpretation—thereby employing a news-is-controversy philosophy.

Also, by this approach, newspapers sought to convince their readership of their forthrightness in presenting important questions. By zeroing in on the controversial aspects of news, a newspaper could emphasize its commitment to protecting the public interest.

Within recent years, the news-is-controversy philosophy has been encouraged by unrest, protest, and general discontent among the young and the counterculture people. These groups have constantly berated an entity broadly termed the "establishment," and to achieve their goals, they have demanded more coverage by the news media of their activities. Especially, they have denounced military activities, economic suppression of minorities, maneuverings of big business, deterioration of the environment, and a lack of integrity in the Federal government.

Responding to these demands, the media have given a greater coverage to meetings, rallies, sit-ins, and other forms of protest—accompanied by some attempt to interpret the controversy inherent in the particular situation.

FINDING THE NEWS

The Reporter

The greatest element in the gathering of news is undoubtedly the ability of the reporter seeking it. One reporter may cover a district without finding a single story; a second may glean a dozen from the same area. In seeking a story, one reporter may find barely enough information for a short; a second may get a full column. In each case, the ability of the individual reporter determines the quality and the quantity of news obtained. Many older newsmen would summarize by declaring that a reporter must have a "nose for news."

They would cite case after case where successful journalists obtained stories when others had failed, attributing it all to a congenital newsfinding ability. Yet there is danger in accepting without qualification any argument that reporters are born, not made. Many reporters have been highly successful by learning their job as one would a trade or a profession; that is, by working hard, being alert, and studying the methods of the most successful men in the field.

Undoubtedly those best qualified to pass judgment on the requirements of the good reporter are the newsmen themselves. The student of journalism, therefore, should know what qualities the seasoned newsman looks for in the reporter. The following points represent the attributes of the successful reporter, as given by 45 newspapermen with successful careers on large papers, ranging from 11 to 51 years.

Accuracy. Above all else, the reporter must be accurate, for editors and publishers—in either print or electronic media—have little use for material containing factual errors. Consequently, the reporter must first teach himself the necessity of obtaining unassailable information; he must realize that guesses, surmises, and carelessly checked material can lead only to disaster. In essence, he must ever live by the slogan made popular by a news service: "Get it first, but first get it right!"

The importance of accuracy stands unquestioned because (1) inaccurate statements may easily stir up libel suits; [3] and (2) a medium printing or airing inaccuracies loses prestige with its readers or listeners. A single careless reporter can often embroil his employer in a libel suit, or he can alienate discerning readers or listeners by making them skeptical of everything carried or aired. Further, he can provide substance for the all-too-common misconception that most media are prepared to sacrifice veracity for audience interest or other advantage (such as, aiding a political candidate in his fight for office).

Recognition of a Story. The reporter must be certain that he can always recognize news—in all its implications—as defined by his organization. He must be able to spot immediately those stories upon which his employer sets top priority and to place lesser stories in their proper position on the value scale. He must also be able to find those stories required for supplementary material or shorts. In brief, he must be able to recognize and assess the stories his medium wants.

To learn his medium's concept of news, the reporter should study successive issues or broadcasts for a prolonged period. This procedure will exhibit rather clearly the stories sought by his editors—as well as the nature of the treatment accorded the stories. Thus the reporter can learn the organization's view on the sordid, the seamy, the spectacular, the entertaining, and the other stories which involve a subjective judgment.

In all his endeavors, the reporter must remember that occasionally the real story lies deep beneath the superficial facts—as, for example, when the real

---

[3] See Chapters 2 and 7 for discussions of libel.

story of a murder lies in the perpetrator's family history. In handling any involved data, the reporter must be able to sense the real story in the manner that a good hunter senses the presence of game.

Handling a Story. When working a story, the reporter must know the facts to seek, their order of importance, and where to find them. He must get all important names—with correct spellings, addresses, and occupations (even though these may not be used), as well as any other pertinent detail (for example, the hold-up victim is a relative of a prominent judge). All these facts, of course, contribute authenticity and interest to the story.

Further, the reporter must build up a background of knowledge concerning the relative value of people as news subjects. He must know, for instance, that professional men are generally stronger news-story material than businessmen, and that mugged clergymen are more newsworthy than mugged steelworkers. These and similar facts he can learn through careful observation.

In addition, the reporter should know that startling facts outside the story itself can often lift the story above the routine. Some examples are: a 77-year-old man injured slightly in an automobile accident is a triplet, and all three live in the same house; the foreman of the newly empaneled jury has 17 cats at home; the newly elected president of the small local union once won a clam-eating contest.

In summary, the reporter must always know the procedures and the devices necessary to obtain and present the best story.

Clarity of Expression. The reporter must have the ability to express himself well both in writing and in speech. The need for effective written expression is obvious. The need for effective oral expression exists because the reporter does so much interviewing and because he often gathers news for a rewriter, to whom he must make clear and vivid, usually by telephone, every point in the story. Also, frequently the reporter must give the editor a quick, incisive picture of a situation or happening that he believes to be newsworthy.

Pleasing Personality. Because so much newsgathering involves personal contact, the reporter must have a pleasing personality. The importance of personality, however, is not limited to gathering news; it is also highly important in contacts with fellow newsgatherers. Frequently reporters must work in pairs or in teams, under intense pressure, to get a story, and in such instances a pleasing personality obviously helps to make the team work more smoothly. The reporter, in short, must be one who can "get along" with other persons—one whose personality "wears well."

Adjusting Approach. The reporter must develop versatility in handling people. He must be able to handle with equal facility the residents of the so-called "tough" neighborhoods and those from the politer sections. Furthermore, he must attempt to speak the language of the person he is interviewing—if he can do so without affectation or other trait likely to alienate the person involved. And he must be especially careful not to imitate the melodramatic television-story version of the reporter in action.

This ability to adjust approach must be developed at the outset, for strange though it may seem, the lowliest reporting assignments (cub reporter, district man, or the like) often require dealing with the widest range of personalities.

Speed. The reporter must be one who can work efficiently at top speed, one who does not break under the pressure of time. This ability to work rapidly is indispensable because much news breaks fast and must be handled fast, especially for the electronic media. The reporter, therefore, must be able to handle accidents, disasters, and other spot news in the minimum time, or the story may miss the deadline.

Gaining the ability to work quickly is largely a matter of knowing what to do. Hence the reporter must construct a plan of attack for every conceivable kind of story. In covering an apartment-house fire, for instance, he should seek to learn the following in the order stated: the number of people injured, the extent of their injuries, the amount of damage, the cause of the fire, the problems met by the firefighters, any possible deviation from fire-code regulations, residents' reactions and plans (if the house is uninhabitable), and finally spectators' reactions.

By having a plan like this for every kind of story, the reporter decreases immensely his chances of becoming rattled and therefore less efficient when news breaks.

Ingenuity. The successful reporter must be well blessed with ingenuity. He must strive constantly for originality in newsgathering procedures—especially in investigative reporting—and must always be alert in procuring photographs and other material helpful to his story. He must never forget that the news world, like other highly competitive fields, is one wherein intelligence is an essential. The reporter who is constantly outwitted by a rival or outmaneuvered by someone involved in the news source stands little chance to succeed. Ingenuity is also vastly important in finding new and different angles to handle otherwise dull and routine material.

Knowing News Sources. The reporter must remember that persons in a position to give news frequently want to withhold stories, either temporarily or permanently. This is especially true of the central figures in scandals, thefts, and other stories likely to provoke unfavorable publicity. It is also true, however, of public officials striving to conceal politically damaging information, police officers not wanting to tip their hand in lengthy investigations, people involved in litigation whose lawyers have recommended "no comment," and many similar instances.

Thus the reporter often has a special problem in knowing news sources: he must know the person likely to divulge the necessary information—either unwittingly or as a personal favor. The ground-crew foreman at the airport, for example, is often the one who can tell the reporter when the dignitary's plane is to leave; and the nurse's aide at the hospital can say whether or not the ill statesman is under heavy sedation.

Checking Names. Since persons not wanting their names publicized sometimes give false information to the reporter, he must know how to check names and addresses against a source likely to be correct. Especially, the reporter must beware the person likely to give someone else's name in place of his own. This practice, obviously, presents the possibility of legal action against the newspaper.

Among the best on-the-scene sources for checking authenticity of names and addresses are driver's licenses, employee identification cards, and social security cards. ("Can I see how you spell it?") Among the secondary sources are police blotters, telephone and city directories, and private listings (club membership lists, institution catalogs, private directories, or the like).

Building Contacts. The reporter should maintain a long list of friends and acquaintances who may be of help when stories break, and he should know intimately persons who can give authoritative information on every kind of story. Among the most desirable persons to have on a contact list are police officers, labor leaders, attorneys, government employees, and persons associated with hospitals and other places where stories are likely to be found.

These contact lists, incidentally, are especially important to the investigative reporter. They can open closed doors, gain inaccessible information, and create advantages not obtainable otherwise.

Retaining the Favor of the Police. Because the police are involved in so many situations that become news, the reporter must know how to obtain and retain their favor. This can be accomplished primarily by giving the police favorable publicity when warranted, or in the words of the veteran district reporters, "taking care of the cops." Consequently, whenever the police make an important arrest or do other creditable work, the reporter should get police names into the story. The officers are grateful because this publicity often attracts the attention of their superiors, thereby aiding in their chances for promotion.

Many a reporter has received a scoop by virtue of help from a policeman grateful for a past favor. And many a reporter has failed to obtain a story because he did not have the necessary help from the police.

Respecting Promises. The reporter must be painstakingly careful in making promises, especially promises to persons who are news sources. If the reporter knows, for example, that he cannot withhold a name from publication, he should not promise to do so. And if someone gives him a story with the understanding that certain facts are to be included, he must make certain that the stipulated information gets into print or onto the air. Broken promises invariably threaten the continuance of many news sources.

The matter of promises becomes most important, of course, in situations where the reporter must maintain a frequent contact with the news source—for example, make regular calls on certain public officials and spokesmen for hospitals and other institutions. The reporter, naturally, must be very careful in these instances because of the long-term relationship.

Knowing the Area. The reporter must know his area in order not to lose valuable time in handling stories. He must know the streets, the important buildings, and the fastest routes to all places at all hours. He must familiarize himself especially with the locations of hospitals, police stations, morgues, firehouses, public auditoriums, and similar news sources.

Working Agreement with Rivals. Whenever a reporter agrees to exchange information or co-operate with a reporter from a rival organization, he should make certain that the agreement is beneficial to him and that it is clearly understood by the rival. If an agreement is not beneficial to a reporter, he is actually helping the competitor to hurt him. If a working agreement is not clearly understood by both reporters, unpleasant relations are certain to follow and the co-operation necessary on big stories that break fast will be threatened.

Getting Names in the Story. The reporter must get as many names as possible in the story without obviously overloading it. Names are important because they generate reader interest and because they give stories a note of authenticity. They are also important because the person who likes to see his name in print is more prone to help the reporter, now and later.

Direct Quotations. Whenever a direct quotation is to be printed or broadcast, the reporter should exert special care in getting the exact words.[4] This caution is important because occasionally the quoted person later denies having made the statement—even under oath in court. To forestall difficulty, therefore, the reporter often must read the quotation back to the person, as is frequently done in interviewing high public officials.

The significance of accuracy in handling quotations is, once again, that (1) quotations may be the cause of expensive and prestige-damaging litigation, and (2) preciseness of quotations creates an atmosphere of veracity in the newspaper.

Editing the News. The reporter must not trespass on the domain of his editor by acting as a field editor, or one who assumes the task of editing the news at its source. The reporter's job is to find news; the editor's job is to pass upon it. When the reporter draws the fire of his editor by assuming the latter's prerogative, strained relations generally arise.

Professional Respect. If the reporter is to be successful, he must have genuine respect for the whole field of journalism. He must realize the significant role that the news fills in society and the importance of his work as a reporter. All too often, a reporter feels that he is doing routine work for an unappreciative public. When this attitude is adopted, the reporter's work is certain to take on a tone of mediocrity.

Improvement. The reporter must always strive to improve, even after long years of varied experience. As in other professions, the reporter will slip backward when he ceases his efforts to improve. A constant effort to be a better reporter is, therefore, imperative.

---

[4] See "Note Taking," later in this chapter, for a discussion of the use of recording devices.

Sources of News

Newspapers in large cities usually obtain their news from the sources listed below. These sources are also used in varying degree by small dailies, trade publications, weeklies, and electronic media.

District Reporters. District reporters patrol an assigned beat or geographical area, commonly a section of the city or a group of suburbs, watching for any news that may originate in it. "Leg men" was once the appropriate label for them; now they are quite likely to be women and also likely to use wheels more than legs. They routinely check the firehouses, hospitals, morgues, or other places in their districts likely to have first knowledge of events that make news. When the district reporter has a story, he calls his editor to learn whether it will be used and, if so, what "play" it is to receive. He may dictate the facts to a rewriter in the newsroom or to a tape recorder; he may even write the story or, if he works for a broadcast organization, phone in the finished story for the air. The district reporter may also be called upon to check tips or stories given him by the desk or to gather information on a story emanating from a source outside his district.

However, some changes are occurring in the concept of assigning reporters to patrol geographical districts.

More and more, metropolitan news media are finding that the intricacies of urban news demand specialists, even teams of reporters with complementary skills, to handle certain common stories. Therefore, the nature of the story, rather than the place of origin, becomes the basis for making assignments.

The protests of neighborhood residents against zoning changes, for example, are seldom the disorganized, extemporaneous, emotional complaints of the past. They are now more likely to develop under the direction of a professional expert. Similarly, the demands of national and ethnic groups for their legal rights are rarely made through informal assemblies. Instead, the demands are voiced by lawyers and efficient public relations firms. Hence these stories have become more complex and more challenging to cover and interpret— thereby eliminating the jack-of-all-trades reporter who handles any story that may arise.

Today the reporter, like the specialist in other professional fields, must often focus competently on situations that demand extensive training.

General and Special Assignments. The news that emanates daily from a particular place (a city hall, a court house, a Federal building) is often so significant that a reporter is given the special assignment of watching over that one spot for stories the minute they break. Furthermore, a single story from a special-assignment source may be so demanding that it consumes the reporter's whole day.

For example, the special-assignment reporter covering the state legislature may spend his entire day following the maneuverings and politicking involved in having a single bill passed or defeated. The story is so valuable as news that it must be presented fully and competently. Therefore, the reporter must be present for committee sessions, the wheeling and dealing, the arm twisting, and every other behind-the-scenes movement of the bill. Meanwhile, he must remain alert for any spot news such as a spirited encounter on the assembly floor.

There is also, however, a second type of special assignment work. This particular type can be understood easily in the light of the increasing need for specialized abilities.

From their first days in news work, most reporters train themselves to be specialists in certain types of stories. Thereafter, as they demonstrate their ability to handle material in the particular category, they become part- or full-time specialists in that field.

A few kinds of stories that require specialized knowledge—and hence provide opportunities for specialization—are those that treat politics, labor, education, religion, stamps, and highway construction. When the reporter writes with great frequency on one of these topics, he is often designated the "education editor," the "stamps editor," or whatever other "editor" title is appropriate.

A final point concerning "special assignment" is that the term is opposed to "general assignment." The general-assignment reporter is on call to handle any story to which he or she may be assigned.

Roving Reporters. The roving reporter is an experienced worker assigned by his editor to roam the city for news—especially for material for human interest and other feature stories. He usually seeks stories at building construction sites, downtown shopping areas, waterfronts, and other places where news is likely to exist, and he relies on friends in varied walks of life to supply tips. The success of the roving reporter naturally determines his right to this attractive assignment—an assignment that is eagerly sought because of the pleasant nature of the work and the customary by-line.

Because some reporters handle this kind of news daily—as opposed to those who receive this kind of assignment only occasionally—their stories may be placed in the same position in the newspaper every day. Therefore, they are often viewed as columnists specializing in local material.

Futures File. The futures file is the repository for notices, letters, programs, and notations of events to come. This file is especially helpful in making assignments, planning the news schedule for the week, and maintaining coverage of local events. The file, usually at the city editor's desk, generally covers the coming three months.

Tipsters. Newsgathering organizations frequently maintain a group of "tipsters," persons paid for informing the editor of anything that may be newsworthy. The tipster, who is usually paid in proportion to the space or air time given the story or to the importance of the tip, must demonstrate both integrity and the ability to furnish valuable information. Tipsters are most often persons whose industrial or governmental positions enable them to have the first inkling of newsworthy events.

Tipsters are usually associated with columnists but are also used rather widely in general newsgathering. Furthermore, some media make tipsters of their readers and listeners by awarding prizes to people who phone in tips that lead to stories. Newspapers following this practice generally use a standing box on the front page to offer the prizes, state the rules and procedures, and give the telephone number. Electronic media stations generally announce the rules from time to time.

Stringers. The stringer is so named because he was once paid according to the length of his "string"—the number of columns that his stories filled. The name is still used although the conditions have changed. The modern stringer, man or woman, is usually only a part-time employee, but is an employee nonetheless. He may have other employers, and may even work full-time for one of them. He should not be confused with the tipster—he is a much more important figure, his service is continuous, and he does more than merely locate tips.

Usually, the stringer operates primarily by lifting material from the publication or station for which he works full-time and reworking it for the string employer. He may, however, submit material he has unearthed on his own or material he has obtained on direct order. He generally phones in his news material for rewrite but may write out the story and transmit it by wire or telephone. Feature stories may be mailed in. The stringer is paid on a per-story basis or a salary.

The two great advantages gained by the newspapers that employ stringers are: (1) they can obtain widespread coverage by competent journalists equipped with the contacts necessary to procure valuable news and (2) they can effect substantial savings because the stringer works for less than a full-time salary.

Handouts. The handout is a statement presented to news people in mimeographed form or by spoken delivery in places where important stories are being pursued.

The best-known examples of handouts are the statements released daily by the White House staff. When, for example, the newspaper and electronic media reporters are seeking the President's reaction to a threatened nationwide transportation strike, the reporters are often handed copies of a prepared statement, or they are read an authorized quotation by a presidential assistant. Similarly, when reporters are seeking progress reports from police working on an important case or when they try to speak with an industrial tycoon being sued for illegal dealings, they frequently must settle for a handout from a spokesman who can release nothing more.

For the newspaper, the distinct advantage of the written handout is that chances for misquoting are minimal. The disadvantages are several. Before all, the handout contains only what the source wants to reveal, not what the public wants to know. The data, obviously, are always limited by lack of enlargement. And the handout tends to make the treatment of the story in every newspaper similar to that of the others.

Publicity Releases. Any institution, organization, or group that desires publicity distributes publicity releases. In some instances, these releases are done in a distinctly amateurish manner by a member of the group itself. However, in the case of larger and therefore wealthier groups, the work is more often executed by a publicity professional or agency.

Although many of these releases have little value as news, one occasionally has genuine appeal. Usually these releases are most valuable when they come from such nonprofit organizations as museums, scientific associations, and charitable agencies. When they are distributed by business houses and other commercial enterprises, they often sound more like material for advertisements or commercials than for news.

Space Writers. To save money, news media frequently employ writers to contribute stories on a space basis. The space writer is paid by the column inch for material accepted and used, regardless of amount of material submitted. Space writers are usually aspirants to the newspaper business, students who write of events in their schools, and persons who act as correspondents from their home towns for newspapers located elsewhere.

In some instances, the space writer is actually a stringer because he submits his material on a regular basis and is viewed by the newspaper as its representative in that particular area.

Unsolicited Calls. All newspapers and newscasters receive unsolicited telephone calls and letters telling them of potential stories. These calls most often tell of accidents, deplorable neighborhood conditions, or illicit activity.

Although the caller's motive is often selfish—as when a homeowner complains of holes in the street that the highway department refuses to repair—many callers seem motivated by a desire to be a part of the newspaper's activity. They sense a satisfaction in seeing in print a story which they reported to the paper. Whatever the reason, however, some of the best stories in the paper may result from checking these unsolicited tips.

Death Notices. By checking published death notices in the paper, the editor sometimes finds one that should be followed up or enlarged into an obituary (as when an elderly once-prominent educator, now almost completely without family ties, dies practically unnoticed in a nursing home). Or the person who died may have figured in an earlier story (for instance, as an important witness in a famous murder trial). Death notices are also checked against the various "Who's Who," the social register, and the clippings in the newspaper or station reference library.

Stories from Other Newspapers and Newscasts. Editors for newspapers and broadcast news programs systematically monitor the output of their rivals—read their papers, watch their programs, listen to their newscasts. If they find a good story they haven't covered, they often assign a reporter to work on it, if possible. In some cases they simply recast the story for their own use. Consequently, local stories can be exclusive for no more than a few hours unless the source of the news can be kept away from rivals. Any story that has a "follow" (that is, a story that will create more news in the near future), is as a matter of course worked over by newsgatherers who missed it in the beginning.

New Services. In addition to the sources discussed above, newspapers and newscasters rely on the wire services to supply news from other parts of the state, the nation, and the world. The two prominent wire services in the United

States are the Associated Press and the United Press International. In addition to the wire services, newspapers use the news bureaus of such large papers as the *New York Times,* the *Chicago Tribune,* the *St. Louis Post-Dispatch,* and the *Los Angeles Times.* Also, some newspapers have individual arrangements with papers in other cities to use each other's material under stipulated conditions. Thus readers in Cleveland, San Francisco, and other American cities get local news from other parts of the nation.

THE WRITING AND STRUCTURE
OF THE NEWSPAPER NEWS STORY

The newspaper news story is a communication form shaped by more than two centuries of experience. It is special both in the way it is written and in the end results. Magazine news stories are different. Television and radio news stories are even more different (they are considered in Chapter 13). The rest of this chapter concerns only the newspaper news story—its structure, its style, its special requirements, and what it demands of the writer.

The Lead in the News Story

The news story is normally written in a structure unique to newspaper journalism—in two parts called the *lead* and the *body.* In contrast to the short fiction story wherein events build to a climax, the news story generally states the climax at the outset and then enlarges on it.

The lead is exactly what its name implies. It is the part that comes first. And it tells the essence of the whole story in a sentence or two. (Other kinds of stories may have different kinds of leads; see Chapter 5 for examples of feature-story leads.) The news story itself may be several columns long, but the lead must summarize it. The lead tells the *where, when, what, how, why,* and *who* of the story. Some leads may not need all six of these, but no lead should be without the necessary ones it needs.

Here are four typical leads:

Teamster Unit To Give Car To Palsy Victims

The 23 children suffering from cerebral palsy who attend South Side Training Center school in the Tuley Park fieldhouse, 90th st. and St. Lawrence av., will be presented with a specially equipped station wagon today by Teamsters Joint Council No. 25, Ray Schoessling, president of the council, announced today.

—*Chicago Tribune*

5th 'Rock Out' Of Season Set At Civic Center

The youth dance committee of the Bridgeport Jaycees has announced that this coming Saturday evening at the Benedum Civic Center in Bridgeport the fifth "rock out" of the summer will be held.

—*Clarksburg* (W. Va.) *Exponent*

Furniture Surplus Up For Sale

The Cheektowaga-Sloan School Dist. will hold a garage sale of surplus school furniture Aug. 2 and 3, from 8:30 a.m. to 3:30 p.m. in the new maintenance building at the John F. Kennedy High School, 305 Cayuga Rd., Cheektowaga. The first day of the sale will be open only to school district employes.

—*Buffalo Courier Express*

Revised Tax Plan Delayed

LAKELAND—Implementation of tax assessment procedures on citrus groves has been postponed for further study by the State Department of Revenue at the request of Florida Citrus Mutual.

Tom Osborne, mutual general manager, said county tax assessors will continue using present tax guidelines instead of newly revised ones which he said would be inequitable to grove owners.

—*Tampa* (Fla.) *Tribune*

Before composing his lead, the writer must settle on the facts to be used and the arrangement of those facts. In the conventional lead, the writer usually selects and arranges detail according to order of importance—as he sees that order. Meanwhile, he concentrates on presenting his facts as clearly and as interestingly as possible.

To illustrate the process, here are the facts of a typical story, followed by the actual story in a representative daily newspaper.

Three boys—ages 18, 16, and 16—involved in a one-car accident on Garden State Parkway; car hit a guard rail and turned over at 4:15 yesterday afternoon; car had run off southbound lane about a mile south of Asbury Park, N.J., exit; Stephen Garboski, 16, Staten Island, N.Y., injured badly, condition fair; driver, Ralph A. Dipalma, 18, also of Staten Island, treated at Jersey Shore Medical Center and released; Steve Dipalma, 16, brother of driver, uninjured; cause of accident being investigated by State Trooper George Wheeler; all information supplied by Parkway and State police.

YOUTH INJURED ON TOLL ROAD

WALL TOWNSHIP—Stephen Garboski, 16, of Staten Island, was listed in fair condition last night following a one-car accident on the Garden State Parkway yesterday afternoon at 4:15.

According to parkway police, Garboski was a passenger in a car driven by Ralph A. Dipalma, 18, of Staten Island, which ran off the left side of the south bound lane approximately one mile south of the Asbury Park exit, hit a guard rail, and turned over.

Dipalma was treated at Jersey Shore Medical Center, Neptune. His brother, Steve, 16, also a passenger in the car, wasn't injured.

The cause of the accident is being investigated by Trooper George Wheeler.

—*Asbury Park* (N.J.) *Evening Press*

As the lead above reveals, the writer settled on the following selection and order of importance for his lead:

identity of most seriously injured boy
condition of injured boy

    one-car accident;
    place of accident
    time of accident.

Then, in the two remaining paragraphs, he used the lesser details as supporting material for his lead.

And throughout, he has managed to write clearly and interestingly, thereby demonstrating the ability to hold his reader's attention without undue demand on the reader's co-operation.

Learning to write an effective lead is no simple matter. The best of newswriters have had to struggle in this area. And even after years of practice, the newswriter may try three or four leads before he is satisfied.

The Body in the News Story

The body of the story, which is the part that follows the lead, serves to explain and enlarge upon the facts of the lead and to supply the less important information. The most common methods used in writing the body are the highlight, the chronological, and the pyramid.

The Highlight Method. When the writer employs the highlight method, he dwells on the most important parts of the event or the situation, thus "highlighting" the event or the situation. The highlight structure is especially suitable for stories of speeches, sports events, and pageants (parades, celebrations, etc.). The following is an example of the highlight method:

Quebec funding of acupuncture hit

By BILL FAIRBAIRN

Acupuncture Association of Quebec president Oscar Wexu yesterday called on Quebec to re-examine its decision to spend $100,000 to set up an officially recognized experimental acupuncture centre.

Speaking at his Belanger Street East clinic, Wexu asked why Quebec was "launching its own research team from naught when it can already benefit from research completed elsewhere?"

He said specialists in China had been dedicating their lives to the research of acupuncture for thousands of years and had passed on the results to acupuncturists in recognized schools.

Backed up by Hubert Lam, president of the Association of Acupuncturists of Ontario, Wexu advocated instead the "elaboration of complete statistics through the files of thousands of patients already treated by qualified Quebec acupuncturists."

Wexu disclosed details of a memorandum the 18-member association had submitted to Quebec Social Affairs Minister Claude Forget urging that the Acupuncture Association of Quebec be recognised as official spokesman for acupuncturists in Quebec and as adviser to the government in preparing acupuncture legislation.

Wexu said his association claimed

official recognition so that it might put "an end to abuses committed by numerous charlatans—many of whom were physicians—who allege to be acupuncturists and endanger the health of the population."

Wexu and Lam jointly announced that the Ontario and Quebec associations had united within the International Society of Acupuncture "in the hope it will contribute to the expansion and recognition of acupuncture in Canada."

The Quebec plan, as announced last May by Forget and Fernand La-londe, minister responsible for the application of Quebec's professions' code, would set up an acupuncture centre at one or more hospitals affiliated with universities.

The announcement followed a report prepared by the Quebec Professions Board.

The authorized centre would be given a $100,000 grant, would include doctors and non-doctors, and would make public "all information likely to aid the public in recognizing and requesting quality acupuncture service."

—The Montreal Star

The Chronological Method. The term "chronological method" is self-explanatory; it is the method by which the events in a story are presented in chronological order. This method employs the structure of the conventional short story, building directly up to a high point or climax. The following story is an example:

When Boat Fans Meet, They Sail Into Battle

Special to the Minneapolis Tribune

LONDON—In Britain, for centuries ruler of the waves, ships are taken seriously—even model ships.

So there was, as usual, a big crowd around Long pond on Clapham Common when Bob Cordiner launched his model steamboat, Robbie's Pride, and Ken Piper put into the water, from the opposite side, his model yacht, the Tempest.

The two elaborately contrived craft approached each other. Suddenly the Tempest swung in front of the steamship. Robbie's Pride, ignoring the rule of the sea that steam must give way to sail, plowed into the yacht, rending its sail.

The yacht owner ran over to the steamboat owner, grabbed him, and threw him into the pond. The steamboater, fishing out the yacht, carried it ashore and broke the mast over his knee. The two owners closed and came to blows.

It was a fine fight, until spectators and polic broke it up. Then the two model builders were hauled off to court, where the judge imposed fines totaling $22.40 on the pair, both grown men, and gave them a lecture.

—Minneapolis Tribune

The Pyramid Method. The pyramid method derives its name from the fact that the arrangement of details resembles a series of inverted pyramids; that is, the facts of the story are arranged in a descending order, the most important coming first. Study the example in which this structure is illustrated.

The pyramid method, incidentally, is especially appealing to the copy editor because of the ease with which he can trim (shorten) the story. When the copy editor must shorten a story cast in the pyramid method, he can simply lop off pyramids, beginning at the end and working upwards. Thus he can be sure of eliminating the least important detail.

The Zubik barge fleet will be gone from the Allegheny River bank by Oct. 15, according to Arthur V. Harris, president of the Three Rivers Improvement and Development Council (TRIAD).

Harris said he has been assured by representatives of the Zubik estate that the rusting boats and barges will be gone from the area between the Sixth Street and Fort Duquesne bridges by that date.

That would comply with the agreement with the City of Pittsburgh to have the equipment off the site within 90 days after the city made the first payment of a $90,000 purchase price for the riverfront property near Three Rivers Stadium, Harris said.

The first $30,000 payment was made on July 15, he said. It was announced yesterday by the U.S. Department of the Interior that it has approved a $493,000 grant for the construction of the proposed North Shore Park which will be developed in the area.

The park, which cannot be started until the Zubik fleet is gone, will cost about $3 million, Harris pointed out.

Payment for the park will be from a combination of state, federal and local money, he said.

Harris said some of the Zubik fleet already has been removed and all of it has been sold.

—*The Pittsburgh Press*

STYLE OF THE NEWS STORY

Conciseness

Generally speaking, the prime consideration in writing the news story is to say everything in the fewest words possible. Stories must be written concisely because most newspapers invariably have more material than they can use, and they want to print the maximum. The reporter, therefore, must learn to phrase his thoughts succinctly, without loss of details or accuracy. Note the following examples:

Long: The man decided after a great deal of consideration that it was best to act then and there.
Better: The man finally decided to act immediately.

Long: The rays of the light extended for a distance of more than 50 feet.
Better: The light shone more than 50 feet.

Long: They do not have any opening at the present time for a man with the qualifications of a stonemason.

Better: They have no openings now for stonemasons.

Long: This problem is recognized as a very difficult one and its solution is baffling to the best mathematicians.

Better: This very difficult problem baffles the best mathematicians.

Clarity

The second consideration in writing the news story is clarity. Although the event may be complex, the story still must be readable to the normal junior-high-school student. This clarity of presentation is obtained by avoiding intricate sentence structure and by using familiar words. Note the following examples:

Poor: That Judge Sloan's judicial pronouncements on the somewhat complex and frequently enigmatic subject of professional mendicants vacillates is not readily demonstrable, even by lawyers.

Better: Even lawyers would have trouble proving that Judge Sloan is not consistent in his rulings on the difficult question of professional beggars.

Poor: The chemist immersed the ecru redingote in a saline solution.

Better: The chemist dipped the tan coat in a salt solution.

Poor: A cardiologist extemporized upon the systolic and diastolic activity of the patient's heart.

Better: A heart specialist spoke about the beating of the patient's heart.

If the writer is forced to use a term that may baffle his reader (as, for instance, a legal term), the expression can be explained in parentheses, in an "editor's note," or in the context of the story, according to the nature of the explanation. Notice how the writer of the following story has explained a term in the context:

At Brecksville, 41% of those on drugs were taking two or more drugs, a practice called polypharmacy, despite findings that such simultaneous use should be avoided if possible. The VA average for polypharmacy was 32%.

Investigators found a patient at one hospital who was taking eight different drugs—three antipsychotic, two antianxiety, one antidepressant, one sedative and one anti-Parkinson.

When a draft of the report was shown to VA officials in Cleveland, it prompted a review of prescriptions, resulting quickly in a 30% reduction of polypharmacy.

—*The Plain Dealer*, Cleveland

Forceful Expression

The third consideration in writing the news story is the need for forceful expression. Although the demands for conciseness and clarity often result in simplicity of expression, news writing still must be forceful. The writer, therefore, must constantly seek for the most effective way, within the limits set by journalistic writing, of expressing a particular thought. It may lie in words used, or it may lie in skillful turn of phrase. It may lie in an unusual figure of speech, or it may lie in some other rhetorical device. Wherever it is, the reporter must find it. Note the following examples:

Fair: The Governor's car moved out of the drive and away from the spectators' view.

Better: The Governor's car slid quietly out of the drive and disappeared into the night.

Fair: Rain was falling as the jury walked from the Court House for lunch at a restaurant across the street.

Better: Rain was falling as the jury marched in pairs from the Court House for lunch at a restaurant across the street.

Fair: The spectators were trying hard to keep warm.

Better: The spectators stomped, twisted, and turned in their efforts to keep warm.

Fair: The committee left the room to deliberate.

Better: The committee filed out of the room to deliberate.

However, there are two cautions to be noted in stating that the journalist must write forcefully; the first concerns *choice of words,* and the second concerns *coherence.* In choice of words, the journalist, already limited to a relatively simple word choice, is restricted further by the need to recognize localisms and the rules of his newspaper concerning doubtful words. He may, for instance, speak of "redding up" (straightening the furniture, cleaning, and the like) a room in a region where that localism is used, but in other localities he must avoid it. As for doubtful words, the writer must check his paper's stylebook to know whether he is permitted to use such terms, for example, as *bum, flophouse, street walker, ripoff, con man, homo, gay, racket, hooker.*

The writer must also check his newspaper's policies on the use of those words and expressions which are generally covered under the heading of such vague terminology as "vulgarities," "obscenities," "profanity," and "four-letter words." Sometimes a newspaper permits language thus designated to appear in direct quotations but nowhere else.[5] Sometimes a newspaper will permit

[5] In the 1975 mayoralty primary election, Chicago Mayor Richard Daley told an audience that his critics could "kiss my ass." Some papers carried the quote; some did not. See *Newsweek,* March 10, 1975, p. 18.

certain expressions on the sports page but nowhere else. Policies differ from paper to paper.

The caution concerning coherence is simply this: a news story's coherence is different from the coherence of fiction and other nonjournalistic writing.

In fiction and other nonjournalistic material, the writer follows a natural sequential pattern; that is, he arranges his facts to build toward a climax or main thought.

In the conventional news story, however, the writer summarizes his story or places his main point in the lead. Then he arranges his facts to support the lead effectively and attractively. As a result, his arrangement of facts may be so clearly out of sequence that he appears to "jump around."

Furthermore, he often omits transitional elements ("however," "moreover," "in addition") to achieve brevity.

Note the absence of ordinary coherence in the story below. In this story, which is completely acceptable journalistic writing, the writer presents the parts in the following nonsequential pattern: (1) punishment for the action, (2) the action itself, (3) suggestions for a punishment, (4) judicial consideration of the case, (5) explanation of the boy's fulfilling the sentence, (6) a nonparticipant's comment on the episode.

To appreciate fully the differences from ordinary coherence in this story, do this: use the facts as the basis for a traditional short story. Then compare arrangements.

Youth escapes contempt count

Scrubbing erases scratching

By VIRGINIA DELAVAN

Fifteen minutes' work with steel wool and a paintbrush yesterday saved Aubrey Ryans, 18, from a conviction for contempt of court.

Ryans, of 2800 block Bowers St., used the materials to erase his own fingernail scratchings from the back of a wooden bench in Superior Courtroom.

The work detail was suggested by Judge William T. Quillen, before whom Ryans appeared to show cause why he shouldn't be punished for contempt.

Ryans was a spectator Oct. 21 at a trial, conducted under heavy security, of three men accused of shooting at a Wilmington policeman. He was arrested by Patrolman John P. Curran, who was sitting nearby and caught Ryans in the act.

The youth admitted he scratched his initials, "A.R.," on the bench during a lull, for "no reason," but denied a small rectangle scratched there also was his handiwork, as Curran had said.

Bernard Balick, the assistant public defender representing Ryans, asked him whether he meant to "show anger or contempt toward the court."

"No, sir," the youth answered solemnly.

Ryans had not resisted arrest or made any "public display," as he would have if he felt antagonistic toward the court, Balick pointed out. Neither did his actions "interfere with the processes of the court."

Young people have a penchant for leaving their initials in public places, the lawyer said, urging Quillen not to "confuse minor nuisance activities with contempt."

Viewing the episode somewhat differently, Deputy Atty. Gen. James A. Erisman said comtempt was anything "that lessens the dignity of the court, and I think that's exactly what this is."

But Quillen decided the matter was less serious than "I at first thought it might be," since Ryans did the scratching openly, used no "implement" and inflicted only "slight damage."

Within an hour, Ryans visited the Public Building maintenance office for supplies, as Quillen suggested, and applied a coat of brown stain to the scratchings.

"It was a very minor job," said James H. McDermott, maintenance foreman.

—The Morning News, Wilmington, Del.

Factual Accuracy

The fourth consideration in writing the news story is a respect for accuracy and truth. In one sense, accuracy is the overriding consideration, but in this context, it means avoiding the small factual errors that can slip so easily into a story; "truth" means being able to substantiate every statement.

Little mistakes inevitably creep into a story the second the reporter relaxes in his recording of names, addresses, and similar detail. Hence he must be ever-careful in this routine gathering and writing of details.

The problem with truth most often stems from an all-too-common tendency to "improve" a story by using data supplied by the imagination; that is, the writer must beware of a natural inclination to present ideas commonly associated, often incorrectly, with certain kinds of stories.

To illustrate: many of us tend to think of people who escape from blazing buildings as heroic. We picture them as calm, courageous, strong persons facing tremendous odds—people whose great inner strength makes the difference between surviving and perishing. Yet few people fit this pattern. Most are terrified human beings, bent on saving themselves from a horrible death—people who escape safely through a combination of luck and circumstance.

The danger of distortion is that discerning readers detect it. The careful reader accepts only cautiously the account of the flood victim who "never doubted that he would conquer the raging waters" or the description of the bank teller who, "facing a sub-machine gun, calmly hit the alarm switch as he handed over the money." The reader's common sense waves a caution flag on this kind of statement.

To be accurate and truthful, the writer must also make his language behave. Quite often, in his desire to underscore a point, he may exaggerate or employ imprecise language unless he exercises more than routine care.

Note the following examples:

Faulty: The farmer lost a thousand chickens in the fire. (Either the exact number should be given, or such an expression as "about" or "an estimated" should be used.)

Faulty: The car careened around the corner at a 45-degree angle. (The expression "45-degree angle" is both trite and inexact. Only a most unusually constructed car could lean at this angle without overturning.)

Faulty: Educators regard the new method as a surefire cure for poor reading. (This sentence implies a complete agreement on a matter which is anything but settled. This type of flat statement is too often used as a means of parading the writer's unsubstantiated opinion.)

Faulty: The defense counsel never took his eyes off the jury during the prosecutor's questioning. (This statement is obvious exaggeration.)

Dictional Don'ts

The final consideration in news writing is to recognize the standard dictional "don'ts."

Don't Use Bromides. Such expressions as the following have been overworked and therefore are considered trite or hackneyed:

too good to be true	lightning fast
fleecy clouds	pearls of wisdom
raving maniac	host of friends
hall of fame	render a solo
stellar performance	heartbreaking finish
as luck would have it	last but not least
method in his madness	hanging in the balance
few and far between	brown as a berry
a dime a dozen	burning the midnight oil
pleasingly plump	dancing divinely
the flowering of genius	true blue
thick and fast	booming voice
straw that broke the	waxing poetic
camel's back	generous to a fault
slow as a tortoise	never-say-die
sly as a fox	sickening thud
quick as a deer	needle in a haystack

Every day, fashionable expressions grow stale and become bromides. Keep reviewing your favorites for staleness.

Avoid Expressions Not Literally True, or Obvious Overstatements. Some examples:

The plane fell in an absolutely straight line into the sea. (No curves? No flutter?)

In a second, the clerk returned to the customer. (Timed with a stop watch?)

The detective spotted the shoplifter the split second he decided to steal the pen. (He could perceive the split second of decision?)

The hunting dog caught the pheasant in full flight. (Literally impossible.)
Everybody knows this is true. (There is nothing that everybody knows.)
The entire audience was pleased. (Who can be certain of the word "entire"?)
It is the world's most appreciative group. (How can one be certain?)
He is the brightest boy in the school. (Judging by what infallible test?)
There can be no doubt whatever that he is the final authority on the subject. (Too sweeping to be entirely true.)
Like all Irishmen, he has a knack for politics. ("All" should be changed to "many.")

Avoid Overworked Personifications. Some examples:

Mr. Man-in-the-Street	Jack Frost
Mr. Average Citizen	Old Man Winter
Dan Cupid	Mother Earth
Lady Luck	Mr. Would-be
Dame Fortune	Mr. Motorist
John Q. Public	Mrs. Moneybags

Avoid Euphemisms. Some examples:

He passed away July 1.
  Say simply: *He died July 1.*
An odor of perspiration was perceptible about the horses.
  Say simply: *The horses smelled of sweat.*
He was so ill that he lost his dinner.
  Say simply: *He regurgitated* (or *vomited*).
His remains were interred in the earth.
  Say simply: *He was buried.*
An aged gentleman entered.
  Say simply: *An old man entered.*

Avoid Expressions That Editorialize (that give the writer's opinion either directly or by implication). Some examples:

She has the most pleasing voice in this community.
It is going to be a most interesting affair.
Fall is undoubtedly the best time of the year to get work done.
The defendant should certainly be acquitted.

REWRITING

An important phase of the news writer's work is rewriting. The term "rewriting" includes (1) rewriting or revising one's own copy; (2) taking news over the telephone and writing it according to instructions from the "desk"; (3) rewriting press releases and other material sent to the newspaper; (4) rewriting or revising with a view to trimming or improving the copy of other writers within the office; and (5) checking the writing of others for grammar, libel, style, and general accuracy.

The conditions which most often cause a newspaperman to rewrite his own work are: (1) his superior decides that the story is not well written; (2) the story must be trimmed because the paper is too tight; and (3) new facts must be added. If the writer is rewriting because of his superior's objections, he recasts, changes, and deletes according to instructions. If he is rewriting because his story must be trimmed, he may gain his end by eliminating the least important facts or by recasting the entire story. If he is rewriting because of new facts, usually he can accomplish his purpose by writing another lead and inserting the new facts in the appropriate places. In rewriting, the journalist adheres to the qualities of good journalistic writing as set forth in this chapter.

When the rewrite man handles a story telephoned to him by a district reporter, he is not "rewriting" in a literal sense. He is, rather, the writing half of a team of two. The first gets the facts; the second writes the story. This teamwork speeds the story into print. Under this system, an editor first listens to the facts as the reporter calls in. Then he assigns a rewrite man to handle the story, telling him how long to make it, what approach to follow, and what facts to play up. The rewrite man then proceeds accordingly.

In rewriting press releases and other material sent to the paper, the rewrite man is indeed re-writing. Although these releases frequently are written by former newspaper people, they must be recast because they do not suit the style of the paper, are too long, or are too obviously publicity releases. When the rewrite man handles such material, he may achieve his purpose by trimming and changing, or he may have to write the story anew, selecting the facts he wants to use. In such instances, he handles the story just as he would one that was telephoned in.

A rewrite man is called upon to revise the copy of others when the editor wants a second writer to work on a completed story. Perhaps he wants a humorous touch that the original writer is not able to give. Perhaps he thinks that the first writer is not capable of rewriting his own story or that the second writer can do the revision better. In such instances, he asks the second writer to trim, point up, or make any other changes which he, the editor, wants. The second writer then revises the work as though it were his own. He cannot, of course, spare the feelings of the first writer; he must hack and change as he sees fit.

When a rewrite man checks the writing of another for grammar, style, libel, and accuracy in general, he proceeds as if he were a copy editor. In the small newspaper office, he is, in fact, a copy editor. To understand this phase of rewriting, consider the duties of the copy editor discussed in Chapter 7.

The matter of who does the rewriting varies largely with the size of the newspaper. So does the amount of rewriting. On a very small paper, one man or woman may be general editor, copy editor, and rewriter. On a larger paper, any of these functions may be a full-time job for one or several people.

TREATMENT OF NEWS—
SLANTING AND COLORING

Although the manner in which the news story is written should be straight-forward, factual, and impersonal, there are two other treatments which the writer of the news story should know—"slanting" and "coloring." He may need either to avoid them or to use them.

News is said to be *slanted* when the facts of a story are so arranged as to lead the reader to a desired conclusion. In slanting a story, therefore, the writer concerns himself solely with arrangement of facts. The newspaper that cites the progress of the national debt, showing statistically that it is moving toward a danger point, is slanting the news. The newspaper that compares the progress of one city with that of another, even though its manner may be impersonal, is usually slanting the news. The newspaper that gives a front-page spot to an official communication is, by virtue of the placing, slanting the news. In each case, the newspaper wants its readers to draw certain inferences and it slants the news accordingly.

News is said to be *colored* when some facts are stressed and others are made inconspicuous or omitted. The newspaperman speaks of stressing facts as "playing up" some chosen angle of a story. In speaking of making facts incon-spicuous, he uses the terms "playing down" or "toning down." To see a good example of coloring, one has only to compare newspapers that support oppos-ing parties at election time. Their reporters may have covered the same event—perhaps the speech of a candidate—but their versions are miles apart. The paper supporting the candidate emphasizes the ovation as he entered the hall. It refers to the applause as "enthusiastic," "thunderous," "deafening," or "tre-mendous." The other paper merely states that, "after customary applause, the candidate began his speech." The first paper dwells on the strong points of the speech, those likely to win votes for the speaker. The second paper stresses the parts likely to cost votes. Each paper thus gives its colored version of the story. This interesting comparison can be carried further by reading the story in a con-servative or impartial paper.

In order to understand clearly the difference between slanting and color-ing, the student of journalism should remember this distinction: news is slanted when the writer has attempted to influence the reader by arrangement of facts alone; news is colored when the writer attempts to influence the reader by ar-rangement of facts and by choice of words. The student should also remember, however, that many newspapermen consider these terms as synonymous and that many newspapermen believe that practically all news is slanted or colored to some degree.

Furthermore, many journalists contend that because no story involving human conduct can ever be completely objective, the writer should concentrate on fairness rather than on objectivity in his treatment. Examine the following examples of slanting and coloring.

City Deficit Being Reduced

Albert K. Leeds, City Treasurer, announced today that municipal revenue for the past year was $524,829.19, an increase of 12% over that of last year. He also pointed out that for the three years in which the present administration has been in power, the deficit inherited from the former administration has been reduced each fiscal period. At the present rate of reduction, the entire deficit will be removed within ten years.

The above news article is slanted because it leads the reader to believe that the present municipal revenue (which may be the result of an unusually good year in the city's industries) is due to good management and that this revenue will continue. Perhaps the article also ignores the fact that the deficit was caused by the erection of some badly needed municipal buildings. In any case, it leads the reader to believe that the present administration is very economical, while the last was not. Actually, the reverse might be true.

Injured Athletes to Be Compensated

The Inter-scholastic Athletic Association announced yesterday its new schedule of payments for injuries received by members of football teams of the association. Boys receiving broken bones will have medical expenses paid, plus $35. per week for the period of incapacity. Boys becoming permanently disabled (spinal injuries, loss of arm or leg, etc.) will receive a flat sum of $25,000. For loss of life the beneficiary will be paid $50,000.

Payments will be made by the insurance company with which the Association has entered into an agreement.

This news article is slanted because it leaves the reader with the unfortunate opinion that serious injury and loss of life are commonplace in football. Actually, serious injury is not common when a team has been properly trained and coached. Death in football is extremely rare.

Examine the story below for elements of coloring. Remember as you read that the subject is a former senator whose sincerity was challenged strongly by some commentators in the print and electronic media. They questioned his role in blocking investigations of voting irregularities in Cook Co., Illinois, during the election of John F. Kennedy and in Texas during the election of Lyndon B. Johnson. They also scored his attempts to suppress the Bobby Baker scandal and his alliance with the block of Southern senators bent on denying minorities the right to vote.

By SCOTT LATHAM

NEW YORK (UPI)—Sam Ervin Jr., the crusty ex-senator from North Carolina and one of the popular heroes in the constitutional confrontation with former President Richard Nixon, brought his down-home wisdom to New York City Wednesday.

He addressed radio and television

executives, and he couldn't have had a more sympathetic audience.

"You don't hold any public office, but the mission you perform is far more important than that performed by anyone who exercises political power," Ervin told them.

"You make it possible for Americans to be free from tyranny over the mind and you make it possible for our government to work."

Senator Sam, as he became known during the long summer of Watergate hearings in 1973, was in top form. His brows worked up and down and his jowls fluttered with senatorial sternness. His eyes twinkled when he told a joke and his face turned severe when he quoted the Scriptures.

He poked good-natured fun at a mythical preacher and threw in an anecdote about Mark Twain. He recited a brief history of the Bill of Rights and spoke of the seditious and blasphemous libel laws of King George's England.

Through it all, 400 members of the International Radio and Television Society listened as if the hulking, 78-year-old Ervin were more a living oracle than a mortal man. They saluted him with a standing ovation for his chairmanship of the Senate Watergate committee. They laughed at his stories and listened respectfully when he became serious.

Senator Sam returned the favor.

"The great thing about America is that our news media as a whole do not accept the advice which Mark Twain is said to have given us," Ervin said. "Mark Twain is reputed to have said— I'm sure he said it with satire—'Truth is very precious, use it sparingly.'

"But fortunately, the American press digs up the truth. It prints the truth. It broadcasts the truth. The 1st Amendment is the very heart and soul of our Constitution.

"There are a lot of people don't like freedom of the press," the senator went on, his drawl getting more folksy. "Lot of them don't like freedom of speech. And unfortunately, a lot of those people are in government."

Ervin paused for the laughter, patted his snow white hair in place, then turned serious again. "A lot of office holders think that the function of a free press is to praise them," he said, "even when they don't deserve praise."

The senator hadn't mentioned Watergate by name once in his entire speech. But when he finally got around to it, the catharsis was complete.

"And I think that the finest example we have in our history of good investigative reporting was displayed in connection with the very tragic Watergate affair," Ervin said.

"And the press is due the credit for restoring our country and putting it back on the path on which it should travel."

CUT LINES

A picture to be used in the paper is referred to as "art," a "pic," or a "cut." Thus, the newspaperman speaks of a one-column cut, a two-column cut, and so forth. The line that appears over the picture is called the "caption," or the "overline," and the lines under the picture are called "cut lines."

If the picture accompanies a story, the reporter involved usually is called upon to write the caption and the cut lines. Once the reporter has learned to write a news story, the writing of these lines is rarely difficult.

Cut lines, like headlines, vary according to the function they are to perform and the effect which the writer desires.

On some occasions, the cut lines serve as the only reading matter with the picture. In these instances, therefore, the lines must provide all pertinent information about the picture. On other occasions, however, the picture and the lines may accompany a story. In such instances, the lines, obviously, are cast in a different vein.

The effect desired influences the writing of cut lines because the writer

Compassion Wins
Honor for Officer

—The Washington Post

By Charles Del Vecchio—The Washington Post

John W. Littles, "model policeman," wins plaque.

Courier-Post Photo by John Avery

Police study damage to the cars which collided with a tractor-trailer on White Horse Pike in Collingswood last night. A taxicab driver died in Our Lady of Lourdes Hospital, Camden, from head injuries suffered in the accident. Because of a leaking gas tank in one car, firemen were called to the scene.

—The Courier-Post, Camden, N.J.

Michael Steele, dancer with the New York City Ballet, stands on the stairway of his two-story brick cottage at 3½ Cottage Place, Saratoga Springs. Mr. Steele is one of several members of the ballet who have bought homes in Saratoga.
—*Times-Union and Knickerbocker News*, Albany, N.Y.

THE LAST TRIP

After 29 years of treading the streets of West Chester to deliver the mail, Robert J. Finegan of 515 N. New St., made his last trip Thursday. Finegan who took advantage of the recently enacted early retirement act, has seen many changes in the post office and West Chester. He turned in his mail bag in order to have more time with his family.
—*Daily Local News*, West Chester, Pa.

may elect to be straightforward, humorous, satirical, or light in touch. Thus he writes his lines accordingly.

The four pictures shown above are representative of those which appear daily in America's newspapers. Below are pertinent comments on the pictures and their cut lines.

John W. Littles. . . . This picture requires only a single line because it appears immediately over the two-column head shown. The story, of course, relates the facts behind the award being made to the officer. This picture is quite interesting because of the informality of the pose by which the photographer captures a meditative quality in his subject.

55

Police Study Damage. . . . Although the picture of the wrecked cars accompanies a story, the writer has chosen to place extensive pertinent detail in the cut lines. He has done so in order to explain the picture and to generate reader interest in the accompanying story. The photographer has interpreted his material quite well by shooting his picture at a revealing moment. Note how he has caught the investigating officer, clip board in hand, and other detail commonly found at a scene like this.

Michael Steele. . . . Here the cut lines serve two purposes: they explain the picture, and they generate interest in the accompanying story. This picture is especially effective because the photographer has posed or caught his subject against an interesting background. The picture and the lines, therefore, aid considerably in making the story attractive.

The last trip. The lines beneath this picture consitute the entire news item; no other story or explanatory material accompanies the picture. Therefore, the writer must compose what is actually a short news story as well as explain the picture. Also worth noting is the photographer's attempt to obtain a feature shot rather than simply a posed photograph.

"THE JOURNALISTIC STYLE"

What has been said about the writing of the news story and cut lines may help discount a common misconception concerning "the journalistic style."

There is, of course, no such entity as *the* journalistic style. Rather, several kinds of styles are employed in journalistic writing—each being appropriate to the kind of material being handled. The stylistic devices of the column, for example, often resemble closely those of the familiar essay. The styles in the editorial column are frequently as numerous as the editorials themselves. The sports feature story may read like the traditional short story. And this discussion of variation in styles can be extended considerably.

When speakers or writers use the phrase "the journalistic style," they often have in mind the style of the newspaper news story—the concise, terse, often somewhat abrupt presentation of detail discussed earlier under the headings of writing and structure, lead, and body. However, because much writing in journalism is not done in this manner, those who use the phrase are helping to popularize an inaccurate term.

INTERPRETATIVE REPORTING

Overhanging the entire discussion of writing the news story is a very significant concept: interpretative reporting.

Stated in simple terms, interpretative reporting involves explaining the implications of the story—interpreting the story for the reader. An important story often needs this treatment.

For example, a writer recounting a court trial must present the hard facts—names, dates, pertinent legal questions, and similar detail. But if he has the space, he can make a better story by also treating other important matters. He can describe the judge's manner of speaking, the attitude of the defendant, the demeanor of the plaintiff, the appearance of the witnesses, the facial expressions of the jurors, and all related aspects. All this is interpretative reporting because the writer examines facts and explains their meaning—as he understands that meaning.

Writing interpretatively makes heavy demands. It requires an abundance of natural insight and intelligence. To handle even everyday stories, the writer must possess a working knowledge of fields like psychology, sociology, political science, and finance. He must have the background knowledge, for instance, to explain the reaction of the dazed air-hammer operator just extricated from the cave-in, the character of the neighborhood where the murder occurred, the inherent danger of proposed municipal legislation, and every other part of these stories.

The strongest reason, of course, for interpretative reporting is its essentiality. The simple facts of most stories are like the framework of the building; they are merely the basis upon which to construct other necessary parts. Hence if the writer is to present the full story, he must interpret.

This conclusion then leads to another basic thought regarding interpretative reporting: in the opinion of most competent journalists, there can be no "pure" or "objective" or otherwise impersonal writing of the news story. They point out that a writer must select detail, choose words, and adopt an overall approach—all subjective processes that lead inevitably to interpreting. And since he is certain to interpret, he must do so to the best of his ability.[6]

The concept of interpretative reporting has been emphasized vigorously the past few years. Many journalists, especially younger ones, are arguing that the sensitivities and the understandings basic to successful journalism preclude the writing of many news stories as one would write of the art exhibition or the spring blossoms on the parkway. They point to instances such as deceptive legal practices or the razing of urban homes to make space for an expressway. These journalists maintain that the reporter must approach many stories primarily as a sensitive human being, that he must react to the human element and he must write from that angle.

This viewpoint is closely related, almost obviously, to the news-is-controversy philosophy already discussed. Like that philosophy, it springs fundamentally from a reaction against the failure of society to distribute wealth and economic opportunity more evenly. Also, like the news-in-controversy philosophy, this viewpoint exhorts the journalist to become active in making constructive criticisms of society. Hence proponents of this school are frequently termed "journalism activists."

Because many news writers have adopted activist roles, controversies are

---

[6] Note the relationship of this point to the discussion of coloring and slanting discussed earlier.

erupting in newspaper offices everywhere. The pattern is simple to understand. The editor wants to play up one angle of a story, but the reporter wants to emphasize another. The reporter then argues that he should not be fettered, that he must be trusted as a professional writer and citizen of a democracy to speak freely.

Although newspapers sometimes skirt the issue by giving the writer a by-line and hence the right to speak as an individual, difficulties continue nonetheless. Within the past few years, for instance, such prominent papers as the *New York Times* have run editorials to disassociate themselves from opinions expressed by their own writers.

Activism has been spurred further by greater coverage of news of the black communities. This news, which often includes protests against social injustice, is generally covered by reporters who are blacks or who empathize with blacks and feel an obligation to report interpretatively. In fact, according to studies printed in journalism magazines, black reporters largely agree that interpretative reporting and writing of most black-community news is inescapable. They maintain that the very nature of the news precludes impersonal writing. Therefore, they feel a commitment to "tell it like it is."

A final aspect of interpretative reporting concerns a practice that is discussed almost everywhere these days—the "new journalism."

Few phrases stir up more controversy. Some knowledgeable persons see nothing "new" whatever in the practice; they see only an emphasis on old approaches that have always been recognized as bad. Others, however, see a limited redeeming value while still others offer unqualified approval.[7]

Just what does the expression mean? Although a small group use the phrases "journalistic activism" and "new journalism" synonymously, most authorities apply the term to a segment of writers who claim a special corner on this designation. They are a loosely knit group, writing for the print media on either a full-time or free-lance basis, who employ a questionable approach to their subject. Though these "new" journalists are distributed throughout the nation, four names seem constantly to surface in any discussion—Tom Wolfe, Jimmy Breslin, Norman Mailer, and Gay Talese. Of these, Mailer is most widely known for his novels and his critical writings on national policies.

This group contends, fundamentally, that the print media must now become the outlet for writing which formerly appeared only in fiction. It is writing that relies freely on the imagination and concentrates on small detail to make the reader see and feel whatever is described. Further, it clearly substitutes opinion for fact.

New-journalism devotees argue that the straightforward, factual character of standard journalism must yield to their more personalized approach; the writer must discuss the sensations of the people involved in the fire, the accident, the catastrophe. The news story is not to be a clinical report but an ac-

---

[7] For an interesting and revealing collection of viewpoints on the new journalism, see *The Reporter as Artist,* Ronald Weber, ed. (New York: Hasting House, Publishers, 1974).

count of people and their reactions as seen and understood by a sensitive person—the reporter.

Largely because this group relies on the devices of fiction over fact, they have been attacked furiously.[8] Yet they are undaunted. With head high, they stand on their dignity. Their critics, they declare loftily, will eventually see the light and fall in line.

Meanwhile, a statement of the historical impact of these new journalists must be made: they have accelerated the use of the personal element in stories heretofore treated impersonally—stories of setbacks, tragedies, emotional reactions, and similar accounts.

EXAMPLES FOR DISCUSSION

On the following pages are news stories taken from some of the leading newspapers in the United States. Study these stories, noting especially the lead and the manner of relating the facts. Also make note of anything that especially impresses you, either favorably or unfavorably.

JUDGE REVERSES DRIVING DECISION

Acquits Motorist Of Drunken And Reckless Charges

BY A. DAVIS BRASHEARS, JR.

Judge Walter M. Jenifer reversed a magistrate's decision yesterday and acquitted a motorist, who police testified was driving "too slowly," of drunken and reckless driving charges.

Judge Jenifer conceded in Baltimore County Circuit Court that the defendant, Daniel Albert Miley, 42, "may have hit the curb a few times," but he said it was not a "flagrant" case.

Patrolman John Webber testified he arrested Miley at 2.05 A.M. last May 17 after following the defendant's car, which was swerving back and forth, for about a quarter of a mile on Eastern boulevard to Wilson Point road.

The officer said he was first attracted to the vehicle by its slow motion. "Most people speed through that area at that hour," he told the court.

Patrolman Webber said Miley's speech was slurred, on being stopped and asked to get out of his car, and he smelled of alcohol and had trouble walking.

The defendant, a mechanic and part-time welder, told the court he had split a six-pack of beer with a friend before his arrest.

He blamed his erratic driving on eye burns he said he had received earlier from a welder's torch.

Has Speech Impediment

William R. Sutton, Miley's lawyer, pointed out to the court that his client had a speech impediment.

The lawyer emphasized that the defendant had only one prior traffic conviction, for making a prohibited left turn.

Mr. Sutton said he had not represented Miley when he was found guilty of the drunk and reckless charges at an Essex magistrate's hearing.

—*The Sun,* Baltimore

[8] A typical blast appeared in a March 1975 flier advertisement for the *Columbia Journalism Review.* The ad asks, among other questions: "Are you aware that some journalists, without warning to their readers, have 'spiced' their reporting with composite and even fictitious characters—plus compressed time sequences to 'speed up' their narratives . . . and that these practices are defended as being within the bounds of 'the new journalism?' "

Master Plan Meeting Wed.

The first of three public meetings to solicit ideas from residents about the master plan for future development of North Kingstown will be held Wednesday from 7 p.m. to 9 p.m. at the Davisville Junior High School, School Street, North Kingstown.

North Kingstown Town Planner J. Dennis Maloney has arranged the trio of meetings to solicit the reaction and suggestions of the citizens to the master or comprehensive community plan.

The meetings will be held in various sections of town to allow as many residents as possible a chance to express their ideas, especially in relation to their sector of town.

A second meeting is set for July 26 from 7 p.m. to 9 p.m. in the North Kingstown High School Auditorium on Fairway Drive.

A third meeting for Slocum residents is planned but the time and place has not been announced.

The Slocum meeting is expected to be one of the most important since Mr. Maloney expressed concern last week about four major developments planned for the Slocum area which might not harmonize with the proposed land use plan.

The planning department, after two years of work on a master community plan, feels it has a broad plan which could elicit comment from residents who review it.

The master plan is designed to be a guide to help officials plan the developmental future of the community.

An array of maps will be provided for the inspection of residents.

—*The Providence* (R.I.) *Journal*

Drowning victims' bodies discovered

VIRGINIA BEACH—The body of a young boy washed ashore early today at 51st Street and Atlantic Avenue, marking the city's second drowning within a 24-hour period.

The boy's body, as yet unidentified, was found at 8:30 a.m. today by a tourist walking along the beach. A medical examiner was called to the scene about 9 a.m., and police are continuing the investigation.

Monday afternoon, the body of another young boy, Thomas M. Owens, 13, of the 500 block of South Lynnhaven Road, was found in a borrow pit at South Lynnhaven Road and Bow Creek Boulevard.

Police said Owens drowned about 11:45 a.m. Navy and police divers, plus personnel from the London Bridge, Davis Corner and Plaza rescue squads, searched for the body for five hours before finding it.

Police said Owens was swimming with two companions in water about 20 feet deep when he began calling for help.

A passerby, 16-year-old Tom Ringer of the 700 block of Lamplight Lane, attempted to rescue Owens, but, police said, Owens apparently panicked and fought off Ringer before drowning.

—*Ledger-Star*, Norfolk, Va.

SLEET STORM BREAKS STATE POWER LINES

Service to 43 Towns Cut Off; Floods Rage in Dixie

Snow and sleet covered northwestern Oklahoma Sunday, cutting off electric and telephone service and disrupting transportation in some areas.

Oklahoma Gas and Electric Co. officials described the storm as "one of the worst for the company in that section of the state."

Ice formed on power lines and cut off electric service to 43 Oklahoma communities. Southwestern Bell Telephone Co. officials said many of its long-distance circuits were out of order because of broken lines.

TOWNS WITHOUT SERVICE

The power company listed the following communities temporarily without service:

Alva, Woodward, Geary, Greenfield, Loyal, Hitchcock, Eagle City, Oakwood, Canton, Watonga, Ames, Ringwood, Meno, Lahoma, Goltry, Helena, Jet, Nash, Garber, Covington, Lucien, Three Sands, Medford, Douglas, Lovell, Marshall, Billings, Hunter, Lamont, Salt Fork, Deer Creek, Narden, Renfro, Clyde, Gibbon, Wakita, Manchester, Carrier, Hillsdale, Kremlin, Pond Creek, Jefferson and the Medford waterworks.

Residents of Woodward

were not inconvenienced by the storm damage to power lines. The city has its own plant sufficient to meet local needs.

Alva has only a small standby plant which officials said was capable of supplying essential service. Alva's service was curtailed because a feeder line tower was blown down by wind.

Power company officials said 125 workmen and engineers had been dispatched to the trouble area and hoped to restore service within 24 hours.

200 PHONE LINES OUT

The telephone company said at one time as many as 200 long distance circuits were down in the northwestern part of the state including sections between Moreland and Woodward, Woodward and Forgan, Woodward and Seiling, El Reno and Clinton, Medford and Blackwell.

All main highways were open but U. S. 66 in the Texas Panhandle was closed because of storms in the Amarillo area, the State Highway patrol reported. Snowplows cleared some drifts in the Woodward area but county roads were all blocked because of snow.

Southwestern Bell said repairs would take two or three days. Forgan, Cherokee, Alva, Fairview and Carmen were without telephone service late Sunday. Also, service was out at about 40 other communities operated by private concerns.

Over 200 extra repairmen rushed to the area to fix an estimated 300 broken poles, 500 broken cross arms and 5,000 wire breaks.

The official forecast for Monday called for fair and warmer with highs from 45 to 50.

—*Tulsa* (Okla.) *Daily World*

Jaycees Back School Building Bond

The Hamilton Township Jaycees have unanimously endorsed the township school board's proposed $11.5-million building program, set for referendum Dec. 1, Jaycees President Jack Lacy said last night.

Lacy said the endorsement decision came after a presentation of the building program made at the Jaycees' November meeting by George C. Tatter, a member of the school board's citizens' advisory committee.

"From the information we have received," Lacy said, "we wholeheartedly believe that this proposed building program is the best solution to the overcrowding problems our school system now faces and will continue to face in the next 10 years.

"We urge all Hamilton citizens interested in improving our educational system to voice their approval of the school building program when they vote on the school bond issue next Tuesday."

The bond issue facing the voters will finance some $8 million of the overall $11.5-million price tag and is expected to add 41 cents per $100 assessed valuation to the local property tax next year.

The other $3.5 million is coming from surplus funds resulting when the school board changed its financial calendar from a fiscal (June to June) year to a calendar year.

—*The Trentonian,* Trenton, N.J.

Divided House Blocks Road, but Mover Stays in Jail

By TODD SIMON

With its dining room hanging out, a four-room section of house was blocking W. 130th Street, the dividing highway between Parma and Brook Park Village, last night.

And the house mover, Frank Mural, of 2317 Denison Avenue S. W., was in a jail cell in Berea. All attempts to bail Mural out had failed because Brook Park's mayor, Louis J. Mares, would not fix bail.

Mayor Mares was at his home, where he and his wife were entertaining friends in honor of Mrs. Mares' and George Washington's birthday.

And two-thirds of the transient house was waiting 700 feet south of Snow Road, in Parma, to be joined by the last third.

Mural was charged with failing to obtain a license and permit to move a structure on Brook Park property, according to the mayor.

According to Mural, Brook Park police came without warning and, saying they were going to help him get his permit, took him in a police car to the Berea jail and locked him up.

Mural said the house did project over the center line of W. 130th, but that the dolly on which the house rides is entirely on the Parma side of the highway, Route 612.

Mayor Mares said the trucks would straddle the center line.

Marked by two flares and a lantern, the itinerant hunk of housing was making automobiles drive onto the Brook Park shoulder of the road, churning it into mucky ruts.

The house was bought from the New York Central Railroad by Allen Thomas, 14045 Lorain Avenue. Thomas was having it moved to his land south of Snow Road, where he was going to rent it out. Eight rooms have been trucked down to that plot and now stand on cribbing there.

But, complete with L-shaped porch and with wallpaper of a delicate pink floral design, the third part to be moved was stalled just as it was turning out of its driveway into the road.

Mayor Mares told it this way:

"No, I haven't set bond. Mural has not been arraigned yet. Today was a holiday, and it would be difficult to dig up the city solicitor to make out a formal charge.

"Besides, it is my wife's birthday and I have friends here at the house for dinner.

"Mural was warned some time ago when he moved the other two sections. He was supposed to get a license and permit and to post a bond in case of damage. He should have applied to the building commissioner of the village for his permit."

Mural's Story

In his Berea cell, Mural said:

"There was a telephone man waiting down there to raise up a lighting pole and wires to let this part of the house in on Mr. Thomas' lot. I sent Mr. Thomas to get the permit so I could stay on the job.

"Then the police came and told me they'd help me get my permit, but they drove right here and put me in jail.

"My bond with the Traveler's Insurance Co. is still good for six months. And we aren't even touching Brook Park territory. Just a little of the house hangs over, about three feet."

Mike Mural, brother-in-law of the prisoner, and Thomas complained that they had tried repeatedly to find out what was the charge and what money or security bond was required to get Frank Mural free, but that both Mayor Mares and Police Chief Glenn Worsley had refused to tell them.

At dark, nobody had moved into the roadbound vacancy, which has two downstairs and two upstairs rooms and a stairway, but no kitchen or bath and no place to rest.

—*Plain Dealer,* Cleveland, O.

Air Holiday Files for Bankruptcy

A i r Holiday, an air travel club at 4369 S. Howell Ave., filed a petition for voluntary bankruptcy in Federal Court here monday, listing $23,181 in assets and $322,390 in debts.

The firm, which opened in February of 1971, a l s o listed 156 persons as creditors. They had made trip deposits totaling $21,597, the p e t i t i o n said. James B. Leonard was named as president of the firm.

In another bankruptcy proc e e d i n g involving a travel firm, a creditors' committee was formed to oversee the administration of unsecured claims of Travel Ideas, I n c., fornmerly of 775 N. Jefferson St.

Travel Ideas closed in June, 1973. About 150 persons were listed in consumer complaints filed with the Wisconsin Justice Department against t h e f i r m, representing a loss of more than $45,000 in travel de- posits.

—*The Milwaukee Journal*

President Installed

Mrs. Robert Ehrenberg was installed May 27 as president of the Sisterhood of Temple Beth Jacob.

The installation took place at the sisterhood's annual dinner at the Brick Tower Motel.

Also installed were Mrs. Norman Kushner, vice presidant; Mrs. Alan Hamburger, secretary; and Mrs. Barry Kushner, treasurer.

—*The Concord* (New Hampshire) *Monitor*

Assessor Culbertson Wants Out

W. Wirt Culbertson has requested that he be relieved of the Dade Tax Assessor's job and be reassigned to Internal Auditing Department, it was learned Monday.

County Manager Ray Goode said he will recommend the move today to the Metro commission. Culbertson will replace Internal Auditor Thomas Merlo, whose resignation is effective Jan. 1.

Culbertson, who has held the tax assessor's job for four years, was severely criticized earlier this year for raising building assessments an average of 25 per cent.

The 1970 tax roll, however, subsequently was upheld by a Circuit Court judge.

—*Miami* (Fla.) *Herald*

EXERCISES

Practice A

Make the following sentences shorter without sacrificing detail:

1. The color of the house was brown.
2. He then called on a man by the name of Peters.
3. He ran for a long way before he stopped.
4. The course will cover a period that will probably extend over three weeks.
5. All people who are interested should plan to attend.
6. It requires a long time to find out who is the next in line of succession.
7. The opinion of each and every student in the entire school should be considered.
8. We are planning to use the book which we want.
9. He asked his mother, he asked his father, and he asked his brother.
10. He asked us to tell him if we are thinking about or considering the action at the present time.
11. It was decided by the committee to act.
12. The flag was flapping and flapping in the strongly blowing wind.
13. We got our message through to him by the use of the telegraph.
14. He will speak at the convention which takes place on Monday.
15. Mr. Smith, who is the man who lives next to me, gets up early every morning in the week.
16. The man with the red hair was shouting and hollering in John's ear.

17. Mr. Howard, who is president of the club, spoke to the club at the meeting held on Tuesday of last week.
18. He put his glasses on in order to read the paper.
19. He was making an attempt to obtain a coat of tan.
20. He was wearing his hat on his head in a manner that was very strange.

Practice B

From the following notes write news stories:

1. Man arrested this afternoon by Branchtown Police: name, John Henderson; address, 117 Linden St., Heather, Pennsylvania; age 35; charge, attempted larceny of automobile; anonymous telephone call traced to public telephone in drugstore at 16th and Washington Sts. told police that strange man apparently was trying to force open door of parked car across street; surprised in act by police, Henderson said he thought car was his; car actually owned by Howard Hester, 2120 N. 8th St., City; check on records shows Henderson doesn't own a car; held by police magistrate at afternoon session in default of bail of $1,000.; to face Grand Jury Monday morning.
2. Woman found wandering in downtown New York this morning (December 17th) without coat or hat; unable to give name or any other pertinent fact; believed to be victim of amnesia; age, about 45; height, 5.5; weight, 145; hair, gray; complexion, sallow; wearing navy blue, frock type dress; muttered irrelevantly to all questions by police; placed in Harper Memorial Hospital for observation pending identification by relatives; photographer has taken picture to be run with story.
3. Fire broke out at 1:00 A.M. this morning in Heller Department Store, 15th & Harold Sts., Philadelphia; cause, watchman threw cigarette butt in pile of refuse on first floor as he was making rounds; did not discover fire until next visit at 1:45; coming down stairs he saw a bright flame and discovered that entire first floor was blazing; unable to get past stairs; ran back to second floor; telephone miraculously not dead; called operator who called firemen; watchman jumped from second-story window into net; building now a flaming mass because faulty automatic sprayers did not work; fire finally extinguished at 6:00 A.M.; damage over $500,000.; owners considering prosecuting watchman for criminal negligence, although no one injured.
4. At commencement exercises this morning at Louden University, Louden, Ohio, speaker was Dr. Harvey H. Beister, President, Harrow College, Harrow, Indiana; addressed class of 721; advised them to seek positions with future, shun positions without future even though salary be very high; look for security job; work hard; marry intellectual equal, otherwise be unhappy; above all, go to church; church-going people always happiest; honorary degree of L.H.D. given Beister for work as educator and author; only 10 honor students—Harold J. Palmer, Phila., Pa., John I. Jones,

Buffalo, N.Y., Peter H. Boone, Cleveland, Ohio, Robert G. Dietrich, Erie, Pa., Morris P. Lester, Indianapolis, Ind., and Harry U. Powers, Robert Williams, Craig Flint, James Thompson, William MacIntyre, all of Louden; salutatory given by Palmer; valedictory by Boone.

5. Automobile accident at 21st & Race Sts., Kane, Texas, this morning; car driven by John K. Roberts, Dallas, sideswiped car of Paul Kyle, 181 Main St., Kane; Roberts attempting to pass Kyle who was going "too darn slow, you'd think he was in a funeral"; damage, one fender badly bent; no injuries except upset dispositions; Roberts promises to pay damages; released by police on promise to settle privately.

6. Anthony J. Kilpatrick, 28, Bay View, Ohio, has acquired a cheetah which he plans to keep as pet; Bay View is small resort town with regular population of 2,000 and summer population of 14,000; committee of regular population petitions local court to ban cheetah; Kilpatrick, armed with petition signed by "over 1,000" residents, argues that cheetah represents no danger; petitioners stress that (1) cheetah is a very dangerous animal, and (2) signatures are from summer residents; court issues temporary order requiring that cheetah be caged at all times until final disposition of case; Judge is J. Theodore Cantwell; case heard in City Hall courtroom.

7. Walter O. Ritter, President, Ritter Tea Company, died at home in Laurel, Md., this afternoon of heart attack; age, 72; death unexpected; found lying on bedroom floor by maid; widower with one son, Walter Jr., secretary of father's business; Walter Sr. was active in affairs of Trinity Episcopal Church, Old Peoples Home; familiar figure at local opera and other musical events; lifelong member of the Republican party; rose from newsboy to importer; philanthropist and financial "angel" for local boys with musical talent; funeral to be announced.

8. Eleven monkeys escaped from the County Zoo this afternoon; keeper forgot to lock door after feeding; monkeys made way out of grounds slowly; did not seem afraid of traffic outside zoo; too agile for keepers to catch; bounded across tops of cars on parking lot; climbed trees; scaled porch railings of houses; called by neighbors, police unable to cope with situation; neighbors keeping windows closed so monkeys can't get in; keepers finally coaxed five monkeys into net with bananas; "monkey-shines" predicted until remaining six are caught.

9. Entire city block, Chestnut to Locust, 13th to 14th, Devon, Mass., to be razed to make room for new vocational school; building to cost $3,800,000.; to have all latest equipment for every major type of shop work; emphasis to be on practical experience; enrollment will be 2,000; four-year course; some academic work of practical nature; building to start by June of next year.

10. Thomas J. Kearns, Manager of Hotel La Vue, held up and robbed of $100. and watch as he left hotel at 1:00 A.M. this morning; robber was tall and heavy; about 40; spoke in heavy tone; face masked; was standing in doorway four doors away from hotel, apparently waiting; jabbed gun in ribs,

took money, and jumped in car that evidently by pre-arrangement drove down street; Kearns placed with hands in air facing doorway; told if he turned to look he would be shot; no clues; police baffled.

11. Governor Louis K. Lowe, Nebraska, coming to Boston, Mass., to address Republican organization leaders at annual banquet; will arrive at airport 2:13 P.M.; will drive to home of Mayor Glenn L. Jenkins in latter's car; will spend afternoon in conference with party leaders; after banquet will have private party in mayor's home; tomorrow morning flies back to Nebraska.

12. Ralph M. Pelot, 38, escaped convict, caught today by Lansing, Mich., police; was trying to board freight train at west-end yard; escaped from Lowton State Prison, Lowton, Ohio, last Monday by concealing himself in garbage truck; was a trusty working in prison kitchen; apprehended today on tip of railroad police who called local police when they heard that "suspicious-looking character" was hanging around yard; railroad police and city police set out for yard at same time but city police arrived first and had Pelot when others arrived; no shots fired; man surprised from behind; was unarmed; gave up without a struggle; said he was "glad it's all over"; hiding from police was "hell."

13. Thermometer today (August 12) reached 97; 14th straight day over 90; no relief in sight; weatherman says this is greatest heat wave since 1910 when 19 days were over 90; 14 people fainted in downtown section; people taking to parks and swimming pools; death of Joseph Combe, 71, 38 N. Titan St., of heart attack induced by great heat; week-end rush for seashore predicted; hotel reservations at Seaside Hotel, Ocean City, already sold out; ice cream dealers unable to keep up with demand; Dr. Carl O. Hart, Director of Public Health, warns people to watch diet, avoid undue exertion, don't "gulp ice water."

14. Eugene L. Cort, Republican, elected mayor over John E. Roberts, Democrat, in yesterday's election; great surprise; odds had been 2-1 on Roberts; final count, Cort 543,829—Roberts 499,134; Chestnut Hill section voted 4-1 for Cort; East Side voted 2-1 for Cort; vote about even all other sections; Cort declares results "a victory for reform in municipal expenditures"; Roberts says, "People have spoken. I accept their will"; election occasions great excitement at Republican headquarters; Democrats quiet; say they are waiting for "next time."

15. Explosion of gas tank on farm of Hiram L. Weaver, Teper, five miles from city, at 3:00 A.M. awakens hundreds; no one hurt; cause of explosion unknown; shed near tank demolished; 200 calls to City Hall and newspapers to inquire if earthquake had occurred, city arsenal had exploded, etc. Weaver says he was "blown clear out of bed"; doesn't have any idea of cause of explosion.

16. Two boys caught at 11:30 last night in act of stealing from Herten Bakery, 821 Powelton St., this city; boys are Peter Lawson, 14, 482 Lutlow St., and Thos. J. Ryan, 15, 499 Lutlow St.; Policeman Robert Kope patrolling

beat heard noise in building as he passed; investigated and found door had been forced; boys gave up in tears; no police record on boys; placed in House of Detention for magistrate's hearing today; parents are surprised and shocked; believe boys listen to "too many bad T.V. programs, see too many bad movies."

17. Wheels stolen from police car at 2:00 A.M. this morning while officers having a snack in restaurant at 15th & Race Sts.; car jacked up and placed on milk boxes; wheels retrieved at corner of 20th & Arch Sts. by fellow police cruising in locality at 5:30 A.M.; all concerned "red-faced"; police in restaurant were Jacob Stone and Charles L. Ulton, patrolmen attached to 1st District; police have no clue concerning pranksters; suspect local college boys; Supt. of Police Herbert Walton plans to "look into" custom of early morning snack while on duty.

18. Dr. Lyle W. Turner, chief surgeon at Chester Hospital, amputated arm of injured worker in accident today at construction job on apartment at 4th and Locust Sts.; workman heard warning cries too late to avoid having arm caught beneath steel girder that accidentally fell; workmen unable to move girder; no machinery available; police summoned surgeon to unconscious man; arm badly mangled; only hopes to free man lay in immediate operation to remove arm; operation performed on spot; man removed to Chester Hospital, is resting comfortably; excellent chance for recovery; man is Howard Potter, 976 Karter St., this city; father of 4 children; age 48; laborer for past 30 years.

19. Woman committed suicide by leaping from 4th story of Biddle Bldg., 4th and Callow Sts., this morning at 10:00; no marks of identification; had ripped all labels from clothing; about 39 or 40 years of age; 5.5 in height; about 145 lbs., dark hair; swarthy complexion; appears to be of Mexican or Italian extraction; elevator operator, Norgert J. Smith, 45, 398 Haverford Ave., this city, remembers taking woman up, but says he never saw her before; landed in street between two parked cars; no one saw her leap except traffic policeman Elmer O. Hayne, 41, 322 S. 11th St.; says he happened to be looking that way just as she stood in window of lavatory and jumped; battered body taken to morgue to await identification.

20. Kidnaped child of wealthy oil man George K. Johnson found in lonely shack one mile from highway junction at Moylan, Indiana; child is George Jr.; age, 6; taken from Moylan schoolyard last Tuesday morning; no one saw him go; ransom note received Wednesday; father told to drop money from airplane flying at distance of 1,000 ft. over certain section of forest adjacent to Hubert, Indiana; terms carried out, but police found money untouched next day; child remembers only "big dark man" who told him that father wanted him to come home from school; had got in car and was driven "long way" into country; man was "kind sometimes, nasty sometimes"; forced to sleep in little room in attic of shack; cried sometimes; told by man he would put out in underground cave if he didn't "shut up"; child unhurt, although suffering from shock; police refuse to divulge

source of information leading to raid on shack; man not found as yet; police are "hot" on trail; parents overjoyed, but feel man must be apprehended "in order to protect other people."

21. Circus coming to town; parade starting from West St. freight yard at 1:30 tomorrow afternoon; proceeding to Broad St.; turning left down Broad to Poplar; there turning east to circus grounds at 4th St.; elephants, horses, and wagons containing wild animals will be in parade; also clowns, and a few freaks such as fat man; circus to feature usual acrobatics, etc., plus captive gorilla that killed three men when being captured; gorilla named Pete, very ferocious; will be shown in specially constructed cage; circus to stay in town for one week.

Practice C

Select 12 pictures from various newspapers and evaluate the cut lines for general effectiveness.

FOR FURTHER READING

Brucker, Herbert. *Journalist: Eyewitness to History.* New York: Macmillan, 1962.

Coblentz, Edmund D., ed. *Newsmen Speak: Journalists on Their Craft.* Freeport, N.Y.: Books for Libraries Press, 1968.

Copple, Neale. *Depth Reporting: An Approach to Journalism.* Englewood Cliffs, N.J.: Prentice-Hall, 1964.

Effron, Edith. *The News Twisters.* Los Angeles: Nash, 1971.

Harriss, Julian, and Stanley P. Johnson. *The Complete Reporter.* New York: Macmillan, 1965.

Hiebert, Ray Eldon, ed. *The Press in Washington.* New York: Dodd, Mead, 1966.

Hohenberg, John. *The News Media: A Journalist Looks at His Profession.* New York: Holt, 1968.

Lyons, Louis M., ed. *Reporting the News; Selections from the Nieman Reports.* Cambridge, Mass.: Harvard University Press, 1965.

MacDougall, Curtis D. *Interpretative Reporting.* New York: Macmillan, 6th ed., 1972.

Rowse, Arthur E. *Slanted News.* Boston: Beacon Press, 1957.

Weisberger, Bernard A. *The American Newspaperman.* Chicago: University of Chicago Press, 1961.

Requisites for Successful Interviewing
Kinds of Interviews—Qualities and Problems
Note Taking

Interviewing

If the reporter is to be successful in his daily work, he must know how to interview. The reason is simply that most news comes directly from personal contact. From the formal press conference in the White House to the district reporter's conversation with the trash collector who witnessed the automobile accident, gathering news is largely a matter of interviewing people of all sorts and conditions.

Because interviewing is so important in obtaining news, the capable reporter constantly strives to develop his competence. This involves versatility; interviewees differ so sharply from each other that the reporter must develop a variety of techniques rather than a single skill. Some persons welcome being interviewed—the television entertainer seeking publicity, the political candidate fighting for votes, the publicity-hungry individual wanting to see his name in print. Others in no way want to be interviewed—the swindler detected in his crime, the central figures in a messy affair, the arrested patrons of a local gambling joint. There are the well-known personalities—the high government figure, the celebrity, the foreign statesman; these contrast with the obscure individuals—the man who witnessed the stabbing, the clerk in the store that has been looted, the boy who telephoned the police to tell of a suspicious character. There are the persons who themselves are the important news figures—the defendant in the murder trial, the visiting dignitary, the hero in the recent disaster; they are interviewed in a different manner from the figures who are simply news sources—the janitor who can tell the reporter when the celebrity usually comes home, the hospital admissions clerk who knows the exact number of victims in the recent accident, the inconspicuous desk sergeant who can give the names of the people arrested.

The interview may be an acknowledged part of a story, a hidden part, or even the entire story. The story may be a news story, a feature story, a crime or sports or political or social story. The interview may be exclusive, or it may be a press conference. It may be casual or planned, cooperative or antagonistic. The medium may be newspaper, magazine, television, or radio. This variety of types and conditions and objectives necessitates an equal variety of approaches and techniques on the part of the reporter. Journalists' interviews, moreover, are not the only kind; personnel workers, psychologists, counselors, physicians, credit investigators, and innumerable others work by means of interviews. Reporters can wisely seek to share and learn from their experience.

REQUISITES FOR SUCCESSFUL INTERVIEWING

The ability to conduct successful interviews can be learned. How easily or how well may depend in some part on the reporter's heredity or personality, but whosoever would be a reporter must master the skill of interviewing. It is not a simple skill. Yet some aspects of effective interviewing stand in clear relief. A discussion of these follows.

Favorable Impression. Although the reporter in the press conference and the one asking routine questions for small stories (minor accidents, purse snatchings, small fires, or the like) need scarcely have dynamic personality appeal, the more involved interviews demand that the reporter make a pleasing impression upon the person interviewed. The interviewee must respond well to the questions, he must evidence some spirit of co-operation, and he must view the whole interview as a pleasant experience. Naturally, these reactions are always dependent on the reporter's making a favorable impression.

Just how the reporter is to make a favorable impression can hardly be reduced to a formula. He may do so by displaying congeniality, respect, sympathy, fairness, or any other of the many qualities to which the interviewee may react favorably. Generally speaking, however, the reporter succeeds by displaying an agreeable personality, by respecting the dignity of the interviewee, and by encouraging the expectation that the printed story will be complete and sympathetic.

Appropriate Technique. The interviewer must adjust his technique and approach to the situation he faces, especially to the marked differences among the persons interviewed in the course of a normal day. A laborer during a strike may be almost any kind of interviewee—desperate, overconfident, defiant, distrustful, resentful; or, on the contrary, cordially glad to have a listener for his viewpoint. Probably the best way to deal with him is to use a straightforward approach with no attempt to influence or to chide. The mayor of the large city speaking at the noon meeting of the service club requires a quite different approach. The reporter can scarcely expect to be successful by addressing him as he would the laborer. He must, instead, take some cognizance of the mayor's important position as he speaks with him. In all instances, the reporter must be able to vary his technique as the situation may demand.

Certainly there can be no formalized procedure to guide the reporter in varying his technique. His only course is to analyze his successes and failures in other interviews with a view to improving. A critical analysis and a sincere attempt to improve, coupled with practice, are the best ways to gain the "know how" of varying one's technique.

Asking the Reader's Questions. The reporter who is interviewing should always think of himself as an intermediary. He is the representative of the reader; he interviews in order to ask the questions his reader might ask.

The reader presumably wants to know the usual facts of every story— names, addresses, occupation, and similar details—but also wants the answers to other questions. In an account of an unsolved murder, for instance, he usually wants every detail, large or small, in order to try to find the solution. In accounts of disputed issues, he needs every aspect of the case in order to es- tablish an opinion. In accounts of heated verbal exchanges, he presumably wants all the key phrases used by the participants.

To appreciate the importance of answering the reader's questions, any newspaper reader need only recall his own annoyance when searching for miss- ing facts. For example, in a recent wire-service feature story the writer was making the point that some men retain their physical strength late in life. In his supporting evidence, he cited the instance of a man who, at age 103, ran a hundred yards in 17.8 seconds. However, he never stated where the event oc- curred nor did he give the circumstances. He merely presented the man's name and identified him as "an assistant to the great escape artist, Harry Houdini." The newspapers carrying the story were deluged with calls and letters asking for the specific details of the feat.

Avoiding Routine. In interviewing, the reporter should make a strong ef- fort to avoid a routine procedure, especially in seeking feature-story material. In the small stories involving one or two questions, a routine procedure is inev- itable. A routine procedure must also be used frequently in such straight news interviewing as the formal press conference, the questioning of the high gov- ernment official about foreign relations, and the questioning of the lawyer about legal implications. But in the many stories where variety is possible, the re- porter should search for a new approach and treatment. The dull, stock ques- tions should be shelved in favor of novel or striking ones. Examples of routine interviewing are especially visible in stories of actresses and sports figures. The actresses are usually asked the same silly questions about their favorite this and that; the sports figures are always asked to explain their success. Although these stories may be interesting to many readers, too often they have the atmosphere of having been written many times before.

To avoid such routine, the journalist rejects the standard patterns of questioning for recurring stories. Every year, for example, numerous people suddenly acquire unexpected wealth—win lotteries, receive substantial surprise legacies from distant wealthy relatives, or collect large rewards. If the journalist, in his free moments, reflects on these patterns, he can store some original approaches in the back of his mind for the first time when the story breaks. Of those who get sudden wealth, for instance, he is ready to ask more than "What do you intend to do with this money?" He has devised questions to probe the psychological impact on the person, the obvious and subtle changes that the money will effect, and the difficulties (often unanticipated either by recipient or reader) of adjusting to wealth.

Pre-interview Contact. Whenever possible, the reporter should attempt to make a contact before the actual interview. Generally speaking, a person is better able to give an interview if he knows what to expect. Therefore, the reporter should communicate with the interviewee beforehand, giving some inkling of the questions to be asked. In the case of important persons, making an appointment beforehand is almost mandatory. In the case of less important persons, last-minute arrangements are acceptable.

Sometimes, of course, making arrangements beforehand is impossible, as when a dignitary or celebrity arrives from a distant place for a quick visit. In these instances, however, the person to be interviewed frequently expects reporters and is prepared.

Preparation. Whenever a reporter is able to plan an interview in advance, he certainly should do so. He should settle on the questions that he wants to ask, he should make plans for "drawing out" the interviewee, and he should anticipate any lull or change in the conversation. While he can scarcely cross-examine the interviewee, he should prepare his questions so as to get the material desired.

Preparation is especially important when the interviewee's time is limited, as is true of the busy official, the dignitary boarding a plane, and the athlete after the contest.

Knowledge of the Subject. The reporter should always try to be knowledgeable in the interviewee's area of endeavor. Specifically, he should brief himself beforehand on the interviewee's background and position; and he should certainly know the basic nomenclature of the field. A reporter interviewing the conductor of the symphony orchestra, for example, should know something of music; the sports reporter should know the ins and outs of the game involved; and the reporter questioning the scientist should know the main ideas of the particular subject. When the person being interviewed must explain needlessly, or when he feels the reporter's incompetence, the whole interview is certain to sag. Obviously no reporter can afford this kind of failure in very many instances.

KINDS OF INTERVIEWS—QUALITIES AND PROBLEMS

In addition to the requisites for interviewing already discussed, the student of journalism should know the qualities peculiar to interviewing for the major departments of the newspaper—straight news, feature, sports, theater, and society stories.

Straight News. The important points to be remembered concerning interviewing for the straight news story are: (1) this is the largest single field of interviewing; (2) generally the reporter is pressed for time most severely in this field; (3) the news reporter usually has the least foreknowledge of the interview and hence the least chance to plan it.

Straight news constitutes the largest single field of newspaper interviewing because it represents the largest part of printed material. Although much of the interviewing may be done by outside reporters (wire service, syndicates, free-lance writers), news stories still represent more interviewing by the staff than any other kind of material.

The reporter handling the straight news story generally is hardest pressed for time because so much of his material is spot news. It breaks fast, and it must be handled fast. Hence the reporter must accomplish his interview—or interviews—quickly. He must also move rapidly to avoid being scooped by reporters from other papers or other media.

Straight news interviewing gives the reporter least foreknowledge because he can never know beforehand the stories that crop up during his working day. Therefore, he rarely has more than a few minutes to prepare for interviewing the victims of swindlers, the witnesses of accidents or tragedies, the office-holders under attack, the lucky winners, the honored, and the disgraced—as well as the other common types caught in spot news.

Feature Story. The important points to be remembered about the interview for the feature story are that (1) there can be great latitude in approach; (2) the reporter is rarely pressed for time; and (3) the interview usually seeks to reveal a personality or an atmosphere rather than to present straight factual material.

There can be great latitude in approach because the feature story frequently can be treated in sharply different ways. Hence the reporter varies his approach to suit his proposed treatment. The story of the local transit company's decision to reduce or end some service, for instance, can be handled in at least three ways—humorous, sarcastic, reminiscent. If the treatment is to be humorous, the reporter may interview passengers with a view to obtaining facetious remarks about old vehicles; if sarcastic, he may phrase his questions so as to draw forth slightly nasty remarks about tardiness; if reminiscent, he plays up the sentimental angle by interviewing oldsters who "remember when." In short, he forces the interview into the pattern that best obtains the material needed for his intended treatment of the story. This approach is in sharp contrast to that of the news story where the reporter seeks straight factual material.

The reporter is not pressed for time in the feature-story interview, as he so often is in the straight news interview, because usually the feature is planned well in advance. The reporter thus can allow himself ample time for interviewing and for writing. In fact, sometimes a feature story is completed and in type a day or more before it is used.

Because the feature story usually seeks to reveal a personality or an atmosphere, the whole course of the interview is affected accordingly. The reporter becomes highly selective. He looks primarily for the material that will contribute to forming a good picture of the personality or creating depth for the atmosphere. Consequently, he will talk at length with a view to selecting the helpful material after the interview. If, for instance, he is interviewing a West Virginia coal miner with the intention of showing the drudgery of his existence, he may ask many irrelevant questions in order to study the miner's expression as he answers. If he is writing of life on a Mississippi river boat, he may ask many questions of crew members for the sole purpose of gaining atmosphere. Thus, the feature-story interview frequently resembles a conversation between friends rather than a formal question-answer process.

Sports. Two conditions characterize sports interviewing: (1) interviews are generally very easy to obtain and (2) there is a distinct homogeneity in the people interviewed.

Interviews are easy to obtain in the world of sports because athletic organizations are heavily dependent on public favor. Hence, favorable publicity is desired—in fact, the newsman has a distinct advantage over many athletic organizations because, if this favorable publicity is not forthcoming (or, worse still, if unfavorable stories appear), the athletic organization may find itself in a very tight position in more ways than one. For this reason, such performers as major-league baseball players who do not "cooperate" with journalists are frequently pressured by the team's public-relations man to "get in line."

There is a distinct homogeneity in the persons interviewed in sports because they have so much in common. The reporter, therefore, can always work from these known facts: sports figures are all striving to reach the top; they are in constant competition with others like themselves; and they are usually completely devoted to their sport. This homogeneity, however, leads to difficulty, for the big problem of sports interviewing lies in the attempt to gain variety. The entire field is so limited and the facts so often fall into a standard pattern that the reporter finds difficulty in gaining novelty. What, for instance, can a reporter find to ask a baseball player that has not already been asked hundreds of times? What can be said of an up-and-coming athlete that has not been said of many, many others? Many prominent newspapermen have had long and successful careers in the field of sports interviewing, but many have also bogged down in attempting to gain original approaches.

Theater. Like those engaged in sports, the person connected with the theater leans heavily on publicity in order to prosper. As a result, interviews are rarely difficult to obtain.

Once again, however, the interviewer also has difficulty in gaining originality. A nationally known actress, for instance, being interviewed for the local paper, presents a problem because her interviews have been published so many times before. Syndicated features, magazines, and other newspapers probably have dealt with her life at length. The reporter for the local paper, therefore, must struggle for a new angle.

Society. The reporter conducting interviews for material for the society page—which increasingly is being merged with the women's page as "social news"—needs to be well established socially and should enjoy this work. Women reporters often get these assignments.

The reporter himself should be well established socially in order to have an entree into the so-called "best circles." Rarely can he obtain a satisfactory interview with a member of the exclusive social group unless he is established or accepted.

The reporter must enjoy society interviewing if he is to be successful because this work quickly tires anyone not truly enthusiastic. The idea of keeping tabs on the routine doings of such a relatively dull group holds little appeal for most newspaper people.

However, the importance of the society or social-news page is not to be taken lightly. Although the devotee of the sports page may laugh derisively at the two-column cut of the pale-faced, slightly built young man conversing inanely with the somewhat horsy, unattractive young woman, such material represents a strong attraction for many readers, especially among the many "would be's" and the *nouveau riche* of the community. Consequently, the newspaper must include it—which means someone must gather it.

NOTE TAKING

The beginning reporter soon realizes that note taking is both more important and more demanding than he had assumed. Note taking is important for the self-evident reason that notes are the foundation for writing the story.[1] Note taking is demanding because of the strong pressures which often prevail.

The greatest pressure results from the necessity of being two persons simultaneously—one person striving to guide the interview to a successful outcome and the other person attempting to record accurately and fully the information needed for the later writing. In addition, the reporter may face the pressures of working against a close deadline and of recording notes under difficult circumstances (for example, a storm, a noisy background, lack of sufficient lighting).

The method of note taking may differ sharply from one story to another. In some instances, the process may be limited to recording direct answers to direct questions—as in the situation of the reporter interrogating the pedestrian

---

[1] Aside from this natural use, reporters' notes have been accepted as evidence in court. Also, notes have proved very helpful to reporters being questioned in court, refreshing their memory about a particular situation.

who chanced to be looking skyward when the large plane burst into flames. In other instances, note taking may entail a variety of techniques and procedures. Despite these differences, however, some basic guidelines characterize all note taking.

Primarily, note taking should aim at obtaining all essential data in unassailably correct form. For instance, if the story recounts an industrial accident, the notes should contain all pertinent names, addresses, known and probable causes, time, place, reactions, and implications. In essence, the notes should list all the information the reader may seek—or, stated negatively, the notes should never lack the information needed to write a full story. Consequently, the interviewer often jots down questions in advance to insure a sound body of data. Otherwise, under stress of the interview, he may forget to ask some of the necessary questions.

As the interviewer records notes, he should also be thinking in terms of a lead for his story, as well as the main direction which his story will take; that is, he should attempt to visualize his story in print. This process, of course, will influence his interviewing and note taking. In an accident story, for instance, the lead may focus on the fact that a man has been injured in a specific type of accident (for example, one caused by a defect in a piece of equipment). The interviewer, therefore, with his lead in mind, must manage his interview accordingly.

In taking notes, most newspeople use the procedure of folding two or three sheets of copy paper horizontally into thirds. In writing, they hold the paper vertically so as to have six or nine long, narrow pages. Sometimes they number the pages, but usually they simply work consecutively, keeping all notes on one side of the paper. Such notes can be spread out before the reporter as he writes, with no need to turn the paper.

As a substitute for note taking, many reporters have begun to use recording devices. They like the idea of turning on the recorder and being relieved of the responsibility for taking notes.

However, there are certain cautions to be sounded in using recorders. Most important, when the reporter later uses the recording in writing the story, he loses the ease and assistance of notes arranged for convenient reference. He may have to play the recording and make notes just as he would have done in the interview itself. Indeed, he often must play the recording several times to get the facts. A second disadvantage is that the recorder may alienate the interviewee for the very reason that it will record his words in incontestable form. He may prefer, rather, to restrict his statements to the ears of the person with whom he is speaking—probably because this procedure affords the opportunity for later alteration or denial of any statement made. Even a candid interviewee speaking into a recorder may become restrained, embarrassed, or stifled—if indeed he does not refuse outright to be questioned.

A final caution concerns the concealed recorder. Although many reporters use hidden recorders (as inside their coats), publishers in many states fear the consequences of the practice—even though the United States Supreme Court has yet to rule on the matter.[2] They feel that privacy laws can easily be construed to make the practice an illegal invasion. Hence they order their reporters to refrain.

EXERCISE

Examine the feature stories "Fenbergs Sign Bonds" and "Northeast High . . ." with a view to evaluating the interviewing techniques that entered into them. Also, examine the feature-story examples in Chapter 5 with the same thought in mind.

Fenbergs Sign Bonds, Leave Randolph Jail

BY BOB BURCHETTE
Daily News Staff Writer

ASHEBORO—Jerry Fenberg and his pregnant wife left Randolph County Jail Wednesday afternoon—exactly 24 hours after they were jailed for staging a protest to the installation of sewer lines to the N. C. Zoological Park.

"We're leaving because there is nothing more useful that we can do by staying in jail," the 33-year-old Fenberg said. He and wife Charlotte, 32, were allowed to sign their own bonds, and are to appear in court June 11 on charges of "obstructing the orderly flow of traffic."

Mrs. Fenberg's pregnancy was causing concern at the jail, and Sheriff Carl Moore wanted the couple out. But they refused to leave, even when Moore told them that they would be able to sign their own $200 bonds.

"It was causing a lot of trouble with her in here," Moore said. "We had to send somebody to check on her every 15 minutes. We didn't want anything to happen to her in here."

Fenberg decided to leave before his wife did, and eventually had to talk her into leaving. Interviewed while still in jail, Fenberg said, "I'm about to go stir crazy."

But he left the decision on whether they would leave to his wife. She sat quietly, talking in a low voice, while Fenberg was mopping sweat from his brow and trying to decide what to do.

At 4:15 p.m. they departed the jail, with Fenberg's arm around his wife's shoulder and her clutching a freshly cut, red rose in her hand. "Somebody brought me that rose. I don't know who . . . I'd like to thank them," she said.

The action that landed the Fenbergs in jail was their Tuesday obstruc-

[2] For a discussion of litigation, see *Journalism Quarterly*, Autumn, 1974, p. 511.

tion of a giant earthmoving machine being used to install sewer pipe in the Richland Creek section of the county near here. For more than four hours, the couple sat in chairs in front of the huge machine, bringing pipe installation to a halt.

And nobody knew what to do about it until highway patrol officers arrived and decided to use a 10-year-old statute designed to keep demonstrators from blocking traffic.

There the Fenbergs sat until they were removed bodily and taken to the county jail.

Fenberg and his wife said Wednesday that they object to the sewer line being installed in the creek. "We want them to move it up out of the creek," he said.

Of course, he would prefer that the line not be installed at all.

Fenberg, who came here five years from Tennessee, said he came to the area because the county has "a 300-year history of pottery making. It's very attractive to a young potter."

And he became interested in the environmental aspects of water and sewer line installations about four years ago, he said. He has consulted with Randolph officials and state officials in Raleigh in an effort to halt the project here. He said he does not belong to any environmentalist groups.

"I have a lot of correspondence about this," he said, holding his thumb and forefinger several inches apart to designate a "stack" of letters. "But I got more attention by sitting down out there in an act of civil disobedience than in any other way."

The sit-in was staged to "focus attention on the (sewer) project," he said. "We got the response, the television stations have been here and the newspapers, and I had a phone call from Raleigh."

About 12–15 of Fenberg's friends were at the construction site of the sewer lines Wednesday, carrying placards and demonstrating by "standing around."

One of his friends came to talk with him about 3 p.m. Wednesday, and reported that the Fenbergs' two small children (aged 4 and 6) were "doing fine."

And Fenberg admitted later that being away from the children was the main factor in his wife deciding to leave jail. "We need to be with our children," he said.

Fenberg, a slender, bearded man wearing rumpled clothes, left the jail with a battered straw hat in one hand and a handful of newspaper clippings about his escapade in the other hand.

—Greensboro (N.C.) Daily News

Edison Got Only the Walls

NORTHEAST HIGH TOOK THE GLORY AWAY

By RAYMOND C. BRECHT
Of The Bulletin Staff

Near a busy city street
Stands a noble school,
Home of virtue, learning's seat,
Owning honor's rule.
Hail Northeast! Hail Northeast! . . .

● ● ●

Half a century's gone. But still you hear the words—2,000 boys belting out the chorus, the organ pealing joyfully.

That was the old Northeast High School, 8th st. and Lehigh ave., in a golden day that seems a thousand years ago.

On a night late in June, in 1927, you sat in the front row of a graduating class. It was the old school's 50th class. You tried to listen while a solemn judge spoke solemnly—the commencement speaker. The warm evening, the sense of slight bewilderment, made it seem a droning.

Mostly your mind rested and your stare was fixed on the dark wooden lectern the judge was standing behind. Carved in Gothic lettering it said on the front of the lectern: "Whatsoever Thy Hand Findeth to Do, Do It With Thy Might." Words to be graduated by.

Your name was heard. You went awkwardly to the platform, president of the school community, hair parted in the middle and shiny with Stacomb. An honor man, the principal said, and you carried back to your seat a silver loving cup.

• • •

At 8th and Lehigh the other day, a January sun warmed the turreted, gray stone building. Over the doors it said, Thomas A. Edison High School. That was the name they gave it in 1957, when Northeast moved up to Cottman and Algon, much further in the northeast, and carried away its history and its traditions and all its memorabilia. Now the double front doors were painted bright red. Graffiti, black and white, swirled over them.

A boy in a green jacket went in. Across his back yellow letters said, "Edison Varsity Club."

In the main corridor, its floor clean, there was a huge bulletin board topped by the word TOGETHER. It had information about college guidance, vocational guidance, work experience, business education.

On the door of the main office a green sign appealed, "Support a New Edison High School at Front and Luzerne sts."

Next door, in a smaller office, sat the principal, Albert I. Glassman, 48, graying a little, smiling warmly, wearing a checked casual jacket. There was a poster on the wall with a repeated profile of the late Dr. Martin Luther King Jr. and the repeated legend, "They Had a Dream."

Glassman was talking about how it was after Northeast moved out, taking the "tangible and intangible things that contributed to the school's personality."

Northeast, he said, was one of the most prestigious schools in the city. It was the second oldest high school. After it went, with its history and its honors, they "had to organize a brand new high school in this old building."

"In our view," the principal said, "this was a tragic mistake." He called it "callous."

"That's hung over us ever since," he said. "I think it has significantly contributed to the image in the community we've had in recent years—an unfair image.

"It should still be Northeast High School," he said, "with its changing community."

• • •

They used to call the auditorium Morrison Hall, after an earlier beloved principal. On the stage of Morrison Hall, about 46 years ago, this visitor stood to make his pitch to be elected president.

His skinny frame behind the lectern with the Gothic admonition, he promised good government, improved facilities, great teams and a deluxe brand of integrity. The candidate was from Fishtown and he said so. He had lower Susquehanna ave. in his pocket.

Ignoring the upper classes and the elite of the north and west, he beamed his stuff at Norris st. and Dauphin st. and York st., at Memphis and Sepviva and Frankford ave. He spoke the language of the guys he'd played peggy with not too long before. And baseball on the lots and basketball in the churches that dotted all of Kensington . . . It was a landslide of New Deal style and proportion.

• • •

They just call it the auditorium now. The name of the old Northeast principal is gone. So is the lectern with its warning to the slothful.

There's a new lectern—speaking stand—a portable one painted yellow. The visitor stood behind it and looked out over the varnished, light brown, wooden seats, new since that other day. The long balcony, curving around the back, showed spots of peeling paint and cracking plaster. Stained-glass windows contributed by Northeast classes of yore, were bare of identifying legends.

Now, behind the lectern, stood 12th-grader Stanley Davis, 18, president of student government, described by his principal as an excellent saxophonist. Davis had been summoned from music class and the cord of the saxophone was still around his neck. He lives in the 2500 block of Master st.

Less effusive than his predecessor in high office, Davis answered questions straight from the shoulder. He said he was elected by the whole student body. The old president, happily looking back, asked how the campaign was.

"I just talked to the brothers," Davis said.

Well, were there big rallies and stuff? Campaigning in the corridors, maybe?

They had a forum, Davis said, matter-of-factly. "I just told the Edison brothers I was running."

• • •

It was in the spring, a balmy night, and the annual Northeast Revue was on. The president of the school community, no actor, was lending a hand backstage. The auditorium was packed—parents, aunts, uncles, and, of course, little sisters and other girls.

Suddenly the electrical system failed. Every light in the house went out. It was pitch black.

A frantic English teacher grabbed the student president pushed him through the curtain and onstage and whispered fiercely, "Start talking! And don't stop till the lights go on!" With a flashlight he circled the terrified student orator in a pool of yellow light. What to talk about?

Gulping, the victim remembered a fund drive to build a concrete stand at Northeast field. In a trice his bewildered head filled with visions of gridiron glory, Northeast spirit triumphing over tremendous odds, mostly teams consisting of big brutes from wealthy neighborhoods.

As though orating for his life, he told tale after tale of smashing touchdowns, spectacular catches, last-second field goals, opponents lying defeated and ignominious like so many men of sawdust.

Score piled upon glorious score. The frantic English teacher kept hissing, "Keep going! Keep going!" A giggle rolled over the audience (that's what you get when you invite girls). Finally the lights went on and the orator stumbled backstage, a gasping William Jennings Bryan.

Afterward, they took a collection at the doors and dollars were cheerfully given. In time there was a grandstand.

• • •

Principal Albert Glassman was talking about the old auditorium. The seats were good. They were put in around 1958, he said.

But around some windows there were great splotches where rain had come in and the plaster was giving way. A crack crawled its threatening way along a section of the ceiling.

The Board of Education does its best, Glassman said. "But the building is so old, and so tired, it takes an incredible amount of upkeep just to keep it running." He said a fortune had been spent on the roof.

He went back again to when Edison opened in 1957. He said they "had to get an honorary alumni association, so the kids would feel that somebody cared."

Musing, he said, "we try to build a sense of pride in Edison." A pause. "It's tough."

"We've got a lot of problems," the principal said. "All the schools have. But we've got a lot of nice kids in the school. We take a bad rap."

He showed decaying walls in the gym, while husky black and Puerto Rican boys dashed up and down the old basketball floor. He pointed to narrow stairwells. There was a fire drill, and the kids went out in orderly fashion. But, passing an open door, Glassman sniffed. Marijuana, he said.

Sometimes the kids get fed up with the drabness and paint their own rooms. Room 116—a bilingual class for the Spanish-speaking kids—they painted a sultry, tropical violet.

There's an occasional sign in the corridors: "Wipe Graffiti Out." But walls, especially near the gym, are full of it. "When we catch them we make them scrub the walls," Glassman said.

The principal grew enthusiastic when he told of the "Edison Academy of Applied Electrical Sciences." That's intensive, three-year training, sponsored by the Urban Coalition and the Board of Education. The kids get to contract for their work.

A spidery kid showed a button on his jacket: "Still Truckin' Along." He improved on it. "We need a new school," he all but shouted.

• • •

So you ride back along Lehigh ave. thinking of the words. Near a busy city street. And—stands a noble school. And you think: it's not the same. Like they all say: it's not the same.

But the old building's been there 71 years, you know. And you think of Albert Glassman saying quietly "the building's not the school." You remem-

ber, just a minute ago, live students
and live teachers and men and women
like Glassman who know what a school
is and care.

You look at the green bumper
sticker they gave you: "Support A New
Edison High School." The car stops for

a light, and in a moment it turns green.
Go. That's what that judge was talking
about, that night so long ago. Now it's
Stan Davis's turn.

I wonder whatever became of that
silver loving cup?
—The Evening Bulletin, Phila., Pa.

FOR FURTHER READING

Bingham, Walter Van Dyke. How to Interview. New York: Harper, 1959.

Bird, Brian. Talking With Patients. Philadelphia: Lippincott, 1973.

Fang, Irving E. Television News. New York: Hastings House, Publishers, 1972. (See section on interviewing, p. 90.)

Kadushin, Alfred. The Social Service Interview. New York: Columbia University Press, 1972.

Merton, Robert King. The Focused Interview. Glencoe, Ill.: Free Press, Inc., 1956.

Morgan, Henry H. The Interviewer's Manual. New York: Harcourt Brace Jovanovich, 1973.

Richardson, Stephen A., Barbara S. Dohrenwend, and David Klein. Interviewing, Its Forms and Functions. New York: Basic Books, 1965.

Sherwood, Hugh C. The Journalistic Interview. New York: Harper, 1972.

Stewart, Charles J., and William B. Cash, Jr. Interviewing: Principles and Practices. Dubuque: William C. Brown, 1974.

Williamson, Daniel R. Feature Writing For Newspapers. New York: Hastings House, Publishers, 1975.

★ **5** ★   What Is the Feature Story?
Abilities Needed for
    Feature Writing
Sources of the Feature Story
The Lead in the Feature Story
    Literary Devices in Leads
    Grammatical Structures
      in Leads
Examples for Discussion

The Newspaper Feature Story

WHAT IS THE FEATURE STORY?

Although newspaper readers can rarely explain the feature story, they look for these stories in every issue of their paper. They recognize and appreciate them through habitual reading—much as the man-in-the-street appreciates accentuation in architecture without ever bothering to analyze it.

Just what is the feature story? Journalists define it by comparing it with the straight news story.

In the straight news story, the whole atmosphere is impersonal. Cold facts are related in an objective manner. There is no conjecture, no opinion, no delving beneath the surface for a human-interest angle. Except for minor stylistic matters, the straight news story shows no traces of the writer's personality.[1]

In the feature story, however, the tone becomes personal. Parts of the story that have emotional, dramatic, or inner-thought elements are given dis-

---

[1] The news story with a by-line is not a straight news story. The by-line writer may properly interpolate his own thoughts and interpretations.

tinctly subjective treatment. The writer adopts this subjective approach in order to impart the human-interest quality. The difference between the news story and the feature story is therefore a matter of selection and treatment. The news-story writer selects only the straight facts and treats them objectively; the feature-story writer concentrates on the human-interest angle and treats it subjectively.

Naturally, many stories do not lend themselves to feature-story treatment. A writer, for example, would be hard pressed to find a feature-story angle in a routine announcement that public buildings will be closed, as usual, on Christmas Day. On the other hand, this same writer would face equal difficulty in attempting to treat some other stories as straight news. For instance, the story of the old woman defying the authorities by refusing to vacate the condemned house is unquestionably feature-story material. So are the story of the man receiving public welfare who won $50,000 in a lottery and the story of the neighborhood protest against allowing a veterinarian a permit to build kennels for boarding a hundred dogs. These stories are clearly feature material because the human-interest angle must take precedence over the straight facts. Certainly the reader is interested in the personal aspects of these incidents beyond the simple facts of the story.

In many instances a story may be used either as straight news or as feature material. The choice of treatments is generally based on the editorial policy of the paper, the number of feature stories already being used, and the value of the story as straight news as compared with its value as a feature. Consequently, one newspaper may use a given set of facts as straight news while another in the same city may use the material for a feature story. An example of this difference is found in stories concerning new equipment purchased by the local government. Some papers play up the color of the whole story (employees' reactions, changes necessitated, and the like); other papers merely report the details of the purchase in a perfunctory way.

Still another point to be noted in distinguishing between straight news and features is the fact that many stories fall between. An editor, in assigning a story, may tell the writer to give it a "light" touch, a humorous touch, or a satirical touch. The story, in short, is to be neither straight news nor straight feature; instead, it is to have some qualities of each. An example is the following acount of a steer on rampage. This story is really straight news with a very light touch.

Police Corral Steer Roaming Streets and Help in its Last Roundup

Patrolmen in red cars turned cowboys today long enough to capture a steer which broke away as it was being unloaded at a West Philadelphia abattoir.

Before the animal was finally led into a garage at the home of Bernardo Consorto, 5126 Master st., it had romped up and down Lancaster av., and along the side streets and alleys from 48th to 52d st.

Edward Grace, of Townsend, Del.,

and his brother, George, brought the steer with a truckload of cattle to the slaughter house of Alec Crisanti, Lancaster av. near 49th st. They had unloaded the cattle without trouble. Then came the steer's turn.

Halfway down the ramp, the steer leaped into the street and hightailed down Lancaster av., with Crisanti and an employe, Charles Sini, chasing after it. George Grace decided it was a case for the police. He telephoned the 49th st. and Lancaster av. station.

Summoned by radio, four red cars arrived within five minutes. The police-men adopted maneuvers to corner the steer.

Even after they got it in Consorto's garage, the steer balked attempts to be put in the truck.

When George Grace borrowed a shotgun from one of the neighbors and was about to shoot, the steer calmly walked out of the garage and up the ramp into the truck.

The steer was taken to the slaughter house, where it will be kept a day or so before being turned into steaks, roasts, etc.

—*Evening Bulletin,* Philadelphia

To make this story a feature, the reporter would concentrate almost entirely on the humorous aspects of the situation. He would poke friendly fun at the police, relate humorous remarks and occurrences of the chase, and stress any other element likely to draw a smile. If the reporter were to handle the story as straight news, he would make no attempt to capitalize on humor. His story would read like the following straight news account of a deer on rampage. The story, of course, could easily have been given a feature-story treatment.

Deer 'Crashes' Bar, Scares
Rhinelander Shoppers, Dies

RHINELANDER, WIS.—Deer season drama was brought to the downtown area here Friday when a wounded, frightened 175-pound buck broke a tavern window, scared downtown shoppers and had its throat cut by hunters.

The buck, a nine-pointer, was shot in the back legs and in the mouth in swamp areas just outside the city limits. He made his way into Rhinelander, running down the middle of a street. He turned onto Brown street, this city's main thoroughfare, and went onto a sidewalk. Pausing at a tavern, he saw his image in the window and made a lunge for it, crashing the glass but not entering.

The buck then went half a block farther when three men, two of them red-coated "hunters," converged on him. A barber working at a shop close by took the deer by the horns, another man hung onto the hind feet while the third slit the deer's throat.

—*Minneapolis Sunday Tribune*

A final point to be considered concerning the part-news-part-feature story is that practically every newspaper uses several very short ones daily to brighten pages or to serve for filler. These shorts, which frequently are akin to the comedian's jokes, are especially valuable for the inside pages containing advertisements. They often make the reader pause as he turns the page, thus increasing the chance that he will read the advertisements. Although the wire services provide an abundant supply of these shorts, editors encourage their reporters to find local ones because of their proximity.

The following shorts are typical of those found daily:

LOW THIEF STEALS A LADDER, MAN IS MAROONED ON ROOF

The meanest thief of the week was walking the streets of Alton today, congratulating himself on his sly humor.

He stole a ladder yesterday, marooning Gene Thiesen on the roof of the Miller Lime & Cement Co. Thiesen, a clerk in the store, had been on the roof putting a light bulb in the electric sign at the front of the building.

Other employes found another ladder and Thiesen got down.

—St. Louis Post-Dispatch

'Latent' Orleans Cowpoke Strikes

A contemporary cowpoke may still be riding the range in New Orleans after he stole a horse and saddle from the Audubon Park riding stables and rode off into the sunset at 5:15 p.m. Saturday.

Second District police said Sunday that a man who identified himself as James Brown rented the horse from the stables at Exposition Boulevard and Magazine Street earlier Saturday but failed to return the animal.

Police said the beige horse and riding saddle were worth approximately $500.

—Times-Picayune, New Orleans

'Some Body Else Is in My Crypt'

Watsonville

Charley L. Mann Jr., 83, filed suit here yesterday for $60,000, claiming there is a strange body in his family crypt.

His Superior Court lawsuit against the Pajaro Valley Memorial Park in Watsonville also asked $2 a day "reasonable rent" for the unauthorized presence of the stranger's body.

Mann charged the cemetery "unlawfully broke and entered the family crypt where his parents rest" on Dec. 7 to make a place for the stranger.

—San Francisco Chronicle

Assets Unfrozen

QUINCY, Mass.—A sneak thief dipped into the deep freezer which grocer Samuel Jolas used for a hiding place and stole $90—cold cash.

—Maine Sunday Telegram, Portland

ABILITIES NEEDED FOR FEATURE WRITING

The first requirement of feature writing is the ability to recognize feature-story material. The reporter must have a sensitivity to the feature-story possibilities in the *unusual* and an awareness of the dramatic or human interest quality in the *usual.* One kind of reporter might never see a feature story; another might find an excellent one every day he works.

Consider a reporter assigned to cover a routine story of a small warehouse fire. Instead of contenting himself with the usual facts about amount of damage, cause, and similar details, he looks for another angle. In his search, he learns that, for a fireman who has just completed 25 years of service, this is fire number 7,000. Immediately the reporter has not only another angle, but also a really interesting story. He talks with the fireman, learns about his most exciting experiences, gathers some interesting opinions, and obtains some reflections on the progress of fire-fighting methods over the years. Now, instead of having a short of eight or ten lines, he has a story that merits a full column with an appropriate headline and picture. Thus, the ability to recognize feature story material has unearthed a good story and no doubt has helped to strengthen the editor's esteem for the reporter.

A valuable skill in feature writing is the ability to *write humorously* because easily half of all feature stories appeal to the reader's sense of humor. How, for instance, could a reporter successfully handle the following feature story without humor?

Joe Creason's Kentucky

Ball Bounces Differently For a 'Benched' Coach

DEEP CIVIC pride drips from the voice of Elizabethtown Mayor James R. Pritchard when he coins a factual pun by declaring, without qualification, that "We have the best basketball coach in Kentucky on our bench."

What his honor means is that the judges' bench in his town's newly-remodeled city court room is occupied by Hardin McLane, a 35-year-old party who is regarded by many as the most talented high school basketball coach in the state.

Before retiring two years ago, McLane compiled a 264-66 won-lost record in 12 years of coaching at Caneyville and Elizabethtown Catholic high schools. Now, after having been appointed judge a year ago, he presides over city court six mornings a week for a couple of hours and works the rest of the time as an associate in an E'town real estate firm.

A Refreshing Visit

Since city court is on the same level as a county court, McLane, whose trademark is bright red, yellow, blue and green sports jackets, has faced an endless procession of persons charged with drunkenness, speeding, assault, family fights and other misdemeanors. The same firm fairness and logic he showed as a coach has helped him in his new role as judge.

"Like in coaching, I have to stay alert because something unexpected happens every time I hold court," he says.

As an example of the unexpected,

McLane tells about a man who had passed out in the bus station and was arrested. When he came to trial, he was asked if he had anything to say before being sentenced.

"Your Honor," he began in a clipped, precise voice, "not knowing the full facts, I would hesitate to make an assertion, but I was not inebriated. I was traveling from the place of my employment, Detroit, Mich., to the home of my dear parents, Decatur, Ga. Having traveled all night, I was completely fatigued to the point of exhaustion and got off the bus in your fair city to refresh myself.

"Alas and alack, when I returned the bus had departed and I merely lay down for a short nap. I was resting and not passed out drunk when your alert officers arrested me."

"But it says here," McLane interrupted, glancing at the citation, "that your speech was very slurred."

"Well, thir," the man retorted without hesitation, "I have a thlight thpeech impediment and, you thee, I always thspeak that way!"

Some weeks back a man from Glasgow was arrested for drunken driving. When booked, he insisted that the judge be informed he was a personal friend of Gov. Louie Nunn and if he wasn't let go "I'll see that this court is wiped out."

The Last Word

"Is this the man who's a personal friend of the governor?" McLane asked humbly when the man, smirking knowingly, was brought before him. "Sir, I want you to go back to Glasgow and tell the governor that the police judge in the red coat in Elizabethtown really is enforcing the drunk-driving law he keeps talking about because he just took your license away from you for six months!"

McLane discounts the disadvantages of a non-lawyer presiding as a judge.

"John Arnett, the city attorney, always sits at my side," he points out, "and he quotes the law to me and all I do is consider the facts and make a decision."

McLane likes to keep things as informal as possible in his court, but he insists on order and decorum being maintained.

"About the only rule I've adopted is never to wear a red or yellow sports jacket to court on Mondays," he says. "That's the day our weekend drunks stand trial and colors like that might be too much for them!"

—*The Courier-Journal*, Louisville, Ky.

Another demand made of the feature-story writer is the ability to poke fun without being mean. He must show clearly that he can laugh pleasantly but understandingly at man's foibles. Note this quality of gentle satire in the story below.

Like an Oldtime Movie

Crash 'Boxes' Up Broad St. Traffic

By PETER WINTERBLE
Of The Inquirer Staff

Hundreds of stalled mid-city motorists got a good look at the heavy rain Friday afternoon that broke the weeklong heat spell.

But chances are the rain didn't cool their tempers, because they were caught in a mammoth traffic jam that for nearly 40 minutes had Broad st. looking like the scene of a slapstick fire drill from Callowhill st. to the south side of City Hall.

It started at 2:50 P.M., when Russell L. Jenkins, of 1317 N. 19th st., was negotiating a turn from Callowhill into the northbound lane of Broad st.

His truck, loaded with 10-foot-long wooden storage cabinets, hit the cement center island on Broad st., dumping several of the boxes on a car driven by Walter Newlands, 67, of Jenkintown.

Newlands said he was unable to

get out of his car. The truck, belonging to the Spring Garden Institute, was blocking the street, and motorists began to honk their horns.

Jenkins and a helper, Eddie Smith, hopped down and began loading the boxes back on the truck.

They had just finished, when a PTC Route C bus tried to weave between the truck and the center island. The bus missed. It caught the rear of the truck, again dumping the boxes onto Newlands' car.

The collision not only damaged Newlands' car again, but also poked a jagged hole in the side of the PTC bus and slammed an Air Force car, parked in front of Newlands', into the curb.

PTC supervisors arrived and gave emergency tickets to the passengers on the stalled bus.

Commuters milled about, alternately looking at the torrents of rain and the torrents of angry drivers caught in the jam. The temperature, 82 at 2 P. M., dropped to 74 by 4 P. M.

Newlands, whose late-model sedan was dented from front to rear, said, "I'm going to stay in Jenkintown from now on."

"I didn't mind too much when the boxes fell on me the first time, but the second time was too much.

"That, plus all this rain. I just don't know," he said.

After loading the boxes for the third time, driver Jenkins pulled the ill-fated truck to the curb and traffic resumed.

The heat wave was over.

—Philadelphia Inquirer

Throughout all, the writer of the feature story must have a deep *sense of the brotherhood of man.* He must have that feeling for humanity which enables him to appreciate the hopes, the joys, the sorrows, and the disappointments of others. It is this feeling which helps the feature writer to handle such stories as the interview with the mother whose son has been killed in a foreign country, the visit to the brain-damage section of the veterans' hospital, or the tour of the flooded areas along the Mississippi. However, the writer must be careful of exaggerated sentimentality and emotional overflow. Gushing and sobbing have no place in the mature feature.

Note how the appeal of the following story originates in the writer's ability to present the pertinent facts sympathetically and thoroughly—yet without attempting to tug at the reader's heartstrings.

STATE RULES CRACK JIMMY'S NEST EGG

By PETER CLAREY
Times Staff Writer

TOLLAND—A 19-year-old youth whose paralyzing injury three years ago moved Tolland County families to contribute $13,000 to a trust fund, is being forced to expend his savings to pay his hospital bills as a result of a State Welfare Department decision.

Jimmy West, paralyzed from the

shoulders down by a gymnasium accident at Tolland High School Jan. 20, 1969, was the beneficiary of a town-wide campaign to raise money for him through suppers, dances and even an appearance by Detroit Tiger baseball star Dick McAuliffe, an Avon resident.

The fund-raisers, who were aiming at $10,000, went over the top.

However, Jimmy's mother, Alice West of Eaton Road said yesterday that her son's $13,000 has been cut in half in the last six months by hospital bills, and she expects it will be all gone by the end of the year.

Mrs. West said the trust is being depleted (it was kept intact for the past three years) because the State Welfare Department stopped paying Jimmy's hospital bills after his 19th birthday.

Mrs. West said Jimmy applied to the State Welfare Department earlier this year for aid to the disabled, but the application was rejected because Jimmy's assets exceeded the maximum amount of money a welfare client may keep.

Until his 19th birthday, his hospital expenses were covered by money from the Welfare Department under AFDC (Aid for Dependent Children).

Welfare officials say the disabled aid is permitted to single persons who earn no more than $1,900 a year and own no more than $350 in personal property.

Mrs. West, who has three other children living at home and is herself on welfare, says she has been given bills for six months totaling $6,600 for medical care from New Britain Memorial Hospital, where Jimmy is a patient five days a week. On weekends he goes home.

Jimmy's accidents three years ago came only two months after his older brother, Byron, then 20, lost both legs in a land mine explosion in Vietnam.

The double tragedy moved Jimmy's classmates to contribute lunch money and their parents to set up fund-raising events for the stricken family. Three children still live at home. Byron and two other children are no longer living at home.

Now that the fund is apparently slipping through their fingers, Mrs. West laments, "it's a shame he (Jimmy) couldn't do what he wanted with it."

She explained that Jimmy has taken special training at the hospital and last year earned his driver's license for specially equipped autos. He wants a car, his mother says, but the Welfare Department would not permit it.

Mrs. West said she had little hope of preserving the trust fund, although she said its existence alone is a morale booster for her son.

—*Hartford* (Conn.) *Times*

SOURCES OF THE FEATURE STORY

For the sake of convenience, the sources of the feature story can be divided into the 10 groupings discussed below. Remember, however, that these groupings are purely arbitrary. They are intended merely as broad classifications.

The Usual. As already stated, many of the stories handled by the newspaper can be treated either as straight news or as features, and the writer accordingly relates the facts in the straightforward, impersonal style of the news story or he adopts the subjective approach and treatment that characterize the feature story.

Typical instances of such stories are the demolition of a once-famous building, the death of a well-known blind news dealer, the razing of the last covered bridge in the locality, or the implications of a recent election.

The Unusual. In every day's crop of stories come those so predominantly features that they must be treated as such. To treat them otherwise would be almost impossible.

Examples of this type of story are the interview with the new circus freak, the visit to the home of the 400-pound man, the interview with the man who has regained his sight, the antique automobile parade, or the hailstorm in mid-August.

The Seasonal Story. A never-failing source of feature stories is the events that come with each change in the calendar. Even though these stories strongly resemble those of previous years, this kind of feature is popular nonetheless.

Among the common seasonal feature stories are the account of the first arrival of Christmas trees in the big city, New Year's Day celebrations, groundhog day, the Easter parade at fashionable places, Memorial Day celebrations, the July 4th parade, the crowds at the beaches during the heat wave, and the opening and closing of the schools.

The Supplementary Story. Where a story has received a great play, there is invariably another story or series of stories related to this main story. This lesser story, sometimes called a "color" story, is in reality a supplement to the larger one.

Outstanding examples of the supplementary story are the account of the crowd at the Army-Navy game, the biography of the man who has achieved sudden fame, the story on the members of the President's family at his inauguration, the caterer's story of his work at a famous wedding, and the eyewitnesses' accounts of their reactions to such newsworthy events as serious accidents, disasters, and other uncommon sights.

The Dramatic Situation. When a story is high in dramatic quality, it is invariably treated as a feature. Scarcely does a day pass without several such stories.

Examples are the accounts of the tiny terrier that awakened the family when their home was afire, the faithful servant who has been left a fortune by his grateful employer, the physician who is called upon to save the life of a member of his own family, and the man of low estate who suddenly is introduced to the President of the United States.

The Guidance Story. Newspapers frequently have one of their staff members or an eminent authority write a story which gives advice or explains an important problem. Such a writing is appropriately termed a "guidance story."

Examples of this type of feature writing are explanations of hidden issues in a forthcoming election, accounts of proposed legislation, and advice on filling out government forms (income tax, social security, veteran questionnaires, or the like).

Sometimes guidance feature writing on a given topic appears regularly, and the newspaper may treat it as a column. The most common examples of such writing are the buyer's guidance story, advice to the lovelorn, aids to dieting and better health, advice to aspirants in a particular field, etiquette talks, and writings on psychology.

Personal Experience. One of the most popular feature stories is that in which a reporter or someone outside the newspaper field writes from the standpoint of personal experience.[2]

Reporters employ this first-person approach in such stories as those which tell of the meeting with a famous person, the demonstration of a new invention,

---

[2] See Chapter 14 for a discussion of the personal experience account in magazine writing.

and the visit to an interesting or unusual place. The stories by outsiders, many of which are ghost-written, include writings under by-lines of famous baseball players who write of their big games; of military men who recount their experience under fire; and of plain citizens who have been eyewitnesses to major disasters.

Arts and Crafts. On many occasions, a newspaper carries a story which explains a fad or trends in a particular art or craft at a given moment. The story is really a little essay to explain.

The music critic, for instance, writes of the record sales for the past month; the radio-television editor sets forth the entertainment for the coming season; and the social-page editor tells of the crafts which are currently popular among the children's groups of the city.

Popularizing Facts. Rarely does a large metropolitan newspaper appear without a feature story which explains the below-surface facts of an institution, a craft, or an interesting place. Perhaps the reporter has visited a famous restaurant. He tells of the quantities of food, the unusual details of preparation, and statistics regarding diners and their eating habits.

This type of feature story is used extensively in the magazine section of the Sunday paper.[3] Here story after story explains places of historical interest, unusual vegetation, and buildings which the reader passes almost daily without knowing much about.

The Utility Article. When the editor sees the advisability of teaching the readers how to perform in a given field, the utility article is employed. Often, in a special section, one comes upon the article concerning new dishes and other phases of improving the home, articles teaching the reader how to interpret music, how to play an instrument, how to play golf, how to tie flies for trout fishing, or how to understand the various sports.

THE LEAD IN THE FEATURE STORY

Writing the feature-story lead differs from writing the news story lead in that there is much greater latitude. The feature writer can use one of several kinds of leads, depending on the material and the style of the story. One lead, he finds, creates suspense. Another creates sympathy. Another gives just the humorous beginning he wants. He chooses the one that best suits his needs.

It is useful to have names for the many possible kinds of leads. Examples follow, in two kinds of classification that intermingle with each other: by literary device and by grammatical structure.

Literary Devices in Leads

The most common kinds of leads are demonstrated below. In studying these leads, note that not all are strictly feature story leads; several can be used in the straight news story or in the part-news-part-feature story.

[3] See Chapter 14.

The Contrast Lead:

A race in alms giving to promote world peace through the influence of spiritual leaders rather than an arms race for war was called for by Rabbi Samuel M. Segal in his sermon yesterday morning at Mount Neboh Temple, 130 West Seventy-ninth Street.

—New York Times

The Question Lead:

GAYLORD—Why did three boys take turns shooting at a friendly, 66-year-old woodcutter until a bullet in the back killed him?

A psychiatrist will try to answer that question Wednesday.

Probate Judge Frank Libcke said he would take the trio to the Central Michigan Children's Clinic in Traverse City.

—Detroit Free Press

The Astonisher Lead:

Cincinnati, July 8—(UPI)—A Cincinnati sociologist today suggested that people stop "falling in love."

Roy E. Dickerson, executive secretary of the Cincinnati Social Hygiene Society, said it just isn't so—we don't "fall in love." Nor do we "love at first sight."

Dickerson told University of Cincinnati students that love is the product of a growth process.

"It isn't an accident or a sudden visitation," he said. "If there actually were such a thing as love literally at first sight, it surely should be carefully tested by the passing of time."

—United Press story

The Suspended-Interest Lead:

During busy shift times, the notoriously slow elevators in the Police and Courts Building create a crush of passengers assembling in the basement.

A policeman who was escorting a prisoner to the second floor found himself watching helplessly as he was unable to exit after the prisoner because of the mob.

Getting out on the third floor, the policeman rushed down a flight of stairs not expecting to find what he found.

The prisoner was waiting for him near the elevator door, apparently puzzling over what had happened to his escort.

—The Dallas (Texas) *Morning News*

The Figurative Lead:

CUMBERLAND, Md.—Superstition, like toadstools, grows wild in these mountains. Over a hundred years ago the "Hag Seer of Horse Creek" is said to have foretold the assassination of Lincoln. Today a mystic cult writes letters to police purporting to give the location of the bodies of two missing coeds.

—The Washington Post

The Epigram Lead:

By NEYSA STROUP

WELLINGTON—There's nothing like a sudden summer storm to aid a reporter in gaining interviews with three top recording artists.

Pianist Floyd Cramer had just offered shelter to this C-T reporter when the first raindrop struck at the fairground last night.

"Come on in," invited Cramer, as those few drops turned into a blinding, blowing sheet of rain.

Boots Randolph dashed in off the stage and Chet Atkins took a chair in the other end of the room. It was a reporter's dream, with a 9 p.m. deadline and the men all captive in a tiny trailer at the Lorain County Fair.

—Chronicle-Telegram, Elyria, O.

The Parody Lead

Bedford, Pa.—The clock in the office of Bedford county Prothonotary Howard J. Koontz has a face that stops a girl.

Koontz had to pull the plug on the electric clock because a temporary stenographer is allergic to florescent light from its dial. It made her break out in a rash.

So time will stand still in Koontz' office until his regular stenographer returns.

—Daily Local News, West Chester, Pa.

The Quotation Lead:

"We hope to be sailing France against Intrepid in the America's Cup races in September," Bruno Bich, spokesman for the French challenging syndicate for the coveted yachting trophy said Thursday as the wooden 12-meter yacht was towed to the Newport Shipyard here.

The arrival of France I killed rumors of a new aluminum French 12-meter in the Australian 12-meter camps where crews have been sailing the wooden Gretel II and the new aluminum Southern Cross nearly every day for more than a month.

—*Daily News-Record,* Harrisonburg, Va.

The Dialogue Lead:

"Hup, two, three, four!"

No, it's not an army drill sergeant, it's Mrs. Margaret Mingo counting cadence for the Miller Homes Matadors, an all-girl precision drill team.

The Matadors are 22 young black girls, five to 14-years-old, who practice nearly three hours every afternoon after school to maintain their champion-caliber marching in military-type precision and monkey drill.

—*The Trentonian,* Trenton, N.J.

The Cartridge or Capsule Lead:

The baptism under fire has begun for Missouri's new auto safety inspection law which could become one of two things—just a headache for motorists, or a lifesaver on the highways.

Roughly 2.1 million cars and trucks in the state are affected, and almost as many pocketbooks. Fees for inspections, alone, will cost $5.2 million this year. The bill for repairs is anyone's guess.

—*Globe-Democrat,* St. Louis

The Pun Lead:

It's "blast-off" time for the Syracuse Stingers.

First, the Stingers hope to blast the Maryland Arrows, tonight's National Lacrosse League foe at the War Memorial.

Second, the Stingers hope their fans have a blast at the "Beer Blast" to follow the contest, a $1.50 affair in the WM's basement for all those who attend the game.

—*Syracuse Herald-Journal*

The Humorous Lead:

It could have been J. Frank Northcutt who coined the expression: Don't knock the weather, most people couldn't start a conversation if it didn't change once in a while.

Frank Northcutt likes to talk about the weather.

But when he does, he isn't making idle conversation. He speaks with authority.

Northcutt served as a meteorologist with an artillery unit in Vietnam for 27 months.

—*Earl Watson in the Berkshire Eagle,* Pittsfield, Mass.

The Definition Lead:

RETIREMENT: Freedom from drudgery and tension, time to golf or fish or do nothing, tranquility to enjoy the fruits of long years of labor. This is often the dream.

RETIREMENT: Boredom, loneliness, sickness, poverty, fear. This is often the reality.

—Jerry Oster in the *New York Daily News*

The Direct Address Lead:

Please don't be nervous.

But if you live in the vicinity of the South Park fairgrounds, chances are you may encounter a . . . er . . . an animal.

He answers to the name of Carl. He is a capybara.

A capybara is of South American extraction and is the world's largest rodent.

Last seen Friday morning at the Children's Zoo compound in South Park, where he was appearing for the 33rd Annual Allegheny County Fair, he is about a foot tall, weighs around 45 pounds, and has a thick brown fur coat. He disappeared that morning.

He is a vegetarian, and yes, he is aware of it.

Although only a . . . baby . . . he is especially fond of lettuce and carrots. He will stand about two-feet high, weigh more than 100 pounds and mea-sure three to four feet from nose to . . . ah . . . end (he has no tail), when he reaches maturity.

—John Little in the *Pittsburgh* (Pa.) *Press*

Grammatical Structures in Leads

It is often useful in considering leads to identify them according to their grammatical structure. Hence, one finds such leads as the infinitive lead, the prepositional lead, and the participial lead. The reason for these terms is simply that the lead opens with the grammatical form for which it is named. Examples follow:

The Infinitive Lead:

To make the most of West Virginia's resources, and to meet federal regulations, each region of the state (the law set up 11) has its own Regional Development Council.
—*The Pendleton Times,* Franklin, W.V.

The Prepositional Lead:

After more than two months of twice-weekly meetings, the Park Commission has released a progress report on its study of the City Park Department.
—*Springfield* (Mass.) *Sunday Republican*

The Participial Lead:

Asserting that state law requires taxable property to be assessed at full market value, Milwaukee's tax commissioner Monday called upon David W. Adamany, secretary of the State Department of Revenue, to enforce the law.
—*The Milwaukee Journal*

The Dependent-Clause Lead:

Although Calvert County is long on history and tradition, it never has had an official song or seal.
—*Evening Star,* Washington, D.C.

The Compound-Sentence Lead:

Boston to Lincoln, Nebraska, may seem an unlikely route to Montreal, but for little Marcie Ravech, of Newton, it's the first major whistle-stop on the long road to the 1976 summer Olympics to be held in that Canadian city.
—*Boston Herald American*

EXAMPLES FOR DISCUSSION

Study the following feature stories. What makes them features rather than simple straight news? What quality necessary to the feature writer is evidenced in each story?

Prison sign shop points way to new careers for inmates

By BILL HARRIS

FLORENCE—Turning out top quality signs at bargain prices is important, but takes second place to turning out productive members of society in the sign shop of Arizona State Prison here.

"Our quality of work will match that of any commercial shop—bar none," said a prison official.

"But more important than that, and more important than our dollar gross, is the semivocational training this shop offers the inmate," stressed M.E. "Mel" Burrows.

Burrows is prison industries superintendent, working under Ken Murray, State Department of Corrections industries administrator.

Approximately 25 inmates work at a variety of jobs in the sign shop, from manual labor to highly skilled layout and design.

One convict who said he was due for release before Christmas is looking forward to a job with a commercial sign shop in Phoenix.

"I've worked in here two years," he said. "When I got 'short' enough to start looking for a job, Mr. Burrows gave me a good recommendation. Thos shop outside answered my application by saying I can go to work the day after I'm out.

"I don't have any family or relatives left who want anything to do with me," he added.

"With a definite job to go to, I can make it on my own" the convicted robber concluded. "It's one helluva relief."

Burrows said that Murray, whose office is in the Department of Corrections in Phoenix, has been "a big shot in the arm" toward helping industry-working inmates find jobs on release.

"We have one shop in Phoenix that has accepted at least nine men from here in the past two years," Burrows said. They started the men at $2.50 an hour and put the finishing touches on their training. The men then are released to seek higher paying jobs."

"None of the nine returned to prison," Burrows reported. "Nine men out of a population of nearly 1,700 doesn't sound like many, but that's just from one department. We have 100 per cent success with a few rather than failure with the majority."

Excluding the auto license plate factory, the prison sign shop is probably the most productive of any correctional industry now in operation by the State Department of Corrections Burrows said.

And Burrows said his sign shop's goal is for a gross production increase from last year's $70,000 to $750,000 five years from now. He said it is not only realistic but highly possible.

"Technically, our correctional industries program is not one designed to be a profit-making enterprise," Burrows continued. "We are basically concerned in providing gainful work for the inmate while he is here. We prefer to think of surplus funds over production costs as 'net' rather than 'profit.' beheaded.

"These net earnings are reinvested in the industrial program for modernization of equipment, techniques and training facilities," he said.

For emphasis, Burrows pointed to a newly installed automatic silk-screen machine, purchased by open bid for $4,500 by the prison.

"When we say 'reinvesting for modernization,' this machine is a good example, Burrows said. 'Until a few weeks ago, all our silk-screening was done by hand. This is the method by which the bulk of our signs are produced. There is no comparison in the output by hand and this machine."

In keeping with the shop's updating and diversified production, Burrows pointed to a recently purchased photo-decal camera and an area where darkroom facilities will be installed.

"This updated equipment and processing puts us on a competitive basis with a commercial shop of the same size," Burrows said.

Tax-supported agencies, counties or municipalities are potential markets and are eligible to buy prison-made signs. Records in Burrows' industries office at the prison indicate the two best customers are Pinal County and the State Highway Department.

"Our immediate plans are to cultivate the interests of other towns and counties in what we have to offer by adding an outside salesman or two," Burrows added.

"We have bargains here that very few purchasing agents are aware of," said Burrows. "Our quality will match that of any commercial shop—bar none. And prices are considerably less."

—*The Arizona Republic*, Phoenix

By Ozzie St. George

CASEY THE GORILLA'S famous though yet unnamed daughter arrived in St. Paul late Tuesday; wide awake and, it appeared, anxious to make friends.

Or anxious, anyway, to make her presence in St. Paul known.

She began by grabbing Mayor Lawrence Cohen's son, Scotty, by his T-shirt. Scotty was not exactly pleased by that, though later he shook hands with the three-month-old gorilla.

Then Casey's daughter got a handful of Councilman Victor Tedesco's hair, while he stood beside her and the cameras clicked and whirred.

The councilman took this in good part. "It could have been worse," he said. "At least she got my real hair. A little higher up and it might have come off in her hand—and how would that look on television!"

Mrs. Joseph H. Scheunemann of 1510 Holton St., who will care for Casey's daughter in her home for the next several months, was holding the little tyke, more or less, while all this went on.

But Casey's daughter, born April 10 at the Omaha Zoo, has reached the squirming stage. She also has arms that are longer than she is and a grip that a 12-year-old-boy with his first Steel Grip Dynamic Muscle Builder would be proud to own.

Mrs. Scheunemann, Como Zoo Director John Fletcher and Dr. Ralph Farnsworth of the University of Minnesota Veterinarian Hospital flew to Omaha Tuesday to collect Casey's daughter.

Their pilot—who donated his time, plane and 60 gallons of gas—was Jim Voigt of Voigt & Fourre, St. Paul architects.

Casey's daughter, who now tips the scales at 11 pounds, is "a good baby—a wonderful baby," say the people at the Omaha Zoo.

Her mother, Brigitte, was a good mother, too—as gorilla mothers go. She used to hold her other babies up to view when she saw a photographer approaching.

She used to drop them, too, though—accidentally. This particular Casey's daughter, therefore, was taken from her at birth and has been raised by humans.

She drinks formula fortified with oatmeal (a small bottle every four hours), wears Pampers and had a playpen and a hanging toy in Omaha.

She wears T-shirts, too, most of the time, but for her trip to St. Paul, what with all the photographers about, both in Omaha and in St. Paul, she was bundled into waterproof pink pants and a new pink dress.

She also has eight teeth and occasionally bites—people and things.

"When she does that," two Omaha Zoo docents told Mrs. Scheunemann, "just whack her on the nose. And when she starts grabbing things—things she shouldn't—whack her bottom. She's spoiled rotten but she knows what a whack means."

There was scarcely a dry eye—a dry human eye, that is—when finally it was time for the folks in Omaha to say goodby to Casey's daughter.

Half a dozen docents there have been standing six-hour shifts with her, around the clock, in the zoo's nursery. And, as Fletcher said, "It is very easy to become emotionally attached to small primates . . . they are so human."

"In fact," said Dr. Lee G. Simons, Omaha Zoo director, who once raised an infant gorilla and an infant orangutan in his home at the same time, "They are far more precocious than children at the same age . . . and therefore more fun."

Neither Casey nor Brigitte, however, appeared to be disturbed by the departure of their only surviving offspring.

Casey, incidentally, is just about the top attraction at the Omaha Zoo. He also has learned to throw, with either arm, and earlier this year nailed a couple of spectators with rocks people had tossed into his yard.

Now people don't toss rocks into his yard anymore.

Casey's daughter and Mrs. Scheunemann appeared to get on famously, right from the start.

Casey's daughter spent most of the flight to St. Paul—arranged to fall between her feedings—curled up in Mrs. Scheunemann's lap, sound asleep, with a firm grip on a couple of handfuls of Mrs. Scheunemann's smock.

Those feedings every four hours and the fact that Casey's daughter loves to be held don't worry Mrs. Scheunemann.

The hardest part, she thinks, will be keeping all those people who "want to see the little gorilla" out of her house.

That's a must, though, for two or three months yet, because infant gorillas are prone to catch all the childhood diseases children catch, and have almost no natural immunity until about six months old.

—*St. Paul* (Minn.) *Pioneer Press*

—Staff Photo by Craig Borck.

CASEY'S DAUGHTER MAKES MINNESOTA DEBUT AT HOLMAN FIELD
The Gorilla Will Stay Temporarily With Mrs. Arlene Scheunemann
—*St. Paul* (Minn.) *Pioneer Press*, July 19, 1972

SPCA Moving Very Tactfully To Ease Skunks Out of Town

Great Care Taken to Avoid Hurting Sensitive Feelings Of Occasional Visitors Here Sampling City Life

By JACK D. HUNTER

"Dear Mr. and Mrs. Skunk and all little skunks:

"This is to notify you that serious negotiations are under way to evict you from your premises in various sections of Wilmington and environs.

"Inasmuch as your occupation of dwellings under porches, in hedges, and in back yards constitutes a mental hazard and otherwise threatens the well-being of other residents of the area—human, canine, and feline—you, as the English say, have had it.

Very Respectfully

"Respectfully—very respectfully—the SPCA."

It's doubtful whether such a communication will actually be sent out by the Wilmington SPCA, and even more doubtful that it would be read and acknowledged by New Castle County's more pungent citizenry.

But the fact remains: Skunks must go!

Miss Alice Warner, treasurer of the SPCA here, assures that there has been no sudden influx of the odoriferous animals.

Few Requests Each Year

But the society receives from four to six requests for aid a year from Wilmington householders whose homes have become the temporary addresses of skunks with a liking for urban living.

For this reason, Miss Warner says, she has placed an advertisement seeking the services of skunk trappers, so that when word comes from a citizen in distress, the society can dispatch a man equipped to take the animals with a minimum of perfumed ado.

The reason the SPCA can't handle the complaints itself, Miss Warner asserts, is that the only traps it has suitable for the purpose would, quite obviously, need scrapping after one application.

Need for Professional

Since the SPCA traps are needed for other pursuits than evicting the four-legged chemical warfare units, she is negotiating with professional trappers to use their equipment.

The "negotiations" are necessary, she points out, to make certain the trappers would use only humane instruments, and not devices that would cripple the skunks or endanger children, dogs, cats, or other pets.

In other words, the orders are this:

"Trap 'em and get 'em out, boys—but don't hurt 'em."

Man-Sized Task

This is, of course, a man-sized task, seeing that the animals to be trapped are known to defend themselves first and ask questions later.

But Miss Warner says she has received three or four answers to her ad from men "who are obviously very responsible and who would meet the requirements set down by the SPCA."

The trap authorized by the society, she points out, is a box-like affair with a sliding door at one end. The prowling black-and-white atomizer is caught when he enters the box to investigate bait left at its far end.

Theoretical Procedure

When the bait is touched, the sliding door is released, and Brother Skunk is on his way out of town.

How the trip to less populated areas is contrived without the trappee putting up a—that is, exercising his God-given right—is a technical matter, apparently.

Under the arrangements under study, Miss Warner says, the SPCA will act as a sort of clearing house for skunk-threatened householders and the trappers.

"If a resident finds he has a skunk living around his place," Miss Warner explains, "he can call us and we will refer him to our SPCA-approved trappers. Financial arrangements between the customer and trapper are their own affair."

Do skunks damage property?

"Well," Miss Warner smiles, "not necessarily."

Then their main nuisance value is the nervous strain they engender among non-skunks?

Again Miss Warner smiles.

—*The Evening Journal,* Wilmington, Del.

Orioles tell Valinda 'sorry, but no batgirls'

By DAVID L. MAULSBY

Women's lib has suffered another setback—Valinda has been turned down in her bid for the job of Oriole bat boy.

The Oriole management rejected Valinda's application, explaining that a bat boy is required to spend a good deal of time in the dressing rooms.

Valinda, daughter of Mr. and Mrs. Billy J. Burgess, of the 300 block Endsleigh avenue, had written to the Orioles, asking for the job and identifying herself as an enthusiastic Oriole and baseball fan.

Her letter said:

"Orioles,

"My name is Valinda Burgess. I am 13 years old. I will be 14 in March. Please, I would like very much to be a bat boy. I am as strong as any boy my age. I got the presidential award (for a physical fitness program) in school this year. I like sports and baseball as much as any boy.

"I watch baseball on TV more than my brother. I go to the games when I can. I love the Orioles. One time I tried to get a paper route but couldn't, 'cause I was a girl.

"Would you please give me a chance? I know I can do it. I am very athletic and can catch balls and play ball real well.

"Linda Warehime (a member of the grounds crew—and a girl) is in my sister's class. I always liked Jay Mazzone (Oriole bat boy who has hooks instead of hands, the result of an accidental

Valinda Burgess, would-be batgirl.

burning as a child and who is retiring to go to college). I have a problem too.

"I have to take a pill every day for the rest of my life and have to get checked for cancer every 6 months. I had a throat operation in Feb. of 1970.

"Would you please write or call me and let me know.

"Thank You"

Valinda then signed her name, gave her address, zip code and phone number.

Two letters were sent to the Burgess residence.

One was from Jack Dunn 3d, Oriole vice president, to Valinda thanking her for her "application" and her interest in the ball club, but turning her down. The other was from Jerold C. Hoffberger, chairman of the Oriole board, also expressing thanks for interest in the Orioles. Sent to Mr. and Mrs. Burgess, the letter added that Mr. Hoffberger had nothing to do with hiring bat boys.

Mrs. Burgees then wrote to *The Sun*. She said:

"I thought maybe you would like to read and publish my daughter's letter. I think it is cute. She is interested in having fun and participating. It is a shame how fast our children are growing up and what is happening in the schools today. Thank you.

"P.S. We just received a very nice letter from the Orioles stating because a bat boy has to spend a great deal of time in the dressing rooms, it cannot be a girl."

—*The Sun*, Baltimore

EXERCISES

Write a feature story for each of the following sets of facts. Use the supplied material only as a basis. *For this exercise,* you may also supplement the material as you see fit, putting in names and additional facts where you think that they will make a better story. (You would never put such imaginary additions into a real-life feature story.)

1. Two nine-year-old boys have been apprehended by the police in the act of taking a dip in the basin of the large fountain outside the public library. The date is August 10th, the temperature is 91, and the city pavements are sizzling.

2. Write the color story for the Harvard-Yale game. The date is November 19th, the weather is clear and cold, the game is being played in the Yale Bowl, and all tickets were sold two weeks ago.

3. An internal failure in the computer system of a local college has created an astonishingly large number of serious errors over the past week. Many students have been given incorrect grades for courses just completed; tuition bills sent to parents have been both too low and too high; and in several instances, nonprofessional employees (janitors, truck drivers, and the like) have been overpaid. In writing this story, consider any legal implications.

4. A wealthy man has made a 30-year hobby of collecting "firsts" in mechanical devices (the first power mower made by a famous company, the first vacuum cleaner made by another famous company, and the like). Visit his museum, located in a specially constructed building on his country estate, and write the story.

5. A patent has just been issued to a local inventor for an electrically operated

apparatus for reading in bed. The apparatus holds the book at any angle and turns the pages. It is controlled by a series of buttons on a small board at the reader's fingertips.

6. Write a feature article containing advice to a future teacher, doctor, lawyer, or other professional person, basing your remarks on your "years of experience."

7. You are present when a man blind from birth has the bandages removed from his eyes after a successful operation to give him sight. Write the story. Remember, not too "gushy."

8. Visit the dog pound and write a story. The dogs have looked at you imploringly, there has been no end of noise there, and you have seen many, many kinds of dogs.

9. It is Easter Sunday morning on New York's Fifth Avenue. The crowds are returning from the churches, and the Easter parade is at its height. The weather is perfect for the occasion.

10. Write a story about a hermit who has lived in an old shack five miles from your home town for the last 48 years. Known as the "Old Man of the Mountain," he used to come to town only once a year to buy provisions. He was found dead this morning, January 10th, by a police officer who broke down the door when a neighbor reported seeing no trace of life about the house for the last two weeks.

11. You have been assigned to write a feature story on a 14-year-old girl who—according to her parents and many others—can predict the future through an ability to see "visions." Visit the home, interview friends and acquaintances, and then write the story.

12. A very poor laborer, father of seven children, living in the slum section of town, decided to patch the wall in the dining room of the home that he has finally managed to buy. In chipping off the cracked plaster, he came upon a strange opening in the wall. Investigating, he found a small metal box containing $22,000 in old bills and coins. The former owner threatens to sue, but the laborer claims all the money.

13. Write a color story for Christmas, which is just five days away. Visit the toy departments, travel down the main streets, get reactions of merchants concerning purchase of gifts, and any other details you think should be in a story of this kind.

14. A local produce merchant who has just been defeated for his party's nomination for mayor for the fifth successive time announces that he is going to try for the nomination for governor at the next convention. He says that he "might as well lose for big stakes as for little ones." He espouses the payment of pensions for all people over 50 years of age, basing the amount to be received on the amount of "good" the applicant has done. He measures "good" by attendance at church, ability to stay out of prison, and number and quality of character references which an applicant can obtain. Points are to be given for each phase of an applicant's record, and the judging is to be done by an impartial board.

15. Visit the home of a local business man who has 12 children. There is no problem of support because the father has a good income. Write an interesting story on the family at dinner, on the purchase of food, and on all the interesting aspects of their life together.

16. An eccentric spinster, very wealthy, plans to launch a nationwide campaign to restore the bustle to feminine attire. At present she is having literature printed on the subject, and next she plans an attempt to enlist the aid of movie actresses and other prominent people. She plans a speaking tour for herself.

17. An actress now 65 years old—on the stage since she was 12—gives the feature writer an interview. She advises girls and boys to know what career they want and to strive for that career, come what may. She believes that "there is always room for a good one, no matter how crowded the occupation may be." She believes the home and the church are the foundation of society and advises everyone to develop more respect for each.

18. A local insurance broker has heard that his brother who, he believed, was killed in action in the last war is a patient in a veterans' hospital on the Pacific Coast. He checks the report and finds it true. The brother, who has lost both legs and part of an arm, has chosen to allow the news of his supposed death to stand because he doesn't "want to be a burden to anyone." Write the story as if you are with the insurance broker from the time he comes face to face with his brother.

19. This is September 5 and the first day of school. Try to avoid the stereotyped feature story on this subject.

20. Worshipers at the local Baptist Church are in a constant state of unrest during the services because two small blacksnakes are at large in the church. They escaped from the pocket of a 15-year-old boy six weeks ago during a service, and all attempts to capture them have failed. They were last seen a week ago as they disappeared into two of the numerous holes between the floor and the wall, after scaring the women in the church. They have at times appeared during services, at strange places, and under strange conditions.

FOR FURTHER READING

Benét, Stephen Vincent, *Stephen Vincent Benét on Writing*. Brattleboro, Vt.: S. Greene Press, 1964.

Burack, Abraham S. *Writing and Selling Fillers and Short Humor*. Boston: The Writer, 1959.

Engle, Paul. *On Creative Writing*. New York: Dutton, 1964.

Gehman, Richard. *How to Write and Sell Magazine Articles*. New York: Harper, 1959.

Hogrefe, Pearl. *The Process of Creative Writing.* Harper, 1963.

Weeks, Edward. *Breaking Into Print.* Boston: The Writer, 1962.

Weisbrod, Marvin, ed. *A Treasury of Tips for Writers.* Cincinnati: Writer's Digest, 1965.

Williamson, Daniel R. *Feature Writing for Newspapers.* New York: Hastings House, Publishers, 1975.

★ **6** ★   The Photographer
                Photographer Specialties
              Pictures in the Newspaper
                Operation
              Qualities of Effective
                Photographs
              Picture Improvement
              Some Representative Pictures
              Sources of Pictures

Pictures in Newspapers

With the great advances in photography, photographic reproduction, and printing of the last quarter of our century, a trend has arisen that is variously termed "visual journalism," "pictorial journalism," and "photojournalism." Stated in its simplest terms, this trend emphasizes pictures as a means of relating news and other stories. The trend is now so strong that many editors and publishers foresee pictures as half the content of the newspaper of the future. Other media executives regard this estimate as conservative. In any case, pictures are carrying a large and important portion of the newspaper's message in the 1970s.

THE PHOTOGRAPHER

Until well into the 1920s, the photographer in most instances was merely the man who "took pictures" for the paper. He went out on routine assignments with his cumbersome old-style equipment and made shots that followed standard patterns. In the newspaper office itself, he seldom commanded any great respect. He was merely a person who performed something of a mechanical service.

With the improvements in photography from the 1920s onward, however, the role of the photographer changed accordingly. Today the press photographer is essential. He is a reporter as well as a skilled technician, a fact gatherer, an interpreter, and an artist. As an artist he must bring to his work imagination, sensitivity, and a concept of the esthetically appealing picture. Although he shoots most pictures on orders from his desk, he still makes the on-the-scene decisions that determine the quality of the shot.

To appreciate the work of top-flight press photographers, a trip to one of their exhibitions is all that is necessary. These exhibitions are usually staged annually by press photographers' associations across the nation, with awards for excellence in the various fields (sports, action, straight news, or other). In these exhibitions, the photos are not merely pictures of persons, events, and actions; they are pictures which reveal the esthetic nature of the person who made them.

Most authoritative figures in newspaper photography sum up in a single sentence this basic attribute of the top-notch photographer: he must have a *feeling for pictures*. By this statement, they mean that intuitively the photographer must know and recognize the scenes that provide good pictures. Life to the photographer must be one long series of picture possibilities. Every scene, every event, every action must be thought of in the light of the potential picture it presents. The child toddling after his mother, the corner lounger idly blowing smoke skyward, the crowd boarding the train or bus—these and every other scene must be viewed in terms of picture possibilities. In each instance, the photographer must think of how to capture the pictorial aspects that best interpret the essence of the scene.

A second quality the successful photographer must have is the *technical ability* to handle his camera and perform the other skills incumbent upon him. Although the amateur photographer may assume that acquiring this ability is a simple matter, it is not so. Schools of journalism give detailed courses in the intricacies of photography because the mechanics of lighting, shutter speed, developing, printing, and general handling of the camera require detailed study—despite the fact that recent developments in camera technology are making the handling of most cameras a more automatic process.

A third quality needed by the photographer is the *ability to handle people*. Like the pencil-and-paper reporter, the photographer deals with persons of all sorts and conditions, but his difficulties may be greater because of the power and the finality of the camera. While an interviewee can talk with the reporter and hence often guide into print only the facts he wants in print, he has no similar control over the camera. The camera may catch him from an unfavorable angle or at a "bad" time. Yet he cannot know until he sees the actual newspaper picture. For this reason, many persons otherwise disposed to be cooperative do not want to be photographed.

Generally speaking, persons to be photographed fall into three groups: those who are willing to co-operate, those who are unwilling to co-operate, and those who are unable to co-operate.

The group *willing to co-operate* can be illustrated by three common types: the obscure individual elated at the prospect of seeing his picture in the paper—as, for instance, the bus-line employee who found the abandoned baby; the celebrity who needs constant public exposure—as, for instance, the entertainer desiring a plug for his new act; and the person to whom any publicity is a godsend—as, for instance, the lawyer-turned-politician who is seeking a seat in Congress.

The group *unwilling to co-operate* can be illustrated by the bank robber arrested at the scene of the crime, the shy housewife at the supermarket who is asked to register surprise as she looks at the price of vegetables, and the person who has been spattered by mud from a downtown building project.

The group *unable to co-operate* can be illustrated by the participant in the midst of a post-game brawl, the bull fighter making his final thrust, and the parachutist making a landing.

Obviously, the photographer has no problem with the group that is willing to co-operate and the group that is unable to co-operate. It is the second group that demands his attention. Sometimes he can coax; sometimes he can flatter; sometimes he can cajole the subject into being photographed by explaining the importance of the picture. An example is the woman recently victimized by the door-to-door swindler. Convincing this subject that she will be saving many others, the photographer may get her co-operation.

Sometimes, however, the photographer has no chance to reason—for example, in the courtroom. Probably more so than in any other place, photographers have long had to battle with courtroom officials for the rights they claim. Photographers contend that, as working journalists, they have a right to photograph news; judges answer that photographers disrupt judicial proceedings. Photographers counter that they will use candid cameras and eliminate any disrupting influence (case, flashbulbs, etc.); judges retort that the very presence of the photographer is disrupting.

This controversy is part of the free-press-vs.-fair-trial issue that attracted great national attention in the 1960s and still remains thorny. In the 1970s, photographers seem to be winning. Editorial writers have backed them effectively, and they themselves have used their power. A recent example is that of a judge who attacked a photographer for making a shot of him as he left his chambers. After the judge had barred the photographer from his courtroom the photographer waited outside the judge's chambers until he left for lunch. Then, probably to needle the judge, the photographer made his shot, and the judge attacked. As the judge lunged and flailed, a second photographer then caught his honor in a most embarrassing series of pictures that was transmitted via the wire services all over the country. Because the sequence was widely used, judges everywhere were reminded to respect photographers.

Television cameramen have not been accorded even the limited privileges allowed newspaper photographers because judges have ruled, with considerable substance, that television equipment can overwhelm the witness on the stand. TV camera crews, however, are usually granted the right to operate immediately outside the courtroom itself.

A fourth quality the photographer must have is *originality*—a quality that is becoming increasingly important because readers are making, more and more, high demands of newspaper photography. These demands grow from familiarity with popular magazines, brochures, and other publications that show top-grade action shots, portrait work, landscapes, and similar pictures—all characterized, among other things, by originality of approach. Hence readers look for the same quality photography in newspapers.

Because he demands originality, the reader feels an antipathy to the once standard posed photograph. He recognizes as false the canned action shots of the athlete catching a ball while looking into the camera, of the public official supposedly greeting the celebrity, or of the group of children beating the summer heat by eating ice cream cones in unison.

Originality, however, has also become more important because of the demands of modern journalism. As newspapers rely more and more on pictures, they need more creativity in their photography. Stiff, artificial posing looks dull or worse in full pages of pictures. Originality has been further encouraged by the growing use of by-lines for photographers.

But originality is not a matter of mere arty novelty. It involves also originality of journalistic idea and outlook, even in routine stories. The story situation and the cut lines contribute to the originality when the printed picture greets the reader. The examples on the next three pages show originality.

In *Seeing triplicate,* the frankly posed picture is given interest by the camera angle, with two of the three little girls looking up toward the lens. The cut line begins with a slightly off-beat catch phrase and continues with a few lines of pertinent and interesting detail. In *Cyclists pedal . . . ,* the composition of the picture and the unusual subject need little assistance from the cut line, but ''the most expensive bike path in the world'' effectively emphasizes the originality of the photographer's observation. The picture of the fishermen on the railroad trestle evokes, as do its cut lines, some thoughts about railroads as a basis for presenting a feature-story situation. Such use of a railroad trestle is a perceptive allusion to the economic situation of the railroads.

A fifth quality which the photographer must have is a *knowledge of libel.* He must have this knowledge, as any reporter must, in order to protect his newspaper. Libel, as previously shown, is defamation by visible communication—that is to say, by words, pictures, or any other means of visual communication. The newspaper, therefore, must be at least as careful of its pictures as it is of its words.

Indeed, there may be greater risk of libel through the use of pictures. In the instance of the printed word, the ability to prove the statement true is usually sufficient legal grounds to exonerate the newspaper. But a picture can be true yet still be libelous. For example, an accidental or trick shot that makes a man look like a horse is both true and potentially libelous (in one famous instance, a horse had turned his head so sharply that a man standing alongside appeared to have the horse's body).

To demonstrate better the nature of libel in photography, a discussion of some actual cases can be helpful.

Seeing triplicate

—Staff photo by Don Goodaker

Happy birthday girls at Lincoln School today were Lisa Fay, Linda Kay and Lillie May, the triplet daughters of Mr. and Mrs. Paul Willis of 603 W. Illinois. The girls are each in a different first grade, but got together for a playground party.

—*The Evansville* (Ind.) *Press*

A businessman in Idaho sued a newspaper whose photographer had taken a surreptitious picture of him through his kitchen window. The suit was settled out of court, probably because the newspaper held little hope of winning its case. A year later, a gangster's lawyer in New York, facing sentence for a criminal act, was photographed surreptitiously from a neighboring fire escape as he prepared breakfast in the apartment of a woman friend where he had spent the night. In the first instance there were sufficient grounds for a libel suit; in the second there were no grounds because a convicted criminal can scarcely be libeled by such circumstances. (Whether the lessee of the apartment would have a cause of action is not covered by this discussion.)

A prominent society woman on the West Coast was photographed on a mid-city street as she recovered from a sneeze. Because of the peculiarity of her facial expression and the presence of a tap room in the background, the picture suggested that she was inebriated. The victim was satisfied by a printed apology. A year later, a shapely movie actress was the "victim" of a trick photograph which made her appear elephantine from a rear view. She, of course, had co-operated with the photographer, who had told her his purpose. If she were to sue for libel, she would have no grounds because of her willingness to co-operate.

A picture editor refused to run a shot of a 14-year-old boy mischievously drawing a

Cyclists pedal south along most expensive bike path in world.
—*Daily News,* New York. Photo by Jim Garrett.

(The picture and underline above are part of a pictorial essay about New York's West Side Highway, now closed to automobile traffic because of deterioration and collapses in the structure. All attempts to restore the highway to a usable condition have become tangled in a web of litigation, financing, and pressure groups.)

If railroads are having trouble attracting passengers, railroad tracks are doing right well attracting sitters, as this Monona Causeway trestle scene testifies. The site is a perennial favorite of fishermen.—(Staff photo by Dave Sandell).
—*The Capital Times*, Madison, Wis.

handkerchief from the hip pocket of a middle-aged man intently watching a parade. He felt that the picture was potentially libelous because it could clearly be interpreted as a boy in the act of stealing. Two months later, the same editor ran a two-column cut of a known pickpocket as he moved suspiciously in a circus crowd. The shot had been taken seconds before a policeman, recognizing the pickpocket, had moved in for the arrest.

The usual procedure for the photographer is to shoot the picture and decide afterwards whether it is libelous—if no law is violated in the actual taking. All pictures, of course, must be examined carefully for potential libel because many shots not suspected of being libelous prove so when they emerge from the darkroom. Also important is the fact that the responsibility for running pictures is seldom the photographer's; it is usually the picture editor's or some other superior's.

In addition to the qualities already cited, the photographer must have the *general ability* needed to be a capable journalist. He must be as much able to work under the same difficult conditions as any good reporter, with the same degree of success. He must understand the function of the entire newspaper in order that he may understand his part. He must be able to sense the presence of scoops, to display ingenuity in working under varied circumstances, and to be a good working newspaperman in every other respect. His role can be summarized by stating that the qualities of the good reporter are the qualities of the good photographer.

Photographer Specialties

Photographers, like other journalists, have specialties. They specialize in straight news, sports, entertainment, women's page, and every other major source of news. Any decision concerning specializing is usually made by the photographer on the basis of his abilities and his interests.

One photographer, for example, may like to concentrate on the dramatic aspects of news and feature stories. Therefore, he is the one to assign the shot of the painters atop the high bridge, the fire in the tenement district, the riot on the waterfront, the athletic contest. Another may be more interested in politics, labor relations, feature-story personalities, and specialized studies (traffic conditions, shoppers' habits, historical sites, or the like), and therefore may want to specialize in these subjects. In all instances, the photographer needs more than a passing interest to do good work. He must be so interested that he builds up a detailed background of knowledge. A photographer with little interest in politics, for instance, can scarcely know the shots to make at the political convention; nor is the photographer with little interest in baseball likely to know the moments of most import to sports readers.

The need for specialties has affected the work of women photographers. Few men are sufficiently interested in society, fashions, women personalities, and similar subjects to do satisfactory work in these fields. Hence these assignments more often go to women photographers; indeed, a male photographer may need a woman reporter on the assignment with him to suggest shots and write the cut lines. Yet women photographers are not by any means limited to these specialties.

PICTURES IN THE NEWSPAPER OPERATION

The gathering and processing of photographs, like the gathering and processing of reading matter, varies from newspaper to newspaper. On the very small paper, the reporter is frequently also a photographer; in fact, this skill may be a qualification for the job. On the larger paper, the photographer is more likely to be a specialist in pictorial journalism. On a very large paper, the work of the photographic department comes under the jurisdiction of the picture editor, who may have one or more assistants. This editor works co-operatively with the other editors and makes his assignments accordingly.

The picture editor, however, does more than make assignments to photographers, for he has many more demanding duties. His greatest function is to provide the newspaper with the quality of picture that will please readers and hence increase circulation; he is, therefore, primarily a judge of photography. He tells his photographers what he wants in specific instances and he passes judgment on their pictures. If, for example, he is sending a photographer out on a parade assignment, he may tell him to emphasize "stuff for mothers and kids." Thus, the photographer is expected to shoot pictures with this thought in mind. Shots of officials discussing parade routes are to be bypassed while shots of animals, fancy dress, and comics are to be emphasized. The photographer's prints become, of course, a display from which the picture editor, often in conjunction with other editors, makes the choices. In some instances, the picture editor also writes captions and cut lines; in other instances, these lines are the province of the department concerned (news, sports, or other).

The picture editor often attends top editorial conferences if the visual appeal of the newspaper is recognized as important. In these conferences, he functions as an adviser to the top editors (he may be one of them) and executives who must strive constantly to discern reader interests. The significance which journalists attach to pictures is strengthened by recent studies which, although in conflict on some points, agree that more readers look at pictures than at any other single feature.

The photography department, moreover, requires administration—staffing, hiring and firing, budgeting, oversight of supplies and equipment, general direction, control of priorities. In a big department these duties can consume much time and attention; hence they may have to be shared between the photo editor and an administrative assistant.

The Functions of Photographs

Few newspaper readers give extended thought to the reasons for the pictures they peruse. They accept the pictures for information, pleasure or general satisfaction of curiosity, often concluding their reading with the thought that "The pictures today are pretty good," or "not so good," or some other evaluation. They realize vaguely that the pictures add interest and life to the paper, but they do not pursue the thought. Actually, there are five basic reasons for the inclusion of pictures.

The most important function of photographs is *to communicate news*. Indeed, they are often the most important means of news communication in the entire paper. They can show graphically, thoroughly, and frequently with an amazing degree of insight a particular moment in the news. The shot of the Secretary of State, caught as he fields an especially delicate question, reveals the moment as columns of words cannot. The beauty, the grace, and the speed of the high hurdler in action are shown better than the best of sports writers can describe them. The tense faces of the relatives of the trapped miners as they watch the rescue elevator come to the surface are made vivid in a manner that lies beyond anything mere prose can accomplish.

The quality photograph does not tell the reader about a given scene; it does not show it to him; it *brings* it to him. Modern photography, with its ability to reveal minute detail, is often superior to actually seeing the incident. How many persons, for example, have the vision, from any vantage point, to see the aspects revealed by most photographs? The old statement, "A picture is worth a thousand words," is understatement.

A second function of the photograph is *to generate interest*. The shot of the baseball player sliding in just ahead of the tag, the picture of the foreign statesman in native garb, the photograph of the sleek racing sloop under way, and the many other cuts in a single issue of the newspaper create an interest that could not exist otherwise. More persons look at the pictures than at any other single detail of the paper, as scientific studies have often revealed and as newspapermen have long known. They have watched innumerable readers in waiting rooms, coffee shops, airports, railroad trains, hotel lobbies, living rooms, and commuting buses as they open their papers. The eye may be temporarily attracted to a banner line or a startling headline, but inevitably it fastens on the pictures. In fact, many readers go through the paper examining the pictures before anything else. Placing photographs on inside pages, especially pages containing many small advertisements, is done for good purpose—photographs are eye stoppers. The reader notices them and pauses before turning the page.

A third function of the photograph is *to give another dimension* to a newsworthy figure. The person about whom one reads raises the question, "What does he look like?" The central figure in a crime, the principals in the court battle, and every other major news personality—all are photographed to satisfy this question. In those instances where the personality cannot be photographed (courtrooms, closed door sessions, etc.), an artist frequently makes a pencil sketch. The reader's desire to know the face of the personality met in the newspaper also accounts for the use of cuts, usually half-column, of columnists and others who write on a day-to-day basis. The reader, newspapers know, is attracted by the picture of the person whom he reads just as he is attracted by the picture of the radio announcer whom he may hear day after day.

A fourth function of photographs is that of using a portrait *to make a brief but important announcement*. If, for example, a company has promoted its sales manager to vice-president, the newspaper can scarcely make a big story of this single fact. In such instances, however, a portrait becomes an excellent resource for making the announcement. The newspaper simply runs a one-column cut with two or three underlines. Newspapers like portraits in such instances for use on their business page. The business page, as can readily be imagined, is often a difficult one for which to find pictures.

A fifth function of the photograph is immediately understandable; it is *to make the page attractive*. Effective photography can dress up a page, create a note of genuine attractiveness, and give a quality of readability not possible otherwise. To appreciate this fact, only a simple exercise is necessary: Find, if you can, a newspaper without a single cut on page 1 and compare it with another newspaper's page 1 having an attractive pictorial layout. The comparison will leave nothing to be said; the difference in beauty and over-all appeal will be self-evident.

QUALITIES OF EFFECTIVE PHOTOGRAPHS

The central question in any consideration of photography is, "What makes a newspaper picture good?" Because photography is a creative experience, no set of rules, no list of qualities, no criteria can be established to answer this question unequivocally. The best anyone can do is to suggest those attributes that characterize the genuinely effective photograph. Meanwhile, this same person must remember that these attributes represent little more than a basis for discussion of photography.

Above all else, every picture must have *a reason for its existence*. It should raise no doubt in the reader's mind as to why it is there; it should be something that he would miss if it were not there. That readers don't give extended thought to the reasons for pictures is true. Nevertheless, a reader must not be driven to suspect that a picture has been carelessly selected merely to fill a space or decorate a page; and if any such suspicion is warranted, the reader will feel it.

Another essential of a good picture is technically termed *composition*, the arrangement of detail. If, for example, a photographer is shooting a picture of a group of four businessmen conferring, he should think first of arrangement. The men should be placed in natural positions, not in stilted poses that create an impression of artificiality. Next, the photographer must make certain that every detail contributes toward the central meaning of the picture—four businessmen discussing a problem. Any detail that detracts from this thought must be avoided. A coat rack behind the table, for instance, should be removed if it creates a disturbing effect. A sheaf of papers lying idly upon the end of the table should be centralized to create a note of immediacy of use. If a window in the background reveals distracting detail, the curtain should be drawn and the table should be moved away. Every detail must say together, "Four businessmen are discussing a problem." This basic idea of stressing the central idea is frequently termed "emphasis."

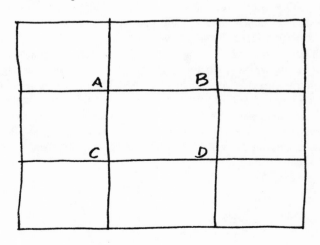

There are many ways to gain emphasis, but fundamentally it is attained by placement of figures and use of tone or color contrasts. The pattern most often employed to gain effective placement is termed "thirds." The area to be covered by the picture is divided vertically and horizontally into thirds. The photographer then locates the object to be emphasized near one of the four intersections of the lines as shown by the letters A, B, C, and D in the diagram.[1] In this manner, the eye of the reader is kept on the object and hence on the picture. Whenever the reader's eye "runs out of the picture," the picture has poor composition.

The proper use of tone and color contrasts can be appreciated by a simple translation of experiences outside photography. A tasteful housewife would scarcely have all-red decorations and all-red furniture in a room. She would strive rather for the color combinations that accentuate attractively. This same principle holds for photography. A white backdrop gives little contrast for a man in a light-colored suit; a granite wall creates insufficient contrast for a gray dog. Therefore, the photographer needs a more effective contrast for these and similar pictures.

In thinking of composition, the photographer must also think of another, closely connected attribute of the effective photograph—*clarity of detail*. This phrase means, essentially, that the photographer has caught the pertinent details so clearly that the reader can identify everything without strain.

Clarity of detail presents special difficulty in scenes where interest centers on small objects like pieces of jewelry. The retiring employee receiving a gold pin, for instance, should not be shown holding the pin because its size and color preclude any chance to exhibit it clearly. Instead, the shot should show someone placing the pin in the employee's lapel or some other movement related to the presentation. Also, the photographer should try to avoid pictures that show secondary figures in side face or part face. The group scene, for example, which shows tops of heads cut off the people in the second row is amateur rather than professional work. Any discerning reader can appreciate the difference between top-quality and second-quality work by comparing the pictures in leading newspapers with those in publications where photographers lack either experience or basic abilities—or both.

When the photographer thinks of clarity of detail, he inevitably comes upon another attribute of the effective photograph, the attribute of *accuracy*.

The day of artificial or stilted posing, staging a scene, or outright "faking" of pictures has disappeared with leading newspapers. Every good picture must possess the unmistakable ring of truth. It must appear as a shot taken without forewarning—a shot caught by the photographer at just the right moment—or a shot that developed naturally from the circumstances of the moment.

Accuracy is most often difficult to obtain in those instances where posing

[1] The pattern of thirds can be very helpful with a wide picture. If the picture is tall (as can be visualized by turning the diagram sideways), the principle must be used cautiously. An outdoor shot, if tall, may leave too much sky when composed according to the thirds pattern.

"run-of-the-mill" citizens becomes a necessity. For example, an obscure married couple has just won $5,000 in a contest, and the paper wants a three-column cut of the couple registering their joy. Unless the couple has histrionic ability—and such is rarely the case—the photographer can spend hours without getting a good shot. Consequently, photographers go out on such assignments wishing it were their day off.

A final statement to be made about the effective picture is broad but important: an effective picture *must attract and hold the reader*. It must possess a magnetic quality that draws and keeps the reader's attention.

Although the qualities that make a picture lure and hold the reader can never be explained finally, some studies have established seven basic attributes: (1) feature-story appeal, (2) familiar persons, (3) familiar sights, (4) information, (5) events witnessed, (6) interest in the activity, and (7) attractive photography.

Feature-story appeal is the fundamental quality in any shot out of the ordinary. For example, a reader coming upon a three-column cut of a child holding a large snake will certainly pause. Similarly, the reader will be caught by the picture of the woman standing beside a five-foot-high cake or the picture of the zebra standing in front of the gasoline-station pump. The appeal in each instance is simply that of the feature story portrayed pictorially.

Achieving feature-story appeal in photographs that accompany straight news stories is a demanding challenge for the photographer; yet this appeal is strongly needed. But it should be found, not forced. Straining to create it can make the subject ridiculous. The governor of an eastern state, for example, was badly embarrassed recently by a shot that showed him visiting a flooded area. There, under a photographer's prodding, he allowed himself to be carried on the back of a policeman at the scene. The picture proved to be politically damaging because the governor was wearing boots while the policeman wore only standard shoes; and the policeman's bulk made the governor look like a small boy in trouble rather than a major public figure coping with an emergency.

Pictures of *familiar persons* attract a reader because, as he scans the paper in his normal reading, he reacts to shots of people whom he can recognize. When he sees a familiar face, he asks "What's he doing now?" This is the response both to persons the reader knows through direct association and to important figures in public life. Readers pause when they see the picture of a friend or an associate, and they generally pause when they see the familiar face of the President of the United States. In each instance, the reader wants to know the individual's significance in the news of the moment.

The appeal of the picture of the *familiar sight* is much the same as that of the familiar person. Wanting to know why this sight is in the news, the reader looks at the picture and reads the lines to learn that the Empire State Building is being cleaned, that the snow is being shoveled away from the steps of the city hall, or that the biggest hotel in town has been sold to an out-of-state corporation.

Editors rely routinely on this kind of picture to show the Christmas shopping crowd in the downtown area, the cindering of the city's streets after the snowstorm, and the great exodus of cars for the seashore at the height of the heat wave.

The power of the newspaper picture which disseminates *information* can be experienced by leafing through any daily newspaper. Every day, the paper gives the reader one or more pictures whose primary appeal lies in the information they present. These pictures show the new-model automobiles, the coming fashions in clothes, the champion golfer demonstrating the proper way to putt, and numerous subjects of a similar type. These photos not only draw the reader; they make him study the picture intensively and read and reread the cut lines.

The attraction of the picture of the *event which the reader has witnessed* can be demonstrated by a simple experiment: think of any big athletic contest, any large fire, or any other major event which you have witnessed. Now simply think of the first picture you look for as you peruse your newspaper that evening or the next morning.

The fact that readers will examine pictures which treat *activities in which they have an interest* is almost self-evident. This interest impels the nurse to pause over pictures of hospitals, the teacher to examine pictures of schools and their activities, the construction worker to scan pictures of building operations, and the winter sports enthusiast to look at pictures of skiing contests. In each instance, the reader examines the picture because of his direct interest in the activity. This condition, incidentally, has an interesting sidelight—the reader often examines the picture as an exercise in professional competence. He looks at the picture critically, evaluating its strengths and its weaknesses.

The role of *attractive photography* in making a reader stop to examine a picture is an easy matter to understand. Even though a given reader may have little knowledge of the qualities of the effective photograph, nonetheless he knows when a picture pleases him. Usually a picture pleases him when it is well done; that is to say, when it has the attributes already discussed. One of the best means, therefore, of attracting and holding readers is to present pictures which mechanically and esthetically meet the highest standards.

Testimony to the importance of attractive photography for many newspaper readers exists in the great number of people who cut photographs from the paper to save or paste in scrap books. Especially appealing, it seems, are shots of bridges, ships, and planes caught against a backdrop of sunset or other unusual light—as well as pictures of small children in unusual circumstances and animals of almost any kind.

PICTURE IMPROVEMENT

The preceding discussion of effective photography treats the qualities which the photographer and the picture editor respect as they work with pictures. These qualities are, in essence, ideals which serve as guidelines.

The photographer, however, can seldom have an ideal situation. As was mentioned earlier, he may have to shoot a picture fast, with little or no chance to prepare (a famous person appears unexpectedly at the entrance to the White House); or he may face poor physical conditions (the prisoner slouches sullenly in the police car, partly concealed by the window post); or he may have no control over distracting detail in the background (the gravedigger stands in clear view behind the family at the burial). Therefore, someone in the picture department applies improvement techniques to the negative or the picture.

The three procedures commonly used are (1) cropping, (2) retouching, and (3) airbrushing.

Cropping means cutting off parts of the picture to restrict the physical detail. Quite often, for instance, the center of interest is crowded off to the side of the negative; or extraneous details lessen the total impact. To alleviate this situation, the art man (or woman) acts accordingly.

The result of cropping is illustrated by two pairs of pictures, each made from the same negative. Note how the center of interest asserts itself in the cropped versions (pages 120–1, 122–3).

The complete shot of the cat that has taken over the dog's house has definite feature story appeal. However, as it stands, it has too much wasted space. The large area in the foreground tends to detract from the central meaning of the picture—the cat contentedly looking out the door while the dog sits dispossessed in the background. Moreover, the wasted area tends to obscure the dog whose color makes seeing him difficult under any circumstances. Now examine the same shot cropped. Note how the whole meaning becomes more dominant, especially now that the dog comes more readily into view.

Retouching means changing a picture to accentuate detail or to cover up distracting items. It may be as simple as a pen stroke to strengthen the outline of an important picture element, or a bit of paint to cover a blemish in the print or negative. The retoucher uses any tool he needs—pen, artist's brush, knife, scraper, or airbrush.

The airbrush is a device like an atomizer that sprays an opacity (basically an ink) to obliterate, soften, or color an object in the background. The retoucher sprays the opacity on the negative or on the print.

Compare the two pictures of a lighted window, both made from the same negative: one has been cropped and retouched; the other is the unaltered original.

The intent of this shot is to reveal a window for the reader. However, the total impact is lessened somewhat by the light casement at upper left, the large amount of unnecessary dark space, and several small white spots.

The picture has therefore been cropped to accentuate the window and re-touched to black out the small amount of white casement that remained in the picture after cropping. The retoucher has also eliminated white spots that appeared in the original.

SOME REPRESENTATIVE PICTURES

The pictures distributed through this chapter, as well as all the others appearing in this book, should be studied and analyzed as examples of the shots that newspapers run daily. Like newspaper pictures everywhere, they represent, in essence, the paper's attempts to meet its readers' expectation for pictures. These shots should also be studied as photographic achievements. They should be seen as each photographer's effort to meet the challenge of obtaining an interesting, informative picture.

This picture draws much of its appeal from the unstaged and unposed effect it achieves despite the microphones—the event was in fact a press conference. A reader could easily believe that it was taken entirely without the subjects' knowledge. Furthermore, the photographer shot his picture from an angle that reveals much pertinent detail in the faces of the three men.

—AP Wirephoto as used by the *Los Angeles Times*

This shot has the necessary detail to support the accompanying news story. The ore truck and the loading hopper make the center of interest; the scarred slope in the foreground and the step-cut terraces behind them convey the irony of a nickel-ore open-pit strip mine being operated in New Caledonia, a French Pacific island.　　—AP Wirephoto as used in the *Atlanta Constitution*

The photographer here has achieved an appealing atmosphere and a pleasing informality. Note how he has had the subject hold the beer can with the label partially concealed so that the picture does not look like an advertisement. Technically, this picture is quite good, although some picture editors might frown on the background detail as distracting.

—AP Wirephoto as used in the *Chicago Daily News*

This picture is a remarkable study in action. It has caught impressively the strain, the effort, and the pervading drama of the finish of a horse race. It also presents a scene which, in itself, is likely to attract interest—even though one may know very little about horse racing. In short, the shot has real esthetic appeal.

—AP Wirephoto

Most picture editors would agree with the photographer's centering interest on the front door as the most humanly interesting detail in this picture. In the mood of this shot, the empty sky at upper right is not waste space.

This photo has excellent optical quality but no better than marginal value for any newspaper because its message is ineffectual. It shows only the backs of the students in cap and gown, while presenting the stage and speaker in a vague and distant background. If the photographer's purpose is to show a rear view of the commencement exercises, or an abstract composition of mortar boards, the photo is acceptable. Otherwise it should be rejected.

126

The above shot of student graduates receiving Marine Corps commissions would probably be rejected by most picture editors because its message is clearly limited. Only two faces are recognizable—that of the awarding officer and that of the student in the foreground. Meanwhile, the furniture covers an inexcusably large space; and the angle from which the shot was made adds little special meaning.

The appeal of this picture arises from the pleasant atmosphere of the whole scene and the angle from which the photographer worked. Newspapers often use this type of picture for adding charm and relaxation to inside pages. Also important, the picture is technically quite good—except for the possible objection that the grass area is a trifle light.

SOURCES OF PICTURES

In addition to the photographs taken by their own staff photographers, newspapers obtain pictures from four other sources. They are picture agencies, publicity agencies, commercial photographers, and amateur photographers.

After staff photographers, agencies provide the greatest number of pictures used by newspapers. The two prominent agencies in the United States are Associated Press and United Press International. They supply newspapers with most of their pictures of persons and events outside the paper's home area. Within a few minutes after these agencies get a picture into their Washington or San Francisco offices, the shot is sent by wire throughout the nation. Because of their specialization, the agencies generally do excellent work and their contributions in photographic research have helped considerably in the advancement of the entire field of photography.

The pictures from commercial photographers are limited almost entirely to portrait work. Many persons who rise in the world of business, industry, education, and similar fields have studio portraits made for distribution upon request. The portraits are generally glossies, so that the paper can have no objection to using them. These persons have the pictures made for the obvious reason that they are thus assured of a pleasing result. Commercial photographers sometimes also provide pictures for groups desiring publicity. Small businesses and charitable institutions, for example, often call in commercial photographers to supply pictures to accompany publicity releases. In days gone by, commercial photographers frequently requested or demanded a credit line, but this practice has tapered off in recent years.

Public-relations agencies and public-relations departments send pictures routinely with most stories, especially those of a brief nature (promotion of officials or the like), because they know the value of a picture in the newspaper. These photographs are generally of top quality to increase their chance of being used by the paper. The larger agencies employ their own photographers, most of whom are very capable. The photographs are always accompanied by cut lines so that they are ready for immediate use.

Advertising agencies, like public-relations agencies, supply top-quality work. The advertising agencies supply pictures for advertisements and also photographs to be used as regular newspaper material. Advertising agencies often operate public-relations services also. Newspapers in large cities, for example, obtain some of their best pictures of the city's major-league baseball team, without cost, from the advertising agency that has the club as one of its accounts.

Free-lance photographers and agencies provide newspapers with material in those instances where the paper cannot get the shot itself. Free-lance photographers are often highly skilled craftsmen who can earn more by working for themselves or an agency than they can as newspapermen. Free-lance photographers are generally successful because they can reach difficult-to-meet persons, because they can unearth good feature story material, or because of the unusual quality of their work.

Amateur photographers are persons who generally take pictures for sheer pleasure but are more than merely desirous of selling their material. Amateur photographers are most often successful when they get a shot otherwise unobtainable. Among the most common pictures sold by amateur photographers each year are shots of accidents at the time of occurrence or immediately thereafter; interesting feature-story material; pictures taken in places inaccessible to photographers (secret conferences, courtrooms, or the like).

In addition to these sources, newspapers get photographs from many miscellaneous sources. Among the most common are families and friends of newsworthy figures, libraries and other repositories of pictures, and files of historical and similar societies.

EXERCISES

1. Select from the Sunday edition of any large newspaper the ten best pictures. What are the reasons for your choices?
2. How would you pose a baseball player and his family of eight children for the picture to accompany a feature story?
3. Examine several issues of a profusely illustrated newspaper for pictures that are potentially libelous.
4. What characterizes the pictures of your favorite newspaper?
5. Write an account of the difference between the pictures used in any two sharply contrasting newspapers.
6. What newspaper shot seen during the last year is most likely to remain in your memory? Why?
7. Find five instances of poor newspaper photography, stating the reasons for your judgment.
8. In what ways do the pictures in the Sunday-supplement magazine differ from those of the news section in a newspaper of your choice?
9. Find three instances of pictures in "poor taste" in newspapers. State their faults.
10. Find five instances of originality in composition. State the elements of originality.

FOR FURTHER READING

Burnell, Walter. *The New Photography.* South Brunswick, N.J.: A. S. Barnes Co., 1968.

Eisenstaedt, Alfred. *The Eyes of Alfred Eisenstaedt.* New York: Viking Press, 1969.

Faber, John. *Great Moments in News Photography.* New York: Nelson, 1960. Unusual news pictures with commentary.

Feininger, Andreas. *Total Picture Control.* New York: Crown, 1961.

Knopf, Aaron A. *Secrets of Taking Good Pictures.* Garden City, N.Y.: Hanover House, 1958.

Logan, Richard H., Ill. *Elements of Photoreporting.* New York: Hastings House, Publishers (Amphoto), 1973.

Loosley, A. E. *The Business of Photojournalism.* New York: Hastings House, Publishers (Amphoto-Focal), 1970.

Magmer, James. *Photograph Plus Printed Word.* Birmingham, Mich.: Midwest Publications Co., 1969.

Miller, Thomas H., and Wyatt Brummit. *This Is Photography, Its Means and Ends.* New York: Garden City Books, 1963.

Schuneman, R. Smith, ed. *Photographic Communication: Principles, Problems, and Challenges of Photojournalism.* New York: Hastings House, Publishers, Inc., 1972.

Spencer, Otha C. *Journalistic Photography.* Wolfe City, Texas: Henington Publishing Co., 1966.

Time-Life Books editors. *Great Photographers.* New York: Time-Life Books, 1971.

Rothstein, Arthur. *Photojournalism,* Revised Edition. Garden City, N.Y.: Amphoto, 1973.

★ **7** ★

Printing the Modern Newspaper
Photocomposition
The Copy Editor
    Functions of the Copy Editor
The Copy Editor
    Handles the Story
        The Copy Editor's Symbols
        A Story that Has Cleared the
            Copy Desk
Headlines
    The Functions of Headlines
    Writing Headlines
    Exceptional Headlines
    The Headline Counting
        Process
    Kinds of Headlines
    A Headline Style Sheet
Other Work of the Copy Desk
    Editing Wire Copy
Type
    Identifying Type
    Type in Newspaper Design

Newspaper Copy Editing

PRINTING THE MODERN NEWSPAPER

To comprehend the whole function of editing copy, some understanding of the printing of the modern newspaper is necessary.

Until the 1950s, almost every newspaper in the United States was printed by *letterpress*. This method, in broad terms, is the process of placing metal type and cuts in a form and then printing the page either directly from the type or from a cylindrical plate that has been cast, via the stereotype process, from the form. Most of the type for the form is set by machines; the remaining small portion is set by hand. This is a sophisticated application of the principle used in rubber-stamping. It is called letterpress even though the printed page may be filled with pictures rather than letters.

With the 1950s, another method of printing became popular—*offset* or *photo offset*. Here, instead of assembling metal type in a form, the reading matter and pictures are arranged in a layout that is then photographed. Eventually the photo image is fixed on a thin aluminum sheet called a plate, chemically treated so that the image will hold ink while the spaces between elements of the image will not. This plate is mounted on a cylinder in the press. Then, when it is inked, it transfers the ink image to a rubber blanket from which it is in turn *offset* onto the paper—in effect blotted off the blanket. This offset method is used in about a third of the newspapers in the United States.

The two processes impose different requirements for the preparation of copy, and both copy editors and writers can better cooperate with typesetters or other compositors when they know something about the two methods.

PHOTOCOMPOSITION

However, anyone studying copy editing procedures on newspapers should also know of another important development occurring today in the printing of the newspaper: it is the use of the CRT (cathode ray tube) and OCR (optical character recognition) processes.

Described broadly, the CRT process operates in the following manner. The reporter sits before a typewriter-like keyboard and types his story. But the story, instead of appearing on a paper in a typewriter carriage, flashes on a television screen above the keyboard. Thus the reporter follows what he is writing by checking the screen. If he needs to alter his material, he can delete, change, or add by using the proper devices on the keyboard. When his story is complete, he signals the editor who presses the necessary buttons to have the story appear on his (the editor's) screen.

The editor then makes changes and edits by operating his keyboard. When satisfied with the story, he flashes it to the copy editor who gives it the final editing. When the copy editor is finished, he turns the story over to the OCR process.

The OCR process is basically a system whereby beams of light scan printed material, "recognize" the letters in each word, and react by punching holes accordingly in a tape. This tape is then placed in a linotype machine or other print-forming apparatus (cold typesetting machine) where it prints the material. This method of preparing the tape is generally termed "photocomposition" for the obvious reason that it employs light.

The great advantages of the CRT and OCR processes are speed, efficiency, and cost. Every stage, from writing to printing, is faster than the orthodox procedure of typing a story on paper, editing by hand, and setting by linotype or other manually operated machine. Furthermore, the new apparatus is practically free of mechanical error—as well as being considerably less expensive than the older system.

What is the present status of CRT and OCR? The American Newspaper Publishers Research Institute estimated at the close of 1975 that about one-third of all newspapers were using the new process in some form; that is, they were using computers or other units of the system to prepare material for printing.

The institute also states that while the growth since 1968 in the use of CRT and OCR has been great, its continued growth will depend upon the financial ability of newspapers to replace the old system with the new. Naturally, as the old equipment wears out, it will be replaced by the new, but few newspapers are financially able to make the complete change overnight.

THE COPY EDITOR

The copy editor has one of the most important functions in the newspaper office: he is responsible for the final checking and editing of copy before it goes into type. He must pass judgment on the accuracy of the facts, the quality of the writing, and the tone of the story. And he must be able to make whatever changes will produce sound, informative, well-executed writing.

In days past, the copy editor sat elbow to elbow with his fellow copy editors around the edge of the big circular desk that graced every large newsroom. Here he worked under the head copy editor whose place at the desk was a section or slot cut inward to enable him to address or throw a story to any editor around the rim. Because of the physical character of the desk, the copy editors were termed "rim men" and the head copy editor, the "slot man." These terms have remained, even though most copy desks are now U-shaped arrangements of desks and tables. Furthermore, these terms are presently somewhat inexact because, more and more, women are also copy editors.

The key words in the copy editor's job description are *responsibility, proficiency,* and *speed.*

Responsibility is essential because the copy editor plays a key role in determining how the writer's story will appear in print. Proficiency is important because copy editing demands a rare combination of specialized abilities. And speed is necessary because the copy editor must frequently work at a dizzying pace to meet deadlines and to stay abreast of a pile of copy that seems to increase faster than it can be handled.

The size of the newspaper determines the number of copy editors and the distribution of specific copy-editing duties. A few copy editors can often handle all the copy for a small daily paper. One alone may do the whole job, even as a part-time activity, for a small weekly. The work load of a large city daily may require each department to have its own copy desk and staff.

As the copy editor takes his place at the copy desk, he becomes part of the team presided over by the director or head copy editor, the slot man, who assigns the stories to be read, keeps a record of their status, and acts as general supervisor of the entire desk.

To be a copy editor, one must be quick, intelligent, well-informed, resourceful, and confident. But above all, he must be a good newspaperman in every sense of the word. He must know the ins and outs of the world of journalism, and he must be thoroughly familiar with every department of the newspaper. In most cases, therefore, the copy editor is a former reporter or rewrite man advanced to this important position.

Because the copy editor is the link between the editorial department and the composing room, he must be especially aware of the problems of both. To

Copy Editors at Work: The Cleveland *Plain Dealer*.

the editorial department, he is responsible for checking and editing the story. To the composing room, he is responsible for making the copy and the wishes of the editorial department clear. To the slot man, he is responsible for the duties discussed in this chapter.

Functions of the Copy Editor

Although the copy editor's work covers a wide range, his responsibilities fall within seven areas. The duties of the copy editor are:

To Make the Story Readable. Where the reporter has written a phrase that is involved or ambiguous, the copy editor must recast it, for journalistic writing must be clear and forceful on the first reading. For example, if the reporter has written, "The witness would not admit he would not identify the suspect because he feared his friends would hurt him," the copy editor must recast it to some such form as, "The witness refused to admit that he would not identify the suspect for fear of reprisals."

The copy editor must beware of vocabulary that may stump the reader. Words like "refraction" and "tort" may be clear to many readers, but in the interest of readability for most newspaper readers, the copy editor needs to find more familiar synonymn.

Making the story readable is difficult because, while newspaper readers represent a wide range of intellectual backgrounds, the story must be intelligible to all without offending any. The laborer will cast the paper aside if it baffles him; the college professor will look for a more mature paper if this one insults his intelligence. To the copy editor, therefore, falls the difficult task of attempting to please readers from all intellectual levels.

To Keep the Story Brief. Since most newspapers rarely have enough space for all the material on hand, the copy editor must make certain that everything is stated as briefly as possible. He may infuriate the reporter, who feels that his art is being weakened, but nonetheless, he must attain brevity.

Obtaining brevity involves two considerations—words and facts. To achieve brevity in words, the copy editor strives to make every sentence as concise as possible. To achieve brevity in facts, he tries to eliminate any data not essential to an understanding of the basic story.

Frequently, there are even occasions when a story already cleared by the copy desk must be re-edited. Here is a typical instance: the paper is "tight"— that is, the reading-matter space is nearly filled—when an important story not anticipated is phoned in by a reporter covering a district. Immediately the make-up editor and the editor confer. They decide to make the new story a column in length, and they instruct the copy desk to cut certain stories already written. The copy editors handling these stories are told to "trim" them or "boil them down"—eliminate facts in order of least importance until the story has been reduced to the desired length.

To Guard against Libel. The copy editor must delete or recast any statement that smacks of libel.

Libel laws and their interpretations vary from state to state.[1] Furthermore, not only errors of facts but even the language of a story can create problems of libel. Hence the copy editor often meets serious difficulty as he examines stories for potentially libelous material.

In watching for libel, the copy editor should remember that his basic guideline is defamation. Where he finds words, for instance, like "liar," "drunk," "cheat," "fake," and "fly-by-night," he must move warily because they are clearly defamatory.

Meanwhile, he has a more subtle but equally dangerous problem with phraseology that is sometimes defamatory and sometimes not. To illustrate: the statement that a local business man is a "card sharp" exudes libel; the same remark made of a professional gambler presents no problem. The reference to a prominent civic leader "smelling of alcohol" is definitely hazardous; the same allusion to a bartender at work is harmless. Calling a football coach "crafty" in his game strategy is a compliment; using the term in describing him as a neighbor or businessman invites a libel suit.

Because the only consistently successful defense against the libel suit is to prove the statement true, mass-media editors often approach potentially libelous material with the question, "If we are sued, can we prove the statement true?" This question, gives another important guideline to the copy editor.

However, when thinking of libel suits, these same editors are usually aware of a very important fact: the significance of libel to the media extends beyond the possibility of financial loss. Any medium sued for libel may lose prestige with the public—even though the medium wins the suit—because

---

[1] See other discussions of libel in Chapters 2 and 6.

much of the public tends to sympathize with a plaintiff. Many also reason that he would never have sued unless he was in the right.

A final thought concerning libel: such prefatory statements as "police say," "it is rumored," and "neighbors declare" have failed, on numerous occasions, to protect the newspaper in the libel suit. The court's reasoning has been that such phrases can be offered as shields for practically any type of defamatory approach.

To Check the Accuracy of Facts. Because the reporter sometimes makes mistakes in facts, the copy editor must be prepared to make corrections. To aid this process, copy editors are frequently given specialties, or kinds of stories on which they are well-informed. One copy editor, for instance, is the specialist in local politics, and all stories in that field are read by him. He usually knows every major political figure, so that if the reporter states that John J. Kelly is political leader in the 27th precinct, whereas it is really the 37th, the copy editor can make the correction. Another copy editor may be the specialist in local crime; he is expected to know the correct spellings and middle initials of most of the police officials and the records, the aliases, and many colorful details of major criminal figures. With this knowledge, he acts as a check on the reporter.

If anyone thinks that small mistakes are inconsequential, he should sit at the telephone of the city room after an error has appeared in print. There he will be amazed at the number of calls protesting small errors—as well as the heat or resentment with which they are registered.

To Make Stories Conform to the Style of the Newspaper. Each newspaper office develops policies regarding use of questionable words, punctuation, spelling, and capitalization. These are usually assembled into a stylebook.[2] Newspaper stylebooks differ according to the publishers' policies, local feeling, and sometimes irrational preferences, but there are good reasons for most of their rules.

The policy covering questionable words governs vocabulary such as *hustler, pimp, gay, floozie,* as well as terms commonly regarded as vulgarities, profanity, and indecencies. Also important to note: as was stated earlier, newspapers often permit certain questionable words in important direct quotations but nowhere else. During the recent past, for instance, many ordinarily conservative papers carried these quotes: Former President Harry S. Truman was recorded as having said that General Douglas MacArthur's difficulties arose from "ass kissers" who would not criticize him; the minority leader of the Senate, Hugh Scott, was quoted as saying that he would "be Goddamned" if he would be a "patsy" in defending former President Nixon in the Watergate scandal; a well-known former priest, Philip Berrigan, was quoted as stating that a specific government program was "bullshit."

The punctuation policies govern the use of the comma, the dash, paragraph indentation, precedes on stories, and any other detail or rule concerning special punctuation marks such as stars, asterisks, or arrows.

---

[2] See Appendix I for a stylebook.

The spelling policy pertains to such words as *thru, nite, boro, catalog, theatre, and catsup.*

The capitalization policy governs all instances where the use of a capital is optional.

To Keep a High Tone to the Stories. The copy editor must always be on the alert for facts that either cheapen the paper or do not contribute to an already established policy of dignity and restraint. Where he is in doubt about killing such a fact, he should consult the slot man. Such facts usually make their appearance in stories about women entertainers, homosexuals, defendants in criminal courts, and in any similar kind of story wherein many readers are likely to appreciate humor or ridicule.

Dubious tone is also likely to result from any tendency to pun on names or to make subtle humorous references based on well-known statements, popular song titles, and other kinds of familiar material.

To Write Headlines. Because of its complexity, this phase of the copy editor's work is discussed at length later in this chapter.

THE COPY EDITOR HANDLES THE STORY

All stories coming to the copy desk are handed first to the slot man, who notes on his schedule the slug, the time of arrival, and the name of the copy editor to whom the story will be assigned. This schedule will also eventually bear the kind of head and the time that the story cleared the desk. After making his initial record, the slot man hands the story to the copy editor to carry out the functions already described.

As he engages in the actual editing process, the copy editor follows the procedure now to be discussed.

The Copy Editor's Symbols

On the succeeding pages are shown the symbols used by copy editors throughout the country, followed by an example of a story that has "cleared" the desk. This story illustrates the use of symbols for the corrections made by the copy editor. Both the story and the list of symbols should be studied thoroughly.[3]

These symbols are a specific professional language—the language employed by the copy editor to give instructions for preparing material for print. This language must be mastered. The best way to learn it is to seek a reason for the form of the symbol. The symbol for transposing words, for example, is

---

[3] The symbols and procedures presented here are standard in the traditional newspaper office and probably will remain so during a good portion of any journalist's career that begins in the 1970s or 1980s. New methods in typesetting and printing are, however, generating new methods of copy editing; people who enter the profession during the development period will have to learn to deal with the new methods from experience, not textbooks.

clearly logical, as are the symbols for moving type. However, when symbols lack a logical basis, like those denoting the end of the story, the learner should strive for some association by which to remember the symbols. Finally, one needs to learn all symbols for every situation, not only those he plans to use. The three symbols for the end of the story, for instance, must be known because all three are employed widely.

The student should also learn to make symbols with the standard pencil used in copy editing. This pencil, appropriately termed a "copy pencil," has a soft lead in order that it may be used easily on standard copy paper. Any harder lead makes too light a mark and often tears the paper used in most newspaper offices. Ink is not used in copyreading because of the difficulty in erasing and because it has a tendency to run on copy paper.

The copy editor's symbols are explained in the following section by first listing each symbol and identifying its function. Then the symbols are used in editing a typical story. The lines in the story have been numbered for easy reference to the list of explanations after the story itself. Obviously the lines would not be numbered in regular newspaper copy.

COPY EDITOR'S SYMBOLS

Symbol	Meaning	Example
⌐ ⌐ ⊬	Start new paragraph	It was then that the man It was then that the man It was then that the man
≡	Make capital letter	Said mr. Smith in answer
∕	Make lower case	Said mr. Smith in answer
⌢	Insert comma	In answer to the Question In answer to the Question
ﾞ ﾞ	Insert quotation marks	across the dull hot desert across the dull hot desert Come, he said loudly

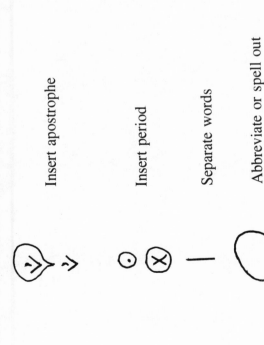

Insert apostrophe

Johns book was lying there

Johns book was lying there

Insert period

That was all he said ⊙

That was all he said Ⓧ

Separate words

He came quickly into the room.

Abbreviate or spell out

Fifth avenue

The prof turned and left.

Write out or use Arabic number

The ③ judges leaned forward

Conner ran twenty-two yards

Indent right; indent left

News Stuns Congress

Symbol	Meaning	Example

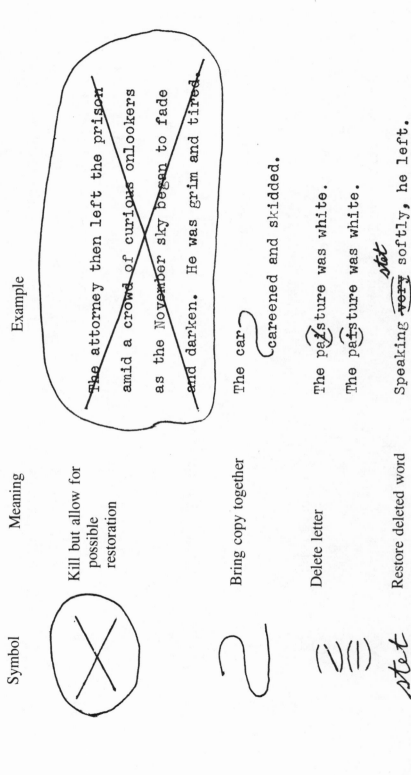

Symbol: ⊗ (circle with X)
Meaning: Kill but allow for possible restoration
Example:

The attorney then left the prison amid a crowd of curious onlookers as the November sky began to fade and darken. He was grim and tired.

Symbol: ⌒ (bring together)
Meaning: Bring copy together
Example: The car careened and skidded.

Symbol: (\/)(\|)
Meaning: Delete letter
Example: The pasture was white. The pasture was white.

Symbol: *stet*
Meaning: Restore deleted word
Example: Speaking ~~very~~ softly, he left. Speaking ~~very~~ softly, he left.

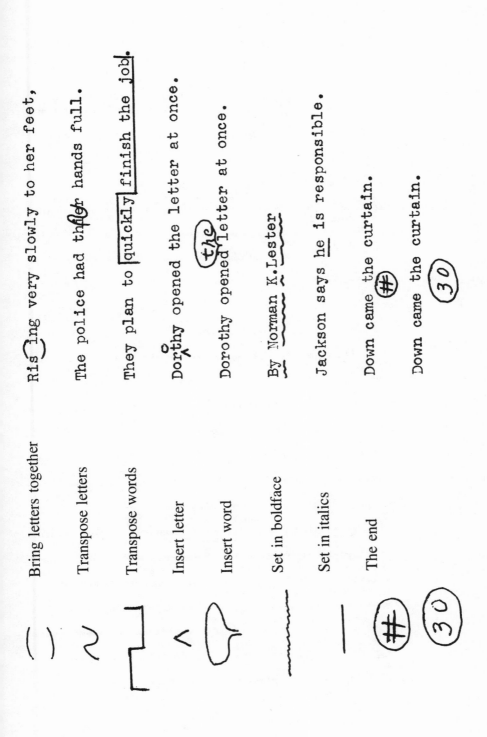

Mark	Meaning	Example
( )	Bring letters together	Ris‿ing very slowly to her feet,
~	Transpose letters	The police had theⁱr hands full.
⌐_	Transpose words	They plan to │quickly│finish the job.
∧	Insert letter	Dor∧thy opened the letter at once.
⋁	Insert word	Dorothy opened ∧letter at once. (the)
﹏	Set in boldface	By Norman K.Lester
─	Set in italics	Jackson says he is responsible.
#	The end	Down came the curtain. #
30	The end	Down came the curtain. 30

Singer — Jones   # 4

1   Facing a battery of news cameras and a mass of
2   cheering people, [Miss] Alma T. Johnson, Montville's well known
3   lyric soprano, returned home in triumph today. The
4   attractive 18 year old brunette appeared at Municipal
5   hall to formally receive the $15,000 [prize] ~~check~~ for ~~winning~~
6   the recent ~~competition to select~~ [contest for] the best feminine voice
7   in the [Nation's] high schools ~~of the Nation~~. The money, according
8   to [Contest] ~~the~~ rules ~~of the contest~~, is to be used in furthering
9   the winner's musical education. Miss Johnson was ~~formally~~
10 presented to the audience by Mayor Richard L. Tompkins,
11 who paid glowing tribute to her ability.
12 Accompanying her were her mother, M rs. Mary
13 Johnson, and her sister, Mrs. Ronald H. Campbell, both
14 of whom were visibly affected by the honor ~~being accorded~~
15 to this famous member of the[ir] family. Miss Johnson's
16 father, Richard T. was confined to his home ~~with a severe~~
17 ~~case of~~ [by] arthritis. Mrs. Johnson reported that ~~that~~ "he
18 certainly wanted to be here with us."
19 Following the ~~introductory~~ speech ~~in which~~ [by] Mayor
20 Tompkins ~~stated the purpose of the gathering~~. Miss Hazel
21 H. Smithers, teacher at the local high school ~~here in~~
22 ~~Montville~~ told of her happiness concerning her former
23 pupil's success. Miss Smithers explained ~~to the audience~~
24 that the unusual quality of Miss Johnson's voice was
25 [always] apparent, ~~from her earliest years~~. Miss Smithers expressed

(more)

her ~~firm~~ belief that ~~international success is in~~ (world fame awaits)
~~store for~~ Miss Johnson.

[After Miss Smithers(') speech, May(no)r Tompkins introduced ~~Mr.~~ Howard L. Wiston, ~~representative~~ of the Sherrill Woodwork Company, sponsors of the contest, who explained briefly the method by which the s(l)election was made. The mayor then presented Miss John son, and while ~~the~~ flashbulbs exploded ~~from all angles~~, she trembling(ly) accepted the check. In an emotion filled voice she thanked(") all who have helped me.(") She modestly disclaimed credit ~~for her-~~ ~~self~~, saying that(') anybody could win when she has such fine, sincere friends.(") Although she was certain ~~that~~ she could not possibl(y) be in voice at such a time,(") Miss Johnson sang(") Thine is my Heart alone,(") from Samson and Delila(h), the composition ~~which~~ ~~brought her to the height of her career in~~ (sung in) winning at New York last week. Miss Johnson's audience ~~wildly~~ screamed for more, but her new teacher, Guido del Ponci, of the Metropolitan Ope ra Co., ~~would not allow~~ (intervened) ~~her to sing~~. He explained to reporters that great harm might be done under the circumstances.

[She has already declined numerous offers to make personal appearances.

Miss Johnson was attired in a blue taffeta gown with a low neckline and full skirt. She wore silver slippers, and in her hair she wore a large diamond bracelet.

Top Line   Slug, writer's name, head number
 1. Paragraph, separate words
 2. Insert word, insert apostrophe
 5. Capitalize, transpose words, delete, insert word
 6. Delete, insert words
 7. Insert word, bring together, insert period, delete
 8. Insert word, delete
 9. Insert apostrophe, delete
10. Insert comma
12. Paragraph, bring together
14. Delete letter, delete words
15. Transpose
16. Insert comma, transpose letters
17. Deletions, insert word
19. Paragraph, restore deletion, insert word, deletion
20. Insert comma, delete words
21. Make spelling correction, insert comma, delete words
22. Delete
23. Delete
25. Insert word, insert period, delete words
Bottom Line   "more" indicates story does not end here.
Top Line   Page number, slug, writer's name
26. Delete words, add words
27. Delete words
28. Paragraph, insert, delete
29. Delete
32. Transpose
33. Bring together, delete
34. Delete, add word
35. Insert quote marks
36. Insert marks, insert comma, delete
37. Delete
38. Insert quotes
39. Delete, insert quotes, correct spelling
40. Insert quotes
41. Capitalize, insert quotes
42. Insert words, delete
43. Delete
45. Bring together, add word, delete
46. Delete
48. Kill
51. Paragraph
Bottom Line   "—30—" indicates end of story.

HEADLINES

One of the copy editor's most enjoyable tasks is writing headlines. This work is creative: it gives an opportunity to express one's personality. With every headline he attempts, however, the copy editor faces the challenges discussed in this section.

The term "headline" (or "head") means the words over the story. The layman, on hearing of headlines, has a tendency to think only of the large lines that cross the entire page. These lines are correctly termed "streamers," "banners," or "banner lines."

Most newspapers identify their heads by giving them numbers; #1 may be the largest, #2 the next size smaller, and so on. Some newspapers identify their heads as "A flares," "B flares," and so on. As the copy editor sends the head copy to the typesetters, therefore, he places in an upper corner the letter or number code that specifies the kind of head and other pertinent information (size of type, family of type, heaviness, caps or caps-and-lower case letters, or the like). If the head is not one of the standard coded kinds, he writes the information in longhand along side the head copy; none of these decisions is left to the compositor. These expressions are explained in the section on type at the end of this chapter.

Whatever the system, the newspaper usually has specimens of all its heads assembled into book form, often printed and bound as part of the stylebook for the copy editors' reference. These specimens are called the "schedule," "headline schedule," or "hed sked." If none is supplied, the copy editor should paste one up for his own use. An example of a hed sked appears later in this chapter.

The Functions of Headlines

A headline has four important functions.

To Summarize the Story for the Reader. Because most newspaper readers have only a fraction of the time they would need to read every item, they naturally want to read the stories that interest them most. Thus, the headline serves the reader by summarizing the story (unless it is written to startle, amuse, or otherwise attract the reader; this kind of headline is discussed later in this chapter). If the headline catches the reader's attention, he begins to read the story; if not, he usually turns his attention to another headline.

To Show the Importance of the Story. As the editor decides upon the size of the headline to be given a particular story, he places a relative importance on the story. Stories with large headlines are expected to be read thoroughly, whereas stories with smaller heads may never be noticed. Generally speaking, the larger the head, the more important the story—or, at least, the more desirous the editor is of having the reader peruse it.

To Attract the Reader. The headline serves to attract the reader to the printed page. Many newspapers are sold because a passerby has been attracted by a headline, or because a bus rider has seen a headline over a fellow passenger's shoulder. And many stories have been read because of an attractively written headline. This is especially true of the feature story, where the head is often humorous, questioning, or astonishing. In the straight news story, however, the writer of the head tries to generate interest in a more conventional manner.

To Give an Attractive Appearance to the Newspaper. Physically attractive headlines, well written, give beauty to the newspaper by presenting a pleasant relief to a field of gray. They serve to break the monotony of looking at column after column of type. In fact, this quality of attractiveness is highly important in causing a newspaper to adopt certain kinds of headline type. It also causes newspapers to use a variety of headlines (full line, stepped line, and other arrangements) on a given page and to employ two or more families of type throughout their pages.

Writing Headlines

Aside from mastering the mechanics of writing headlines, the copy editor must develop the *art* of writing headlines. He must acquire those esthetic qualities necessary to recognize and to write a good headline. Like all arts, headline writing cannot be reduced to a formula, but there are some basic abilities upon which any success in this field is built. A discussion of these follows.

Command of Synonyms. A basic requirement for writing headlines is a command of synonyms, especially short ones for long words. Since many newspapers frown on abbreviations in heads, short synonyms are especially important when a headline demands that a long name or term must appear. (For instance; a one-column headline where the name "Richardson" must appear leaves very little room for any other word on the same line.) Some standard synonyms, many of which are overused, follow:

rob for steal; *quiz* for question; *grill* for question continually; *hit, rap,* or *flay* for criticize unfavorably; *ire* for anger; *vie* for compete; *go* for contest; *rip* for denounce; *flee* for abscond; *laud* for praise; *wed* for marry; *raze* for demolish; *scan* for examine closely; *probe* for investigation; *top* for defeat.

Sometimes there are synonyms for names, as, for instance, appellations given the many athletic teams throughout the country: *Wolverines* for University of Michigan; *Gophers* for Minnesota; *Rams* for Fordham; *Phillies* for the Philadelphia National League baseball team; *Cubs* for the Chicago team in the same league.

Occasionally, the synonym of a city or a state is invaluable in writing a headline, as, for instance, *Twin Cities* for Minneapolis and St. Paul; *Hub* for Boston; *Bay State* for Massachusetts; *capital* for Washington, D.C.

Although abbreviations frequently are prohibited, those that are immediately clear to the reader are often permitted, especially where they replace a title too long to be practical. Examples: *ACLU, IRS, DAR, WCTU, GOP, YMCA, USSR.*

Then, too, many newspapers circulate chiefly among readers who know certain abbreviations immediately. In these cases, journalists use these abbreviations. Examples: *PIAA* (Pennsylvania Inter-Scholastic Athletic Association); *AAU* (American Athletic Union); *PSFS* Building (Philadelphia Saving Fund Society); *NYU* (New York University); *UCLA* (University of California, Los Angeles); *NEA* (National Education Association); *AAUP* (American Association of University Professors).

Command of Vocabulary. The writer of the headline should have a vocabulary that is extensive and attractive. He must know and be able to use words that create interest, that arouse curiosity, that have a picture-making quality about them, and that can summarize concisely.

Imagery plays a part in this quality, and so we find many of the following personifications in headlines. In fact, we find them in too many newspapers, thus wearing them thin from overuse. Examples: *Adonis* for well-built man; *Venus* for beautiful girl; *Man Friday* for faithful servant; *Bluebeard* for wife murderer; *Nero* for one who wastes time in the face of important work; *Alexander* for one who is seeking another field to conquer; *Don Juan* for faithless lover; *Romeo* for ardent lover; *Man in the Street* for every citizen; *Izaak Walton* for ardent fisherman; *GI* for soldier or other serviceman. All these are bromides, the bad writing already discussed in Chapter 3 as the foremost "dictional don't."

An important fact to remember, however, is that there can be no rule of thumb for choosing or finding the right word. The copy editor can only rely on an extensive vocabulary and a carefully developed sense of taste to guide him to the most effective terminology for the particular situation. "Bard" for "poet" may be just right in one instance but hopelessly out of place in another. "Head guy" for "President" would be all right where the effect is meant to be humorous, but it definitely would be out of place in a straight news story. "Yes man" would be permissible in a derisive statement but it could hardly be condoned in any other instance.

Ability to Summarize. The copy editor must have, in addition to the qualities mentioned, the ability to write a headline that summarizes the story. In the case of the news story, the headline is essentially a brief version of the lead. It contains or implies the "w's" and the "h" discussed in Chapter 3. In the case of the feature story, however, the headline may depart from this pattern in order to arouse curiosity, to be humorous, or to do whatever will lure the reader into the story. Consequently, the feature story head does not always summarize.

Although this ability to summarize may appear easy to acquire, it really comes only with long experience.

Ability to Make Headlines Readable. What one of us has not had the experience of reading a headline two or three times before understanding it? Or worse still, of having to read the story in order to understand the headline? Note, for illustrative purposes, the head below; then try to obtain its meaning before reading the two paragraphs beneath the head. (This head and story, incidentally, appeared in a well-regarded neighborhood newspaper.)

Move to lower Serra, Mission speed limits

A campaign to lower the speed limit along Mission St. and Junipero Serra Blvd. is seeking support at City Hall, but the prospects are uncertain.

The Mission Merchants Association and the Project Area Committee, citizens' arm of the Redevelopment Agency, want the limit reduced from 35 to 25 miles per hour for safety reasons and "because it would give the people more chance to see what services are available in these areas."

—*The Record*, Daly City, Calif.

The readable headline must be intelligible. The preceding example lacks this quality. To make sure the head is intelligible, the copy editor needs to ask himself, always: Does this head make sense on a first reading?

The readable headline should also present a satisfying structure. As to appearance, this means that it should look attractive and uncrowded. As to wording, it should make sense, line by line; that is, each line should constitute some kind of logical unit of thought. This logical unit—word or phrase—loses some of its logic if it is split over two lines. Study these examples of good headlines:

Wilson Factory   **Eased Tax Rate**
Changes Policy   **Goes in Effect**
Under New Owner   **With New Year**

Would these headlines be as satisfying or intelligible if they broke in a different way?

Wilson Factory Changes
Policy Under New Owner

Eased Tax Rate Goes in
Effect With New Year

The need for making the headline readable has helped wash out an old-time taboo against *is, are, were,* and *was.* These are now used freely when they help clarity (or fill up the letter count for a line), but they are also freely omitted when not needed. Copy editors obey their own newspapers' standards in matters like these. Consider some examples:

U. S. Skiers Are Among Favorites For World Jumping Crown Today

Coach Hopeful of Placing Three in First Seven at Lake Placid—Swedes, Finns Also Threats to Norse Supremacy

—New York Times

Storm Survivors' Plight In Pakistan Is Grave

—St. Paul (Minn.) *Pioneer Press*

CITY AIRPORTS ARE CLOSED BY FOG BLANKET

—Chicago Tribune

Shooting Death Is Investigated

—Times Picayune, New Orleans

Exceptional Headlines

Though headline-writing rules and standards are important and hence must be mastered, they are often bypassed when there is good reason. Departures from established patterns can sometimes achieve unusual effects, create interest, or make the headline more effective.

Jeffrey Spins
Web Around
Spelling Bee

The writer of this head aims at humor, punning on the fact that a bee was won by a contestant successfully spelling *cocoon* (*The Sunday News*, New York)

It's Enough to Drive
Sober Men to Drink

This humorous headline applies to a story about continuous and unannounced changes in hours of operation for liquor stores throughout the state. (*Maine Sunday Telegram*, Portland)

Stand Up and Be Counted

A familiar statement headlines a story about the national census. Note that the head is cast in the imperative. (*Daily Times*, Woodbury, N.J.)

Bye-Bye Heat

A whimsical observation headlines a story on the passing of a heat wave. (*Herald Examiner*, Los Angeles)

Here's What Law Is
On Auto Inspections

The writer of the headline accepted the need for a direct statement in colloquial language. (*St. Louis Globe-Democrat*)

Can Mayor Of Gretna
Hold Hospital Job Too?

When a story treats a question, the question headline can often be quite effective. (*Tampa, Fla., Tribune*)

Dole: U.S. Will Be Proud
Of Experience in Indochina

Some journalists and readers regard the colon as excessively formal punctuation, but it takes less space than "says." (*Courier-Post*, Camden, N.J.)

Betty Loh Tih Dies;
Hong Kong Actress

The semicolon helps to identify the person named, much more neatly than "She Was a"; and it saves space. (*Kansas City Star*)

How Jordan Christopher
Became a Pigeon Kicker

This headline's strange message is likely to attract the reader. The story tells how an actor came to the leading role in the motion picture, "The Side-long Glances of a Pigeon Kicker." (*San Francisco*, Calif., *Chronicle*)

Shaw Trial
Judge Gets
Heave-Ho

"Gets Heave-Ho" has a tone different from "Is Removed"; it intimates indifference, low-tension disparagement, "good riddance." Supposedly the headline writer aimed for that impression. (*Miami*, Fla., *Herald*)

holy Toledo!
the mayor, yet

This head appeared over a story about the mayor of Toledo, Ohio, when he was fined for reckless driving and had his operator's license suspended. It had timely humor when the exclamation "Holy Toledo!" was in high vogue. It probably did draw readers to the story. Was it appropriate? (*Star-Bulletin & Advertiser*, Honolulu)

The Headline Counting Process

Nothing is so unyielding as type. A headline will either "go"—that is, fit—or it will not. Consequently, the copy editor may find his headline returned by the composing room with the explanation that it "won't go" or that it is "too tight." Even headlines already in type are sometimes discarded because the editor thinks that they look too crowded. The simplest way to know whether a headline will fit or not is to "count in" the letters.

Every kind of headline allows a definite number of units per line, depending on family of type, size of type, and letters involved. Generally speaking, the following facts may be taken as guides in counting the units in a head.

1. If the headline is in *solid caps*, that is, if it is set entirely in capital letters, then every letter is one unit except *M*, *W*, and *I*. The wide *M* and *W* are

each 1½ units, the narrow *l* is ½ unit. The comma, period, hyphen, colon, semicolon, and single quotation mark are each ½ unit; the space between words is ½ unit; the double quotation mark is 1 unit; the dash is 1½ units. Each Arabic numeral is 1 unit. A parenthesis is 1 unit.

LITTLE, REMIRO
FORD VICTORY

The upper of these two all-capital headlines fills 12½ units; the lower fills 11 units.

    2. If the headline is set in *caps and lowercase,* or *up-and-down,* then most of the lowercase letters are each 1 unit. But lowercase *m* and *w* are each 2 units, lowercase *i* and *l* each ½ unit. The comma, period, colon, semicolon, and single quotation mark are each ½ unit; the hyphen is 1 unit; the dash is 3 units. Capital *M* and *W* are each 3 units; capital *l* is 1 unit; all other capitals are each 2 units. Arabic numerals, double quotation marks, and parentheses are each 1½ units. The space between words should be counted as 1 unit, though it may be squeezed to ½ unit.

White House Date

This 1-column 1-line head fills 19½ units.

Atlantic Salmon's
Dramatic Return

In this 2-column 2-line head the first line has 18 units and the second line has 17½.

What
Minority
Women Want

The lines in this 3-line head make 6, 9, and 15 units.

The headline counting process is only approximate, for copyreaders can't split hairs about exact letter width. They come to know that *b, d, p, q, n, u, h,* and *g* are noticeably wider than *c, f, r, s,* and *t;* but counting all such letters as 1 unit each usually evens out. In some novelty typefaces, the letters differ from the usual unit widths.

Kinds of Headlines

A newspaper achieves individuality and attractiveness—two essential qualities—by adopting its own standard method of writing and printing headlines. Complete familiarity with these practices in the particular newspaper is naturally a must for the copy editor.

The most common headlines are presented below.

The Full-Line Head. The basic idea of this head is to make every line full without giving it a crowded appearance.

Plane Crash
Killing Four
Of 23 Aboard
To Be Probed

—The Evening Journal, Wilmington, Del.

The Stepped or Drop Line. The reason for the name of this line is apparent at first glance. This, incidentally, is one of the most popular of headlines.

RAIL WALKOUT
SPREADING TO
OTHER POINTS

—News-Times, Danbury, Conn.

The Inverted Pyramid. Once again, the name of the headline is apparent at first glance.

REDS SHOW NIXON
AS PURE VICTIM

—Springfield (Mass.) *Republican*

The Flush Left Head. This headline, which gives considerable freedom to the copyreader, begins every line at the immediate left, leaving the blank spaces to the right.

Grandparents,
Divorced 3 Years,
Remarried

—Seattle Daily Times

The Hanging Indent. This head is written with a full first line and shorter lines thereafter. The succeeding lines are indented.

Wind Howls
As Vikings
Top Packers

—The Miami (Fla.) *Herald*

The Axis Head. The axis head is so named because each line seems to be balanced on an axis; that is, each line is centered and the centers create an imaginary center line or axis. This kind of head is quite popular for columns and other standing feature material, but is also used frequently for straight news stories—as is the case in the illustration below.

6 Months

For Attack

On Cop

—San Francisco Chronicle

The Jump Head. The part of a story continued on another page is called the "jump" and naturally the head over the continued part is known as the "jump head." Since it is shorter, it strives to take the most important part of the original head. The student should note that some papers use as jump heads a line that more nearly resembles a slug.

SOLONS O.K.
WATER BILL

(Continued from Page 1)
—San Diego Union

Rose Robbery

—Indianapolis News

The Crossline or Keyline. This is simply a one-line head written straight across the column. It is most popular as a subhead or as a jump head.

Lilliputian Rooms

—Christian Science Monitor

The Overline. As the name implies, this line appears over the headline. Its function is to create interest and to add detail to the information given in the headline. Because the term "overline" is also frequently used to denote the lines over a picture, some newspapers label this line a "kicker," a "lead line," or other individualized term.

104-YARD RUNBACK

Alert Harvard Rolls
Over Cornell, 16-0

—The Washington Post

Banks. When a story is very long or very important, some newspapers still use the now rapidly fading practice of banks.

A bank is a unit of material written below the main head, enlarging upon

the details already given or supplying new ones. These banks are also referred
to by newspapermen as "decks." Below is the headline with banks:

SPEEDY REPAIRING
OF STREETS URGED

Epstein Tells Borough Heads
to Get the Jobs Done as
Quickly as Possible

WILEY DEMANDS ACTION

Tells City Hall Conference
He Is Blamed for Traffic
Delays Not of His Doing

—New York Times

Subheads. In long stories, the copy editor frequently is called upon to
divide the story into logical units by writing single lines or subheads that are inserted where they divide the story nicely for the reader. The type used in the
subhead is sometimes slightly larger than that of the story and usually is set in
boldface. Here are two subheads for the preceding story.

Borough Heads' Problem
Cavanagh and Gulick Attend

The Headline Copy

A headline with banks is illustrated as the copy editor would prepare it for
the typesetters (next page) along with the same headline as it appears in
type. The story was slugged "Parley." The copy has a circled note in the upper
right-hand corner to order an A head for the story slugged "Parley."

A Headline Style Sheet

As was said earlier, newspapers usually have a *head schedule* or *hed
sked*—a headline style sheet that shows the standard headline patterns used in
the paper. A part of the hed sked of the *St. Louis Post-Dispatch* is shown in an
illustration (p. 160); it presents two facing pages from the newspaper's stylebook.

Hed skeds are designed for the guidance of editors, make-up editors, copy

West Asks Soviet
To Geneva Parley
Of Big 4 On July 18

(Parley A)

U. S., Britain, France Send
Notes Proposing Conference
of Heads of Government

Preliminary Talks Set L

3 Powers' Foreign Ministers
Meet in New York June 16-17
to Prepare for Session

WEST ASKS SOVIET TO GENEVA PARLEY OF BIG 4 ON JULY 18

U. S., Britain, France Send Notes Proposing Conference of Heads of Government

PRELIMINARY TALKS SET

3 Powers' Foreign Ministers Meet in New York June 16-17 to Prepare for Session

—*New York Times*

editors, typesetters, and anyone else involved in the typographical aspects of the paper. They contain the technical language needed to understand and use type. For some explanations and discussion, see the section on Type at the end of this chapter.

OTHER WORK OF THE COPY DESK

Editing Wire Copy

One specialist on the copy desk of the large newspaper is the *telegraph* or *wire editor*. If the size of the paper warrants, he may have one or more assistants. The principal duty of the telegraph editor is to edit the wire stories that arrive via teletype from news services. Because some wire copy is in capital letters, this editor must distinguish between capital and lower case letters. By pre-arrangement with the composing room, all letters in wire copy are considered as being small unless marked with one of the standard symbols (≡ or Z) for caps.

The telegraph editor, naturally, must be completely familiar with the agreements between his newspaper and the wire services. Some stories may be edited, some may not. Others may be used only under certain conditions—as, for instance, a predated story or one with a "hold for release" order. The telegraph editor must be careful to respect the rules of the wire associations, or the service may be discontinued.

HEADLINE STYLE SHEET

4-Column 36-pt Century Bold Italic Caps (20)

REDS SAY U.S. BOMBING MUST BE HALTED WITHOUT PROMISE OF RECIPROCITY

WAR PAGE HEADLINES

1 col. 13.10 ems on 14.6 slug   4 cols. 57.4 ems on 58.9 slug
2 cols. 28.7 ems on 29.3 slug   5 cols. 72.7 ems on 73.6 slug
3 cols. 43.2 ems on 44.0 slug   6 cols. 86.4 ems on 88.3 slug

All headlines Nut & Thin Left

18-pt kickers with headlines up to 36-pt

24-pt kickers with 42-pt headlines or larger

Decks, when ordered, are 14-pt Bookman c&lc, about 20 units to 13.10 em col.

War Page and Sunday Editorial Title Page leads are set shoulder date, 10-point (8 to 10 lines of type) and the first few words of the first line light caps. A word or two of bold-faced caps begin paragraphs at intervals in the body of the story. Regular subheads are not used. When a two-column headline is used, the lead should be set 28.7 ems on a 29.3 slug.

2/3/30—2 Col. 3 lines (26)
30-pt Bodoni Bold

Horrors of Drug Abuse
And How New Chemical Age
Led to the More Frequent Use

1/36—1 Col. 3 lines (9)
36-pt Bodoni Bold

GOP Seeks
New Image
In Precinct

Some Medicinal Chemicals That Are Produced Synthetically Leave Trail of Deformed Infants, Suicides and Other Tragedies—New Warning

Determining Candidates and the Responsibility

The maximum unit counts (indicated in parentheses) for specific headlines are approximations. Even using 1/2 for m & w, and 1/2 for l, i and spaces, the slight differences in width of other letters, plus any variation in the number of capital letters employed, affect the count.

To keep headlines from reading into adjoining ones, avoid full lines, except when an 8-column streamer is used.

All headlines are flush left, except those with kickers.

Capitalize nouns, pronouns, verbs and all other words of four or more letters.

Capitalize No, Nor, Not, Off, So, Up.

Lower-case a, and, as, at, but, by, for, if, in, of, on, or, the, to, except when connected with the preceding word, as Cared For by His Mother, but He Cared for Nothing.

Capitalize both words of a compound adjective. Example: An Able-Bodied Seaman. But lower-case after hyphen in One-tenth, Twenty-two and in such words as Re-elect, Co-operate.

Capitalize the first word of the second and succeeding lines of each headline.

Set infinitives as follows: to Be, to Do, to

All headlines, unless otherwise noted, are Bodoni Bold caps and lower case. Headlines are designated by indicating the number of columns, number of lines and type sizes, in that order. For example:

5/2/36 to indicate 5 columns, 2 lines, 36-point.
or
3/1/30 to indicate 3 columns, 1 line, 30-point.

For Italic heads use the abbreviation Ital.
7/3/60 Ital—7 columns, 3 lines, 60-point Italic.

For a kicker use the letter K.
6/2/42K—6 columns, 2 lines, 42-point, with kicker.

For Italics and kicker use K Ital.
3/2/30K Ital—3 columns, 2 lines, 30-point Italic and kicker.

However, 1-column heads are designated by number and letters, with unit count in parentheses, as follows:

No. 1—30-pt (9)

Policemen
Caught in
Cross Fire

No. 2—24-pt (11)

$5700 Gone
From Offices
At Stix Stores

No. 3—24-pt (11)

Switch Crews
Strike Here

No. 4—18-pt (14)

Steamfitter Fund
Study to Resume

No. 1 Ital—30-pt (8)

*Escaping
Men Face
Rifle Fire*

No. 2 Ital—24-pt (11)

*New Officials
Inaugurated
A Day Later*

No. 3 Ital—24-pt (11)

*$5700 Gone
From Offices*

No. 4 Ital—18-pt (14)

*Steamfitter Fund
Inquiry Halted*

For other 1-column heads omit the column designation

2/18—1 column, 2 lines, 18-point.

2/18 Ital—1 column, 2 lines, 18-point Italic.

For a 2/18 Ital feature story mark the copy INDENT

No. 7—2 Col. 1 line 18-pt (28)

Steamfitter Fund Study to Resume

No. 7 Ital—1 Col. 1 line 18-pt Ital (28)

Steamfitter Fund Study to Resume

Jump heads are 24-point caps and lower case unless otherwise designated.

When kickers are used, write them on separate sheets and mark the headlines to be indented one pica for each column; i.e., a 2-column headline would be indented 2 picas, etc. A kicker should be no more than half the length of the headline.

When the headline is roman, set the kicker italic; when the headline is italic, set the kicker roman.

Kickers are 18-point for headlines up to 36-point. For headlines 42-point and larger, use 24-point kickers.

Decks are 14-point Bodoni Bold.

One-column folo heads can be either the No. 2/18 Italic for longer stories or 5 Italic for shorter ones.

72-point

Fine

72-point Italic

Still

60-point

Limit

60-point Italic

Born

48-point

Policy

48-point Italic

Police

42-point

Soldier

42-point Italic

Confer

36-point

Arrested

36-point Italic

Confuse

84-point Mid Gothic Caps (25)

IN ATLANTA

72-point Mid Gothic Caps (30)→

60-point Mid Gothic Caps (36)

ON POLICE

8-Column 72-point Mid Gothic Caps (30)→

SNIPERS FIRING ON POLICE IN ATLANTA

Discussion With Cambodians

Diplomatic Windfall for U.S.

But Caution Is Necessary

2/2/30—2 Col. 2 lines (26)
30-pt Bodoni Bold

European Economy Is Faltering

As 4-State Conference Opens

Translating Wilson's Overtures Into Practical Gains May Be Difficult in View of Problems

2/2/30 Ital—2 Col. 2 lines (24)
30-pt Bodoni Bold Italic

European Economy Is Rising

Despite Row With Asiatics

2/2/24—2 Col. 2 lines (29)
24-pt Bodoni Bold

European Struggle Is Going Ahead

To Help Britain With Its Economy

2/2/24 Ital—2 Col. 2 lines (29)
24-pt Bodoni Bold Italic

European Struggle Is Going Ahead

To Help Britain With Its Economy

New Plan

For Voters

In County

1/30—1 Col. 3 lines (13)
30-pt Bodoni Bold

Artists, Critics

Praise Painting

In New York

New Work Hailed As Best to Appear Since Start of Competition

1/30 Ital—1 Col. 3 lines (12)
30-pt Bodoni Bold Italic

Helping Hand

From Court on

Foreign Ties

1/24—1 Col. 3 lines (14)
24-pt Bodoni Bold

European Nation

Is Under Attack

In Berlin Parley

1/24 Ital—1 Col. 3 lines (14)
24-pt Bodoni Bold Italic

European Nation

Is Under Attack

In Berlin Parley

Within the last several years, the wire services have increased the practice of using by-lines on their stories. Consequently, the names of their top-flight writers are now familiar to thousands of readers. The wire services have also sought after famous writers outside the newspaper field to handle assigned stories.

A typical piece of edited wire copy is illustrated.

¶ NEW ORLEANS, DEC. 21 - (AP) - JEROME L. KENT, WEALTHY
CHICAGO IMPORTER, ARRIVED HERE TODAY FOR THE ~~ANNUAL MEETING~~
ANNUAL MEETING OF THE NATIONAL AUDØBON SOCIETY.   ALTHOUGH
HE SPOKE CORDIALLY WITH REPORTERS, HE REFUSED TO DISCUSS HIS
RECENT TRIAL FOR FRAUD.   AT THAT TRIAL, HE WAS FOUND GUILTY
AND GIVEN A FIVE YEAR SUSPENDED SENTENCE.   TO ALL QUESTIONS
REGARDING THE CASE, HE REPLIED SIMPLY, "NO COMMENT."

TYPE

Identifying Type

Type is identified chiefly by its (1) size, (2) family, and (3) heaviness.

Type Size. Type size is measured in points, each point being approximately $1/72$ of an inch. Thus, 18-point type is ¼ inch high, 36-point type is ½ inch high, 72-point type is 1 inch high. These heights include a minimum white space between lines. The smallest type used by most American newspapers is 5½ point, often called ''agate.'' This smallest type has been traditionally used for setting classified advertisements (although other type sizes are also used on the classified advertising pages). The larger type sizes are used in headlines. Most reading matter—stories—is printed in 7-point or 8-point type, though important stories may be printed partly or wholly in larger sizes. An illustration shows how some type sizes compare with one another.

This is 5½-point, also called Agate.

This is 6-point.

This is 7-point.

This is 8-point.

This is 9-point.

This is 10-point.

This is 12-point.

This is 14-point.

This is 16-point.

This is 18-point.

This is 24-point.

This is 30-point.

This is 36-point.

This is 42-point.

The type sizes in the past were called by various names before the point system came into use. Some of these names are still used. For instance, advertising people refer to *agate* lines (5½-point). *Pica* (12-point) and *nonpareil* (6-point) survive to designate sizes of spaces between lines. Picas also measure line length. Type sizes in some other countries are measured in different units, including metric.

Type Families. The expression "family of type" refers to its design style, the word "family" thus covering all the variations within a given style. Most newspapers limit the use of type to two or three families. They base their choices on attractiveness and on families already in use by rival papers, this latter because the typographical appearance of a given paper is a distinguishing characteristic for the reader. Some common type faces are shown here, set in 12-point:

Bodoni Book	Goudy
Bookman	Karnak Lite
Bruce	Modern
Caslon	**Scotch Roman**
Century	**Spartan Medium**
Erbar Light	**Tempo Medium**
Franklin Gothic	Times Roman
Garamond	**Vogue Bold**

Heaviness. In appearance, type may be "heavy" or "bold" as distinguished from "thin" or "light." These terms pertain to the thickness of the line forming the letter. Some families of type are obviously heavier than others, but there are also variations within a given family. These variations enable the editor to emphasize by using types of contrasting heaviness. Some newspapers, for instance, always accentuate the name of the paper in the body of a story by setting it in boldface; some emphasize all titles by setting them in boldface or italics; some always set subheads in boldface.

The width of letters may vary within a family. Thus type can be

Regular   **Extra Condensed**

Condensed   **Extended**

The heaviness of type may vary within a family. Thus, for example, type can be

Regular   Lightface

Boldface   **Extra bold**

Type may also be varied by italicizing.

This sentence is italicized.
This sentence is not.

Type in Newspaper Design

One of the important functions of the headline, as stated earlier, is to give the newspaper an attractive appearance. This appearance is provided not only by the headlines but also by the reading-matter type and by the over-all typographic design and make-up of the paper.

These matters are discussed in the next chapter.

EXERCISES

For practice in copy editing, retype the following stories, including their errors. Use standard copy paper, and double space. Then copy edit them, correcting all their errors as well as any that you make in typing. Write headlines in whatever style you think fitting, using the head schedule illustrated in this chapter.

1. Bayonne, New Jersey, police are seeking a dangerous intruded these days. It is a mouse with an unfortunate appetite for the most important papers in the desk drawers at police headquarters in city hall.

   He has caused already no ned of embarrassment to city officials. Last Saturday, for instance, ,Police Captain John O'Donnell had to race allover town to get the signature of District Attorney Lewis J. Kolb on the committment papers for Joseph Torrence, convicted of larceny and sentenced to five years in the State Penitentiary. Imagine the embarrassment of the captain when, as he reached for the paper in his top desk drawer last Monday morning he found that the mouse had eaten a hole right through the signature.

   Then there was that sad occasion on Tuesday when Patrolman George Potter stood red faced in the court room of Judge Oliver T. Rosen where Thomas Warren, 312 S. 2nd Street is being tried as an accomplice in the numbers racket. Patrolman Potter declared that when he arrested Warren he found five slips of paper in the latter's possession. On the papers were numbers and names and addresses. Those papers, Potter sadly declares, were taken from my top desk drawer or else that mouse ate them.'' With this the courtroom burst into laughter and Potter slunk back in abject misery.

   Thus far all efforts to capture Mr. Mouse have failed. A trap baited with cheese has been spurned, a little wire house with an inviting piece of bread inside has not been visited, and a big cat imported for the sole purpose of capturing the criminal has reported "no progress."

   In the meantime, Captain O'Donnell has ordered that all important papers be kept in the metal filing cabinet.

2. The study of American Literature is neglected in colleges and universities throughout the United States and as a result students are unaware of many of the significant fields of their native arts and culture, according to a survey conducted under the auspices of the National Council of Teachers of English. Few of the seven hundred colleges that responded to the councils questionnaire require courses for B.A. or B.S. degrees.

   However, 30 per cent of the universities and colleges require American literature for majors in English and for those who are perparing to teach English. But the total number of students who fall in those catefories is less than 10 percent. Emerson, Hawthorne and Whitman are teh three most popular of the older American authors judging by the frequency with which they are studied. Others are Peo, Thoreau, Mark Twain, Franklin, and Washington Irving.

   Many of the educators who attended the recent convention of the Council in Minneapolis, Minnesota expressed genuine concern over this situation. They feel that if we are to hold the things for which we have fought, we must increase respect for our nation and its heritage in the arts.

3. Smarting under a ver poor batting average for the past week, Harold Upton, Weatherman for the town of Harshaw, Pennsylvania refused to predict the weather for more than a day at a time in the future. Upton has been wrong for six of his last seven predictions. For Monday he prophesied snow; it rained. For Tuesday he forecast continued showers; it was clear. For Wednesday he saw countinued fair weather; again it rained. For Thursday he announced continued rain; again it cleared. Friday, said he will be clear and cold; it was cloudy all day. For Saturday, he foresaw contineued cloudiness, but he didn't go far enough for that day saw the heaviest snowfall in years. His prediction for today is bound to be correct; he says the snow is going to remain for a while before it melts.

4. The first Chirderen's Concert presented yesterday morning by Jacques Marteau and the Philadelphia Orchestra, was as full of surpreses as a christmas stocking and equally delightful. Even the Academy of Music wore an unespectedly festive air with Christmas trees and a colorful winter scene on stage and many eager youn members of the filled auditorium looking like Christmas cherubs themselves.

A bust of Beethoven directly in front of the podium reminded the audience that the great composer who would have been 20 to-day was sharing honors with the coming holiday event.

The program was composed of "The Nutcracker Suite, Beethoven's first piano Concerto in C major, and the traditional C h ristmas carols.

5. The fourth speaker in the regular college assembly lecture series will be prof. Franklin J. Leonard, Professor of History, who will speak in Auchinloss auditorium next tuesday morning at 10 a. m. Professor Leonard's topic will be Are We Prepared for the Current international monetary Problem."

Professor Leonard hold the bachelor of Arts degree from Baylor and the Master of Arts and Doctor of Philosophy degree from Yale. His special field is American Economic History.

He is also the author of a book named America's Econnomic Dilemma, published by the Yale University press in 1974.

During the year 1972–73, he visited the Brookings Institute in Washington, District of Columbia, where he studied and served as a consultant on the staff.

Proffesor Leonard will be availabl for individual discussion in the lounge of the Adams Student center between the hours of two and four on Tuesday afternoon, the same day as the lecture.

FOR FURTHER READING

AP-UPI Stylebook. New York: Associated Press; United Press International. Published annually.

Ashley, Paul P., *Say It Safely: Legal Limits in Publishing, Radio, and Television*. Seattle: University of Washington Press, 1966.

Bain, Eric K., *Display Typography*. New York: Hastings House, Publishers, 1970.

Bremner, John B., *HTK: A Study of News Headings*. Topeka, Kansas: Palindrome Press, 1972.

Crowell, Alfred A., *Creative News Editing*. Dubuque, Iowa: Wm. C. Brown Co., 1975.

Croz, Peter. *Graphic Design and Reproduction Techniques*. New York: Hastings House, Publishers, 1968.

Dangers of Libel. New York: The Associated Press. Revised and published annually.

Garst, Robert Edward, and Theodore M. Bernstein, *Headlines and Deadlines; A Manual for Copy Editors*. New York: Columbia University Press, 1961.

McNaughton, Harry H. *Proofreading and Copyediting: A Practical Guide to Style for the 1970's*. New York: Hastings House, Publishers, 1973.

New York Times Style Book. New York: McGraw-Hill. Published annually.

Rivers, William L., *The Mass Media; Reporting, Writing, Editing*. New York: Harper, 1964.

★ **8** ★

Make-Up as an Art
Principles and Patterns of
  Make-Up
    Attractiveness
    Readability
  Balanced Make-Up
    True or Perfect Balance
    Inverted Pyramid Make-Up
    Weighted Make-Up
  Unbalanced Make-Up
    Horizontal Make-Up
    Broken-Column Make-Up
    Panel Make-Up
  Using Make-Up Patterns
  Other Guiding Points
  Examples of Make-Up

Make-Up

MAKE-UP AS AN ART

The most casual reader of newspapers senses differences in newspaper formats. He recognizes some by their big headlines, frequent banners, and pictures, others by their sparing use of such devices. He senses moods or tones conveyed by the types that various newspapers use. He learns to look for late flashes in boxes or panels on one front page and as precedes or inserts on another. He is aware, vaguely or clearly, that pictures and stories appear in characteristic patterns—balanced or in some other attempt at orderly arrangement. To the reader, all these differences are part of "appearance" or "looks." To the newspaperman, they are designated by the self-explanatory term "make-up."

Although newspaper make-up has much science about it, fundamentally it is art. It is art because it is distinctively creative work, work wherein one relies on his innate sense of order and beauty, work wherein one expresses his artistic personality. Stated in other phraseology, make-up is an activity which, like composing music or painting pictures, demands a knowledge of technical controlling principles to serve as guides in producing an aesthetic creation.

As with all other artistic activities, disagreement and controversy over make-up abound. A page that one newspaperman considers genuinely appealing another views with disdain; the readers' guides (arrows, borders, asterisks, or the like) favored by one newspaper are taboo with a second; and a photo arrangement scorned as bizarre by one picture editor is praised by an equally competent colleague. Further, opinions differ sharply concerning such common devices as the eight-column streamer, the bleeding cut, the read-out line, and the shifting of the name plate or masthead. These arguments are not likely to be settled easily—no more than are the arguments concerning the well-dressed man, the properly furnished living room, the world's most beautiful woman, or the greatest musical composition. As long as newspapermen are human beings, there will be the disagreement about make-up that characterizes creative work.

The procedure for making decisions regarding make-up varies from paper to paper. On the very small newspaper, staffed by an editor and two or three assistants, the editor makes the decisions. On larger papers, one man, appropriately called the make-up editor, handles this work. He, however, is not the absolute authority, for he must be guided by the established policies of his paper and his work must be approved by his superiors. Usually, he attends the editorial conference that reviews the day's news so that he can draw up the dummies for the important pages (generally the front, the editorial, and the split pages). Then he must have these dummies okayed by the top editors. The make-up of the other pages containing general news is his decision. The make-up of the specialized pages—sports, women's, theatre, for examples—is usually done by the top editor in the particular department.

A large newspaper has a team of make-up editors. One handles the editions that appear during his shift while others cover the remaining editions. Each make-up editor has one or more assistants, according to the size of the paper. These assistants usually make up the inside pages under the direction of the editor.

PRINCIPLES AND PATTERNS OF MAKE-UP

Even though, as stated above, opinions vary regarding the well made-up paper, three considerations become central in any authoritative discussion of effective make-up: (1) attractiveness, (2) readability, and (3) balance. Hence differences of opinion concerning specific make-up patterns are really differences of judgment about these three attributes.

Attractiveness

Attractiveness is the first consideration of make-up because the reader knowingly or unknowingly looks for a pleasantly arranged page; that is, he looks for a creation that pleases his aesthetic sensibilities.

In his initial encounter with a page, the reader renders a critical judgment like that which he makes upon entering an unfamiliar hotel lobby. With the page as with the lobby, he automatically feels a sense of pleasure or revulsion, however slight or great, regarding the scene before him.

In this first reaction, the reader is not likely to favor a page as black and unassertive as the listings in the telephone directory or as jumbled and illogical as the unassembled puzzle. Rather, he will probably respond most favorably to a page that exudes the atmosphere of neat, refined, well-ordered creation—the atmosphere that emanates from the fittingly planned garden, the reposeful cluster of homes, the interestingly plotted model city, or similar arrangement characterized by an appealing sense of decor.

Attractiveness of newspaper make-up lies beyond any precise formula or tight definition. Like attractiveness in other fields, it can only be described broadly or sensed. Readers are aware of it when they meet it, and they note its lack when it is absent. Therefore, the make-up editor must always strive for it.

The opportunity to make a page attractive is naturally affected by editorial policy. A very conservative paper, for example, rarely uses streamers, large heads, or more than a few small cuts on page 1. As a result, the make-up editor has limited options in his attempts at variety. The sensational paper, on the other hand, may demand so many cuts and banners that the editor is pressed to find a really attractive arrangement.

Nonetheless, the skilled make-up editor can arrange almost any collection of material into an appealing entity. He can manipulate, contrast, and experiment with his type and pictures until he gains a pleasant and relaxing quality. In this respect, he is like the capable automobile showroom manager who so places his cars that each one exhibits itself and the others to maximum advantage.

Readability

Readability is important in make-up because the reader likes to examine his newspaper in an intuitive or second-nature manner. He wants to be able to "take in" the entire page in one first sweep so he can read stories in the order of his preference. Then he wants to read without being forced to think about how to follow the material before him.

The reader becomes distinctly annoyed by closely placed lines of type, poor placement of heads and jump material, and similar impediments to ease of perusal. In fact, he sets a much higher value on ease of reading than is commonly realized.

To appreciate the significance of readability, an observant person need only compare a highly respected metropolitan daily with a poorly executed neighborhood weekly. The act of reading the first paper is a pleasant and trouble-free experience. But often in reading the second, the reader must scan a given column two or three times to find the continuity of the story; he must solve puzzles in trying to identify the people shown in a picture; and he must grope through a maze of ill-done typography to read a story intelligently.

Undoubtedly, the need for readability is forcing newspapers, more and more, to adopt a larger body type; to avoid difficult-to-locate continuations; and to use more pictures and other devices that help to make reading the newspaper a simpler and hence less overwhelming experience. The need for readability is also the major reason that most newspapers have discarded the old eight-column front page in favor of a six-column page that uses white space instead of column rules (lines that separate columns from each other).

BALANCED MAKE-UP

Balance is the attempt to arrange material so as to gain a symmetry and hence a beauty in the finished page. Headlines, cuts, boxes, and type are selected and placed with a view to balancing and therefore to setting off each other.

The concept of balance in newspaper make-up is quite similar to an idea respected by interior decorators in furnishing a room. The decorators seek balancing effects by making each piece of furniture the counterpart of another. They counterbalance a grand piano, for instance, by putting a large sofa against the opposite wall; and they space pictures and small items with the same goal in mind. Thus they can avoid a one-sided or lopsided result.

As might be assumed, variations exist within the realm of balance. The most common are presented below.

True or Perfect Balance

The first of these variations is referred to simply as balanced make-up; actually, it should be called true or perfect balance. Under this pattern, an attempt is made to approximate a perfect pairing of material. Each item is the counterpart of another in head, position, and length, and everything may be ruled over by an 8-column banner. The great advantage of balanced make-up is the orderly appearance given by the regularity of the page. The great disadvantage is that it tends to subordinate news values to make-up—for example, a minor story may be assigned a #1 head in order to balance a far more important story with a #1 head.

Inverted Pyramid Make-Up

A variation of balanced make-up is the inverted pyramid. Under this pattern, material is so arranged that a triangle can be constructed with its base across the top of the page and its vertex near or at the center of the page.

The material below the vertex can then be balanced or arranged is some other appealing form.

Inverted Pyramid Make-Up

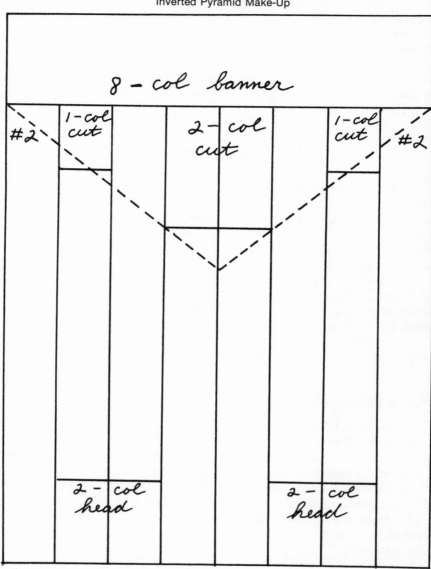

Weighted Make-up

A third variation within the concept of balanced make-up is weighted make-up. This pattern can be understood easily by invoking, once again, the comparison of the making-up of a page with the furnishing of a room.

Sometimes the interior decorator "weights" rather than balances the furniture in a room; that is, he positions the furniture with the thought of distributing

Balanced Make-Up

2-col head	#3	2-col cut	#3	2-col head
1-col cut				1-col cut
#3		1-line head		#3
	#2		#2	
2-col head		2-col cut		2-col head
1-col box	#5		#5	1-col box

the psychological weight evenly throughout the total area. Hence his primary goal is an appealing distribution.

When the make-up man employs this principle, he uses heavy items (long stories, large type, strong pictures) to hold down specific parts of the page while placing lighter items in the areas between. Such a page, when done competently, presents an attractive dispersion of weight.

Weighted Make-Up

Note how, in the dummy above, the three stories at the bottom of the page hold down the entire page in an appealing manner. Also, note the overall atmosphere of appropriateness.

UNBALANCED MAKE-UP

Although balance was once widely regarded as an attribute of effective make-up, a large segment of the newspaper world now deliberately avoids it. They argue that some unbalanced forms are more attractive, impressive, and readable than the conventionally balanced page.

The patterns endorsed by this group are appropriately termed "unbalanced make-up." Among the most common, three are especially popular: (1) horizontal make-up, (2) broken-column make-up, and (3) panel make-up.

Horizontal Make-Up

Horizontal make-up can best be understood by thinking of its central or controlling idea: it is make-up conceived in terms of horizontal rather than vertical effects. Consequently, unlike the many patterns constructed on up-and-down guidelines, horizontal make-up employs across-the-page concepts.

Essentially, horizontal make-up originated with the magazine. Magazine art directors or designers, because of the physical nature of the pages, developed this particular system to obtain more attractive and more readable layouts. Then the newspaper people, seeing the overall appeal and the general efficacy of the layout, adapted it to their own needs.

The most striking use of horizontal make-up is the variation which makes the front or main page look like two pages—one above and one beneath the fold. A more common use, however, carries an eight-column story, with an eight-column banner, across the top of page one and may even drop the nameplate beneath the story. The material below the nameplate is then also arranged in horizontal concepts.

The great argument for horizontal make-up is ease of reading. Because the human eye functions more easily in horizontal than in vertical movements, the reader feels more comfortable in examining and reading a page in horizontal as opposed to vertical arrangements. Also, the large heads and extensive white space make the reader's initial encounter with the page a less awesome and hence a more relaxing experience.

A danger of using horizontal make-up is that, unless handled carefully, it may create the appearance of a series of layers: it may give the reader an impression of looking at the shelves of a closet.

Throughout all discussion of horizontal make-up, stands one all-important fact: it is easily the most widely used make-up pattern of the present time. The majority of the nation's newspapers favor horizontal make-up for their front and other main pages, as well as for many of their inside pages.

Broken-Column Make-Up

Broken-column make-up derives its name from the fact that each column is broken by two or more heads. Its purpose, as a first glance demonstrates, is to place as many stories as possible on the particular page.

Horizontal Make-Up

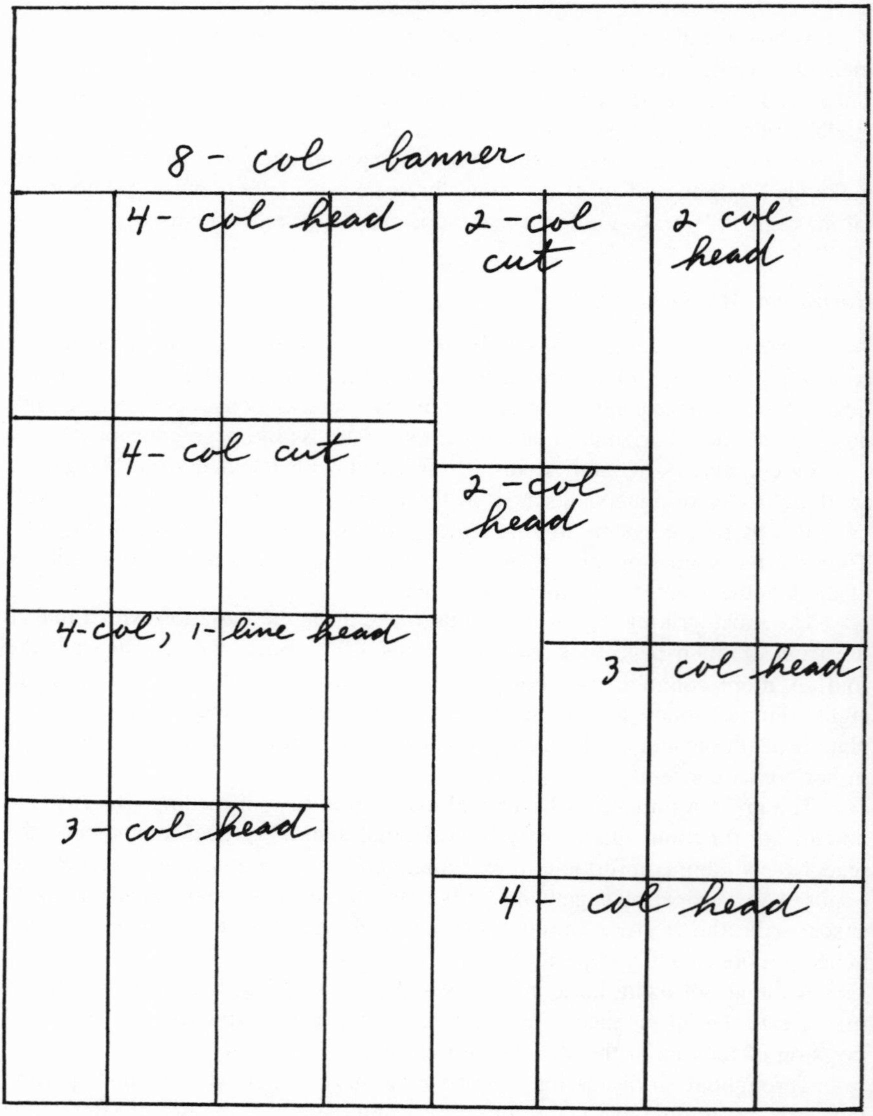

8 - col banner

4 - col head   2 - col cut   2 col head

4 - col cut

2 - col head

4 - col, 1-line head

3 - col head

3 - col head

4 - col head

The advantage of this make-up is that it provides an extensive assortment of stories for perusal—without making the reader turn pages except for those stories with jumps. The disadvantage is that it may overwhelm the make-up editor in his efforts to obtain order and beauty. If he has an excessively large number of stories to force onto the page, he has trouble avoiding a badly cluttered effect.

Broken-Column Make-Up

When the amount of material is not unreasonably large, the capable make-up editor can often achieve an attractive and effective broken-column page because he knows how to place and contrast type, to juggle stories, and to arrange boxes and similar material to gain a pleasing atmosphere. But in less skilled hands, the page can easily look like the overstocked furniture store that shows no semblance of order.

Panel Make-Up

Panel Make-Up

Panel make-up is the procedure of using a two-column panel along one side of the page.

The primary value of the panel is that it attracts the reader. Many newspapers, for instance, use the front-page panel for especially appealing material—

last-minute dispatches, late-breaking developments, brief but significant stories—because this practice habitually draws the reader to the page. Similarly, papers use panels on inside pages to present standing features (regular columns, sports results, and the like) because regular readers want to locate favorite reading without any problems. Panels are also used widely as guides for the reader. In these instances, the panels give summaries much like headlines, of the main stories in the particular section, along with the location of the stories (for example, "p. 3, col. 4").

In addition, many make-up people feel that the panel has the advantage of undergirding or stabilizing the entire page. They see the panel as the builder sees the keystone in the arch.

USING MAKE-UP PATTERNS

A student reflecting on the make-up patterns discussed in this chapter must recognize certain significant facts.

Most important, he should note that the make-up editor generally employs the patterns described as points of departure to create his page; or stated in other terms, he seldom pursues a specific pattern routinely. Instead, he starts with a standard pattern, say balanced make-up, but improvises as his creative impulses direct. Thus he may intend at first to use horizontal make-up—only to decide later that the lateral lines are too severe. To lessen this effect, he then introduces a "chimney" to "straighten things out." His page therefore becomes, technically speaking, horizontal make-up with variations. In practice, he never bothers to designate his make-up with a single label; he simply works in terms of his aesthetic sensitivities.

This particular point can be made clearer by an analogy. The make-up editor is not like the housewife who makes a dress in complete conformity to a tissue-paper pattern purchased at a local store. Rather, he is like the clothing designer who alters or deviates from established patterns to improve upon or add a touch of individuality to the finished garment.

A second fact is that nearly all newspapers use several of these standard make-up patterns—with appropriate deviations—in every issue. They do so because of the nature of the material in the various sections and the variety obtained. For example, in a random sampling of copies of the *Washington Post,* the *New York Times,* the *St. Louis Post-Dispatch,* and the *San Francisco Chronicle,* this author found every make-up pattern discussed in this chapter.

A third fact is that make-up patterns must be adjusted for the tabloid page. Although such patterns as horizontal make-up can be used in modified form on inside pages, the size and nature of the tabloid demand a special brand of make-up for its main pages. The kind most often used is "poster make-up."

With this make-up, the editor arranges his material as if he were preparing a poster. He places his pictures and overlines as attractively as possible—in the manner of the display artist preparing a commercial poster.

Poster Make-Up

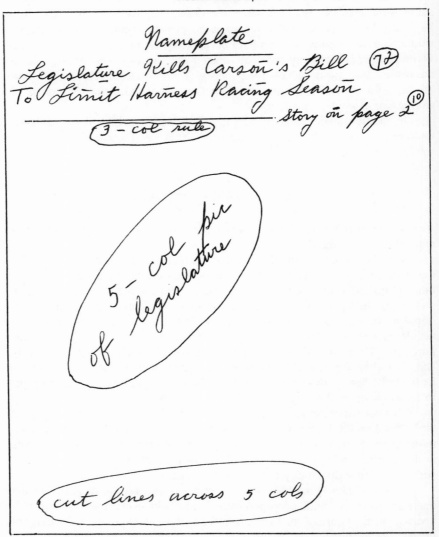

The final fact is that make-up procedures are forever shifting. Everywhere, editors are searching for more original, more appealing make-ups; and frequently they discover striking and valuable patterns. Thereupon other make-up editors, impressed with their colleagues' innovations, adopt their practices.

This experimenting with new patterns is eliminating the column rule more and more; and it is encouraging large areas of white space and novel arrangements of pictures. Meanwhile, it is hastening the end of hard-to-read body type, tightly spaced paragraphs, and similar impediments to ease of perusal.

OTHER GUIDING POINTS

Despite the fact that many systems of newspaper make-up are currently in vogue, there is a general acceptance of certain guiding principles applicable to all. A discussion of these principles follows.

Headlines. The size of the head should be proportionate to the length and the importance of the story. In making up a page, the editor must be careful that heads do not cancel out each other. If, for instance, there are too many heads at the top of the page, they tend to crowd each other out of the reader's attention. If in three or more successive columns there are similar heads side by side, they tend to obscure or "tombstone" each other.

When placing headlines on the page, the make-up editor should try to blend families of type together smoothly—or to state the matter negatively, he should beware clashes of type families. A Scotch Roman head beside an Old English head, for instance, can jar the reader's sensitivities.

𝔅𝔯𝔦𝔢𝔣𝔰 𝔦𝔫 𝔱𝔥𝔢 𝔑𝔢𝔴𝔰 Drivers Hospitalized After Head-On Crash

Position. Where a story is placed in a newspaper should be determined by its relative importance and by the department in which it logically belongs (straight news, sports news, society, business, or the like). With one exception, therefore, the biggest stories get the most prominent positions in their respective departments. The exception applies to the story that isn't straight news but is so important that it must be placed on page 1. Examples of such stories are those about high-interest sports events (World Series, Army-Navy game, Kentucky Derby, or the like), major or unexpected developments in church affairs, weddings or divorces of prominent people, and "best of the year" awards in entertainment or literature.

In arranging stories and pictures on the page, a make-up editor must avoid any layout that tends to "push a story off the page"—to divert a reader's notice away from it in his ordinarily superficial scanning. If a story in an outside column is short, some broken-column make-ups can make it vanish from attention—be quietly "shoved off the page." Similarly, a small story with a light-face headline can be obscured if it is placed between large items.

Accentuation. The ideal achievement is to place all material so as to accentuate all else. On every page there must be an abundance of white to offset the black, and heads must be so written and placed as to set off each other. Cuts and boxes should be used to brighten the page, especially the dull ones. Line after line of close type should be relieved by the generous use of slugs and subheads.

Also troublesome is the problem of two or more pictures on the same page. Before deciding on any pictorial layout, the editor should try the pictures side by side in order to obtain the most comfortable effect. He must, for example, avoid such unpleasant mismatching as a two-column cut of a man's head and shoulders placed beside an equal-sized shot of children at play. The contrast in the size of the figures generates an unusually disturbing aura.

Accentuation, one must always remember, lies at the very center of the overall attractiveness necessary to sound make-up.

News Value. The make-up of the newspaper, especially of the front page, should be adapted to the importance of the news; the news should not be adapted to the make-up. The editor, for example, should not decide to have an 8-column banner, several large heads, and a generally sensational make-up until he is certain that the news justifies these devices. The newspaper that uses banners and large heads every day is hard pressed to label really big news properly when it occurs. The make-up editor must always remember that make-up evaluates news.

Inside Pages. Inside pages must not be neglected. All too often, the emphasis on make-up is confined to the front page while the inside pages are composed with little thought. This is especially true of the pages which contain advertisements.

The most important points to remember about inside-page make-up are: (1) cuts should be used to brighten the pages; (2) as many pages as possible should have some genuinely lively news stories; (3) if filler is to be used, it should be interesting; and (4) dead ends of type (type without heads) should be kept at a minimum. (However, dead ends of type are practically impossible to avoid when ads cover almost the entire page.)

Also, if an inside page is to contain a large group of single ads, some attempt should be made to blend the ads together and to avoid a scenery silhouette (jagged edges protruding upward). The make-editor should step the ads or gain some other interesting or attractive arrangement.

Clarity. Make-up should always be devised with the aim of forestalling any strain on the reader as he seeks material. Therefore, banner lines and the related headlines must be so arranged that the reader locates the story immediately; pictures and their accompanying stories must be placed properly; guiders (arrows and the like) should be used when needed; and every attempt should be made to present material in clearly discernible patterns.

A main function of make-up, the editor must always remember, is to guide the reader unerringly to the material being sought.

Section Make-Up. Make-up must vary according to section; similar make-up in all the sections of a newspaper is undesirable. The sports section, for one example, is generally the most sensational—it uses more and larger cuts and uses the large heads more profusely. The obituary page, in contrast, generally has the most conservative make-up—its news is of such nature that sensational make-up would be in quite bad taste.

Furthermore, the choice and arrangement of pictures in some sections demand a special knowledge. Wrestling pictures in the sports pages reveal almost nothing unless a facial expression is shown. Hence the make-up editor must know this fact—as he must know the pertinent facts that characterize each section of the newspaper.

Individuality. The make-up of a given newspaper should reflect a note of individuality. It should not be so like the make-up of another paper, especially that of a competitor, that the reader can note no difference. In addition, it should be an individuality that appeals to the reader.

Individuality in newspaper make-up is like individuality in dress and in furnishing a home. It emanates from a careful, ceaseless effort to present an atmosphere of originality permeated by good taste. It is not being different for the mere sake of being different. It is, rather, a characteristic that results from reflection and deliberation.

EXAMPLES OF MAKE-UP

Several pages from newspapers are now presented, with comments on their significant make-up characteristics, to demonstrate some of what has been said.

The creator of this page 1 of the *Evening Journal* has relied on horizontal make-up with accompanying chimney effects.

The three stories in the upper half ("U.S. Concedes . . . ," "Moslems Close . . . ," "UD Tells . . .") and the story across the bottom ("Wilmington Area . . .") generate horizontal overtones. The editor has then lessened these overtones by stacking a two-column picture above a two-column story and running a single column up the middle of the page.

This page, incidentally, is representative of the six-column front page which more and more is replacing the traditional eight-column front page. Readers favor the large type, ample white space, and general ease-of-reading of this make-up.

This front page of the *Boston Sunday Globe* is basically a panel make-up with horizontal and vertical devices in the remaining areas.

The two stories along the left side form a panel which tends to accentuate the rest of the page, thereby making it appear as a page in itself. The story across the top ("Gen. Franco . . .") and the story across the bottom ("Taunton Gets . . .") create horizontal effects while the remaining material produces vertical effects.

The feature page of the *Pittsburgh Press* employs a horizontal make-up accompanied by a special kind of balance achieved through the use of pictures and a line drawing.

The three stories on the page are laid out in a generally horizontal arrangement. Meanwhile, the three-column shot (the horses) tends to balance the four-portrait arrangement on the right, while the two-column picture at the bottom and the two-column box with the line drawing become counterpoises.

Further strength for the make-up comes from the story and picture at the bottom. They serve to create a base for the whole page.

EVENING JOURNAL

WILMINGTON, DELAWARE / THURSDAY, DECEMBER 11, 1975 / VOLUME 43, NUMBER 277 / FIFTEEN CENTS

Spills and Damage to Shellfish Forecast

U.S. Concedes Perils in Offshore Drilling

WASHINGTON (AP)—While minimizing the potential danger faced by Maryland if oil drilling proceeds off New Jersey and Delaware, the Interior Department has raised the possibility of shellfish damage and economic hardship if support facilities are located in the state or drilling moves closer.

The department, in a statement on its plan to allow petroleum exploration 50 to 100 miles off the mid-Atlantic coast, also forecast unavoidable but limited oil spills and other problems.

These problems would be multiplied, however, if the Interior Department went ahead with another mid-Atlantic offshore sale in 1977 as tentatively proposed, the report said.

The study contends onshore development will be centered in New Jersey because it is closer to the drilling area and already has a large refining industry.

The major dangers to the Atlantic coast would stem from near shore spills from tankers or a pipeline break, according to the report. But spills, drill cutting, the laying of underground pipes and other related activities could lead to extensive killing of shellfish, the report says.

"The geographic areas most susceptible would be along tanker routes (possibly into New York harbor or Delaware Bay and, more remotely, Chesapeake Bay) and pipeline routes (possibly into New Jersey, Delaware or Maryland)," the study said.

If development were centered on the Eastern Shore instead of New Jersey, the report predicted, "prices in the country could increase astronomically, the pace of life could increase — causing certain emotional impacts . . . and tensions between newcomers and minority and elderly members of the population could occur."

"Adverse economic impacts could be caused in Ocean City (where more than one-fifth of the county employment may be tourist-generated) and to a lesser extent in the Rehoboth Beach, Del., area," the impact statement noted.

The study predicted from 4,200 to 15,400 jobs could result from the proposed mid-Atlantic leasing, in-

See PIPELINE—Page 5, Col. 1

Moslems Close In on Holiday Inn

BEIRUT (AP) — Moslem forces closed in today on Christian fighters in the 500-room Holiday Inn, the last obstacle in a leftist drive to take over Beirut's fire-blackened luxury hotels.

A night of the heaviest fighting in Lebanon's eight-month-old civil war brought the Moslem militiamen to within a grenade's throw of the former traveling businessman's palace.

The Moslem youths occupied the St. Georges and Phoenicia Intercontinental Hotels and surrounded the Holiday Inn on three sides. They covered the only escape and resupply route with sniper and machine gun fire.

Young leftist gunmen knocked holes in the walls of surrounding apartment buildings and blasted away with their Soviet-made weapons. they said they had ventured right up to the door last night in an armored car captured from the army but had to pull back when the vehicle came under rocket fire.

Spent cartridges from the armored car's .50-caliber machine gun littered the area.

Troops from an 850-man commando unit dispatched to the downtown battleground two days ago pulled out of the Phoenicia, leaving its soot-covered debris to adolescent Moslem street fighters. A charred body lay on the gutted ground floor and at least three more bodies sprawled on upper floors, covered by a layer of black dust.

The heaviest overnight fighting swirled around an office building called the Starco Center, where Christian gunmen of the rightwing Phalange party repelled a Moslem assault to pinch off their lifeline to the besieged Holiday Inn.

"The armed men were fighting five or 10 yards apart in the street there," said a Phalange spokesman. "And from behind they were using rockets and 120mm mortars."

The explosions rocked Beirut all night and into the morning, but tapered off during the afternoon to machine gun and rifle fire.

"The Holiday Inn is practically ours," claimed Moslem chieftain Abu Abed, leading the leftist charge. "If the state does not intervene today, it will inevitably fall completely into our hands."

UPI Telephoto

Lines are forming at airline ticket counters

Young traveler waits with parents in Des Moines

Sponsoring Prof Required

UD Tells Moon Followers To Obey Its Regulations

By DAVID HOFFMAN

The University of Delaware has warned disciples of Korean evangelist the Rev. Sun Myung Moon to follow university regulations or face loss of official sanction for their campus activities.

The university said it was "inappropriate" for any of Moon's followers who are not students to seek new converts on the campus.

Assistant Dean of Students Richard M. Sline also told Moon's campus followers to find a sponsoring professor by Dec. 19, as required by the university. They have been without one since September, he said.

The group's dozen or so members at the university are known as the Collegiate Association for the Research of Principles, (CARP), an affiliate of an army of about 7,000 converts to Moon's Unification Church across the nation.

The university's official recognition allows Moon followers use of college classrooms and access to the 12,800 undergraduate students on the Newark campus.

A religious and political organization that teaches strong anti-communism, Moon's church has become increasingly controversial as some parents attempt to "rescue" their children by kidnaping them out of the cult.

The movement's street solicitations nationwide are estimated to bring in $10 million a year and Moon controls a number of South Korean industries.

In a letter this week, Sline told the University of Delaware chapter not to look to the university for help if its members get in trouble with local authorities.

In another development this week, several "moonies," as they are called, have been ordered evicted from a ranch house at 305 Webb Road in Newark, rented since last July for $270 a month as a recruitment center.

The house, less than a mile from the campus, is owned by Rodney N. Reeder, a lieutenant with the university's security force at the College of Marine Studies in Lewes.

Reeder said yesterday his real estate agent, John F. Kelleher, issued the eviction order last week "with my approval" after reading an Evening Journal series of articles on Moon and the Unification Church.

Reeder said he was concerned the Moon followers were overcrowding a house that was meant to be a single-family dwelling.

A spokesman for Kelleher said the youths were told to leave by Jan. 3 because some neighbors had complained about the overcrowding last summer but the group had done nothing about it.

Dan Ciami, the 19-year-old president of the local chapter, could not be reached immediately for comment.

Meanwhile, the university's stu-

See MOON—Page 2, Col. 1

Ford's Fiscal Fights Could Shorten Trip

WASHINGTON (AP) — President Ford may cut short his annual Christmas skiing vacation in Colorado because he and Congress have some unsettled differences over tax cuts and government spending.

White House aides indicate Ford now has scheduled only a week in Vail, Colo., from Dec. 23 to Dec. 29. Originally, the President planned at least a two-week holiday stay.

Congress is expected to give final approval next week to a bill extending this year's tax reductions. Ford is expected to veto the bill because it probably will lack a spending lid he has sought. Congress then will attempt to override the veto.

Ford also is planning to salute Congress at a big White House Christmas ball to which all Senate and House members are invited. The black-tie party Dec. 17 is the big event on the Fords' Christmas social calendar.

The Fords also are plannig special parties for the White House press corps, children of foreign diplomats and volunteers from Williamsburg, Va., who helped provide this year's old-fashioned Christmas decorations at the White House.

The Dec. 17 date for the congressional ball originally coincided with the day the legislators picked to recess for a year-end holiday. But now congressional leaders think they may have to stay in session until Dec. 23 to clean up pending bills.

The White House is festively decked for the holidays. An 18-foot Douglas fir, grown in Michigan and transplanted to Garrison, N.Y., is the First Family's Christmas tree.

Victim Compensation Passes Pa. Senate

HARRISBURG, Pa. (AP)—The Senate has passed a bill that would permit state grants of up to $15,000 for crime victims.

The bill, approved 45-2 yesterday, provides for awards of up to $100 for each week of lost earnings or to a maximum $10,000. In cases of death, the victims' survivors would receive $15,000. The Senate sent the bill to the House.

Jurors Being Selected In Sussex Murder Case

From the Sussex Bureau

GEORGETOWN — Jury selection began today in the first-degree murder and rape trial of 17-year-old Linwood L. Shields in Superior Court in Georgetown.

Shields is being tried in the May 22, 1974, strangulation death of Phyllis Lenhart, 54, of near Millsboro.

Miss Lenhart was an assistant secretary of the Millsboro branch of the Bank of Delaware. Shields, 15 at the time of his arrest, lives near Millsboro where he was a student at Sussex Central High School.

Police were led to the youth after neighbors reported seeing him in the area of the Lenhart home on the day of the crime. After the arrest, investigators said an undisclosed amount of money, allegedly taken in burglary of the house, was recovered.

Shields is one of the youngest persons ever tried as an adult for first-degree murder in Delaware.

Today's Chuckle

More than 50 of every 100 Americans wear glasses. Which gives you some idea of how important ears can be.

N-Power on Rise, Soviet Scientist Says

NASHVILLE, Tenn. (AP) — The Soviet Union is accelerating construction of new nuclear power plants to provide up to half the country's total electricity needs within 50 years, a Russian scientist says.

Tadeush Adamjats, a faculty member at a technical institute in Moscow, says the speedup in nuclear plant construction in the Soviet Union parallels a similar program proposed by President Ford.

2 Lines Shut Down

Strikes Threaten Yule Air Travel

WASHINGTON (AP) — The nation's largest air carrier, United Airlines, is canceling all scheduled flights through Christmas Eve because of a breakoff in talks with its striking machinists Union.

Federally mediated talks between the airline and representatives of the International Association of Machinists, which has 18,000 members employed by United, broke off yesterday.

The United shutdown raises the possibility that many holiday travelers will find airline seats hard to get during the peak holiday season. United flies 90,000 passengers a day.

National Airlines has been shut down by striking flight attendants since Labor Day.

A United spokesman said also all charter flights have been scrubbed through Jan. 1. United has a substantial charter business and flies 19 of the 26 National Football League teams. Those teams now will have to find alternative transportation.

The United strike began at midnight Friday in a dispute involving both economic and non-economic issues, a Federal Mediation and Conciliation Service spokesman said.

The talks can be resumed at the request of either party or the mediation board, a board spokesman said.

Jobless Rate Dips In Pennsylvania

HARRISBURG (AP) — Fewer Pennsylvanians were laid off last month than expected, resulting in a dip in the state's seasonally adjusted unemployment rate, the Labor Department says.

The rate went from 9.7 per cent in October to 9.4 per cent, but was still high compared to the 5.9 per cent rate reported for November of 1974.

IN TODAY'S JOURNAL

Stephen Andretta, a New Jersey Teamster, is being questioned by a Michigan grand jury today on the whereabouts of his brother and two union associates on the day Jimmy Hoffa disappeared. Page 6

Homicide inspectors says investigation indicates slain millionaire John S. Knight III was bisexual. Page 10

Sunshine is something two Oklahoma sisters will never see. It would kill them. Page 11

General Assembly wasn't even asked by Gov. Tribbitt to cut its expenses, but Democratic leaders pledge a 10-per-cent reduction. Page 15

Democratic legislators have joined Gov. Sherman W. Tribbitt in asking for an investigation of comments made by U.S. District Judge John J. Gibbons in Wilmington's desegregation hearing. Page 17

Kidnaped Detroit bank manager James Crawford is still missing but three men have been arrested for extortion in the case. Page 20

With the acquisition of veteran pitcher Jim Kaat, the Phillies are already being projected as pennant winners. Page 24

The Oblates of St. Francis de Sales begin celebrating the 100th anniversary of their order tomorrow. Page 37

Gov. Mandel insists he'll hold taxes despite gloomiest budget prediction in his seven years at Maryland's helm. Page 41

INDEX

Arts	56-58	Ecology	38
Astrology	71	Editorials	34
Bridge	71	Health	44
Business	21-23	People	39
Comics	71	Record	60
Datebook	53	Sports	24-33
Deaths	59, 70	TV	54-55

Diamond Replay Winners 13

WEATHER

TONIGHT: Mostly cloudy, lows 30 to 35.

TOMORROW: Mostly cloudy, continued cool, highs low to middle 40s.

(Weather map, details on Page 3)

Each Resident Paid $1,547 in Fiscal 1974

Wilmington Area 11th in Per-Capita Income Tax

The Greater Wilmington area has missed — but just barely — being on a top 10 list.

The Wilmington area wound up with the No. 11 spot in a survey of average per-person federal tax payments made in 123 metropolitan areas across the country, according to the Tax Foundation Inc. of New York City.

Wilmington area residents paid an average of $1,547 in total federal taxes during fiscal 1974, according to the foundation.

That put the Wilmington area just behind 10th-ranked greater New York City with per-capita tax payments of $1,570.

Helping put Wilmington in the relatively high bracket was a 5.3 per cent unemployment rate for fiscal 1974. The areas' unemployment rate in October, the last month reported, was 8.1 per cent.

And, as in the case of a number of top-ranked areas, Wilmington apparently got a boost from the number of highly paid corporation executives and other well-to-do persons living in the area.

The figures include all federal income, gift, estate, excise, Social Security and corporation taxes.

The greater Wilmington area is defined by the federal Office of Management and Budget as including all of New Castle County and Salem County, N.J., and Cecil County, Md., a foundation spokesman said.

The survey dealt with what are known as Standard Metropolitan Statistical Areas which generally include more than one county, he added.

Leading the list with the highest per-capita tax payments was the Hartford-Bridgeport, Conn., area with a $1,841 figure.

Following in order were Hartford-New Britain, Conn. — $1,740; West Palm Beach-Boca Raton, Fla. — $1,723; Washington, D.C. — $1,721; Rockford, Ill. — $1,654, and Fort Lauderdale-Hollywood, Fla. — $1,594.

Washington led the list in fiscal 1973.

On the bottom of the list with the lowest tax payments of those areas surveyed were Charleston, S.C. — $721; El Paso, Tex. — $882; Corpus Christi, Tex. — $885, and Johnstown, Pa. — $890.

Hub's unfulfilled love affair—'75 World Series photo album, Section C

Today's section
Complete indexes for today's edition on Page 2

Boston Sunday Globe

The weather
Cloudy, 60s
Complete details on Page 96

Vol. 208, No. 118 © 1975, Globe Newspaper Co. ® * | SUNDAY, OCTOBER 26, 1975 * | Telephone 929-2000 | 75 CENTS

If American League loses, will Ford fall?

By Jon Margolis
Knight News Service

WASHINGTON — As all serious students know, four elemental forces shape human behavior — religion, sex, politics and baseball.

The first two will not be discussed here. But now that a most extra ordinary World Series has ended and a presidential campaign is beginning, the relationship between the last two merits examination.

First, there is the matter of expertise and prediction. Before the recent tournament began, the experts almost unanimously declared that the Cincinnati Reds would not simply beat the Boston Red Sox, but would demolish them.

Forecasts of an easy five- or six-game Cincinnati victory were heard across the land. A few certified experts even predicted a four-game sweep.

The experts, of course, supported their predictions with hard facts. The Reds had more power, more speed, a tighter defense. Those meaningless position-for-position comparisons were made, all giving the edge to the Reds.

Well, they did win, but they didn't demolish anybody. On a bloop single, the Reds managed a one-run win in the last inning of the last game, the fifth to be decided by one run. Two of the games went into extra innings.

A certain amount of crow-eating and apologizing to the Red Sox commenced even before the Series ended.

Now the same thing is about to happen in politics. Predictions will be made. They will be based on facts, facts about which candidate has raised the most money, gotten the most prestigious endorsements attracted the most volunteers. The predictions will be wrong.

After they are proven wrong, those who made them will explain that they were wrong because of unforseeable developments. This will be true. Sen. Edmund Muskie's 1972 crying jag could not be foreseen. Neither could Bernie Carbo's pinch-hit home runs.

GAME PLAN, Page 27

Old comic book store is no laughing matter

By John B. Wood
Globe Staff

There is a hint of embarrassment in Chuck Wooley's voice when he talks about comic books.

Comic books, after all, are not something people are expected to talk seriously about — at least not people who, like Wooley, have reached the age of 22 and have acquired a Harvard degree along the way.

Wooley, however, is quite serious about "the books" as he calls them. He has been collecting them, more or less professionally, since he was 13, and wrote his thesis on comic book superheroes — Superman, Wonder Woman, et al. — as modern myths.

Last year Wooley culled about 10,000 duplicates from his collection and opened the Million Year Picnic, the Boston area's first bookshop devoted entirely to comic books and paperback science fiction.

Most days he can be found sitting cross-legged on the floor of the shop in Harvard Square, quietly appraising stack after stack of Captain America, The Avengers, Iron Man, Superman, Conan the Barbarian, The Incredible Hulk, Swamp Thing, and a host of others too bizarre to contemplate.

"I read most of these," he said, indicating a pile of slightly more than 700 books which have been brought in for sale. "There's nothing really exciting here. Collectors are hanging on to their good stuff because the market is, you know, crazy, and they just bring in the junk."

COMIC BOOKS, Page 16

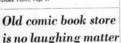

Chuck Wooley, Jerry Weist and their Million Year Picnic—a comic book feast. (Michael Cheers photo)

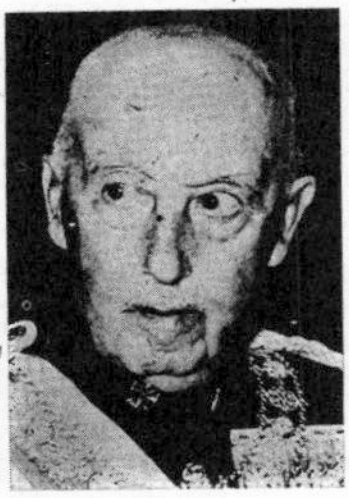

GENERALISSIMO FRANCO
. . . suffers third attack

Mourners gather at palace

Gen. Franco receives last rites

By Julie Flint
Associated Press

MADRID — His heart growing ever feebler, Francisco Franco received the last rites of the Roman Catholic Church yesterday and the nation's leaders gathered at his palace.

Prince Juan Carlos de Borbon, Franco's chosen heir, rushed to the Pardo Palace last night with his wife, Princess Sophie. The full cabinet of Premier Carlos Arias Navarro waited there with them.

The 37-year-old prince was named by Franco in 1969 to succeed him as chief of state and to become Spain's first king in 44 years.

Juan Carlos and Arias had visited the 82-year-old generalissimo briefly in the afternoon. A crowd of Spaniards kept vigil outside the palace, 10 miles north of Madrid.

Franco, ill for the last eight days, asked for the last rites of the church at midday, shortly after a team of doctors reported his heart had shown signs of failing twice in the course of the morning.

Officials at Pardo Palace said Franco, tranquil in the presence of his closest family, received the Sacrament of Extreme Unction from his military chaplain. He also heard Mass with his wife, Dona Carmen Polo de Franco.

After the rites, relatives and high officials began arriving and leaving later in tears. A vast crowd gathered outside the gates.

An evening medical bulletin reported "a slow and progressive deterioration" in his condition. It said: "Signs of myocardiac suffering have intensified. Fever has appeared. Blood pressure had dropped and heart beat and breathing have increased."

The doctors said, however, he was still conscious much of the time. After the noontime bulletin, doctors had said privately they expected him to live no longer than 72 hours.

Premier Carlos Arias Navarro visited Franco with Juan Carlos. All 18 cabinet ministers also arrived. Franco's elder brother, Nicolas, 85, paid a last visit, and Franco's sister Pilar stayed at his wife's side.

FRANCO, Page 19

She decided to let her husband die

By Richard A. Knox
Globe Staff

Though she had no doubts about it, the sad-eyed young widow wanted to talk about her decision to authorize doctors to "pull the plug" on her husband's respirator.

"People usually associate death with old age and just avoid the subject," she said, "but they should be prepared. If your number's up, it's up, and there's nothing you can do about it. The machines are wonderful, but they can't make you live."

It has been 41 days since Kristin Kramer of Concord, the mother of two little girls, made the decision to relinquish hope for the recovery of her 35-year-old husband, Robert, who died Sept. 15, 1975.

Since then, the case of Karen Quinlan, a 21-year-old New Jersey woman who has been in a coma since April, has focused attention on the painful issue of when to stop "extraordinary" care of brain-damaged patients. It was the Quinlan case — which may be decided by New Jersey Superior Court Judge Robert Muir Jr. this week — that prompted the Concord woman to share her feelings.

"I know something of how the Quinlans feel," Mrs. Kramer said last week. Watching her husband breathe with the aid of a respirator when the doctors said there was no hope of recovery "was like going to a funeral parlor and seeing the body breathe," Mrs. Kramer said in an interview.

Like Karen Quinlan, Robert Kramer was an active person who was free of sickness — until he was felled suddenly by a mysterious ailment. A versatile, athletic man, he had a political science degree from the University of Paris, and had held diverse jobs as a toy designer, a self-employed businessman, a design consultant for Polaroid and as the top regional salesman for a tool-and-die manufacturer.

His genial good looks brought him a little income on the side as a model — thousands of Boston subway riders saw his picture last summer in a Globe advertisement.

On Sept. 13, the Kramers drove to Gloucester for a weekend picnic with friends. While Robert was checking on his 16-foot sailboat in Gloucester harbor, he felt a sudden devastating pain in his head, an internal sledge-hammer blow so intense it brought him to his knees.

Dr. Joseph Arena, a neurosurgeon at the Salem Hospital, later established a diagnosis of massive subarachnoid cerebral hemorrhage—the rupture of a blood vessel in the brain and subsequent outpouring of blood — which caused such intense pressure inside Kramer's skull that it killed billions of brain cells. It was probably due to an aneurysm — a balloon-like defect in the wall of a cranial blood vessel, a sort of biological time-bomb that may have been present since birth.

By Sunday, Arena was convinced that his patient's brain had been destroyed by the hemorrhage. Two separate electroencephalograms, or brain-wave recordings, revealed no electrical activity in the brain at all. Kramer was without reflexes

DILEMMA, Page 7

Kristin Kramer in her Concord home with Kara, 3, one of two children she is raising alone since her husband's death. (Globe photo by Michael Cheers)

ROBERT KRAMER
. . . died in September

Disillusioned, says Rolling Stone

Patty was ready to reject SLA

United Press International

SAN FRANCISCO — Patricia Hearst was on the verge of rejecting the Symbionese Liberation Army when she was arrested, according to Rolling Stone.

The magazine, in an article being prepared for publication, says the FBI found her because of her arguments with fellow fugitives William and Emily Harris.

A go-between trying to mediate between the 21-year-old newspaper heiress and the Harrises was trailed by the FBI to the two San Francisco houses where

Patricia Hearst's former boyfriend, Steve Weed, although ignored by the jailed heiress and her family, hasn't forgotten. Stories, Page 18.

the long-sought fugitives were hiding out, the magazine reports in the second of two long articles about the case. A copy of the second article, due to reach the newsstands in about 10 days, was obtained by UPI yesterday.

Rolling Stone also says sports activist Jack Scott knew of Miss Hearst's disaffection with the SLA and was working with her father, Randolph A. Hearst, president of the San Francisco Examiner, to bring her home. It says Miss Hearst's mother, Catherine, told the FBI of two negotiations and they were ended.

"By late summer 1975, she (Patricia) had lost almost all "fascination for the intrigue of the underground," say authors Howard Kohn and David Weir. "Most of her time was spent away from the Harrises, who no longer seemed like the brother Teko and sister Yolende she once admired."

While hiding out in the San Francisco house where she was arrested, Miss Hearst came under the influence of her roommate, fellow fugitive Wendy Yoshimura, a militant feminist.

"When Wendy initially criticized the SLA as sexist, Patty had defended Cinque (original SLA leader Donald DeFreeze) and Teko (Harris)," Rolling Stone said. "But over the summer her opinion changed. She was beginning to view the SLA as a gun-toting gang heavy on machismo."

HEARST, Page 18

Taunton gets used to boiling its water

By Norm Lockman
Globe Staff

TAUNTON — For the last 27 days, the 43,000 residents of this southeastern Massachusetts city have been warned against drinking the community's water without first boiling it because the water is contaminated by coliform bacteria from an undetermined source.

Yesterday, while comparatively pure water poured down on the city in the form of rain, a fleet of National Guard trucks towed more of the squat, 400-gallom mobile tanks from filling points in neighboring towns to strategic locations here, where people could draw fresh water.

By midday, there were 26 of the water tanks spotted around Taunton, including one which was parked at the green in the center of the shopping district, a baleful reminder that drinking the water in Taunton could be harmful to one's health.

Since Sept. 30, city residents have been told to boil all drinking water from the tap. At least three surrounding towns have attached faucets to fire hydrants near the Taunton city limits to allow their neighbors to fill up jugs of drinkable water.

Taunton officials have added large amounts of extra chlorine to the water, but even that has not made the water safe. It has, however, loosened rust in water mains and caused discoloration of water in some sections of the city.

Samples are being taken daily from about 85 checkpoints in the city. All the samples have to pass a rigid test for three consecutive days before the water can again be declared safe. Last Wednesday and Thursday, the samples were clean, but on Friday, one sample, taken from a source near the center of town, had an unusually high coliform count and the drinking ban continued into the weekend.

Except for Mayor Theodore Aleixo, optimism is running a poor second to stoicism among the people in Taunton. Aleixo is hoping that yesterday's, today's and tomorrow's samples will be clean and that the water drinking ban can be lifted by Tuesday.

TAUNTON, Page 4

Found something?

If you're running an hour ahead of schedule today, it's probably because your friends set their clocks back one hour last night, and you didn't. Daylight Saving Time officially ended early this morning (2 a.m. to be exact) in the United States. Standard Time will remain in Arizona, Hawaii and part of Indents of Arizona, Hawaii and part of Indiana, however, won't enjoy the hour gain because, under local legislation,

Hub facing bankruptcy?

Can Boston go bankrupt? For answer see a report by Robert Lenzner, Page A-1.

The Pittsburgh Press

Sunday, June 15, 1975

Features • Food

• Food 2-15
• Gallup Poll 5
• Golden Weddings .. 16
• Veterans News 16

More Aid Awaits Vets Through Maze Of Red Tape

By RAY CROMLEY

WASHINGTON — Congress has voted substantial new benefits for veterans in the past two years.

The Senate and House are now considering additional assistance.

But a warning is in order. As a veteran, you will all too often run into red tape, inefficient or bumbling bureaucrats—and meet some private operators who will attempt to fleece you or your VA allowances.

Veterans attending colleges and universities complain they don't get checks on time. In one VA office, an investigation revealed a backlog of 5,400 checks.

Veterans with entitlement have been turned away from some VA hospitals during holidays by staff members confused as to the rules. But regulations say that even where admission eligibility is questionable, a veteran should be taken in for 72 hours to give time for observation and a proper decision.

A serious complaint has been made that when a VA hospital is near a medical school and the dean of that school is strong-willed, he sometimes influences admissions to the hospital, giving priority to patients expected to provide profitable clinical experience to his students.

The Committee on Veterans Affairs of the House of Representatives reported this year that "an average of 45 per cent of veterans applying for (medical) care are being rejected."

The committee says investigation reveals that some of those rejected are in serious need of care. The panel says it has noted "many instances where needy veterans have experienced long delays in being examined in connection with their applications for hospital admission . . ."

The eligibility laws are too complex for the veteran to understand and impossible for him to apply, according to a special survey ordered by the committee.

The committee goes on to explain that these laws "define his eligibility as varying with cause, diagnosis, severity and indicated treatment of the condition for which he is seeking care."

The physictan who sees this patient at the hospital cannot necessarily give him the care required for his condition, but "only that care for which the veteran is determined eligible."

Once in a VA hospital or clinic, however, the survey reports, "The majority of patients . . . receive health care of a quality which meets or exceeds the standards of nationally recognized professionals."

In a number of instances, the quality of care that is provided has been categorized as outstanding.

EDUCATIONAL BENEFITS: If you are an eligible veteran, and single, a law enacted in December, 1974, gives you $270 a month for going to a college or university full-time.

You will receive $388 if married with two children. Each additional child increases your payments $22.

You also have 10 years from your date of discharge to finish your government-aided schooling, instead of eight years as before.

If your eligibility expired on June 1, 1984, you have a grace period until June 1, 1976. Eligibility rules have not been changed.

If you have exhausted your 36 months of entitlement, assuming your service entitled you to 36 months, and have not finished work toward a standard undergraduate degree, you are allowed an additional nine months to achieve that goal.

If you are having troubles with your lessons, you may receive individual tutoring for 12 months instead of nine.

You may have an allocation of $60 a month for this purpose instead of $50. And you may draw a total of $720 instead of $450. This is in addition to your normal education allowance.

You are no longer barred from enrolling in courses teaching skills you already have.

Under the new law, you will receive payments for up to six months for refresher training and to study technological advances which have occurred in your field during your active military service.

You may now count toward your eligibility time a period of Reserve or National Guard active-duty training—usually six months—provided that training is followed by one year or more of full-time active duty.

The new law sets up a supplementa loan program under which you may b row up to $600 each academic year eligible.

This money will be available only veterans unable to secure adequate fu from other federal loan programs.

There is now no limitation on the nu ber of veteran-students the VA may sist through employment at VA offi during or between periods of school rollment.

The number of hours a veteran n put in under this arrangement is creased to 250 a semester and the ma mum a veteran may receive is rai from $250 to $650 a semester. Advan may be made under some circumstan

[For Ray Cromley's "Benefi for Veterans," a 96-page guid book with an eight-page suppl ment on recent benefit increase send $1 plus 25 cents for po age and handling in care of Th Pittsburgh Press, P. O. Box 48 Radio City Station, New York N. Y. 10019.]

Newspaper Enterprise Association

TOMORROW: Hospital Care Expand

Benefits For Veterans

Billions of dollars worth of educational, medical, financial and professional aid have been mandated by Congress for honorably discharged veterans.

Many are unaware of the special benefits available or how to claim them. This is the first of a series advising veterans, their families and survivors what they've got coming, where to seek it and how to cut bureaucratic red tape.

Wagons Roll To Blairsville's 150th

Press State Wire

BLAIRSVILLE — The Blairsville sesquicentennial celebration slips into high gear Saturday when the nearly 100-wagon Appalachian Wagon Train rolls into town.

The wagon train, which is to leave Somerset this morning, has grown from a 19-wagon effort in 1970 and now rates as the largest annual tour by covered wagons in the United States.

On arrival at Blairsville, the modern-day pioneers, dressed in the garb of their early ancestors, will participate in square dancing and other frontier pastimes.

The Armstrong County Mounted Sheriff's Posse will entertain the wagoneers and other spectators with a horsemanship exhibition.

Highlight of the community's year-long observance of its 150th birthday will be the presentation July 20-26 of the original play, "A Place of Consequence."

The play, co-authored by former Press historical writer George Swetnam and Mrs. Helen Snyder Smith, is the story of the lives of Sam and Mary "Polly" McAnulty, early settlers of Blairsville.

Gwynne Dean will play the part of Sam McAnulty and Cheryl Ralston has been cast as his wife.

Other sesquicentennial activities include:

July 12, Karate tournament; July 18, departure of the Tri County Pony, Horse and Mule Association trail ride for the Salem Crossroads Celebration; July 20, community-wide religious services; July 21, historical tours, celebrities auction, and firemen's carnival (tours and carnival will continue through the week.)

July 27, community-wide religious services and Towpath Exchange Arts and Crafts Fair; Nov. 11, Veterans Day parade; Dec. 31, burial of sesquicentennial time capsule.

The Appalachian Wagon Train, **which has over 500 men, women and children aboard, has grown steadily since the 1970 train was organized to help celebrate the 175th birthday of Somerset County.**

In 1971, the train grew to 30 wagons and 75 horseback "outriders" and covered the route from Ligonier to Bedford to help observe Bedford County's bicentennial.

Cumberland's Heritage Days drew the dedication of the 1972 train which started out as a 52-wagon cavalcade but, thanks to the interference of tropical storm Agnes, finished with only 19 wagons still in line.

In 1973 the Westmoreland County bicentennial was the attraction and 72 wagons with over 500 "pioneers" made the trek from Bakersville to Old Hanna's Town near Greenville.

Last year the Appalachian train, which at its inception was patterned closely after the annual "Daniel Boone Wagon Train" in Kentucky, drew 87 wagons and 250 outriders for the 55-mile trip from Bakersville to Meyersdale for that community's centennial observance.

This year, Donald "Boots" Miller is president of the train with Jerry Hershberger as wagonmaster and Jim Crosby as chief scout.

Using back country roads as much as possible, the wagon train will "fort up" tomorrow night at Fern Lodge, the summer estate of the C. B. Korns family, about nine miles from the starting point.

Tuesday, the train will be in Ligonier; Wednesday and Thursday nights at the Roy Dunlap Farm near Derry, and Friday at the Ed Deavers Farm near Blairsville.

Though their transportation is rustic and their horsepower is the real thing, the only "Indians" these pioneers are likely to see are Boy Scout Order of the Arrow dancers who will entertain at one of the evening campfires.

It's off for Blairsville with the Appalachian Wagon Train for the Bill Graff family.

Cheryl Ralston will portray Mary "Polly" McAnulty.

Gwynne Dean will be Sam McAnulty in play.

7 Years Later, 'Faceless GI' Makes Strides—And Can Smile

By GREGORY GORDON

LAGRANGE, Ill. (UPI) — Becky Bailey, age 4, bounced in her Uncle Leroy's lap, beaming proudly.

She hugged her "Uncle 'Rory," oblivious to the surgical patchwork that represents his face.

Traces of a smile formed where Leroy Bailey's mouth used to be.

The scene seemed to epitomize the transition Bailey has made in the seven years since the darkness came.

Cynicism and self-pity still linger. Bailey, 28, has much to be cynical about.

Rocket Victim In '68

His face was "shot off" by an enemy rocket in Vietnam nine days after he began his tour of duty in 1968. One doctor said his injury was "so severe it is almost unbelievable."

Bailey was sleeping in a tent with about 25 other American soldiers when the rocket hit. A piece of shrapnel flew into his mouth and lodged behind his nose and eyes, touching his brain.

Some said it was a miracle he survived. A medic apparently performed an emergency tracheotomy at the scene to allow him to keep breathing until the shell could be removed.

When Bailey regained consciousness at Walter Reed Hospital in Washington, he was blind and his face was gone. For what, Bailey wonders now, after the South Vietnamese government's surrender to the Communists.

"At the time, to be honest, I did not know why I was there," Bailey says. "Who wants to be killed? If we went there with the idea of knocking the North Vietnamese out of there, then okay. But you can't hold a territory by day and lose it by night. Why waste our time, destroy the American people . . . tear down this country?"

The Veterans Administration (VA) performed at least 36 operations on Bailey over a three-year period, trying to help him chew solid foods again so he wouldn't have to squirt liquid meals down his throat with a large syringe. Bailey said the blindness wasn't "much of a hangup." It was not being able to taste or chew his food that was unbearable.

The surgery brought little improvement. Bailey's brother, Eldon, with whom he lives, said, "It appears Leroy would have been in a mental ward," if he wasn't removed from the hospital in 1971.

Bailey began to seek help from a private plastic surgeon. But the VA told him his injury was not "service connected," and he would have to pay the bills himself.

President Nixon read about Bailey's plight in a column by Mike Royko of the Chicago Daily News in late 1973. Nixon told the head of the VA to "get cracking," and "get that boy in a hospital."

The VA readmitted Bailey, but specialists again offered little hope he would be able to chew. This time, the VA agreed to pay for any private help he might seek.

Nixon even invited Bailey to visit the White House. Before he could accept, Nixon had resigned as president. "I wonder how much Nixon got for stepping down. That's what I'd like to know," Bailey says today.

More than a year has passed, and Bailey has made great strides. His medical progress is encouraging.

"We have been gradually reconstructing him," said Dr. Charles Janda of Oakbrook, Ill., who performed three operations on Bailey in the last year.

For the first time in six years, Bailey found he could chop up soft cooked foods such as spaghetti and meatballs and drop them down the back of his tongue with a spoon.

Doctors cautioned him not to be too optimistic, but Bailey talks of the day when he will wear false teeth and eat and taste as a normal person.

Janda is frank. "We have a prosthedontist (a dental specialist who handles prosthetics) constructing an upper appliance to improve the appearance of his upper lip and to give better form to his nose," he said.

"I think the chances of his being able to wear false teeth are virtually zero. He's lost so much tissue and bone that there's nothing there. But we are always hoping we will be able to pull something off, that we can put something in there."

Even if Bailey can't be completely rehabilitated, the fact that someone is trying seems to have changed his outlook.

He often can be seen hurrying al the streets of Lagrange at a fast clip hind his seeing-eye dog, "Chip."

He has taken woodworking cla and recently finished constructin large toolbox complete with locks smoothly finished jewel box he rings out "Come All Ye Faithful."

He knits and sells handsome stock caps, doilies, and potholders. He i member of a blind bowling league. has a girl friend, a volunteer who him at Hines Veterans Hospital and him regularly. One day the two of th started from scratch and baked a c On another occasion, they went t movie.

'Loyalty Day' Parade

In early May, Bailey rode in "Loyalty Day" parade in nearby C tryside, Ill.

"If you could have seen him when saw him in Walter Reed (Hospital) see him today," Bailey's older bro Eldon said, "it would be like seeing different people."

Bailey listens and the trace smile forms.

Bailey's face is comprised of f eyeballs, a flat patch of skin where nose used to be and a series of grafts which gives him a semblanc cheeks. He is able to talk by combi the slight movement of his tongue his voicebox.

"I'm convinced it's by the grac God that I'm here," he said. "I n lost my faith in people. All the let that I got . . . I knew there were m good people."

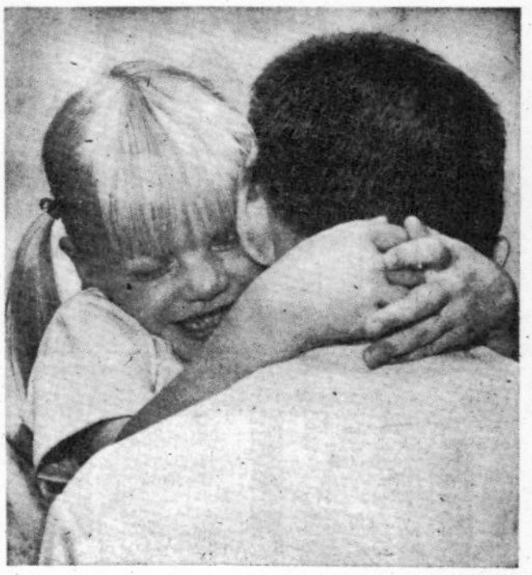

—UPI Telephoto

Faceless veteran Leroy Bailey gets a hug from niece Becky.

The New York Times

Founded in 1851

ADOLPH S. OCHS, *Publisher 1896-1935*
ARTHUR HAYS SULZBERGER, *Publisher 1935-1961*
ORVIL E. DRYFOOS, *Publisher 1961-1963*

ARTHUR OCHS SULZBERGER
Publisher

JOHN B. OAKES, *Editorial Page Editor*
A. H. RASKIN, *Assistant Editorial Page Editor*
A. M. ROSENTHAL, *Managing Editor*
SEYMOUR TOPPING, *Assistant Managing Editor*
MAX FRANKEL, *Sunday Editor*
JACK ROSENTHAL, *Assistant Sunday Editor*
•
CHARLOTTE CURTIS, *Associate Editor*
CLIFTON DANIEL, *Associate Editor*
TOM WICKER, *Associate Editor*

Rededication

On July 3, 1776, John Adams wrote to his wife: "I am well aware of the toil, and blood, and treasure, that it will cost us to maintain this Declaration, and support and defend these States. Yet, through all the gloom, I can see the rays of ravishing light and glory. . . ." One year later, as Adams walked about Philadelphia on the night of July 4 and saw lighted candles in thousands of windows, he said: "I think it was the most splendid illumination I ever saw."

At a time that calls for hard decisions rather than vain smugness, Americans might benefit from a recollection of how matters looked 199 years ago. Thomas Jefferson's historic document was not the ceremonial capstone on a victorious rebellion. At the time, Washington's forces were outnumbered four to one. When the roll was called as daylight faded on July 4, 1776, Pennsylvania and South Carolina voted "No"; Delaware was divided; and New York abstained.

Despite doubts and fears, the signing of the Declaration marked more than the birth of a nation. It was made memorable because, in Henry Steele Commager's words, "it set forth, with matchless eloquence, the basic philosophy of democracy and liberty."

• • •

The period that began with the drafting of the Declaration of Independence and ended twelve years later with the ratification of the Constitution represented an era of political genius rarely, if ever, equaled in the affairs of nations. A meaningful commemoration of the founders' courage calls for a rededication to their dreams.

It calls for a new determination to place equality and freedom above those material values which have corrupted the nation's public and private morality.

It calls for a recognition that concern for "the General Welfare" is not a radical distortion of the Government's function but the mandate of America's original charter.

It calls for a rediscovery of Jefferson's belief that there can be "no safe depository of the ultimate powers of the society but the people themselves; and if we think them not enlightened enough to exercise their control in a wholesome direction, the remedy is not to take it from them, but to inform their discretion by education."

It calls for a return to statesmanship that shares the contempt this nation's early leaders had for all tyrants.

• • •

These principles, spelled out in the Declaration of Independence, can flourish only in a society that, dedicated to remaining open, jealously protects the citizen's right to privacy and refuses to give to any sector, including the Government itself, powers that abridge freedom and curtail equality.

Bruce Catton wrote: "The central reality in this great act that brought a nation to its birth was the living, aspiring, struggling people. . . . It was a struggle, furthermore, that was fought out by people very much like ourselves; which is to say that they were often confused, usually divided in sentiment, and now and then rather badly discouraged about the possible outcome of the tremendous task they had undertaken."

In the end, what mattered then, as it matters now, was that enough of the people had more faith than fear, and were ready to fight for the new principles. The question, one year short of America's 200th anniversary, is whether faith still outweighs fear. The Fourth of July commemorates a Revolution that electrified the world with its message of unalienable rights. The challenge to Americans today is to reaffirm that Declaration by once again making of its faith and its spirit a living reality.

Ford vs. Solzhenitsyn

Does President Ford know the difference between détente and appeasement? This unlikely question arises in light of the news that President Ford decided not to receive Nobel laureate Aleksandr I. Solzhenitsyn because to do so would be inconsistent with détente. Thus one of the world's leading writers, the most eloquent contemporary Russian enemy of dictatorship, was snubbed by an occupant of the White House who finds time to receive eminent soccer players and lovely cotton queens.

Yet the Soviet Union has repeatedly indicated that it regards détente as perfectly compatible with the most exaggerated ideological warfare against the United States. Neither Leonid Brezhnev nor any other high Soviet official has ever been known to refuse to receive American Communist party leaders for fear of upsetting détente. Quite the contrary, major foreign Communists (including American) are normally given red-carpet treatment in Moscow.

Basically, détente seeks to avoid military confrontation and to reduce risk of World War III. It even heightens the importance of the peaceful competition of ideas and accentuates the desirability of free exchange of information—points the Russians have been resisting in the current negotiations over the European security treaty. Instead of rebuffing Mr. Solzhenitsyn, Mr. Ford ought to have welcomed him as the most noted spokesman for a subterranean but important element of Soviet public opinion.

In contrast to Mr. Ford's confusion was the refreshing example of détente at work given by the group of United States Senators who have just completed a trip to Moscow, during which they spoke at length with both Mr. Brezhnev and his veteran Politburo colleague Mikhail A. Suslov. There was evidently blunt speaking on both sides, with no effort to avoid what either the Soviet or American leaders regard as the truth in order to spare the others' sensibilities. Mr. Suslov, for example, complained about what he regarded as United States failures to honor its commitments in the fields of arms limitations and expanded trade; the Senators in turn emphasized American suspicions of Soviet intentions and the moral importance of the issue of free emigration.

The Soviet leaders' friendly attitude toward their Senatorial visitors suggests that the Kremlin chiefs respect most those partners in détente who face issues directly as the prelude to finding mutually satisfactory solutions. It is unlikely that Mr. Brezhnev in his heart has any more respect for appeasers than does Mr. Ford.

Playing Games

With an assist from illegally striking sanitationmen and other fractious city employes, Mayor Beame appears to have scored a victory in his stubborn fight for new taxing powers—but at heavy cost in civic disorder, continuing labor unrest and future fiscal uncertainty, to say nothing of the added burden of punitively high municipal levies.

The $330-million tax package that has been negotiated in Albany offers less than the Mayor had demanded. Nevertheless, it contains more than Senate Majority Leader Warren Anderson had been offering and substantially more than the $150 million in added taxes that had been the basis of the Mayor's "near-crisis" budget, adopted June 19.

If endorsed by the Legislature next week, the new taxes suggest a level of city spending that will mean fewer layoffs than the 40,000 projected by City Hall under its "crisis" budget. But it certainly will not mean no layoffs at all—if the Mayor and union leaders still cling to their rigorous rejection of a pay freeze or other more humane payroll economies. Even the "austerity" budget, envisioning more funds than are likely to be forthcoming, entailed dismissal of more than 13,000 city workers, including nearly 800 sanitationmen.

It is impossible to understand in these circumstances how the Mayor could promise to put all the sanitationmen back to work. No wonder laid-off employes in other departments are puzzled and angry. Are the sanitation workers to be rewarded for their breach of contract at the expense of other employes—and of the taxpayers?

The Mayor is playing cynical and dangerous games with the city and its employes. If he is going to extract still higher taxes from New York citizens in order to save some jobs, he has a duty to tell city workers and their intransigent union chiefs honestly and bluntly that there is still not enough money to save all jobs unless they, too, make some sacrifice through a pay freeze or share-the-work arrangement.

Don't Destroy—Restore!

In the decade since New York City first established its landmarks law and Landmarks Preservation Commission, after a long battle against real estate hostility and public indifference, much has changed.

The destruction of landmarks that was routine in cities everywhere is now opposed and often stopped by a public newly aware of the values of the urban heritage and increasingly sophisticated about the politics of protest. The kind of urban renewal that once turned historic neighborhoods into windfall profits with the backing of the authorities has been fought to a standstill, with a near-total reversal of policy and practice.

It is easy to be heartened—even in the face of problems as large and complex as New York's legal setbacks in the Morgan Library and Grand Central cases—by the overwhelming number of cities and towns engaged in active, visible restoration and reuse of fine old buildings. Cities are finding economic and environmental strengths in the recognition of their past.

A current wave of "recycling," with factories and warehouses turned into housing and handsome old public buildings refurbished that were slated for the bulldozer, has been spurred by inflation and the energy shortage. Preservation has become fashionably practical in terms of the greater costs in money and energy of demolition and new construction.

But every silver cloud has its lead lining. With the recession, construction costs are now dropping—a threat that preservationists, in their current euphoria, might overlook. If it becomes a better deal again to destroy rather than to save, the battles will start all over. Can those hard-won historic, esthetic and environmental values survive a return to conventional investment economics? Will cash flow triumph over community character? In preservation there are no victories; only spoils.

Slower Is Saner

Out of the unlamented long lines and "No Gas Today" signs at service stations last year came a genuine effort to economize fuel consumption by reducing speed limits on the highways. The 55-mile-an-hour regulation brought the realization to many drivers that going like sixty (or seventy) didn't make all that much of a time difference. It even became almost pleasant to return to what used to be called motoring, instead of instinctively stepping on the gas.

Gradually, old habits revived and speedometers inched upward. The Fourth of July weekend is a reminder that slower is safer and saner. New York State highway deaths this year showed a slight decline over last year; still, there have been 912 deaths in the first five months of 1975. This kind of slaughter on the highways can be sharply reduced in the next few days if motorists obey the rules of the road, do not consider the car ahead the enemy, and, especially, avoid speeding.

Letters to the Editor

On Solving Our City's Problems

To the Editor:

With constantly mounting unemployment in New York City, it seems to me more important than ever for the Federal Government to provide an adequate "public works" program similar to the W.P.A. instituted during the Roosevelt Administration. Legislation was recently enacted that will give New York City $26.5 million for recreation and summer jobs for our young people, but this is far from sufficient.

While I realize that many municipalities face a similar financial crisis, the situation here is unique. New York City is the gateway to America—with visitors to our country, both official and tourist, making this their first stop. Their impressions of New York may very well color their impressions of the entire country. It is clear that our city is, physically, in a deplorable condition. I strongly urge that the Federal Government make a special grant to the City of New York for a specific project, such as repairing and cleaning up our streets, restoring the beauty of our city and at the same time putting thousands of unemployed to work. The potholes throughout the city are a disgrace and a menace to public safety—both pedestrian and motorist. Judging by the slipshod work of those responsible, this important job could be done satisfactorily, with minimal training and adequate supervision, by those who desperately need employment.

I hope that other concerned citizens will join in pressing for action in this area, where the beneficial effects would be widespread.

EDITH A. LEHMAN
New York, June 20, 1975

•

To the Editor:

A major and ever-escalating expense in New York City's budget is pension costs. Admittedly pensions should be adequate; but they must also be realistic and reasonable. City pension systems came into being long before the advent of Social Security. The city should take a look at industry pension plans which incorporate Social Security into their benefit programs. It would be interesting to have the city publish the benefits of the various plans including contributions, if any, of the employes.

These pension benefits include generous medical and dental plans for life, even the payment of Medicare "B" premiums. In fact, it costs the taxpayers almost $5,000 per year per employe for pension, medical and dental expenses. In addition, it is quite common for those about to retire to be given extra "overtime" in the last year of employment, not necessarily productive, to give retirees even higher benefits. And many retire young enough to take on state or Federal jobs, thus perpetuating themselves on government payrolls while collecting pension from another agency.

More than 40,000 city employes and their families live outside the city which gives them their livelihood, thus depriving the city of needed revenue in the form of direct and indirect taxes, and the usual benefits derived by city business establishments generated by the purchasing power of these families. In the very sensitive Police Department 40 per cent, or 12,200 families, indicate their utter disregard for the good and welfare of the city by residing outside the five boroughs. In addition, those city employes who are nonresidents and whose employment began prior to January 1973 do not even pay New York City income tax. Instead they are subject to the nonresident earnings tax, which is only a small fraction of what the income tax would be. Can't you just hear them say: "Yes, New York City is a great city to work for, but we would not want to, nor do we, live here."

Of those who must be fired for budgetary reasons, it is suggested that Mayor Beame discharge these nonresidents first. Not only is this equitable, but it is even good politics, for they have no vote, by their own choice, in the City of New York.

SAMUEL S. LEVINE
Flushing, N. Y., June 23, 1975

•

To the Editor:

Your June 18 editorial "The Efficiency Option" criticizes the city for failing to prepare a program that would eliminate "fat" in the budget rather than people. But a definition of "fat" is needed, because in practice it means much more than a mere lack of efficiency. What has to be weeded out is the imbedded system of "legal corruption," by which I mean the payoff system of hiring and promoting, from handouts to relatives and buddies to large-scale empire building within various bureaucracies. In this way high salaries are paid out for mediocre or unnecessary personnel who are, of course, expected to repay their benefactor not in services rendered to the city but by providing loyalty for Mr. Big, who gave the goody (from tax money) and from whom further rewards may be expected.

An honest inspector general's office in this city, busy at all times with the process of auditing outlays of public funds of each agency, could unquestionably save hundreds of millions per annum. I am sure that such an agency, while eliminating some of our highest-paid freeloaders, time-servers and tax robbers, would make unnecessary the current meat-ax approach to saving money by the firing of thousands of lesser civil servants.

STANLEY W. PAGE
Professor of History, City College
New York, June 18, 1975

•

To the Editor:

I have just read in a Times news story that New York City police officers receive two days off with pay when they donate one pint of blood—costing New York City taxpayers $3-million annually. This is inexcusable. I know of no business organization that gives employes even an extra hour off for donating blood. In a time of fiscal crisis (or any time, for that matter), let's call on New York City's finest to cease this ridiculous practice.

RONALD FRIEDMAN
New York, June 16, 1975

'This Country Needs The Mind of Nixon'

To the Editor:

"A mind is a terrible thing to waste." That truism reminds me of Hjalmar Schacht, who was president of the former Reichsbank of Germany, and in a way of William Safire's recent column on Nixon.

Dr. Schacht was a financial genius. He invented the depreciated currency system of Germany in the late 1920's and early 1930's. He was not a Nazi, and at dinner I heard him make derogatory remarks about Hitler and the Nazis; I asked him whether he was not afraid to do this because of the possible dire consequences, but he was not, and nothing serious ever happened to him except he lost his position in the bank.

I spoke to Dr. Schacht in the period after the war, and he was unhappy because he was unemployed. He was so brilliant a financial mind that no private interest would employ him. I suggested he announce that he would never own stock in a company, only consult, and his great mind divorced from authority was again used and not wasted.

I have read Theodore White's "Breach of Faith," the articles in the New Yorker, and other articles about the evil doings of Mr. Nixon, but no matter how evil his acts are painted, no one has yet claimed that he does not have a great mind. I know of no one in our public life, or in any other country, with the mental capacity, planning ability and mental adroitness of Mr. Nixon, whom, incidentally, I have never met or seen except on television.

This country sorely needs the mind of Mr. Nixon, but, as in the case of Dr. Schacht, divorced from power. I do not agree with Safire, who tones down what Mr. Nixon did by comparing him with other Presidents. It is too much like saying, "Every politician does it."

I hope Mr. Nixon can be brought back to advise our Government, because it is a terrible thing to waste a mind—especially a great one.

IRVING ROSSI
New York, June 27, 1975

•

The Impossible Choices

To the Editor:

This is the time to remedy the major weakness in our election process, i.e., eliminate the stacked deck provided for our choice at primary and general elections. As indicated by the last Presidential election, we are sometimes offered an impossible choice of nominees for elective positions.

In order to give everyone a reason to vote, let's include a box to indicate non-selection for any position to be filled in the election. If the number of voters rejecting any choice for office exceeds 30 to 40 per cent, the selection process for such office must be repeated. This additional option would help prevent nonrepresentative nomination for office by a determined minority and refute the argument of nonvoters that their lack of choice is the reason for their failure to participate in the election process.

This additional choice will offer everyone an opportunity to influence the outcome of elections and make these actions more truly responsive and representative of the will of the people.

HENRY M. SAFFREN
Randolph, N.J. June 25, 1975

The New York Times Company
229 West 43d St., N.Y. 10036
(212) 556-1234

ARTHUR OCHS SULZBERGER
Chairman and President
HARDING F. BANCROFT, *Vice Chairman*
•
JAMES C. GOODALE, *Executive Vice President*
SYDNEY GRUSON, *Executive Vice President*
WALTER MATTSON, *Executive Vice President*
•
JOHN McCABE, *Senior Vice President*
JOHN MORTIMER, *Senior Vice President*
JOHN D. POMFRET, *Senior Vice President*
•
CHARLES B. BRAKEFIELD, *Vice President*
BENJAMIN HANDELMAN, *Vice President*
JOHN R. HARRISON, *Vice President*
FRED D. THOMPSON, *Vice President*
•
MICHAEL E. RYAN, *Secretary*
RALPH BOWMAN, *Treasurer*

World Hunger: The 'False' Hope

To the Editor:

Harold Geneen would no doubt grimace painfully if I were to suggest that poverty could be solved by simply printing more money and distributing it to poor people. As an educated businessman, he would know that such a suggestion is ludicrous; printed money has to be backed by gold, silver or some other tangible material. Yet, he proposes [Op-Ed June 16] an equally nonsensical solution to the problem of world hunger—micro-organism "printing presses" producing an abundant supply of food—without consideration of the "backing" necessary for food production.

Janice Stapleton

Besides the raw material necessary to produce food (nitrogen, phosphorous, potassium, etc.) and the expensive trace minerals necessary for high-quality protein, food production requires energy, a commodity in increasingly short supply. Preliminary results indicate that the type of food production Mr. Geneen refers to would require even greater amounts of energy than we are now utilizing for food production and distribution.

The American food system requires six calories of energy to put a calorie of food on the table. By contrast, a so-called "primitive" agricultural system could produce over one hundred calories of food with the same six calories of input. To feed the whole world with an energy-intensive type of food system such as ours would require almost all the energy currently being used for all purposes around the globe.

It is interesting to note that the country which has made the most dramatic strides in increasing food production has utilized a system that would most likely be unacceptable to a man of Mr. Geneen's position. The People's Republic of China, with a population four times that of the United States and with only two-thirds of the arable land, is rapidly approaching the point of self-sufficiency, chiefly through the use of traditional agricultural practices coordinated through a tightly controlled and well-organized national system. While the Chinese system is not without its inherent dangers, Mr. Geneen's contention that our only hope lies in space-age technology is false.

DAVID SAROKIN
Brooklyn, June 17, 1975

•

Of Pupils, Teachers And 'a Little Love'

To the Editor:

It is unfortunate when mellifluous phrases and beautiful style becloud an issue. It is serious when that issue happens to be as important as the education of youngsters growing from childhood into adolescence. It is unconscionable when such obfuscation is created by a practicing educator.

James P. Jacob, in his June 14 Op-Ed article, "The Awkward Age," carefully and correctly emphasizes the complex nature of middle school children, the pressing need for good teaching based on high standards of pupil work and the critical importance of proper adult guidance for obtaining pupil growth.

But how can he allow teaching to take place without an emphasis on good human relationships—rapport (or love)—between pupil and teacher? The young person, caught on the tightrope between childhood dependence and adult self-dependence, needs the kind of support that comes from emotional ties to others.

Yet Mr. Jacob is ready to "swap" work for love. He also throws in "growth" as part of his trade-off. As Mr. Jacob's value system is described, love is at the bottom of the scale when, in reality, it should be somewhere at the top for this age group.

School violence was mentioned in the same issue of The Times as being the norm in the nation's schools. Sydney Cooper, the Board of Education's director of New York City School Safety, has told me that violence exists to a greater degree at the middle school-junior high school level in New York City than at any other level.

If that is so, children at this level need all the love and understanding that can be provided by a supportive staff of sensitive teachers and behavior and guidance counselors who are experienced in working with them.

Billie Holliday, in "Lady Sings the Blues," said, "You've got to have something to eat and a little love in your life before you can hold still for any damn body's sermon on how to behave."

JACK BLOOMFIELD
President
Junior High School Principals Assn.
Staten Island, N.Y., June 18, 1975

In making up this editorial page of the *New York Times,* the editor has made several decisions worth analyzing.

First, he has chosen to separate the editorials from the letters by using a column rule. Then, in placing his editorials, he has elected to break one editorial ("Ford vs. Solzhenitsyn") over two columns—thereby creating a dead-end of type at the top of column 2. He could have avoided this dead-end by running "Playing Games" at the bottom of column one and moving "Ford vs. Solzhenitsyn" to the top of column two. However, that would have put two identically sized heads ("Rededication" and "Ford vs. Solzhenitsyn") side by side—thus tombstoning the heads. This editor evidently preferred the dead end to the tombstoning.

In placing his letters, the editor has grouped those concerning the city's problems at the top of the column, separating them by solid bullets (heavy dots). At the end of this group, he has left white space to tell the reader that the other letters are on other subjects.

Also worth noting is the little line drawing in the outside column. This lightens the page—and helps to rout a phrase long associated with this particular newspaper, "The good gray *Times.*"

EXERCISES

Directions: In doing the exercises below, submit the actual newspaper pages with your answers.

1. Select a front page from a large metropolitan daily and evaluate its make-up.
2. Choose four headlines from four different newspapers and discuss each headline from the standpoint of physical composition and over-all effectivness in the total make-up of the page.
3. Discuss the make-up of any page containing a panel.
4. From a newspaper of your choice, compare the front page and the first sports page. Watch especially for the size of head and length of treatment given local athletic contests as compared with those of the international story.
5. Discuss the make-up of any split page (sometimes called the break page) of your local newspaper.
6. Select any newspaper page having at least four pictures, and discuss the over-all effectiveness of the pictures in the layout.

7. Discuss any page that employs weighted make-up.
8. Find an especially appealing arrangement of side-by-side headlines and explain the reasons for your choice.
9. Discuss any page that has perfect-balance make-up.
10. Find three examples of stories where you feel the headline is not proportionate to the value of the story as news. (You may feel that the story deserves a larger or a smaller headline.)

FOR FURTHER READING

Arnold, Edmund C. *Modern Newspaper Design.* New York: Harper, 1969.

Burt, Cyril. *A Psychological Study of Typography.* London: Cambridge University Press, 1959.

Butler, Kenneth. *Practical Handbook on Headline Design in Publication Layout.* Mendota, Ill.: Butler Typo-Design Research Center, 1954.

Croy, Peter. *Graphic Design and Reproduction Technique.* New York: Hastings House, Publishers, 1968.

Dair, Carl. *Design with Type.* Toronto: University of Toronto Press, 1967.

Hohenberg, John. *The New Front Page.* New York: Columbia University Press, 1966.

Johnson, Alfred Forbes, *Type Designs: Their History and Development.* London: Grafton Publishing, 1959.

Paterson, D. G., and M. A. Tinker. *How To Make Type Readable.* New York: Harper, 1940.

Ruder, Emil. *Typography: A Manual of Design.* New York: Hastings House, Publishers, 1970.

Turnbull, Arthur T., and Russell H. Baird. *The Graphics of Communication.* New York: Holt, 1964.

★ 9 ★

What Is Editorial Policy?
Conditions Affecting Editorial
  Policy
Finances
Responsibilities of the Press
  Responsibility to Society
  Responsibility to Individuals
  Responsibility to Government
The Tone of the Paper
Demands of the Readers
Political Outlook

Business Considerations
Religious Considerations
Ethnic and Social Considerations
Patriotic Considerations
Personal and Group Consider-
  ations
Whims of the Editor
Sectionalism
Taboo Subjects
The Publisher's Role in the Com-
  munity
Crusades
Effect of Editorial Policy on the
  Editorial and the Column
  The Editorial
  The Column

Editorial Policy

WHAT IS EDITORIAL POLICY?

The habitual reader soon comes to know his newspaper as thoroughly as he knows a close associate. He learns to recognize the kind of stories used, the stylistic practices employed, and the attitude of the paper on all the prominent questions of the day. He also discerns a pattern in the use of headlines, banner lines, punctuation, and typography; and he sees a story-to-story and a day-to-day similarity in the presentation of news. Further, he is quick to react to any change in appearance—such as a new family of type in the nameplate—just as he would note a new suit in the wardrobe of a friend. Eventually this reader tends to think of the newspaper as a personality, as a collection of writings emanating from a single mind rather than from many minds; and he quotes his newspaper as if it were a person, approving or reproving it as he would a member of his family.

This consistency in outlook and in publishing practices which the reader perceives arises from a totality of thought and practices termed "editorial policy." Editorial policy is the course a newspaper elects to follow as it answers the two all-important questions: "What shall we print?" and "How shall we print?" It is composed of the practices, rules, and principles which the newspaper sets as a guide for itself in doing its work. Editorial policy, therefore, governs every phase of the newspaper from the kind of news it seeks to the size of type it uses in printing. The editorial policy of the conservative daily makes it reject the story of a gangster's love affair; the editorial policy of the tabloid causes it to give the story a big play. The editorial policy of the Southern daily rejects the Associated Press story that portrays the Southern cotton industry in an unfavorable light; the editorial policy of the New England daily displays the story prominently in a main section. The editorial policy of one metropolitan paper permits an acid denunciation of a political fraud; the editorial policy of another restricts the writer to dignified phraseology in handling the same story.

Rarely are the most important phases of editorial policy expressed in writing; they are simply understood. Consequently, the newspaperman comes to know by experience, rather than by directive, the editorial policy of his paper. Thus, after working for a relatively short time on a given paper, the reporter can determine almost immediately the importance of a story; the feature editor can evaluate a proposed comic strip at a glance; and the copy editor can write a head consistent with the others in his paper. Each has learned to sense the pattern of editorial policy. The smaller details of editorial policy, however, are recorded in the stylebook. There the newcomer may learn the paper's policy regarding writing stories and preparing them for print.[1]

The editorial policy of a particular paper is established when the paper is founded, and it is maintained or changed over the years as a result of editorial conferences. These conferences, as one might assume, are gatherings of publisher and top editors to discuss the day's news, the successes and the failures of recent editions, the editorial view to be taken on leading questions, and means of increasing circulation. Usually the conference is held just before the beginning of the working day so that the various editors may instruct their subordinates accordingly.

The conferees discuss the day's news to determine the coverage to be given the various stories and the slant to be taken. (Even the so-called "impartial" papers discuss slant because there can be no pure impartiality in handling most stories.) The successes and the failures of the recent editions are discussed with a view to improving the paper. (One phase of this discussion is the invariable comparison with rival papers.) The editorial view must be discussed so that the portrayal of news may be consistent with the editorials; and means of increasing circulation are discussed for the simple reason that financial condition is the all-important consideration of the newspaper.

CONDITIONS AFFECTING EDITORIAL POLICY

The editorial policy of most newspapers is affected by the 15 conditions now to be discussed. Although some of these conditions are far more signifi-

---

[1] See Appendix I, "The Stylebook."

cant than others, all usually have some bearing on the choice of material for the paper and on the manner in which it is presented.

These conditions are essentially guideposts or warning signs—whichever may be the case in the particular instance—which lie in the path of the newspaper as it does its work. They are entities, therefore, which the newspaper must see as the building engineer sees firm ground and marshy ground, rock deposits and shale deposits, hills and valleys. The newspaper, in brief, like the building engineer, must work in terms of conditions which it neither has created nor can control.

In reviewing these conditions, the student of journalism must beware of oversimplification. He must realize that there is no single formula for editorial policy everywhere because the exact strength of the conditions varies from paper to paper and from day to day. In fact, one can safely say that no two papers have completely similar editorial policies because no two papers are affected in the same manner by these 15 conditions.

The 15 conditions interact with each each other, and the response to any one of them may affect the options available for dealing with the others. Each will be examined in some detail. But it is useful to have them listed first, for over-all impression:

Finances
Responsibilities of the press (to society, to individuals, to government)
The tone of the paper
Demands of the readers
Political outlook
Business considerations
Religious considerations
Ethnic and social considerations
Patriotic considerations
Personal and group considerations
Whims of the editor
Sectionalism
Taboo subjects
The publisher's role in the community
Crusades

FINANCES

The dominant influence on editorial policy is finances. The newspaper is ever the business proposition; it must make money or retire. Such papers as New York's *Herald-Tribune* and the *Chicago Sun* were operated over long periods of financial loss, but they were carried in the vain hope that eventually they would become solvent.[2]

---

[2] Some newspapers can continue over long periods of financial loss because they are part of a chain. Even though losing money in their individual operation, they may be of value to the chain and the other papers in it.

Because the newspaper must be financially profitable, the publisher usually demands that editorial policy be directed primarily toward increasing circulation. The coverage of news must be all-inclusive, a constant attempt to satisfy readers of all levels must be made, and new elements of appeal must always be sought. The publisher may make further demands upon his editors. He may call upon them to justify an established editorial practice, or he may insist that they adopt new features which he thinks will increase circulation. The financial consideration is especially important in the choice of syndicated features (columns, puzzles, comics, and the like) because they are chosen primarily for their ability to increase circulation.

So serious is the financial question that many papers hold regularly scheduled three-way conferences of publisher, business manager, and top editor to discuss the general condition of the paper. Each hears the reports and the opinions of the others in an attempt to increase revenue and reduce expenses through co-operative efforts.

The importance of the financial consideration may be summarized by saying that, generally speaking, every line of type and every feature must be pointed toward increasing the appeal of the paper. Old readers must be held and new readers must be gained, for circulation is the lifeblood of the newspaper.

RESPONSIBILITIES OF THE PRESS

Editorial policy is deeply influenced by the newspaper's conception of its responsibilities to (a) society, (b) individuals, and (c) government. According to its conception of these responsibilities, the newspaper varies in its view of what is to be printed and how it is to be printed. In fact, the view taken of these responsibilities gives rise to the most striking differences between newspapers. Thus, as a given newspaper formulates its attitude toward these three responsibilities, a major influence on editorial policy is determined.

Responsibility to Society

The responsibility of the press to society is tremendous, for the newspaper can be an impressively good or a horribly bad influence on the reading public. The newspaper that runs an exposé of a political swindle, that constantly sets a tone of calm rationality on important issues, that treats unsavory scandal merely as a news item is working a good influence on society. The newspaper that constantly plays up stories of crime, divorce, and sexual exploits, that puts a romantic note on the activities of gunmen and robbers, that runs stories filled with malicious innuendo is working a bad influence on society. These are the extremes; between them are gradations of good and bad.

An important aspect of the newspaper's responsibility to society concerns the interpretations of news, especially stories of great import.

Two long-running stories of the mid-1970s illustrate the point—the Vietnam involvement and the Watergate break-in.

In treating the Vietnam involvement, most newspapers abrogated their responsibility in the early stages by failing to interpret the story properly. Fundamentally, they failed to expose the implications of the whole situation because they did not study the facts in sufficient depth. Although these same newspapers, in retrospect, charged the Federal government with deception, the conclusion stands that harder digging and more intensive interpretation would have exposed the conditions that eventually surfaced.

In the instance of Watergate, many newspapers displayed an irresponsibility by demanding President President Nixon's impeachment before pertinent facts were demonstrated or, more important, before any definition of impeachable conduct was formulated. Hence they contributed to the unsound emotional climate that pervaded the country.

Another facet of the responsibility of the newspaper to society is this: making decisions can be troublesome. What, for instance, should a newspaper do with rumor? To illustrate: during the heated arguments over President Nixon's possible impeachment, rumors circulated that the President had cracked emotionally and was under psychiatric care. Under the circumstances could a paper serve society better by discussing the rumor, by attempting to discredit it, or by ignoring it?

Newspapers are also baffled about printing pessimistic stories of diseases. Should the public be told the discouraging facts about research in incurable diseases, or is society better served by printing only the good news? The editor's answer to these questions hangs in part upon another: What are the other media going to do? If one paper prints a story or a news broadcast carries it, a paper frequently has no alternative. It must run the story or leave some readers wondering why.

A final thorny problem for newspapers in settling on their responsibility to society arises with the manner in which the paper imparts information likely to constitute negative lessons. Among such facts are the names of poisons used in suicides, quack procedures in abortions, techniques of burglars, and methods of evading the law. Journalists can often agree that some facts should clearly be omitted, that others may be mentioned without elaboration, and that others can be treated fully without serious damage. But since there is no standard guide for every situation, decisions about this phase of the responsibility to society are certain to vary.

Responsibility to Individuals

The responsibility of the press to individuals should be divided into (1) the responsibility to public figures and (2) the responsibility to the obscure man.

The responsibility to public figures is a far more troublesome question than a first glance indicates. Editors disagree sharply on such questions as: Is the public figure entitled to any privacy? When should his wishes be respected concerning withholding stories? Should he be given special treatment in print, for example by always including his official title? If the public figure is a high government official, he or his staff may sometimes pressure the newspapers, but generally the editor decides on the treatment to be given. Nevertheless, as any news story about a public figure arises, some decision must be made regarding the use of the story and the slant to be taken. Naturally, this decision varies from paper to paper. Among the stories on which newspapers differ are those which tell of questionable activities of the public figure's relatives (as when a senator's brother-in-law figures in a tavern brawl); unfavorable opinions of the public figure as voiced by those who deal with him (as when a service-station owner from the governor's home town says that the governor is a tightwad who always made unreasonable demands on tire guarantees); and off-guard moments of the individual himself (the mayor is heard raising his voice to his wife as the couple enter the official car at the City Hall).

The responsibility to the obscure man, or the figure who is newsworthy for the first (and probably the last) time in his life, rests on the use of any and all data in such stories as cases of criminal attack, juvenile delinquencies, and serious embarrassments. Here are the facts of three stories, followed by questions which the editor must answer.

1. A 16-year-old girl baby sitter has been criminally assaulted by an intruder. The intruder has stolen nothing, and there is relatively little chance that the police will ever detect him. Should the story be used? If used, what details should be included? What names should be printed?
2. A first offender in juvenile court is the 13-year-old son of a small business man. The boy has fallen into bad company and has been arrested for shoplifting in a department store. All concerned are agreed that the boy is not likely to stray again. Should the local paper in this town of 18,000 do anything at all with the story? If so, what?
3. A local clergyman has been forced by an armed depraved intruder to remove all his clothing, to shout obscenities over the telephone, and to prepare food for the intruder. What parts, if any, of this story should be used?

The editor's answers to these questions will show his conception of his responsibilities to the obscure man, and thus they will show also a field in which newspapers may differ sharply.

Responsibility to Government

The responsibility of the press to government is difficult to analyze because of the vagueness of the entire question. To draw the line between allegiance to one's nation and freedom of speech is a very difficult task. Where one paper feels justified in revealing information or in criticizing the government, another may withhold a story because, in the opinion of its editor, the welfare of the nation is involved.

Some specific examples can illustrate the problem.

Many newspapermen knew of the U-2 flights over the Soviet Union in the 1950s before the downing of one of these high-flying planes made the fact common knowledge.

Several Washington journalists had considerable information about the Bay of Pigs invasion before it became a reality.

A small group of newspapers had some of the most important facts detailed in the Pentagon Papers before the *New York Times* and the *Washington Post* broke the story on June 13, 1971.

In 1973, several newspapers obtained classified information involving SALT (Strategic Arms Limitation Treaty) negotiations. Some of the newspapers did nothing with the story because of national-interest considerations. Others released some of the most important facts. Hence different interpretations were made regarding responsibility to government.

In early 1974, a State Department employee leaked information to a few newspapermen about a very sensitive treaty being negotiated by Secretary of State Henry Kissinger. If the papers having this information had printed it, international relations could well have suffered badly. In this instance, every editor withheld the story until after the treaty was signed because each saw clearly the issue of national interest.

In 1975, few newspapers even delayed publishing stories about the connection between the Central Intelligence Agency and the Hughes companies' ocean salvage effort on a Soviet nuclear submarine. Their reasoning was that preserving secrecy in this instance was impossible, however much national interest may have been affected.

The subject of responsibility to government has recently become especially troublesome because of a growing tendency to challenge the tenets upon which our government is built, the approach to handling our civic affairs (police activity, for an instance), and the whole conduct of our legal system. Many radically inclined groups have openly attacked ideas and procedures heretofore considered sacrosanct; and they have vigorously repudiated such practices as the salute to the flag, the honoring of heroes, and the celebration of patriotic holidays. Using such phrases as "the establishment" and "government by legal tyranny," they have called for serious changes—to be effected by violent means if necessary. How does a responsible newspaper deal with stories of this kind?

In addition, a spate of political scandals in high national circles between 1973 and 1975 deepened an already strong suspicion about honesty in government.[3] This, in turn, has lowered esteem for our most important officeholders and institutions, thereby causing many citizens to wonder about the efficacy of our political system.

This whole situation has posed a rather serious question for editors. They must re-assess their responsibility, if they recognize any, to uphold the values

[3] A Harris Poll study published in November 1973 revealed that only 22.8% of the population believe officeholders are honest.

of the "American way of life." They have been forced, in short, to accept the philosophy and the motives of the dissenters and the disquieted—either by open declaration or by silent acquiescence—or to "stand up and be counted" in opposition.

THE TONE OF THE PAPER

When a newspaper is established, its founders attempt to define the predominant atmosphere or tone of the paper; that is, they decide on the adjective which they want the public to associate with their paper. Thus, the paper becomes radical, belligerent, brash, conservative, scholarly, crusading, hairshirt, or whatever else the founders may desire; and it assumes a position in the gamut that runs from ultraconservatism to extreme sensationalism, or yellow journalism as it is still frequently called. Once this tone has been decided, editorial policy must be so constructed as to obtain and retain it.

Although tone is closely related to several other conditions affecting editorial policy, it is interwoven especially with the responsibilities discussed above. In fact, tone and responsibilities are really inseparable because tone results largely from the paper's view of its responsibilities.

The tone of the paper is affected by (1) the kind of stories used, (2) the manner in which the stories are written, (3) the approach or treatment of the subject, and (4) the makeup of the paper.

To see how the kind of story used affects tone, we need only examine the atmosphere of the tabloid with its sensational and risqué stories as compared with the tone of the conservative paper where such stories are conspicuously absent. The stories in the tabloid often generate the air of a cheap gossip while the material in the conservative paper projects refinement and restraint.

To see how differences in treatment of subject affect tone, only a perusal of the same story as handled by several newspapers is necessary. For example, when the governor of Maryland and his wife separated a few years ago, the traditional or conservative newspapers gave the story a restrained, dignified treatment. More sensational papers spelled out numerous details behind the story—for example, the wife's refusal to move out of the official mansion, the snide remarks made by citizens of the state, little sidelights on the governor's new love. In each instance, of course, the treatment of the story contributed to an over-all atmosphere or tone of the newspaper.

To see how make-up affects tone, a simple comparison should once again be made. Place a conservative paper such as the *New York Times,* the Baltimore *Sun,* or the Dallas *News* against a typical Hearst paper. The Hearst paper makes great use of the streamer or banner, it uses many large heads, and it carries numerous large pictures. The result is that tone is profoundly affected.

Another important phase of tone is the art (pictures) that the paper uses. Readers soon notice that newspapers vary sharply in amount of pictures used. The tabloid usually makes a heavy use of pictures, covering the two outside and the two center pages completely and placing cuts generously elsewhere. The conservative paper habitually uses much less art per line of print. But in kind of pictures used, the difference between papers is more pronounced. The ultraconservative paper, on the one hand, uses only the most conventional of art. There are the usual photographers' portraits of people in the news, the customary pictures of dignitaries, and the conventional shots of important events. At the opposite extreme is the tabloid with its pictures of the slain gangster lying in his coffin, the pretty girl displaying her well-curved legs, and the aggrieved wife exhibiting her blackened eye in the police court. These obviously are the extremes. The position between these extremes elected by the newspaper shows something of the tone it desires.

A further thought on tone and pictures used is this: selecting and handling pictures can be quite difficult. In early 1974, for instance, there was an outbreak of "streaking" (running nude) on college campuses. Readers, naturally, wanted pictures and hence newspapers had to comply. As a consequence, picture editors had to decide just how much each picture should reveal. Sometimes they were cropped; other times they were blurred or retouched in some places; other times they showed only rear views of males; and on some few occasions, they left nothing to the imagination. As was to be expected, the tabloids showed most, the conservative papers least.

DEMANDS OF THE READERS

Since any successful business handles the merchandise its customers want, editorial policy is influenced by the readers' demands.[4]

Newspapers try to learn what readers want by many methods. One is to study the contents and the practices of the most successful newspapers with a view to establishing a correlation with circulation. (A rather interesting result of such a study is the fact that many people buy a newspaper largely because of its comics.)

Another method is to send investigators from door to door asking subscribers to name the features they like best and the ones they read regularly. The great disadvantage of this procedure is that readers give false answers. A man attempting to appear intellectual, will declare that he always reads every editorial—actually, he may rarely read one. A woman will deny reading the celebrity gossip column—in reality, she devours it.

A third method is the "pull out." This is simply the procedure of removing a feature without notice, and then keeping an account of telephone calls and letters protesting or inquiring. (This method should be used cautiously with the comics. When a favorite comic strip failed to appear in a Chicago newspaper one Sunday, the switchboard was jammed all day.)

Over the past decade or more, the procedure of having professional orga-

---

[4] For further insight into readers' demands, see "Mass Audience" in Chapter 2.

nizations analyze reader interest has increased. These organizations have evolved scientific approaches similar to those of such professional political and social analysts as the Gallup and Harris polls. Their findings have proved to be quite sound, especially in areas where newspapers serve a widely diverse readership.

Editors and publishers also try to analyze reader demands by checking the letters to the editor and by having staff members conduct casual interviews with fellow passengers on buses, patrons in restaurants, and others from whom a ready opinion is available.

Despite the newspaper's unceasing attempt to determine reader demands, the subject remains fairly enigmatic. There always seem to be present certain shifting conditions that make a final analysis impossible. A feature, for instance, such as a column, that is highly popular for a prolonged period may suddenly sag, and an approach, such as a sentimental treatment of a story, that pleases readers in one instance may fail in the next.

This enigmatic nature of readers' demands can be illustrated pointedly with a single condition. Currently, sales of Sunday newspapers have dipped seriously in many sections of our nation. In the Chicago area, for example, better than a half million people read no Sunday paper whatever. What is the reason? Thus far, only personal opinion and theory have provided answers.[5]

Because of the imponderables of this question, many newspapermen, especially the old timers, rely on a continued use of material that has proven successful—and on their own innate judgment.

POLITICAL OUTLOOK

Because many of the questions in the news must be presented and interpreted in terms of a political philosophy, the newspaper feels the inescapable impact of political considerations on its editorial policy.

This political outlook can assume, of course, a variety of forms. On the one hand is the independent paper which usually weighs every election and every issue very carefully before giving its restrained, qualified support. On the other hand is the newspaper that is violently in favor of one political party. Its editorials screech censure or praise and its headlines and stories ring loudly for its candidate. For the opponent, however good he may be, there is routinely the screaming, denunciatory banner and the acid comment concerning his shortcomings. Between these extremes are all shades of support and opposition.

Furthermore, many newspapers line up with political parties in order to survive. A paper supporting Republicans in many Southern cities would once have found hard going, just as a pro-Democratic paper would have difficulty in many a New England town.

Editorial policy is influenced most directly by political outlook when a

---

[5] This matter is discussed under "Mass Audience" in Chapter 2.

newspaper openly admits its affiliation with a political group. It is influenced least when a paper seriously attempts to be impartial in all political questions. Yet, however great or small the influence, it is always present.

BUSINESS CONSIDERATIONS

Although the fact is not always to be condoned, editorial policy is sometimes affected by the firms or the individuals to whom the paper sells advertising. The publisher and his top editors, for purely practical reasons, make certain that the department store and other large advertisers are not treated adversely. Hence accidents and similar news items that break within a specific place may never make the paper. The same paper may run a story simply because the big advertiser asks. In this category are stories of new products, buildings to be erected, and similar items reflecting favorably on the advertiser.[6]

Certain qualifications, however, must be placed on the concept of the newspaper favoring advertisers. One is that the very large newspaper—such as the *New York Times,* the Chicago *Tribune,* and the *Milwaukee Sentinel*—need not fear advertisers' reprisals because the advertisers need the newspaper at least as much as the paper needs their revenue. The large department store, for example, depends heavily upon newspaper advertising to attract customers. Therefore, it cannot withhold ads—however much it may desire. Another qualification is that ads are frequently handled by an agency that makes every decision regarding the ad. Hence the decision to insert or withhold an ad may not rest with the advertiser unless he takes extraordinary action. A third qualification is that only the small newspaper is likely to suffer severely from the loss of a single ad; the large paper, with its proportionately larger budget and circulation, can absorb a loss more easily even when substantial money is involved.

A more serious instance of business considerations influencing editorial policy occurs when a specific commercial interest may gain control of a paper. On January 2, 1975, for example, the editor and several of his immediate assistants resigned from the Wilmington (Delaware) *Morning News* and *Evening Journal.* They charged that the publisher and Board of Directors were constantly insisting on a favorable treatment of the du Pont family and interests— even when the treatment was not merited. (The du Pont interests held the controlling block of stock in the papers.)

---

[6] The idea that advertisers seriously affect editorial policy was given wide popular currency in the early part of the present century by the muckraking writers. Since that time, the idea has persisted, despite the qualifications that must be imposed.

RELIGIOUS CONSIDERATIONS

Whenever any unfavorable comment might be made concerning a religious organization or a clergyman, the reporter sees a rapidly flashing caution light. Where he misses the light, the copy editor sees it. A large segment of the churchgoing public, newspapers have found to their sorrow, will tolerate no unfavorable criticism of their church, however sound the criticism may be. People who, on other occasions, are fair and objective close their minds to adverse comment about their religion.

As a result, a strong influence often comes to play on the source of news. This influence usually varies according to the size of the particular organization involved. When, for example, Chicago police raided a local gambling den and arrested a prominent clergyman among 18 patrons, only one paper in the city decided to use the story. As it called to check facts, it was advised to "beware the well-known weight of the church." The paper persisted, however, and when the story appeared in print, the members of the organization were told by their clergymen to refrain from buying the paper because of its "anti" sentiments. Thus, a newspaper was brought to the realization that a reporter is not free to report facts without reprisal where religion is concerned.

The influence of religion also works in another direction; it causes many stories to be printed that are not especially newsworthy. The small-town daily, for example, reserves space for religious news in order to retain the favor of the various denominations. This principle also functions in the large city where the newspaper, to prove its impartiality, includes stories of all large groups.

Another influence of religion upon editorial policy lies in the pressure exerted by organizations. Committees for the observance of Good Friday, for better interfaith relations, and for similar causes constantly bear on editorial policy. They want more publicity for their work; they object to a story that was printed; or they want the paper to take a particular editorial stand. Sometimes these organizations have an uphill battle, but usually they are relentless in their struggle.

ETHNIC AND SOCIAL CONSIDERATIONS

When a paper runs a story that is distasteful to a large racial or social group, it faces trouble. The protest may come from an organized group or from scattered citizens, and it may be concerted or sporadic. But it is usually strong, and it invariably makes itself felt to some degree. When the representatives of the offended group are not satisfied with the newspaper's explanation or apology, a boycott of the paper is often begun.

This boycott varies according to the seriousness of the offense, the number of people offended, and the effectiveness of the structure of the boycott. (Naturally, the most feared boycott is the highly organized one.)

The impact which carefully planned protest can achieve is evident in the work of organizations like the NAACP, the Anti-Defamation League, and such nationality societies as the Sons of Italy or the Polish National Alliance. These groups, all of which have the well-being of a particular people as a primary goal, have forced newspapers to avoid slurs on ethnic groups, to promote the interests of other groups, and all in all, to steer a cautious course in many controversial matters.

Because strong protest of any kind can cut sharply into circulation, the editorial policy of most newspapers calls for eliminating any statement likely to offend a large group; or at least, it calls for the exercise of caution.

Ethnic and social considerations are most likely to influence editorial policy in stories of large urban disorders, persecution of minorities, and class struggles. In such instances, the newspaper must be especially careful of its presentation because some members of each involved group are certain to be offended. The ideal solution, obviously, is to offend as few as possible.

Also important is the fact that many newspapers include features and stories designed to increase circulation among ethnic and social groups in their areas, and many papers strive to convince their readers of their tolerance of all races, nationalities, and groups.

PATRIOTIC CONSIDERATIONS

Throughout the United States, many patriotic organizations have appointed themselves watchdogs over all the media. They scrutinize newspapers, theatrical productions, motion pictures, radio, and television for anything that resembles a lack of loyalty to the country. Once they find a quarry, they pursue swiftly and decidedly.

As a result, newspapers must be careful to display some modicum of patriotism. Parades, celebrations, and all other events commemorating great moments in history must be given a prominent play, and no fact or innuendo must appear that can be challenged effectively as disloyal.

One must not conclude, however, that organizations alone are responsible for the influence of patriotism upon editorial policy. Actually, many newspapers display loyalty because the editors feel so minded or because it may be good business.

The degree to which the newspaper shows its loyalty varies from mild to rabid. While most papers are restrained and dignified, some flaunt their patriotism. They may use American flags in prominent positions and print patriotic quotations in their mastheads.

Furthermore, some papers occasionally use patriotism as a guise for other motives. In the name of loyalty to country, these papers call for investigations of schools, penal institutions, local governments, and similar agencies.

There is also a sharp difference in the loyalty of a given newspaper during peacetime and wartime. During the latter period, almost every newspaper becomes more vociferous in its patriotism. In this they are usually prodded by the government, even though they may need no help.

PERSONAL AND GROUP CONSIDERATIONS

Very often, a story or a picture must appear in the paper simply because an interested individual or group wants it there.

Someone known and respected by the newspaper calls and begins with the customary "I want you to do me a favor." The result is a story or a picture, or both, of a wedding, a prize won at a distant college, or an anniversary. Although most stories in this category have little value as news, one occasionally appears that deserves space. Examples are stories about the local charity drive, an event to raise funds for a worthwhile cause, or the activity of a public-spirited group.

Also appearing in the paper as the result of this kind of pressure are many of the press releases of such large organizations as labor unions, fraternal societies, and lodges—as well as pictures, especially in small-town newspapers, of celebrations, presentations, and guest speakers at civic associations and similar places.

Stories appearing in the newspaper because of personal or group considerations usually appear in proportion to the prestige or the friendship of the person or group seeking the publicity.

WHIMS OF THE EDITOR

No small matter in the determination of editorial policy is the whim of the editor. By virtue of giving commands to a large force and heading a successful paper, the editor rarely lacks confidence in his own judgment. In fact, he frequently overrides the judgment of his subordinates in choice and treatment of stories, thereby making the paper reflect in some way his little whims and peculiarities. One editor may like stories of the seamy side of life; another may like subtly humorous stories; another may like tales of horror. The reporters, striving to please the editor, look for his favorite stories; and the paper is affected accordingly.

The top editor also plays the dominant role in make-up, choice of features, pictures, and cartoons. Hence his personal likes and dislikes have strong bearing on every phase of the newspaper.

SECTIONALISM

The editorial policy of a given newspaper is always affected by the part of the nation in which the paper circulates. The newspaper must show some pride in its section; it must evidence concern for the welfare of its section; and it must handle news in keeping with the over-all atmosphere of its section. A paper in a heavily industrial area, for example, must emphasize news of its industry. It is also expected to support editorially any attempt to improve the position of that industry. Helpful tariffs, regulation of imports, and government aid to the industry must be approved. Conversely, any attempt to weaken the position of the section's industry must be fought.

An interesting example of this situation occurred a few years ago when an employee of the Ford motor plant in a small New Jersey town was fined by his union for buying a foreign-made car. Because most residents of the town were dependent economically on the plant, the union felt any such purchase undercut everybody concerned. A local newspaper wanted to support the employee on the ground of his legal rights, but the editor, fearing repercussions, by implication sustained the union. This, of course, is an isolated illustration of a significant condition that affects the inclusion and treatment of news. Broader illustrations can be seen in the agricultural districts where the newspapers not only support everything designed to help agriculture but also include features designed to attract the farmers.

Sometimes, of course, sectionalism combines with one of the other 15 influences discussed in this chapter to affect editorial policy. For example, the impact of sectionalism and business considerations on editorial policy was dramatized on June 6, 1975, when the newspapers in the Daytona Beach, Florida, area were embarrassed by local television personality John Montazzoli.

Throughout the week of June 2, sharks had been sighted in the Daytona Beach bathing areas; and on three occasions, bathers had been attacked and seriously injured. Yet the newspapers, mindful of the tourist trade, carried no stories whatever. In fact, the reporters were said to have joked among themselves that no sharks were in the vicinity—only large fish with sharp teeth.

The story emerged only after Montazzoli made shots of the sharks from a low-flying plane and exhibited his pictures to his television audience. The newspapers were then forced to face up to the story also.

Sectionalism is also defined very clearly in political matters wherein one section of the country differs with another. Editors of newspapers in or near coastal regions that are likely to feel the effects of off-shore drilling for oil, for example, are naturally concerned when such drilling is proposed; and invariably they have editorial comment on such occasions. Meanwhile, gasoline-starved residents of the hinterland are likely to advocate the drilling as a remedy for a bad situation; and their editors are likely to support them.

One should not suppose that conscious decision is the only conduit of sectionalism. There is no doubt that a person's thinking is influenced by the section of the nation in which he lives. As a result, sectionalism affects editorial policy by influencing the thinking of the men who direct the policy of the paper.

TABOO SUBJECTS

Some newspapers, probably motivated by extreme sensitivity, prudishness, or false modesty, have drawn up lists of subjects which their writers are barely permitted to mention. Examples are falsies, contraceptives, and specific names for various forms of sexual perversion. Some other taboos are: a prostitute is never to be mentioned as such; crime stories may not be on page 1 unless they are of national significance; obscenities must never be used—not even by the old process of using the first letter and a dash; reputable persons may not be referred to by last names only; an infant is not to be spoken of as "it"; "*Playboy* stuff" (pictures of shapely women displaying themselves) is always to be omitted.

Some taboos are plainly foolish but some have been very important in the history of journalism. For instance, William Allen White forbade the naming of a juvenile delinquent on the first offense. Now his taboo is almost standard practice.

THE PUBLISHER'S ROLE IN THE COMMUNITY

Because the publisher is an important man in his community, usually he is invited to join many prominent organizations. At the meetings and in the other activities of these organizations, he meets people who have axes to grind or desire publicity. These people, and in many cases the organization itself, strive to influence editorial policy by having the paper support or oppose some plan before the public. Perhaps the exclusive golf club has been told that the right of eminent domain is to be exercised, and a highway is to bisect the course; the publisher is asked to spearhead a protest. Perhaps an organization is staging a membership drive; the newspaper is asked for space. Perhaps the local businessmen are fighting against the installation of parking meters; the newspaper is asked to aid in the battle.

The publisher consequently may find himself influencing editorial policy by dictating a stand for his paper.

CRUSADES

When a newspaper is conducting a crusade, its whole editorial policy is frequently affected seriously. The best spots in the paper are reserved for stories related to the issue; stories helpful to the cause are used while otherwise good ones are discarded; art and cartoons lean toward the particular question; and editorial after editorial beats the drum for the cause.

Crusades, as any competent observer of newspapers can attest, have had a resurgence. With the recent renewed emphasis on investigative reporting, more and more newspapers have found themselves involved in campaigns for reform in local government, better educational opportunities, recreational facilities for inner-city children, and similar causes.

Some famous crusades of the past have been: the *New York Times* and the *Harpers Weekly* crusade against Boss Tweed and Tammany; the *New York World's* campaign throughout the 1880s and '90s for free ice and medical care; the *Kansas City Star's* campaigns for community improvement programs; the many current crusades throughout the nation for better housing; and the innumerable campaigns for combating juvenile delinquency.

EFFECT OF EDITORIAL POLICY ON THE EDITORIAL AND THE COLUMN

The Editorial

The most obvious manifestation of editorial policy is naturally in the editorials of a paper. Here, as the paper openly states its opinions, the reader sees how it stands on a given issue. Most editorials, therefore, are really statements of phases of editorial policy.

Because every issue that arises cannot be measured readily against the established policy of the paper, a daily conference of editorial writers is often held to discuss the slant to be taken on leading issues. This conference, usually attended by the editor, his immediate assistants, and the writers themselves, generally decides by a vote upon the view to be adopted. When an editorial writer does not agree with the slant decided upon, he naturally is not asked to write the editorial pertaining to that question.

The Column

The relationship of the columnist to editorial policy is both interesting and somewhat involved.

When a newspaper assigns a staff member to write a regular column, it usually learns his political outlook and major philosophical tenets beforehand—thereby avoiding any serious conflict between his column and editorial policy.

The same is generally true with the syndicated columnist. His material is studied carefully before the paper adopts his column. Then, if the paper later disapproves of his approach or ideas, it may omit a day's column on occasion, or it may even terminate the contract. This has been the fate of numerous columnists across the years.

Yet many newspapers do not restrict themselves to columnists whom they approve. Three common situations can illustrate this point.

In some instances, newspapers print columns by diametrically opposed writers—for instance, a conservative like William F. Buckley and a liberal like Max Lerner—in order to present contrasting ideas or viewpoints. This practice, they feel, is essential to openmindedness in interpreting issues. Naturally, one of these writers is certain to run counter to the editorial policy of the particular paper.

In other instances, a newspaper may carry a specific columnist because he is a spokesman for a group that deserves to be heard—even though the paper may frequently disagree with the viewpoint expressed. An example is the black columnist on the metropolitan daily who is given a free hand to interpret black issues. On many occasions, the black columnist advocates a militancy that meets the paper's editorial policy head on. Yet the paper, in an attempt to be openminded, respects his opinion.

In still other instances, newspapers feel compelled to carry certain columnists—such as a nationally syndicated gossip columnist—because he or she draws readers. One such columnist, for instance, is currently widely published, even though his record for truth is low and his use of gossip, hearsay, and innuendo is high. This writer's material and tactics go against the fairness of interpretation to which most papers are committed. Yet these same papers use this column because it appears to attract readers.

Some papers run a little box on the editorial page explaining that "the opinions of the columnists are their own and do not necessarily reflect the opinion of this newspaper." This explanation, the editors believe, gives a note of impartiality to the whole paper.

Meanwhile the fact stands that the freedom given the columnist sometimes enables the newspaper to print material that common politeness might otherwise withhold. On many occasions, for example, columnists who specialize in gossip, small talk, and unsupported statements reveal little tid-bits that a self-respecting newspaper could never print while making any claim to ethical responsibility. They tell of little domestic differences within the household of the President of the United States, locker-room arguments between important legislators, the drinking habits of dignitaries' wives, and similar material. Usually such stories are played down or omitted in the news pages out of deference to the persons involved, but when the columnist breaks the story, the newspaper has a clean bill to print it—or so the paper reasons. Hence the paper can run material which, for one reason or another, it is reluctant to sponsor but delighted to see in print.

EXERCISES

Keeping in mind what has been said about editorial policy, write your answer to each of the following problems. Explain your stand fully.

1. A man comes into the city room of a New York daily to protest a deception by a large department store. There is unmistakable evidence that the store is not selling several of its products as advertised, and hundreds of people are being cheated. The store, of course, is a heavy advertiser.

    What do you, as a member of the editorial policy committee, suggest that the paper do?

2. The rector of a fashionable church in your city is a godly but hot-tempered man. Last night he became angry with a parishioner who was visiting him in the rectory and struck the parishioner over the eye. Six stitches were required to close the wound. The parishioner prefers "to let the matter drop." Your district man got the story at the local hospital to which the parishioner was taken.

    What do you, as editor of your local paper, plan to do with the story?

3. A new conservative daily is about to be launched in Detroit, Michigan, a typical large American city.

    What do you as publisher say about including information concerning (1) horse racing, (2) dog racing, (3) major league baseball "runs for the week," and (4) daily Treasury Department figures?

4. Imagine yourself as editor of the only paper in a town of approximately 45,000. A local resident has just been appointed to a high position in an organization which calls itself the "American Nazi Party." He wants a feature story, accompanied by a picture of himself in a uniform modeled precisely on that of a Storm Trooper in Adolf Hitler's Third Reich.

    What should you do?

5. The most important charitable organization in the United States has a rather lax director of your local unit. You, as editor of a large daily, have been given an exclusive story showing that this director has spent an exorbitant amount in furnishing his private office.

    What are you going to do with this story?

6. As editor of a Democratic paper, you have just been told via the telephone that the wife of the Republican governor, a staunch teetotaler, is "rolling drunk" at a local night club. You have a good reporter and the paper's best photographer on hand.

    What are you going to do?

7. The 18- and 20-year-old sons of a local college professor have been arrested and fined at a distant seashore resort for drunkenness and disorderly conduct. The professor is admired and respected in the community and at the college. His wife, however, is a badly class-conscious social climber whose come-uppance is long overdue. You are the editor of the only newspaper in this community of 10,000. If you do not use the story, it will not appear in print, and consequently it will go unnoticed.

    What are your plans?

8. A group of local clergy and civic leaders in your town of 20,000 have just visited you, the editor of the paper, asking for its editorial help in closing a local drive-in movie that specializes in X-rated films.

   What stand should you take in answering them?

9. You are the editor of a Republican paper during a very heated political struggle for the mayoralty of a New England town. A reporter has just learned that a distant cousin of the Democratic candidate, a resident of Utah, has been jailed for drunken driving in his home state. Except for his connection with the Democratic candidate, the cousin would not rate a second thought.

   What should your paper do with this story?

10. A local quack doctor has just been arrested. His particular specialty has been "beating" the insurance companies. He has a list of simple yet effective methods of concealing cases of high blood pressure, diabetes, and liver ailments. Over a two-year period he has obtained medical approval for almost 500 people who should have been rejected. The complete story would make highly interesting reading as a feature article.

    How should a self-respecting paper handle this story?

11. The picture editor of a large metropolitan daily must pass judgment on the one available shot of a young mother who has just been told that her only child has been killed by a truck. Upon being told, the woman became hysterical. She fell to the ground and began to scream and kick wildly. The picture shows her arms and legs flailing the air, her clothing disarranged, and her face contorted into a maniacal expression.

    Thinking of yourself as picture editor of a newspaper of your choice, make and defend a decision.

12. A local dentist has been unfortunate enough to have three patients die in his chair within a month. Since all three were chronic heart cases, the dentist obviously was not at fault.

    How would you, as editor, have your reporter write the news of the third death?

13. The discharged housekeeper of the very able governor of your state has a wealth of embarrassing but highly readable stories about the private lives of her former employer and his family. You are editor of a paper that respects, but does not support, the governor.

    What should your paper do with the story?

14. The Governor of a Northern state has just refused to sign extradition papers for a man wanted by a Southern state. The man, who is now a serious heart case, broke out of a jail three years ago where he was serving a 20–30 year sentence for the only robbery he ever committed. The Governor says, "He's paid his debt to society. Let's leave him alone."

    What slant should a New York daily take on this action?

15. The research director of the largest medical clinic in the United States has just given a press conference to speak about the progress in combating the leading incurable diseases. His picture is strongly pessimistic—he sees only the slightest hope of checking the most dangerous incurable diseases within the next decade.

How much of the story should be printed?

16. A once-brilliant scientist of national renown, a man who has contributed greatly to the welfare of society, is now completely senile. When a reporter was visiting a nearby home yesterday, the scientist accosted him and engaged in all sorts of childish behavior before being taken into custody by a nurse. The public has already been told that the scientist has failed mentally. The reporter, however, wants to write a long account of the experience as a feature story.

Which parts of this story, if any, should be used by a self-respecting newspaper?

17. The paper has just stumbled across absolute proof that a local garage owner, known and respected in this community of 15,000 for over 25 years, is a fugitive from justice. Immediately before coming here, he had been sentenced to a 10- to 20-year term for his part in a drunken brawl in which a neighbor accidentally had been killed. No local resident has ever known him to drink; he is strong in his support of the town's churches and civic affairs; he has shown genuine altrusim in helping less fortunate citizens.

What should the paper do?

18. A committee representing nearly every parent-teacher group in this city of 500,000 has just visited the publisher of the paper to demand the discontinuance of a daily comic strip. They insist that this feature is seriously demoralizing to their children because it portrays a majority of disreputable people. They are backed in their judgment by many prominent psychiatrists, psychologists, educators, and children's leaders. The comic strip, however, is distinctly popular with children and adults alike, and its presence is a decided help to circulation. Requests to the cartoonist to change his material have always elicited the unofficial answer that he "would be crazy to cripple a going proposition." Officially, he uays, "There's nothing wrong with this comic—it's what people read into it. I can't be responsible for people's thoughts."

What would you, as publisher, do in this instance?

19. A notorious gangster, high on the "public enemy" list for many years, has been sentenced to life imprisonment. A wire service which sells its material locally to your paper has bought his autobiography, a serial of 12 episodes. Although the gangster hits hard in the last chapter the idea that crime does not pay, the earlier chapters are filled with braggadocio, explanations of how to evade the law, and various methods of safecracking. The

autobiography makes fascinating reading, especially in the light of the gangster's recent news value.

What would you have the paper do about using this material?

20. The state police have just staged a surprise raid on a suburban barn where a cockfight was in progress. Because cockfights are illegal, the 54 patrons arrested were fined $50 each and given a stern lecture by the local magistrate. Among those arrested were the Boy Scout leader for the entire city, a member of the local charity board, several executives of large firms advertising in the paper, a high school principal, and a layman prominent in his church's affairs. Naturally, there were also the usual gamblers.

As editor, what names would you print?

FOR FURTHER READING

Agee, Warren K., ed. *Mass Media in a Free Society*. Lawrence: University Press of Kansas, 1969.

Daly, John Charles. *The Media and the Cities*. Chicago: University of Chicago Press, 1968.

Edwards, Verne. *Journalism in a Free Society*. Dubuque, Iowa: Wm. C. Brown C., 1970.

Emery, Michael C., and Ted Curtis Smythe. *Readings in Mass Communications: Concepts and Issues in the Mass Media*. Dubuque, Iowa: Wm. C. Brown Co., 1972.

Gerald, James Edward. *The Social Responsibility of the Press*. Minneapolis: University of Minnesota Press, 1963.

Gilmor, Donald M. *Free Press and Fair Trial*. Washington, D.C.: Public Affairs Press, 1966.

Hynds, Ernest G. *American Newspapers in the 1970s*. New York: Hastings House, Publishers, 1975.

Kreighbaum, Hillier. *Pressures on the Press*. New York: Thomas Y. Crowell Co., 1972.

Larsen, Otto W., ed. *Violence and the Mass Media*. New York: Harper, 1968.

Liebling, A. J. *The Press*. New York: Ballantine, 1964.

MacDougall, A. Kent. *The Press: A Critical Look at the Inside*. New York: Dow Jones, 1972.

McLuhan, Marshall. *Counterblast*. New York: Harcourt Brace Jovanovich, 1969.

Merrill, John C., and Ralph D. Barney. *Ethics and the Press: Readings in Mass Media Morality*. New York: Hastings House, Publishers, 1975.

Reston, James. *The Artillery of the Press*. New York: Harper, 1967.

Rivers, William L., and Wilbur Schramm. *Responsibility in Mass Communications*. New York: Harper, 1969.

Seldes, Gilbert. *The New Mass Media: Challenge to a Free Society*. Washington, D.C.: Public Affairs Press, 1968.

Tebbel, John. *Open Letter to Newspaper Readers*. New York: James H. Heineman, 1968.

★ **10** ★

What Is the Editorial?
Writing the Editorial
    Language
    Consistency in the Editorial
Classification of Editorials
    To Influence Opinion
    To Call Attention to a Wrong
    To Enlighten Readers
    To Help a Cause
    To Praise or to Congratulate
    To Present an Editorial Essay
    To Comment Lightly on the News
Guiding Points for Editorial Writing
    Thinking the Issue Through
    Consistency of Viewpoint
    Aggressiveness
    Dignity
    The Note of Authority

The Editorial

WHAT IS THE EDITORIAL?

To most newspaper readers, the familiar term "editorial" denotes a strongly worded argument for a specific course of action or a ringing denunciation of an undesirable condition. These readers associate the editorial with such discourses as the impassioned plea of the legislator for a new law and the vigorous demand of the prosecutor for a guilty verdict in a murder trial.

Although many editorials fit this pattern, the majority do not. In fact, editorials are so diversified that they fall into seven categories; [1] and even then, some specialists see a need for additional classifications. Furthermore, some journalists now argue that the opinions expressed by section editors (sports, theater, or the like) are editorials or "editorial writings" rather than simply personal opinions appearing in columns. Consequently those endorsing this concept of an editorial would make an already broad definition even broader.

As a prelude to any detailed consideration of the editorial, the student of journalism should understand the manner in which editorials differ as to purpose, structure, and treatment.

The editorial column of a metropolitan daily, on any typical day, will

---

[1] Listed and discussed later in this chapter.

demonstrate how editorials differ in purpose. It will probably present at least three of the seven types of editorials discussed in this chapter. Perhaps the lead editorial is a militant call to support a particular candidate for office. This may be followed by one that congratulates a prominent citizen on a recent success. And the column may close with a little humorous essay on how to kill mosquitoes or how to beat the heat.

The manner in which editorials differ in structure will become evident through examination of a representative sampling of editorials from various newspapers. One may be cast in the conventional structure discussed below. Another may employ the suspended-interest approach. A third may be written in the chronological (short-story) style. In short, the writer of the editorial, like the writers of the news story and the feature story, adopts the approach that best suits his purpose.

A sampling of editorials will also display differences in treatment. Even a quick examination will show that the writer of the editorial, like the effective writer in other fields, must vary his treatment according to his subject and his purpose. Hence, the reader may find an earnest, passionate treatment in the editorial that is attempting to influence, a sarcastic treatment in the editorial that is attempting to deride, and a whimsical, cavalier treatment in the editorial that is attempting to amuse. Thus, he easily can see that treatment of subject is as varied in the editorial as in other prominent types of writing.

In view of the preceding discussion, the only all-inclusive statement to be made of the editorial is this: it is an official expression of a newspaper's argument, opinion, or observation—so prepared and placed in the paper that its essential role is clearly apparent.

WRITING THE EDITORIAL

The conventional editorial generally is composed of three parts. The first part, which resembles the lead of the news story, makes a statement of a situation or of an argument to be defended. The second part, appropriately termed the "body," then proceeds to develop the statement. The third part, or the "conclusion," suggests a remedy, makes a plea for action, or attempts to summarize the writer's main purpose in a short, forceful paragraph. Although some writers prefer to incorporate the conclusion with the body, this three-part arrangement is the general pattern of the conventional editorial.

"What Are Guidelines?" is an example of the conventional editorial.

What Are Guidelines?

Recent developments in agencies of federal and state bureaucracies and in the courts, in our opinion, recommend substitution of another word for "guidelines" in official decisions, directives and other governmental documents.

Either usage has changed radically the meaning of guidelines since publication in 1966 of Webster's Third New International Dictionary, Unabridged, or the word is being abused.

An action by the federal government in forcing Louisiana to pay $200,000 for allegedly diverting surplus commodities from human consumption to feed for animals is a case in point. The diversion, contended the bureaucracy, violated guidelines of the United States Department of Agriculture.

Just in what way were these guidelines violated? Commodities such as surplus corn meal, flour and dried beans furnished free to the state for use in hospitals, nursing homes and schools were judged by medical doctors to be unfit for human consumption. They were fed to animals raised by the Louisiana Department of Hospitals.

This violated the guidelines, the Washington agency ruled, because a doctor rather than a registered sanitarian was judge of the fitness for human consumption of the surplus supplies.

Webster describes a sanitarian as "one skilled in matters of sanitary science and public health." If doctors employed by the state hospital agency aren't "skilled in matters of sanitary science and public health," what are they doing on the public pay roll?

Judging by their application, guidelines contained in directives from some of the bureaus and in decisions handed down by some of the courts bear no resemblance to established definitions of the word. Rather, they have become edicts or ultimatums.

As defined by Webster's 1966 dictionary, a guideline is "a cord or rope to aid a passer over a difficult point (as on a trail) or to permit retracing a course (as in a cave) . . . an indication or outline of future policy or conduct (as of a government)."

The true guideline, it seems to us, is a piece of material or written outline intended to be of help. It says, in a manner of speaking, "Follow me and I'll help you."

The word has been abused or corrupted to really say, "Follow me, or I'll get you put in jail or fined $200,000."

All of us should recognize that times and conditions probably are changing more rapidly than in any earlier period of recorded history. The meaning of the English language, in our opinion, is being changed by people in public office more rapidly and more arbitrarily than it deserves.

—*The Times-Picayune,* New Orleans

If the editorial is not of the conventional type—that is to say, if it is written in the suspended-interest approach or in another style wherein the writer does not state his main facts or stand at the outset—then obviously the lead and body differ accordingly. Note how the editorial "The Conscience of CBS" does not employ the conventional structure.

The Conscience of CBS

One of the angels of the Prince of Darkness came rushing up to his Prince with the breathless announcement, "Hark, noble Prince, someone on earth has just had a good idea."

The Evil One brushed the messenger aside. "Never mind, never mind," he replied. "I will teach him to organize it and that will be the end of it."

Obviously, Columbia Broadcasting System executives had not heard this story when they decided to "organize" the CBS conscience.

Working on the premise that "business cannot be governed by the profit motive alone," CBS has formed a department of corporate responsibility which will "advise the management of CBS . . . on activities which further the corporation's policy of displaying good citizenship in conducting the various businesses in which it is engaged."

CBS spokesmen said the new department would address itself toward establishing "a sense of fulfillment on the part of employes . . . a sense of satisfaction on the part of the consumer with the goods he receives and an affirmative climate of public trust, confidence and respect in which the enterprise can expand."

Trying to be more specific, another official said of the new executive chosen to head the department: "I would guess that he's sort of a roving conscience for the corporation."

Roving? Yes, this is the problem in "organizing" the corporate conscience—and lots of other things. For example, imagine how easy it will be to respond when these questions come to CBS management: How can you present so many violent programs for children and so many slanted newscasts and documentaries? Why do you glamorize criminals, offer inane "soap" series, and give gross overpayment to incompetent talent? Why are you so preoccupied with triviality?

Now the answer will be: "Our conscience is out of town."

—*The* (Phoenix) *Arizona Republic*

As is true of the news story, the lead of the editorial is very important because it can hold or lose the reader. The writer, therefore, must strive mightily for a lead that generates interest. Thus he may open his editorial with a short, crisp sentence, with a long sentence, with a question, or with whatever other device he regards as most effective.

Consider the leads of four editorials, all taking the same stand on one of the most significant legal rulings of recent years—the "Pentagon Papers" decision.

Free Press Alive and Healthy

The United States Supreme Court has sustained the freedom of the press. It has warded off an attempt by the United States government to impose a gag upon newspapers publishing government documents stamped "Secret."

There must never be star chamber censorship in America. Ever since Blackstone there has always been an unshakeable law against "prior restraint of publication." The First Amendment unqualifiedly made that a sacred foundation stone in American democracy.

—*The Plain Dealer,* Cleveland

'The Governed' Are Winners In That Supreme Court Ruling

The unprecedented outpouring of separate opinions in the Supreme Court case on the Pentagon papers not only adds up to a historic victory for press freedom but offers some eloquent and timely reminders of why that guarantee was written into the Constitution in the first place.

As The New York Times itself has observed in an editorial ". . . this is not so much a victory for any particular newspaper as it is for the basic principles of freedom on which the American form of government rests."

That message came through loud and clear in some of the concurring opinions as the justices took the occasion of this landmark decision to teach a history lesson.

—*The Philadelphia Inquirer*

The Pentagon Papers: Free—At Last

"Our democracy depends for its future on the informed will of the majority, and it is the purpose and the effect of the First Amendment to expose to the public the maximum amount of information on which sound judgment can be made by the electorate. The equities favor disclosure, not suppression. No one can measure the effects of even a momentary delay."

This passage from the ruling of U.S. District Court Judge Gerhard Gesell on June 21, 1971, comes close to summing up our own views in the case of the United States Government vs. The Washington Post—and, frankly, we would have preferred to leave it at that. Instead, the issue moved up to the Supreme Court and yesterday the government's plea for a restraining order against this newspaper and The New York Times was dismissed by a vote of 6-to-3.

—*The Washington Post*

The rekindled light

It is being called "historic" and a "landmark," this decision that the New York Times and the Washington Post have the right to publish the classified documents known as the Pentagon papers. It was, in a way, neither of these things. Rather, it was a reaffirmation by the Supreme Court of what had been assumed to be true between the time the First Amendment went into effect and the time President Nixon and Atty. Gen. John N. Mitchell came along. This assumption, not lightly held, was that government could not dictate in advance what the free press might publish.

—*Chicago Sun-Times*

Although the lead of the editorial is highly important, the development and the summation of the main purpose are even more so because therein the writer succeeds or fails in his main purpose. If the writer is attempting to influence, these parts carry the weight of his argument. If he is attempting to inform, they convey the main facts. If he is attempting to amuse, they sustain or weaken his humor. Thus, the writer must be especially careful with these parts of the editorial.

To see the function of every part of the editorial, the student of journalism should study the complete examples given in this chapter. He should then evaluate the writer's ability to correlate the parts effectively.

Language

Anyone studying the actual composition of editorials must remember two important facts about language: (1) many words are relative in meaning and (2) choice of words largely determines the tone of the editorial.

The fact that many words are relative in meaning is immediately obvious in any study of language. Words, for example, like "big," "rich," "building," "difficult," and "heavy" have such broad meanings that, unless helped by other words, they can never convey precise meaning. The editorial writer, therefore, often faces a real problem as he attempts to express to all readers the exact idea he has in mind.

The fact that choice of words largely determines the tone of the editorial must be recognized because the writer naturally wants to create a specific tone. If, for example, the purpose of the editorial is to condemn a tax collector found guilty of graft, one of several tones may be desired, and that tone will result largely from the language used. If the tone is to be dignified, the editorial might call the convicted man "an office holder who has betrayed the confidence of the electorate." If the tone is to be caustic, he might be referred to as a "common ward heeler," "a henchman of an arch political boss," or even worse, "a traitor to his public trust." If satire is in order, he might be referred to as a "public servant who has gathered in a few dollars on the side by assisting a taxpayer."

A good example of varying language to suit the desired tone is afforded by two editorials ("Sinking feelings . . ." and "Yet more appalling . . .") taken from the same issue of the same newspaper.

Sinking feelings about Alaskan oil tankers

The human race is now quite adept at firing men into orbit around the earth at speeds that enable them to circle it about once every 90 minutes. The Concorde has flown from Boston to Paris and back in six hours. A televised event may be viewed by North Americans a fraction of a second after it occurs in Europe.

The curious thing about all of this is that most of us are still closer to the 80 days of Jules Verne than the 90 minutes of the National Aeronautics and Space Administration. The prevailing instinct is still to think of the world as immense and everlasting, so big as to be almost indifferent to the touch of man's hand on its surface.

In spite of challenges thrown at traditional scales by such concepts as the global village, the notion of unassailable size remains. This is evident in most references to the land mass of the globe—and even more evident in the way we regard the oceans which cover three-quarters of the earth's surface. We have not even begun to talk in terms of the global lake—a dangerous lag in view of the rate at which technology is undermining the old scales of size.

The urgency of applying new concepts finds its sharpest focus for Canadians in the matter of oil spills. Here we have a really fast way to do vast damage to coastal areas. Barbara Ward, writing in The Economist, noted that as recently as 1948, no cargo ship weighed more than 26,000 dead weight tons. By 1973, more than 400 oil tankers weighing more than 200,000 tons were operating or under construction.

But let us for the moment concentrate on the four tankers built or being built for the Alaskan oil trade. They are of more modest size (120,000 to 130,000 tons) and are capable of carrying 10 times the quantity of oil that was spilled by the Liberian tanker Arrow when she ran aground in Chedabucto Bay in 1970. The Alaskan tankers are likely to be threading their way delicately—well, as delicately as a 120,000-ton tanker can do anything—through the waters of Georgia Strait and other hazardous waters off the coast of British Columbia and the State of Washington.

The awful consequences of mishap would scarcely seem to need emphasis, and yet there is a curiously casual attitude in evidence. We learned the other day, for example, that the best type of radar will not be installed by the time the tankers begin plying the route.

Not one of them will be double-bottomed as a safeguard against spills in the event of collision or grounding, nor will they be fitted with double screws which would offer greatly improved maneuverability in the difficult waters they have to negotiate.

The whole world has been slow to come to grips with the reality of the grief that an oil spill can bring (Canada has not always been fussy about the safety of oil tankers whose operations it could control) but surely we should be entitled to expect more foresight than has been apparent in the design and guidance of the Alaskan oil tankers.

Solutions to problems of the energy crisis in the United States and Canada will call for a spirit of co-operation on both sides—a much more constructive spirit than is present in this situation.

Yet more appalling . . .

Hey, you voters! Here it is—chapter two of the election speeches of Pierre Trudeau rushed to our office by the Post Office—at public expense, of course.

(Fade to italic preamble. . . . You will remember how the last instalment left off . . . with the Prime Minister savagely putting down the New Democrats—likening them to wild geese "honking at excess profits"—in a Vancouver speech on July 3 and delivered to us on July 16. Now read on. . . .)

The latest batch—delivered on July 19—has the text of the PM's words in Granby on June 25 and Niagara Falls on July 5.

Did you know—*did you know*—that in Niagara Falls Mr. Trudeau said that Conservative Leader Robert Stanfield was trying to bamboozle the people by selling them snake oil to cure everyone's ailments? You voters who voted Tory—if you had known that, would you have voted the way you did on July 8?

Well, you'll get another chance. Perhaps in 1978. In the meantime, watch this space for more election 1974 coverage. Brought to you by Mail Canada.

—Globe and Mail, Toronto

Because tone is such an important consideration in the editorial, the writer generally attempts to set a dominant atmosphere with his opening sentences. Note, for instance, how the tone of the editorials below emanates from the start.

Both those who applaud and those who are made anxious by the decision of the Supreme Court of the United States in the case of the Pentagon papers should take notice that the court by no means authorized an unbridled press.

The decision itself was on narrow grounds. Judgment was passed only on the question of whether in this case the government had made its claim of possible damage to national security so clear as to justify "prior restraint."

The court, by a vote of 6-to-3, said that the government had not made a good enough case.

—The Christian Science Monitor

As Albuquerque moves into a new era in its dynamic history, with a new form of municipal government to provide responsiveness and flexibility in municipal service, it would be thoughtless to let the old regime pass into history without an expression of appreciation.

The old commission—Chairman Richard G. Vaughan and Commissioners Robert Poole, Ray Baca, Louis Saavedra and Mrs. Nancy Smith—merits commendation first for its initiative in setting the stage for a new form of municipal government and, then, for facilitating a smooth, orderly, and quiet transition. Under terms of the new charter Commissioners Poole and Baca will continue to serve on the newly created City Council for about 17 months to help the larger representative body find its bearings.

—Albuquerque (N.M.) *Journal*

Heroes and villains share a common trait: both have singlemindedness of purpose and the energy necessary to attain their goals. Instantaneous gratification gives way to self-denial as they struggle toward their ultimate dream.

Unfortunately, when that dream is greed, the two often combine efforts with disastrous results. One such effort was reported this week, when the SEC cited the Home-Stake Production Co., a tax shelter scheme, with fraud. Among the many heroes who were caught up with the villains was the White Knight of Wall Street, Adam Smith, of "The Money Game" fame. Adam Smith, alias George J. W. Goodman, was considered to be among the most savvy of investors. He added to the financial vocabulary such terms as "the gnomes of Zurich," and "Scarsdale Fats."

Readers roared as they read his rapier thrusts at managers of go-go funds; his deft analysis of analysts left many a reader astounded at his audacity and amused at his irreverence.

Oh, how the mighty have fallen! When the SEC charged that a Ponzi-type scheme tripped up such notables as Goodman, Walter B. Wriston, chairman of First National City Bank, Senator Jacob Javits, Judge Murray Gurfein and a pride of lions from every sector of the performing arts, it underscored the gullibility of even the great as well as the paternalism of the government toward the small investor.

—*The Commercial and Financial Chronicle,* New York

Women's libbers are not born that way. The latest batch has emerged from the ruling by the State Department of Industry, Labor and Human Relations ruling that boys can caddy at age 12 but girls must wait until they're 14. Isn't that silly?

Girls can carry golf clubs just as easily as they can manage a stack of newspapers or (ask any mother) a baby brother. They have proved just as dependable and competent as boys. Yet, job by job, girls must fight for the right to work that has traditionally been reserved for boys. That should be answer enough to the question, "How did a nice girl like you become a militant?"

—*The Milwaukee Journal*

In all American cities, small boys want to grow up to be garbagemen, or firemen or policemen.

But in San Francisco, and nowhere else in this country, there is a vocation of vehicular operation that invades the dreams of many small fry.

Probably, very few boys who live in the Bay Area have not, at one time or another, wanted to be gripmen, the rugged individualists who guide the cable cars up and down the fog-shrouded hills of what columnist Herb Caen calls "Baghdad-by-the-Bay."

—*The Courier-Post,* Camden, N.J.

Consistency in the Editorial

The kind of editorial, the style of writing, and the attitude taken are determined for a newspaper by its editorial policy committee. Therefore, a definite consistency is usually reflected in the editorials of a given newspaper. Those of such conservative publications as the *New York Times,* the Philadelphia *Evening Bulletin,* and the *Christian Science Monitor* are generally quiet and thoughtful in tone. The editorials of the sensational papers, the papers consistently supporting a political party, and the tabloids are likely to be vigorous and loud.

The devices of the editorials are also determined by the editorial policy committee. Hence, some newspapers use heavy sarcasm; others avoid it. Some newspapers give nicknames to such high figures as the President of the United States; others use only accepted titles. Some newspapers present heavy, scholarly editorials; others use short, sprightly ones. These devices, naturally, are consistent with those used in the other sections of the paper.

CLASSIFICATION OF EDITORIALS

The only satisfactory way to classify editorials is by function. Even this approach, however, presents difficulty because function is not always immediately clear. An editorial, for example, which appears to be a light, humorous treatment of a serious subject, written for the sole purpose of entertaining, may in reality be a vicious attack; and an editorial written for the announced purpose of clarifying a difficult question may actually be a veiled attempt to influence opinion.

However, when purpose is fully clear, editorial writers classify editorials under seven headings:

To influence opinion
To call attention to a wrong
To enlighten readers
To help a cause
To praise or to congratulate
To present an editorial essay
To comment lightly on the news

To Influence Opinion

When a newspaper wants to influence the opinions of its readers, it generally runs an editorial for that purpose. This, the most common type of editorial, outlines the paper's position and the supporting evidence. The editorial usually closes with a plea for action.

The editorial to influence is used to support political candidates, to arouse backing for or against proposed legislation, or to sway the reader's opinion on any other controversial issue.

The writing of this editorial demands primarily the ability to analyze and present arguments forcefully. Because it is the most important kind of editorial, it usually precedes the others.

"Insulin isn't enough" is an example.

Insulin isn't enough

With the discovery of insulin, half a century ago, the healthy portion of the public assumed comfortably that diabetes as a menace had been ended.

Not so.

Medical experience over the years has revealed that insulin, wonderful and useful as it is, is not a cure.

Even with use of the drug, it has been found, the patient is too likely to develop blindness, heart trouble and other diseases. On the average, his life expectancy will be substantially reduced.

A tragic case was that of Jackie Robinson, the baseball player, whose untimely death was ascribed to heart failure. This was true, in a way. But Mr. Robinson had had diabetes for many years, and this, the doctors believe, was responsible for his physical degeneration, which included blindness.

While the incidence of diabetes, now estimated at towards 10,000,000 cases, has been increasing—insulin keeps its victims alive longer—Federal grants for research into its cause have not kept pace.

Bills providing for such research now languish in congressional committees. They should be pushed along. This disease is a still unconquered killer, and millions spent to overcome it will be far less expensive than what it now costs every year.

—*Boston Sunday Globe*

To Call Attention to a Wrong

Frequently, a newspaper sees something that it believes to be a serious wrong, and it calls attention to this wrong editorially. It may be a dangerous aspect of a new law, a threatening condition in sanitation, or an error committed by a person in high place. When possible, the editorial is expected to suggest some constructive way to eliminate the wrong.

This kind of editorial differs from the editorial to influence opinion in that it concentrates on factual material rather than on a viewpoint; that is, it is really a straight presentation of facts rather than an argument.

"Lincoln Blockbuster" is an example.

Lincoln Blockbuster

In what some members of the City Planning Commission have called "a carefully orchestrated shell game," the developers Paul and Seymour Milstein have bounced plans for a building for the Lincoln Square area back and forth between the commission and the Board of Standards and Appeals. The builders' purpose is quite clear: they are after a variance that will give them a structure 33 per cent larger than anything legally permitted in the Lincoln Square Special Zoning District. That kind of blockbuster means appalling density. It is also quite clear that the whole city loses if the Milsteins win.

The developers apparently have no intention of building what the commission has approved. They intend, instead, to bounce the plan right back to Standards and Appeals (where they had it before) for a "hardship" decision and the right to build a 43-story tower with no design controls.

The "hardship" argument is a particularly dangerous one in this case. The Milsteins are claiming that the design restrictions of the special district, even with its bonuses, make it impossible to build profitably. Maybe other builders in the Lincoln Square district know something the Milsteins don't. At least they seem to ignore the fact that four similar buildings are being constructed there under the necessary regulations, with no claim of hardship at all.

The effect of granting a variance to the Milsteins under these circumstances would then inevitably be to put all of the special zoning districts in jeopardy and threaten the city's basic right to plan. This is a shell game all right—of carefully orchestrated cynicism and greed.

—*The New York Times*

To Enlighten Readers

When a newspaper feels a need to explain to the reader some pertinent question or event, it often runs the editorial to enlighten. The subject may be a proposed constitutional amendment, a distant war, or any other issue which the newspaper wants to make clear to the man in the street. Thus, in its true form, this editorial is an unbiased explanation. The reader, however, must often beware the identity of the paper running the editorial, for sometimes the writer may color or slant the material. Politically affiliated newspapers, for example, are rarely impartial in political matters, and regional papers seldom present an unbiased picture of Federal legislation concerning their areas.

"World Wide Communion" is an example of the editorial to enlighten.

World-Wide Communion

Members of Christian churches all over the world join tomorrow in the observance of the sacrament of Holy Communion, thus signifying the bond of Christian fellowship that unites hearts and hands in the work of Christ's church in every part of the world.

World-wide Communion is just what its name implies, the distribution of the sacred elements to all believing Christians and in accord with the plan instituted by Christ Himself when He met with His disciples in the Upper Room centuries ago. As the disciples looked to Him for comfort and guidance in a time when men plotted against His life, so do Christians today look to the same Christ for inspiration and leadership in a time when the forces of evil in the world seem bent on destroying the very foundations upon which our Christian faith rests.

And so throughout the world wherever the name of Christ is honored men and women will gather at the Lord's table tomorrow and again dedicate their lives to the furtherance of His kingdom here on earth.

—*Daily Local News*, West Chester, Pa.

To Help a Cause

Whenever a newspaper desires to aid in some worthwhile cause such as a charity drive, a safety campaign, or a memorial program, it frequently uses its editorial voice. The editorial informs or reminds the public of the importance of the cause and makes a plea for help. Thus, this kind of editorial is actually an advertisement or "plug" for the cause involved.

An example is "Red Cross Blood Supply Is Running Low."

Red Cross Supply of Blood Running Low

January is National Volunteer Blood Donor Month and it comes not a moment too soon, according to local Red Cross officials.

All local hospitals are totally dependent on the Red Cross for their blood supplies, but a serious drop in collections in December has put the local program in jeopardy. In fact, December was one of the worst months for blood collecting in the area in years.

President Ford, in recognizing the importance of blood donations, proclaimed the month-long observance. In so doing, he noted that the gift of blood "is an offering for which there is no substitute and which annually helps restore to good health countless fellow citizens."

Some persons are reluctant to give blood because they fear the pain or the inconvenience. But neither is as great as one might expect. And neither is great enough to prevent some regular donors from giving gallons and gallons of the precious fluid over a period of years.

According to Dr. Robert Langdell, president of the American Association of Blood Banks, American hospitals need 7 million pints of blood a year. The need is great in January because holidays, winter illnesses and even the weather keep donors away from the blood banks.

There is an economic side to persons donating their blood to blood banks. About 80 per cent of our national supply of blood comes from such institutions at a saving of some $100 million a year for hospital patients. Ironically, only about 3 per cent of Americans who qualify by age and health actually provide this vast amount of the life-giving fluid.

If an adult is in good health, he can make a donation of blood to a blood bank and very possibly be a key factor in saving a person's life. When looked at in this manner, it's just about the perfect gift.

And January is the month to do it.

—*The Scranton* (Pa.) *Times*

To Praise or to Congratulate

When a citizen or a group has performed an outstanding deed or received an honor, the newspaper may run an editorial to praise or to congratulate.

''Mr. Ashe: a Virginia 'first' '' furnishes an example.

Mr. Ashe: a Virginia 'first'

In moving up to the chairmanship of the State Board of Welfare and Institutions, Norfolk's Victor J. Ashe reaches a new peak in his own career and breaks significant ground for his race.

This lawyer and long-time political figure here in Tidewater is the first black to serve in the top capacity on the key Virginia agency. Moreover, his is a degree of individual distinction pre-dating the sizable array of black appointments by the Holton administration, having been appointed to the state board in 1968, by then-Governor Mills Godwin.

Mr. Ashe's service on that body since, as well as the qualities which made him a respected public figure in his home community, suggest that in his difficult, complex new duties he will perform most ably, while reflecting credit on himself, the black populace he has championed so responsibly over the years and on the entire citizenry of this area.

—*Ledger-Star*, Norfolk, Va.

To Present an Editorial Essay

The editorial essay is a reflective writing on a serious subject which appears in the editorial column. In this writing, the editor discusses an important or timely topic as an interested, concerned individual. He does not attempt to approve or condemn, to influence opinion, or to defend an argument or course of action. He merely approaches his subject with an attitude of concern, respect, and humility. He says, in effect, "Here is a question we should all be thinking about, and here are the considerations, as I see the matter, on which we should focus attention. A satisfactory answer will be hard to find, but we must proceed nonetheless.

This editorial is especially appropriate for such topics as the discontent of young people with existing institutions, the financial plight of the large cities, and the rising crime rate in many urban areas. On such questions, the editorial writer, obviously, dares not claim omniscience. Hence the editorial essay becomes an attractive and practical approach.[2]

The success of the editorial essay—as is true of all reflective writing—stems from the quality of the writer's mind and the appeal of his personality. This writing, therefore, makes heavy demands on intellectual capacity and attractiveness of personal attributes.

In a sense, the editorial essay is the most valuable writing in the entire paper. When well done, it helps the reader to see a timely or controversial question in a clear outline, as well as casting light into the recesses of the subject itself. Hence it opens a door for the reader to begin reflection on an important issue.

Furthermore, the editorial essay often performs the role of the gadfly. It provokes readers to think about a topic that should concern them. And finally, it often contributes to the newspaper an intellectual stimulation found only in the best of our current quality magazines.

"Thoughts on Grade-Grubbing" is an example of the editorial essay.

Thoughts on Grade-Grubbing

Reports are filtering back from campus that the current generation of students has reverted to a form of behavior that so many pop sociologists had thought died forever in the Great Cultural Revolution of the late 1960s. They are grade-grubbing with an intensity that shocks their elders. And according to a recent New York Times article, some professors believe that the pressure in pre-law and pre-med courses has grown so great that it has produced a surge of cheating.

So we checked with some of our academic friends. They agreed that students are more job-minded and worried about grades than they have been for years. But

---

[2] One of the most successful users of the editorial essay was Norman Cousins who, for almost 30 years before his resignation as editor of *The Saturday Review* in November 1971, wrote a "Report to the Readers." This particular series of signed editorials was composed largely of editorial essays that were read and quoted throughout the world. When Cousins resumed his association with the magazine slightly more than two years later, he also resumed his editorial essay.

the alleged increase in cheating was news to them. One teacher told us he was more inclined to trust his students now than in the late '60s. The paper-writing mills of five years back seemed to have died out, he said. And even though it was harder to excite students about knowledge for its own sake, at least they were conscientious workers.

The conclusion we draw is that whether or not you believe in the "cheating surge" depends on whether or not you approve of the new student attitudes. For those who applauded the student activism of the late '60s, today's generation has sold out to crass materialism, and all the dishonest activity that implies. But those who thought the campus rebellions were shallow, thoughtless and simply destructive are inclined to welcome the new mood, narrow-minded as it may be, as a return to at least some form of responsible and serious-minded endeavor.

—*The Wall Street Journal*

To Comment Lightly on the News

Almost daily, the editor or the director of the editorial page finds a need to lighten the editorial column. He sees that the serious nature of the main editorials and the generally ponderous atmosphere of the page make the column hard reading. As a result, he inserts an editorial writing that comments pleasantly or humorously on an item in the news.

The importance of this editorial should not be dismissed quickly. This editorial does more than lighten the column: it frequently attracts the reader to the column itself, thereby inducing him to read the other editorials.

Note "Normal Abnormality" and "Smile, Please" as examples of the editorial that lightens.

Normal Abnormality

Two meteorologists studying long-term weather trends claim they've discovered that it's normal for weather to be abnormal.

Floods, droughts, hurricanes and the like are to-be-expected aberrations of climate, they say. In short, the unexpected convulsions of nature that are routinely expected.

There's no use hazarding friendly rapport with the weatherman by unseemly nit-picking.

But it looks very much as if the forecasters have contrived a slick theory that will help them tut-tut away those mishaps of weather they sometimes aren't able to foresee.

That 30 inches of unpredicted snow? Nothing to it, under the new theory. Simply a perfectly normal abnormality.

Next, probably the economic soothsayers will adopt the theory as their own. They need it at least as much as the weathermen do.

—*The Pittsburgh Press*

Smile, Please

It strikes us as a bit inane for State Highway Department clerks to tell an applicant to "smile" when being photographed for a new driver's license.

There is seldom anything amusing about those occasions when a motorist is required to produce his license for inspection. Perhaps the driver would be more recognizable if his likeness portrayed a silly grin rather than a genuine smile.

—*The State,* Columbia, S.C.

In thinking of the editorial to lighten, however, one must observe a special caution. Sometimes the writer may employ this approach as a means of disarming the reader; thus he may use the light commentary as a front for arguing a serious point.

In the editorial "A Rat's Diet," for instance, the writer is ostensibly commenting humorously upon a recent research finding. Yet in the process, he is establishing a rather startling fact—the fact that the nutritional quality of American bread is far lower than is commonly realized. Classifying this editorial, therefore, is not a facile procedure.

A Rat's Diet

The learned and generally reliable Encyclopaedia Brittanica appraises the common rat—whether brown, barn, sewer or wharf—as "aggressive, omnivorous, adaptable and fecund—immensely successful as a biological organism."

For all that, recent scientific research now reveals, the rat is no match whatever for the limp and flabby loaf being hawked across this Nation under the designation of bread. The ordinary white bread of commerce, laboratory tests indicate, is of such meager nutritional value that it will do in the witless rat that attempts to exist on it exclusively for 90 days.

This does not necessarily mean, of course, that the human animal who depends upon the pre-sliced product as the staff of life is necessarily leaning on a broken reed. It does suggest that in casting his bread upon the waters, he has little to gain nutritionally if it does indeed come back sevenfold. Furthermore, it permits him to remark with confidence, whenever he descries a rat that is aggressive, omnivorous and fecund, "There goes a rat that does not live by bread alone."

The San Francisco Chronicle.

GUIDING POINTS FOR EDITORIAL WRITING

Although editorial writing is fundamentally a matter of individual ability, five significant guidelines demand the attention of the best of writers.

Thinking the issue through
Consistency of viewpoint
Aggressiveness
Dignity
The note of authority

Thinking the Issue Through

If the issue is at all controversial, the writer must think the question through before so much as making an outline. He must make certain that he has all the facts—in a clear, undistorted form; and he must be logical and sound in his reflection. Whenever possible, he should allow a day or more to think about the issue because of the wider perspective on controversial questions which the passage of time provides.

In many instances, however, there is simply not time to reflect at great length; the nature of the topic demands that an editorial be written almost immediately after the story breaks. For example, many debatable decisions by the President of the United States are often completely unexpected. Perhaps he initiates a move to devalue the dollar or he calls for an increase in import tariffs or he suggests military support for a foreign country—all without any forewarning whatever. In situations like these, the editorial writer may have, literally speaking, only a few minutes to think before beginning to write. Yet he must prepare the editorial because tomorrow's readers will be looking for it.

Consistency of Viewpoint

The editorial pronouncements of a given paper must evidence a note of consistency. If the editorial of today is inconsistent with that of yesterday; if the editorials on the same day are inconsistent with each other; or, worse still, if the editorial itself is inconsistent, the newspaper faces trouble. The reader does not merely look for consistency; he demands it. When inconsistency exists, he immediately suspects a poor mind or a base motive.

The word "consistency" naturally admits of several definitions. One view of the word may mean a blind support of a political party. Hence, a newspaper may be consistent in its political outlook but inconsistent in an announced intention to expose corruption. Another definition may mean opposing every act of a particular public official. Hence, the newspaper may be consistent in its opposition but inconsistent in its announced intention to be fair. To most readers, however, the term means an honest attempt to be consistently impartial, sincere, and straightforward.

Aggressiveness

If the editorial is a serious writing about an important subject, it should have a note of aggressiveness without belligerency. The editorial should reflect the attitude of fighting for what is right in a fearless, unhampered manner, rather than simply fighting for the sake of being in the midst of a combat. Although the editorial should imply that the writer has examined all aspects of a given question, it should take a firm stand one way or the other. Very few readers, newspapers have learned, are interested in innocuous editorial writing.

Dignity

For the self-respecting paper, dignity is indispensable. Although tabloids and other papers leaning toward the sensational frequently transgress the limits of good taste in language and approach, a good editorial demands a note of dignity. The dignified editorial, like the dignified man, creates a note of calm, authoritative judgment; the undignified editorial, like the undignified man, too often creates a note of belligerent, reckless thinking. Even in the lighter editorials wherein the writer unbends, a certain note of dignity is essential.

The importance of dignity has been underscored by a series of studies made recently by several large schools of journalism. These studies re-inforce the self-evident truth that the presence of dignity conveys an impression of being in command of the situation. Conversely, the absence of dignity exudes the atmosphere of an emotion-laden situation.

The Note of Authority

As the reader follows the editorial, he must have the feeling that the writer knows his subject. Very few persons will read an editorial if they get the impression that the writer is not well informed and intelligent. Without a note of authority, an editorial cannot be stimulating. Consequently, it stands little chance of being read.

EXERCISES

Write editorials on the following subjects:

1. Condemn a resolution just passed by City Council to levy a sales tax on all purchases made in the city.
2. Uphold or refute the statement of a leading educator that parents are largely to blame for juvenile delinquency.
3. Enlighten your reader on a dangerous amendment to a recent tax bill in your municipality. The amendment provides an additional tax on property if present revenue is not enough to meet all budgetary items. There is to be no public hearing before the tax is levied.
4. A society of educators is making a drive to put all public schools completely under Federal control. Express your view editorially.
5. The fact is established that radio and television do not enjoy the same freedom of speech enjoyed by the newspaper because the Federal government controls the airways. Write an editorial on this subject.

6. Condemn or uphold the Governor in his granting of a parole to a man who has served only two years of a 50-year sentence for murder. The prisoner had a long record of petty thievery and unlawful entry before being convicted of shooting an accomplice in a dispute over spoils received in a hold-up. The Governor acted against the advice of the Board of Pardons, contending that the evidence in the trial showed that the man had shot in self-defense.

7. A university in your city wants to take over a large public park for a new building. There are no other parks in the immediate neighborhood. Comment as you see fit.

8. Write an editorial on the subject of any need—as you see the matter—to reform a local election code.

9. Write an editorial in which you advance a plan for slum clearance in a large city.

10. Write an editorial on the need of a vocational school in a community where there is none.

11. Defend or attack the mayor of a large city for his oft-repeated belief that the city is as nearly perfect as it is possible for it to be.

12. Condemn a city for its failure to support an orchestra or some other cultural institution.

13. A small child has been electrocuted by a wire blown down during a storm. The equipment of the electric company is old, the city is not forcing the company to replace it, and this kind of accident easily can happen again. Write an editorial.

14. Write an editorial supporting a particular candidate for the office of Mayor, Governor, Senator, or President of the United States.

15. Condemn the present laxity of the police in enforcing the laws against double parking, overtime parking and illegal parking in downtown streets.

16. Write a light editorial on the recent announcement by the Chairman of the Park Commission that the city parks need at least 200 more benches.

17. Over 500 of the city's 725 high school seniors have received shockingly low grades in a simple American history examination given by a national magazine. This is the month of May, so that in three weeks these people will be high school graduates. Write an editorial on this subject.

18. There has been some agitation to reduce the size of the Art Museum on the grounds that few people visit it. The space saved is to be used for storage purposes by the highway department. Write an editorial as you see fit.

19. Write an editorial in which you explain to the readers how much additional tax each person is going to have to pay under the recently approved tax bill.

20. Write an editorial congratulating a distinguished citizen for an outstanding contribution to the community, the state, or the nation.

FOR FURTHER READING

Daniels, Jonathan. *They Will Be Heard: America's Crusading Newspaper Editors.* New York: McGraw-Hill, 1965.

Editors Forum. Atlanta, Georgia: Georgia Press Association. A monthly publication for editors.

Grassroots Editor. Carbondale, Illinois: Southern Illinois University Press. A quarterly containing examples of outstanding editorials.

Hulteng, John L. *The Opinion Function: Editorial and Interpretative Writing for the News Media.* New York: Harper, 1973.

Ingersoll, Ralph M. *Point of Departure: An Adventure in Autobiography.* New York: Harcourt, Brace & World, Inc., 1961.

Kemler, Edgar. *The Irreverent Mr. Mencken.* Boston: Little, Brown 1950.

Kreighbaum, Hillier. *Facts in Perspective.* Englewood Cliffs, N.J.: Prentice-Hall, 1956.

MacDougall, Curtis D. *Principles of Editorial Writing.* Dubuque, Iowa: Wm. C. Brown Co., 1973.

Masthead. Washington, D.C: National Conference of Editorial Writers. A quarterly dealing with the editorial page.

Pool, Ithiel de Sola. *The Prestige Papers: A Survey of Their Editorials.* Palo Alto: Hoover Institute Studies, 1952.

Waldrop, A. Gayle. *Editor and Editorial Writer.* Dubuque, Iowa: Wm. C. Brown Co., 1967.

★ **11** ★

Sources of Material for the Column
Attracting Readers to the Column
The Style of the Column
    The Unified Style
    The Anecdotal Style
    The Departmental Style
    The Unrelated-Facts Style
    The Question-&-Answer Style

The Column

One of the most pleasant, satisfying, and rewarding assignments in journalism is the writing of the column. The task is pleasant because the columnist generally has a free hand to compose as he pleases; it is satisfying because he is doing highly creative work; and it is rewarding because some of the highest salaries in the newspaper world are paid to columnists. This being true, the position of columnist is eagerly sought after by many, many newspapermen. The path to success, however, is a hard one, and columnists, like other writers catering to a fickle public, often rise quickly and fade quickly.

Columns are written on a multitude of subjects. There are syndicated and nonsyndicated columns on politics, sports, news, gossip, religion, radio, movies, television, music, stamps, words, general information, legal advice, and a host of other subjects. In fact, the newspaperman is seldom surprised to hear of a column on a new subject, for just about any field is fair game for the columnist.

The great criterion for measuring the success of the columnist is his ability to attract and hold readers. To be successful, he must possess that magical quality which forces readers to continue after perusing his opening sentences; and even more difficult, he must be able to make his readers return to his column day after day with undiminished enthusiasm. Like the famed Pied Piper, he must have a large and attentive audience.

232

Just how can a columnist achieve this end? That remains one of the most enigmatic questions in journalism. Some specific instances can illustrate the complexities of the enigma.

For some 20 years before his death, Arthur Brisbane (1864–1936) wrote a daily syndicated column containing nothing but capsules of the day's news. Undeviatingly, he followed a simple formula. Each day, he scanned the wire service copy and the several newspapers within his reach, extracted between five and twelve items, and re-hashed them in capsule form. He added no comment, and he attempted no evaluation or interpretation; he simply presented settled fact in précis. Yet his column was very widely read, despite its utter lack of identifiable originality. Upon Brisbane's death, a host of newspapermen rushed forward to garner his audience by following his simple formula—only to meet resounding failure in every case. Brisbane, therefore, stands as a kind of oddity within the history of journalism. No one has ever explained how he acquired his vast readership with such a transparent device.

Will Rogers (1879–1935) was a leading motion-picture actor, homespun philosopher, and humorist before turning to the writing of an unusually successful syndicated column. Although many nonjournalists have attributed Rogers' success to his appealing rustic humor, journalists themselves are not so sure. They point out that many other writers have had Rogers' attributes, but none of these has ever attracted such a following. Hence these journalists regard Rogers as a special case. They contend that like the comic journalists of the last century,[1] he seemed to have a special gift that defies academic analysis. His success as a columnist, therefore, can be explained only broadly as the reflection of a unique personality.

Walter Lippmann (1889–1974) had one of the greatest impacts of all American columnists. The startling aspect of his success, oddly enough, is that he took very strong stands on issues that were largely political. In other words, he moved into an area where readers tend to follow only columnists with whom they agree, and succeeded in drawing and holding readers of all political stripes. His audience, it seems, was impressed with his message, even though it may have disagreed with his politics. Lippmann, in fact, was so influential that President Lyndon B. Johnson was forced to answer, through a spokesman, Lippmann's arguments against the Vietnam involvement.

Both in his person and in his work, Lippmann stands as a journalistic phenomenon. Critics can cite the high quality of his mind, the clarity of his prose, and the subtle drive of his arguments; but they cannot explain with any real finality the basis of his success.

To appreciate further the difficulty of analyzing the success of columnists, journalists and others need only try to find the formula of prominent columnists. James Reston in political writing, Red Smith in sports, Art Buchwald in humor, William F. Buckley in social criticism—the appeal of these writers is

---

[1] Writers like Artemus Ward (Charles Farrar Browne) and Petroleum Vesuvius Nasby (David Ross Locke).

not a matter for facile analysis. And if they have successors, analysis of their appeal will be no more easy.

SOURCES OF MATERIAL FOR THE COLUMN

The source of material varies with the nature of the column for which it is being sought. Consequently, gathering material may be a very simple or a highly complex task.

The least difficult material to gather is that used in the reflective column: the column wherein the writer reflects, lightly or seriously, on an event, a change, or some other part of the vast canvas of life. The material is easy to gather because the writer merely turns within himself for his subject matter. Perhaps an old theater building is being razed; the columnist reminisces. He writes of famous performances he saw there, of little anecdotes in its history, or of the great actors who trod its boards. He, of course, is successful in proportion to his ability to make his reflections appealing. When well done, this type of column is always highly popular. It is employed by the sports columnist to rehash past baseball seasons, by the political columnist to evaluate the great figures of past or present times, and by all other columnists who write appraisals.

Also fairly easy to obtain is the material for the specialized column (health, stamps, books, or the like). Much material for this column is easily gathered because it is always readily available. The physician writing the health column simply gives information on current illnesses; the philatelist writes of the recent issues of stamps; the book columnist tells something of the new books; and the scientist explains some seasonal or topical subject such as the spring rains or the unusually loud noise of this year's locusts.[2]

The material for the column of anecdotes, tidbits of news, gossip, and patter is much more difficult to gather. The columnist, like the reporter, must dig hard for material, for the competition in this field is keen. The syndicated columnists who use this kind of material have staffs of reporters to do their leg work; the lesser lights must do their own. The columnist in this field, however, is usually helped by friends who supply tips, by publicity agents of those persons (such as actors or entertainers), who must stay in the limelight to prosper, and by tipsters who are paid in proportion to the material used.

Still more difficult to gather is the material for the philosophic column, the column wherein the author probes into the complexities of life. To be successful, the philosopher-columnist must have an air of originality about his work; that is to say, the reader must not be able to trace the writer's ideas directly to

---

[2] The reader must not conclude that the writing of the specialized column is a coast-in because material may be abundantly available. Quite the contrary. The successful writer of the specialized column must have an extensive background of knowledge upon which to draw and he must have unusual ability in interpretation. The physician, the scientist, and the book columnist, for instance, all need considerable expertise and understanding in order to write their columns.

other sources. Because presenting philosophy in an original way is a most difficult feat, especially when the writer must turn out six columns a week, very few columnists have been highly successful in this field.

Another column for which material is extremely difficult to gather is the humorous one. The difficulty exists because genuinely humorous material is hard to find or invent. Few persons can do it consistently. Like the comedians of stage, screen, and radio, the columnist who relies chiefly on humor is usually short lived. There have been, however, columnists who have been very successful over long periods, as for example, Will Rogers, Irvin S. Cobb, and Franklin P. Adams in the distant past and Art Buchwald and Harry Golden more recently.

The material for the column which answers readers' queries is, contrary to popular belief, frequently difficult to locate. This condition is true because writing this column is not always a simple matter of extracting questions from the mail and answering them. Too frequently, the questions mailed in cannot be used by the columnist because (1) they have been asked and answered very recently, (2) they are too stupid to be given a reply, (3) the phraseology is so badly muddled as to be unintelligible, (4) important data are missing in the question, or (5) there is no answer available. Where the columnist cannot get his questions from readers, he must invent them. Although this may seem a simple process, it entails a constant effort to unearth interesting material and is, therefore, a real challenge to the columnist. Furthermore, if the columnist invents his questions, he is unable to use the names and addresses that give the question-and-answer column the ring of authority which so many newspapers desire.

ATTRACTING READERS TO THE COLUMN

Since the necessary aim of the columnist is to have the greatest attainable number of readers, the student of journalism should know the five common ways in which a columnist can attract readers.

First, he can accomplish this end by *originality*. If, in his column, he constantly strikes a new note, he is likely to draw readers. He may have new material, a unique use of language, the ability to coin new words, or an unusual twist of thought. If this quality is attractive and he can maintain it consistently, he will hold his regular readers and draw new ones.

An important caution in this area, however, concerns the danger of imitation. An aspiring columnist, in his all-pervasive ambition to succeed, may suddenly conclude that he can perform in the pattern of a highly successful figure. He decides, for example, that he can philosophize with the capability of a Walter Lippmann or that he has the appealing touch of such past great writers as Heywood Broun and William Allen White. He forgets—or he has never learned—that these men were among the greatest columnists of the current century because of an unusual combination of personal attributes. As such, they are not subject to easy imitation.

Second, a columnist can attract readers by coming through with an *occasional scoop*. In the past several years, some columnists have divulged stories that have precipitated national scandals and congressional investigations. One syndicated columnist has been instrumental in arresting top-flight criminals; another has sent a congressman to prison; another has blocked presidential appointments. A columnist cannot hope, certainly, to have a scoop every day, but when he does, he will have many readers. Between scoops, he must rely on his other abilities to hold these readers.

Nationally syndicated columnists often obtain their scoops through tipsters and friends on the "inside." Local columnists must rely on whatever contacts they can establish in the right places. Both kinds of columnists, however, frequently receive "tips"—solicited or unsolicited. Someone wants to expose a dishonest practice, to embarrass a political administration, to "let the public know the truth," or to achieve a personal objective. In these cases, he simply contacts the columnist who, quite often, profits handsomely by using the information.

Third, a columnist may build up a large following by exhibiting an *attractive personality*. Because "attractive" is too broad and nebulous for a tight definition, the idea can be explained best by citing some illustrative personalities.

One of the most popular columnists of all time was H. L. Mencken, who exhibited a strangely attractive personal quality in the midst of devastating scorn and irony. His readers were charmed by his ability to smash cherished idols with a strong mixture of savage fury and intellectual scorn. One of the most appealing humorists in American writing was Franklin P. Adams, whose "The Conning Tower" for many years carried delightfully tart quips and light verse, especially as it all touched his metropolitan New York scene. The most widely read columnist from the battlefields of World War II was Ernie Pyle, whose writings gave out the ring of a genuinely likable man. His readers responded especially to his deep humility and his appealing sensitivity.

Today, in our leading newspapers, others are carrying on in these traditions; and if their reputations are not yet so great, they are still highly successful because of the appeal of their personalities.

Generally speaking, when the column is largely personalized, as for example, the column of humorous observations, an attractive personality is an essential. When the column is strictly factual, as is the general information column, the demand on personality is at its lowest.

Fourth, a columnist can gain readers by exhibiting a note of *authority*, by consistently showing that he knows whereof he speaks. The columnist with this attribute is like the widely respected newspaper: he is regarded as the essence of soundness, and he is esteemed and quoted accordingly.

Because this quality is so important, the columnist must beware rash judgments, immature thoughts, half truths, and obvious propaganda. These cautions are especially important with respect to any column designed primarily to impart facts. Examples are columns on general information, answers to queries, and legal advice.

Fifth, a columnist can win readers by attaining a position of *eminence* before turning to the writing of a column. Syndicated columns have been written by a widow of a former President of the United States, a former presidential cabinet member, a high ranking churchman, a prominent educator—and of course by dozens of authors from other fields. Meanwhile, there are numerous columns by well-established figures in the sports world, the theater, the business world, and similar places familiar to a large portion of the reading public.

THE STYLE OF THE COLUMN

In writing the column, there are five general styles which can be employed. In each case, of course, the columnist chooses the one which best suits his material and his personality.

The Unified Style

When the columnist wants to speak on a single subject throughout, pointing everything toward convincing the reader of his central idea or thesis, he employs the unified style. This column is really an essay, formal or informal, according to the topic and the approach. The unified style is employed by the political columnist, the sports columnist who discusses a single subject each day, and others who cater to readers interested in reading columns that dwell upon one main idea. Two well-known columns furnish examples of the unified style. "A Line o' Type or Two" [3] exemplifies *reflective writing;* "Don't Take My Word for It" illustrates *serious discussion.*

A LINE O' TYPE OR TWO

Hew to the Line, let the quips fall where they may.

Reg. U. S.
Pat. Office

WHO NEEDS MORE HOLIDAYS?

If the rigors of holiday living grow much worse, somebody is going to get wise and organize the International Brotherhood of Factory Workers, Office Employes, and Professionals [UFO-CIA], dedicated to longer working hours and fewer so-called holidays.

Surely today's version of a day off is not what the late Sam Gompers had in mind when he led the struggle for shorter working hours, better working conditions, and more paid holidays. What the workingman deserved, he said, was more leisure.

Leisure? Week-ends are bad enough at any time of year. They are when everybody else thinks you have plenty of time to stop by and discuss the future of the PTA, or take part in a neighborhood pick-up-and-clean-up drive, or umpire a neighborhood ball game, or raise money for the local epizootic society. They are when the American male is expected to remedy the defects in the household gadgets which have liberated the American female, or

---

[3] Columns do not often survive their creators, "A Line o' Type or Two" is an exception. It was originated by Bert Leston Taylor, who died in 1921.

more likely try to get hold of what is sometimes inaccurately referred to as the repair man [who collects a substantial holiday fee for examining the ailing device and informing you that it can't be fixed until next Thursday, when he can get the necessary parts].

Days off at this season are even worse. They are when you examine your checkbook and wonder how you ever get your tax figured out, change the car license plates [the bolts, of course, have to be sawed thru], and contemplate the icy expanse of ruts, crevasses, and seracs which you call your driveway.

During the Christmas "holidays" we are jounced, dragged, shoved, or otherwise propelled from one festive occasion to another. We stagger to bed, exhausted, only to be aroused at 7 a. m. because this is the day the lady of the house has chosen to change the bedding and do the laundry. After all, she explains, she has to do this on your day off so that you will see how hard she works.

Only 12½ per cent of men, according to an informal survey of eight colleagues, find the leisure which they look forward to on their days off. Another 12½ per cent have no opinion. The remaining 75 per cent admit that they work harder on days off than they do at the office, and that they secretly look forward to getting back to work, after a holiday, for some rest.

Yet the unions keep on pushing for shorter work weeks as well as easier working conditions. It doesn't make sense. The easier our jobs get, the more eager we should be to stay at them. It won't help to devote more days off to doing all of the things we have to do on days off. As Prof. Parkinson has probably discovered, the number of things to do on days off rises twice as fast as the number of days off. There is no balm in that direction. What the American worker needs is a seven-day work week, a card room in the personnel department, comfortable beds in the restrooms, and tennis courts built over the office parking lot.

JOHN T. McCUTCHEON JR.
—*The Chicago Tribune*

Don't Take My Word For It

By FRANK COLBY

Let's Learn A New Word

In the December, 1949, issue of "Word Study," a publication of G. and C. Merriam Company (Webster's dictionaries), Dr. Thomas Elliott Berry, a college professor, coins a most interesting and useful word to designate the literary device of naming fictional characters after their occupations, appearances, or personal traits, such as Mrs. Malaprop, a character in Sheridan's "Rivals." She is noted for her blunders in the use of words. The word Malaprop was coined from the French phrase mal a propos, "inappropriate."

Dr. Berry's new word is charactonym, formed from the Greek charakter, "impression, mark, characteristic," plus onyma, "name." Charactonym is pronounced: KAR'ik-tuh-NIM, the first syllable as in carrot, carry.

Dr. Berry observes that charac-

tonyms are as old as literature itself. He cites many such interesting examples as Aaron Thousandacres, Admiral Bluewater, and the seaman Harry Ark, from the works of James Fenimore Cooper, Ben Jonson's Cutbeard, a barber, Lady Haughty, and her servant, Mistress Trusty.

Greek fables are rich in charactonyms, and they are to be found in the folklore and legends of almost every race. Indeed, untold millions of persons today bear surnames that began as charactonyms: Little, Strong, Bernard ("bold as a bear"), Leonard ("strong or brave as a lion"), Philip ("lover of horses"), Wise, Goodman, Handy, Long, Short, Longfellow.

In a manner of speaking, then, charactonyms are nicknames.

Teachers of literature will, I feel sure, be very happy to discover Dr. Berry's new word charactonym. And I am more than glad to pass the good word on to the readers of my column. Here's a paste-in item for your dictionaries:

Charactonym: KAR'ik-tuh-NYM. A name given a person or fictional character in keeping with his occupation or most pronounced characteristics. Charactonym, from the Greek charakter, "impression; characteristic," plus onyma, "name," was coined by Dr. Thomas Elliott Berry, State College, West Chester, Pa.

The Anecdotal Style

The term "anecdotal style" explains itself. It is used by the columnist who wants to tell a series of little unrelated stories or make several observations which have no bearing on each other. The writer usually has between six and ten of such anecdotes or observations in a column, and he generally separates them from each other by asterisks or other typographical devices (stars, dashes, bold type, extra space, short lines, or other). "Paul Crume's Big D" is representative.

Paul Crume's

Big D

ONE OF THE guests at the opera ball a week ago at the Fairmont was rudely interrupted when a small, soft, cuddly dog fell out of the heavens into her lap.

The dog turned out to be Snoopy, the boon companion of Mark Schnallinger, the 3-year-old son of the Fairmont manager. Just before bedtime, Mark and Snoopy had sneaked down from the penthouse to the lighting booth of the Regency Ballroom to get a look at the great things.

Mark had become entranced with all the fine gowns, jewels, the W. T. White High School marching band and the waiters with flaming swords and pheasants under glass.

Snoopy had just fallen over the railing.

Everything turned out all right. This was a very understanding guest.

A man tells us that the local wags have quit telling Aggie jokes and are now laying them to the Cowboys.

AT PARIS, says Bill Thompson, a tiny kindergarten lass appeared at the Calvary Methodist Church in a new leather miniskirt, and everybody spoke admiringly about it.

After the playground period, the youngster came into the classroom without the skirt. As a matter of fact, she was stripped down to her panties.

"Honey, where's your skirt," asked Mrs. John Good, the teacher, who does not get too upset at such capers from her tiny charges.

"Well," said the little girl, "everybody said it was so pretty that I didn't want to get it dirty playing in it."

A DALLAS TRANSIT bus driver was driving along the other day on one of the downtown streets where the righthand lane is a bus lane. He was slightly shaken up when a Volkswagen driver cut in ahead of him from the left, zoomed around in front of the bus and attempted to turn at a street.

The bus driver barely kept from hitting the car, but it didn't keep from creating a commotion.

The Volkswagen driver was incensed.

"If there's anything I can't stand," he said, "it's somebody who doesn't know how to drive a bus."

On Division Street in Arlington is Woody's Drive-Thru Pawn Shop. Presumably, you can leave anything but the car.

MRS. BEN NABORS of Carollton bought the first real, whole, hairy coconut that she can remember the other day.

She took it home, and Ben, her 6-year-old son, was properly amazed.

"That," he exclaimed, "is the biggest pecan I ever saw."

—The Dallas (Tex.) *Morning News*

The Departmental Style

When the columnist has material that is easily separable into "departments," he often employs the departmental style. The departments may be given such names as "In the Mailbag," "Lest We Forget," "Things to Remember," and "Passing Parade"; or they may simply be separated by asterisks or some other typographical device. The departmental style is especially effective for random observations, little-known information, and provocative bits of news of general interest.

Departmental style columns are highly popular with readers because of the ease with which they can be read and the interest they often hold. Consequently, most newspapers have at least one such column. An example is Herb Caen's column in the *San Francisco Chronicle*.

HERB CAEN

One Thing After Another

CAENFETTI: Remember when you could see the gifted pantomimist, Robert Shields, performing free in Union Square? You may now place that memory in your "That Was San Francisco" file, for Robert and his equally talented wife, Lorene, are being featured for the next three months at Vegas' Flamingo Hotel—at $3000 a week . . . I was half-kidding last year when I predicted our troubled ball club would some day be the Tokyo Giants, but the rumors grow stronger that Japanese money will speak louder than Bob Lurie's yen to own the team . . . Perhaps you noticed Matthew Kelly's daily photo in the society pages yesterday. If you particularly admired his shirt, The Shadow Knows that Mr. Kelly is in receipt of the following communication from his London shirtmaker: "We are disappointed that you have not acknowledged our recent memorandum concerning this account for we expected confidently that in view of the time already allowed you would have sent us your cheque, and we must now ask that you be good enough to give the matter your urgent attention" . . . In Keeping with the tenets of modern journalism we fished the foregoing out of Mr. Kelly's garbage can.

★ ★ ★

BIG NIGHT: Nadine Dennehy, sniffing the air at the Cow Palace Tues. night: "The Rolling Stones may gather no moss but they do draw a lot of grass." It was like old times at the Fillmore plus Winterland times 10— Haight-Ashbury Medical Clinic volunteers treating kids who had OD'd on something stronger than grass, good vibes mingling with bad trips, Frisbees flying, and a million-dollar sound system achieving the death knell of the electronic age: the music was so loud you couldn't hear it . . . Is Mick Jagger's appeal bisexual or unisexual? Remind me to ask the next bison or unicorn that crosses his path. It was more fun and less confusing backstage, where Bill Graham was happily nuzzling his new love, a 23-yr-old with a seven-yr-old son, and Bianca Jagger, a vision in dazzling white, paraded around as Rolling Stones' great Annie Liebovitz flashed her bulbs . . . The news, if any: rock'n'roll is dead.

★ ★ ★

ONWARD: Re decibels, Dr. A. Alan Weber is thoroughly confused to read that the new Fireman's Fund bldg. in Novato has a "white sound" system "which provides a constant inaudible hum that industrial psychiatrists say is better to work under than Muzak." Inaudible? That may account for all the dogs gathered at the front door . . . Add newlyweds: S. F. Atty. Wm. Fazio

and Princess Lepeti Malo Tuitele, dghtr of American Samoa's Super Chief. The bridegroom's brother, Joe Fazio, who made the 6000-mile trip to attend the wedding, almost missed it; he was stuck for two hours in an aerial tramway that suddenly went dead, 1000 feet over Pago Pago harbor, and That's Not Funny . . . If you happened to see Chub Feeney, Pres. of the Nat'l League, and Peter Lomax, owner of Monroe's on Lombard, bursting out of that place and racing madly around the block, they were settling a bet. Nice Guy Feeney finished last.

★ ★ ★

MORE NAMEDROPS: Frances Ford Coppola is backing Geo. Moscone for Mayor but Dianne Feinstein's campaign is moving ahead by Leeps and Bounds. That would be Harry Leeps and Charlotte Bounds, who have joined her volunteers and may I join you in becoming slightly ill? . . . A new and probably meaningless poll shows Ms. Feinstein slightly ahead of George, Milton Marks slipping, Barbagelata sliding and Ertola scrambling. At this point, nobody's winning, as usual . . . Middle-of-the-roader Ertola has hired a liberal (Maxwell Arnold) to handle the media, and a conservative (Harvey Hukari) as campaign manager.

★ ★ ★

TEA FOR TWO: Nancy Welford, the one-time musi-comedy queen who now lives at Parkmerced, celebrated a Golden Anniversary last week. It was on July 7, 1925, that she opened at the Curran in "No No Nanette," scoring a smash that carried her and the show to Broadway stardom. "I was only 20 at the time," she giggles enchantingly, "but I won't tell you may age now— you'll have to guess" . . . Okay. Fifty.

—*The San Franciscio Chronicle*

The Unrelated-Facts Style

When the object of the column is to present a mass of facts which have little or no bearing on each other, the unrelated facts style is generally the best approach. This style enables the columnist to present his facts without any apparent order. He simply separates the facts with one or more periods, depending on the length of pause desired. To relieve the monotony of the reading, the writer or the copy editor may use an occasional subhead.

The success of the unrelated-facts-style column springs from its author's ability to sustain interest by variety, surprise, or whatever other device may be suitable.

An example is the *Boston Herald American's* D. Leo Monahan column.

D. Leo Monahan

WBZ-TV's No. 1 choice for Celtics' commentator is Bob Cousy. Meanwhile, Kenny Hudson, another candidate, also is under consideration for a TV job in Washington, D.C. . . . I talked with Rick Wise last October the day of the Sox-Cards deal. He seemed unhappy then. Apparently things have gone downhill since . . . Sox Veep Dick O'Connell had a hair transplant. Hockey's Bobby Hull had one, but it didn't take. Hull recently tried another, this time a "hair weave," whatever that is.

Spalding, one of the top producers of tennis balls, is expanding production facilities to supplement output at the Chicopee plant, which has to tell you something about the sport's growth . . . The tennis this week at Bretton Woods, N. H., received a big play in NY journals. The Times even carried a map on how to get there . . . The Nat'l Blind Golf is a good take this weekend at Nashawtuc CC, Concord. Proceeds go to eye research . . . Former 49ers QB John Brodie, now a sportscaster, didn't need the NFLPA, it seems. He's now collecting $75,000 per annum for the next decade as a souvenir of the AFL-NFL armistice.

BC's hard-working sports PR man Eddie Miller is moving up, taking over the school's overall publicity program, an ambitious undertaking. It was a wise move on the college's part since Eddie is one of the real pros in the field. Of course, AD Bill Flynn now must find a worthy successor, and that won't be easy.

The Storer people have looked into pro lacrosse to fill Garden dates. The Nat'l Lacrosse League is backed largely by NHLers in Philly, Montreal, Toronto and recently voted to expand. Further, B's GM Harry Sinden is buddies with Montreal's John Ferguson, part-owner and coach of Les Quebeccois. Lacrosse is akin to hockey with speed, contact, fights, etc. and player's salaries are peanuts—$4000 a season average. Montreal has drawn crowds upwards of 10,000, but Toronto recently drew 749 and is considering a move to Long Island.

Team Canada '74, the WHA-backed entry which will play the Russians next month, has a couple of ringers—Mark and Marty Howe, Gordie's kids, who are Americans born in Detroit. Mark, indeed, played for the U.S. Olympic team in Sapporo, Japan . . . Pawtucket Red Sox angel Joe Buzas is reportedly allied with others in an effort to get major league baseball into Toronto with the moribund Baltimore and Oakland franchises the most likely candidates to shift. . . . Major league players now are using souped-up Japanese bats at $15 a copy. The bigs lowered the mound, reduced the strike zone and substituted cowhide baseballs for horsehides to hypo hitting. Now this. Little wonder the pitchers are beefing . . . or is it cowering?

—*Boston Herald American*

The Question and Answer Style

The reason for the term "question and answer" is immediately apparent—the columnist gives a question and then answers it. This style is employed in all columns answering questions for readers and in columns where the author poses questions. An example of the author-posed question is to be seen in the bridge column, where the writer answers the questions which he believes are most often asked.

The *Boston Globe's* "Camper's Corner" is an example of a special-interest question-and-answer column.

Camper's Corner—

Q. We have just acquired a new, small travel trailer equipped with bottle gas tanks. A friend has warned me that if these are overfilled by the gas dealer, it could be dangerous. Can you explain how to avoid this? Mrs. R. D. Lowell.

A. Most dealers know better than to overfill such tanks. But if you're in doubt, warn your dealer. He'll probably explain to you that these systems are of the vapor-withdrawal type, and that 10 to 15 percent of the tank's capacity must be left for the vaporization and expansion of the propane gas during temperature rises. This is a safety measure. In other words, when you fill a 20-pound tank you'll probably receive only 17 to 18 pounds of gas. If you insist on a full 20 pounds, the dealer will probably refuse. He knows that overfilled tanks can cause appliance malfunctions and leakage through the safety valve.

———

Q. I know it's not a wilderness stream, but I'm planning to canoe the Connecticut River in mid-July. How far up can I start? Can one paddle from the Connecticut Lakes into the river? G. T. Marshfield.

A. During mid-summer, the water may be too low and rocky above West Stewartstown, N.H. This is probably your best starting point.

———

Q. What is sassafras tea and how is it made? Mrs. O. T., Newton Highlands.

A. Sassafras tea is brewed from the bark of the roots of the sassafras tree. Springtime roots produce the best flavor. Seal the bark in a cloth envelope and simmer vigorously in water until this attains a dark root beer-like color. The longer you simmer, the more pronounced the flavor. Sugar can be added during the simmering. The tea can be served hot or cold. The northern range of the sassafras tree extends into southern Maine. It can be identified by the variety of leaves—with three lobes, unlobed, and mitten-shaped, often on the same branch. The further south you go, the bigger the tree. In some areas, it is as prolific as a weed.

———

Q. My brother-in-law insists that some canoes are equipped with a "bilge keel" to keep them from side-slipping in a high wind. His description of a bilge keel is pretty vague so I think he's putting me on. Is he? J. T., Saugus.

A. No. But "bilge keel" should be plural—"bilge keels." These were supplemental keels, one each side of the regular keel on canvas canoes of a generation ago. Most were added by trappers who wanted to protect their craft when dragging them across beaver dams. The last time I saw bilge keels in use was 1941. Modern canoe fabrics—aluminum, plastic, and fiberglass—have eliminated the need for them.

———

Q. A friend of mine just returned from a trip down the Allagash Wilderness Waterway where he claims his party was charged $2 per night per person. How come a charge for canoeing in the wilderness? N. J., Rutland, Vt.

A. The "Allagash Wilderness Waterway" is a misnomer. It is not a true wilderness. Rather it's a state park accessible by canoe. The state of Maine has to pay rangers to patrol it, to clean up campsites, to move overused camping sites, to maintain the dam at Churchill Lake to provide adequate water in the river, plus an occasional rescue or emergency mission. At $2 per day per person, the Allagash is a bargain, even if it's not really a "wilderness." This word should be deleted from the name.

—*Boston Sunday Globe*

EXERCISES

Write a column for each of the following:

1. Discuss the last major election in the nation, the state, or your city, with a view to its implications.
2. Think of yourself as an ardent devotee of the theater (legitimate stage) and write of the offerings of the current season.
3. Compare the leaders of the United States Senate of the moment with those of 10 or more years ago. Are they of as fine quality? Are they as shrewd? Do they have as much vision and grasp of current problems?
4. Write a column for a school paper in which you advocate either complete student control or partial student control over choice of outside speakers for all-school assemblies.
5. As a columnist for a metropolitan daily, discuss the strength or the weakness of the modern high school or college education. Remember that you are writing for laymen.
6. As a columnist for a large college publication, write a column composed of observations made about the campus on a particular day.
7. As radio and television editor on a newspaper serving a town of approximately 40,000 people, write a reflective column on Saturday evening offerings on one or both media.
8. Visit the opening of the opera season and write a column on what you see.

9. Write a humorous column on your inability to make your morning bus, the baffling questions that your four-year-old son asks, or how to avoid helping your wife with the spring housecleaning.
10. It is January 20 and there is little doing in the world of sport. Rehash last year's World Series.
11. Give a round-up of the nonmalicious gossip of your school, your neighborhood, or your town.
12. As a columnist of natural reputation, write a column on some important current question.
13. Picture yourself as a columnist who has lived in your town or city for the last 25 years or more. Write a column of reminiscences concerning changes of all sorts.
14. Gather six or seven interesting anecdotes and put them in a column.
15. Write a humorous column on some trivial subject such as how to get rid of door-to-door salesmen, how to retain the status quo of your waistline, or how not to slip on icy pavements.
16. As a roving reporter, write a column on the very interesting places in your city of which many residents are not aware.
17. Write a sports column in which you discuss the problem of subsidizing college athletes.
18. Write a column in the departmental style composed of material concerning your school or your community.
19. Write a column on the subject of the changing position of women.
20. Write a column in which you discuss some major speech that has been given recently.

FOR FURTHER READING

Bulman, David, ed. *Molders of Opinion*. Milwaukee: Bruce, 1945.

Carlson, Oliver, *Arthur Brisbane: A Candid Biography*. Harrisburg, Pa.: Stackpole, 1937.

Childs, Marquis, and James B. Reston, eds. *Walter Lippmann and His Times*. New York: Harcourt, 1959.

Dam, Hari N. *The Intellectual Odyssey of Walter Lippmann*. New York: Gordon Press, 1973.

Fisher, Charles, *The Columnists: A Clinical Survey*. New York: Howell, Soskin, 1944.

Johnson, Walter, *William Allen White's America*. New York: Holt, 1947.

Kramer, Dale. *Heywood Broun*. New York: Current Books, 1949.

Mayfield, Sara. *Constant Circle: H. L. Mencken and His Friends*. New York: Delacorte Press, 1968.

Williamson, Daniel R. *Feature Writing for Newspapers*. New York: Hastings House, Publishers, 1976.

★ **12** ★

Basics for the School or College
  Paper
Operation of the School Paper
Problems of the School Paper
  Personnel and Staff
  Financial Situation
  What to Print
  What Not to Print
  Instruction
  Schedules
The School Paper and the Un-
  derground Press
Recent Changes in Coverage
Advisers' Problems and Respon-
  sibilities
Sources of News
The Column and the Editorial

The School Paper

Educators have long since come to recognize the school paper as an indispensable part of a well-balanced school life. An effective paper properly interprets the newsworthy events in the life of the institution it serves; it helps to build the pride that is the basis of school spirit; it provides a medium of expression for students interested in writing for publication; and it gives students pointing toward careers in journalism an opportunity in practical experience. As such, the paper is one of the most important activities outside the classroom. But if the paper is to fill its important role, all concerned must recognize certain basic facts.

BASICS FOR THE SCHOOL OR COLLEGE PAPER

Above all, everyone from adviser to lowest staff member must realize that the paper, however small, *must be a real work of journalism,* not merely a toy for the amusement of a privileged group. The paper must always aim for the highest standards of the good publication, toward being approved completely by those competent to judge. Every phase of the work—coverage, writing, content, make-up—must be executed carefully, and the staff must think of the paper as highly as if it were a professional undertaking. All too often, a little clique gains control and uses the paper in an immature or selfish manner. It prints the small talk its members consider sophisticated, it takes malicious digs at other students and faculty, and all in all it defeats the purpose for which a paper should exist.

Equally important, the *school paper must fill a need;* or stated in another way, it must make the student population regard it as an essential of school life. Like the traditional football game, the senior prom, and the spring class day, the paper must be eagerly anticipated; it must be thoroughly enjoyed; and it must be discussed vigorously afterwards. The readers must be brought to rely on the paper for material they consider meaningful—whatever it may be. They may be seeking important announcements, pleasant observations, background information on athletics, news of their classmates—or all these, and more. The effective school paper somehow finds the elusive formula that explains reader interests and builds a sound journalistic creation on those interests. Meeting this requirement may be almost overwhelmingly difficult, but the paper's staff must exert the maximum effort.

A third basic fact is that the school paper *must have competent faculty direction,* for without mature guidance and instruction, it seldom points toward high ideals. It is not patronizing to state the reason: the student staff rarely has the perception, judgment, and journalistic experience necessary to handle a paper expertly. Such being the case, sympathetic direction is vital. This direction, as the faculty adviser soon learns, may entail numerous difficulties because students tend to believe that a school paper should be completely unbridled. Athletic teams have coaches whose words are law; musical organizations have conductors who rule with absolute authority; and dramatic productions have directors who approximate the dictator. Yet school newspaper staffs often want absolute freedom of decision.

When the adviser meets this attitude, he should try to help the staff see the light of good journalism rather than attempt to censor the paper—however deft his censorship touch may be. Most good papers, faculty advisers attest, experience little or no friction because adviser and staff have learned to "talk things through." [1]

Another important point concerning faculty direction is that the adviser's role varies according to the particular situation. In the case of the secondary-school paper, the adviser usually has complete jurisdiction. He is the final authority on every question, and he is expected to be, in the exact sense of the term, a censor—although even this situation is now changing (see the discussion under "Recent Changes in Coverage," later in this chapter).

In the instance of the college paper, however, the adviser's role may vary from that of absolute censor [2] to that of pure adviser; that is, the adviser may be in complete control, or he may be a bystander who gives advice when

[1] See the several Press Association handbooks for a substantiation of this point.

[2] Although the number of colleges and universities where the faculty adviser is an absolute censor is very small, such institutions still exist.

requested. Between these extremes, various degrees of control are to be found throughout the nation.

Generally speaking, private universities and colleges are most likely to have uncensored papers. Consequently, many of their papers exhibit a complete freedom of speech. When the administration feels that the newspaper has gone too far, the editor may be called to task, but these occasions are generally rare. In state-controlled institutions, however, the newspaper must sometimes be wary of offending the taxpayer. The paper, for instance, must be careful of aiding one political party at the expense of another, offending a religious group, or straying outside the bounds of good taste. Taxpayers, it seems, believe they have the right to pass judgment on any agency supported by their money, and college administrators, in their desire to keep the public satisfied, often attempt to exert a control on the handling of editorial policy.[3]

The main philosophical bases for censorship are well known. The school administration contends that the paper is an "official" part of the school program, and as such, must be subject to some official control. The administration further contends that staffs, especially on the secondary level, are not sufficiently mature to forestall unfair treatment of individuals or damage to the prestige of the school. Finally, the administration contends that it has an obligation to safeguard the investment—in finances, goodwill, and tradition—which has been handed to the newspaper staff.

Against these arguments stands one very important belief: that students must have the unrestricted right to express their thoughts on their school. They maintain that unless allowed to criticize policies which directly affect them, they are being denied fundamental rights as citizens of a democracy and as members of an institution of which they are the largest part.

OPERATION OF THE SCHOOL PAPER

To understand the school paper, we must first see how it differs from the ordinary newspaper.

The most striking difference is that the school paper, like other house organs, *relates news of a single institution.*[4] Practically every item comes from the school and its related activities, and the item is valuable in proportion to student interest in the particular story.[5] Because the school paper recounts news of a single institution, the whole procedure of gathering and handling stories differs from that of the standard paper.

---

[3] The matter of taxpayer resentment is not a subject to be dismissed as a series of harmless howls. As a result of the student protests and disturbances of the late 1960s on the campuses of California colleges and universities, state legislators reacted to a public pressure against those institutions by drastically reducing their appropriations, thereby seriously threatening all their academic programs.

[4] The term "house organ" refers to the publication of a business house, a church, an industrial organization, or similar place which produces its publication primarily or exclusively for its own "family."

[5] Some college publications carry some local, state, and national stories.

A second difference is that the school newspaper *serves a distinctly homogeneous group.* Unlike the general newspaper, its principal readers are generally in the same age bracket, on the same intellectual level, and of relatively similar backgrounds of interest. Thus the editors can be certain, in normal situations, of some common denominator of reader interests and concern. Moreover, these leanings do not vary sharply from year to year. Students are always interested, for example, in stories about upcoming assembly programs, curriculum changes, and unusual student personalities. Satisfying reader interest is simplified by this homogeneity of background.

A third basic difference is that the school newspaper *operates in a manner sharply different from that of the ordinary newspaper.* Most noticeable is the longer time lapse between writing and printing. The school paper, except in the large colleges where a daily is maintained, generally has a 24-hour period between writing the last news and seeing the paper in print. Other items may be in type three or four days earlier. This situation poses the problem of giving a "hot-off-the-griddle" aspect to news that may be a week old. Another noticeable difference in operation is the ever-changing personnel of the school paper; positions are usually held for only one year or one term. No sooner does one staff become reasonably competent than its term ends and another takes over. A final difference in operation concerns repercussions. Where the regular newspaper operates with a view to avoiding censure from many quarters, the school publication is responsible almost solely to the school authorities.[6] Hence, the problem of avoiding censure is much easier to analyze.

PROBLEMS OF THE SCHOOL PAPER

By virtue of its essential nature, the school paper differs markedly from the professional newspaper. Most noticeably, it has a more rapid turnover of editorships, a greater percentage of novice writers, and a less substantial financial structure. It also carries a more predictable kind of news because school and college activities tend to move in cyclical patterns—that is, class elections are held the same time each year, class days are staged the same week each spring, and most other events are scheduled on traditional days. All this being true, the school paper faces a set of special problems.

Below is a discussion of the major issues encountered in operating a school paper on any level. These, therefore, are the problems which constantly beleaguer anyone charged with handling the school paper.

Personnel and Staff

In staffing the school paper, the success or the failure of the publication is often determined. A competent, eager staff can raise the paper to new heights,

---

[6] An exception to this statement must be made regarding some college and university papers. Recently, many such newspapers, especially in the large universities, have become, legally speaking, entities apart from their institutions. Therefore, their institutions have no control over, and hence no responsibility for, the contents of the publication.

while an incompetent, diffident staff can relegate the paper to a surprising depth. The greatest care naturally should be given the choices of editor and business manager. The former is important because on his shoulders rest the responsibilities of publishing a good paper; the latter is important because to him falls the task of providing the finances for printing the paper.

The Editor. The editor should be a person who has risen from the ranks, one who has *earned* this important position. In addition, he should know thoroughly the business of turning out this particular paper; he should be capable of handling other students so that friction may be kept to a minimum; he should be well acquainted with every phase of life on his campus so that he can catch immediately any error in fact or procedure made by his reporters; he should be able to write well so that he can help others and correct bad copy; he should have vision and good judgment so that the editorial policy of the paper will reflect a high tone; and he should be absolutely reliable in order that schedules may be respected, deadlines may be met, and accuracy may be maintained. But, above all, he should be a person who is doing the work of editor because he is deriving great satisfaction from his labors. Without enthusiasm, he can rarely do acceptable work.

Clearly, the above statement of attributes presents an ideal situation; it describes a person with a rare combination of rare characteristics. Yet if the statement is idealistic, it is also realistic because a first-quality editor must at least approach these requirements closely.[7]

The Business Manager. The business manager must be a person with a sound business sense, one who can handle the problems entailed in keeping a school paper solvent. He must have an understanding of the intricacies of budgeting expenses and balancing receipts and expenditures, and he must be able to keep accurate records, to operate his department smoothly, and to maintain a close check on an endless number of small details. He must be able to appraise changing business conditions, and he must be able to handle his staff efficiently. Above all, however, like the editor, he must be a person who is doing work that appeals to him.

Other Staff Positions. The positions immediately below the two top offices of editor and business manager should fall to the runners-up. They, like the winners of the top positions, should possess in great degree the qualities already discussed, and they, too, should have earned their positions. Also important, these first assistants should be given significant responsibilities. Too often an unsuccessful candidate for the highest position feels that he has been defeated completely, that he must now serve as a mere clerk for his successful rival. The answer, therefore, is to make the subordinate office really significant.

In filling the lower positions, the central consideration should be the student's potential value to the staff. A serious attempt should be made to evaluate the student's interest, ability, and reliability. Interest and ability can be ap-

---

[7] For further thought on the matter of choosing the editor, see the discussion "Merit System" under "Adviser's Problems and Responsibilities" in this chapter.

praised by the tryout method; reliability can be determined by appraising the student's work after he has been given some responsibilities. Because the tryout is an important phase of staffing the paper, some discussion is necessary.

When the would-be-staffers report for tryouts, the entire process of selection should be outlined in order to convince any doubting candidates that the selection will be fair and open. The actual tryout can evaluate the candidate's interest by asking leading questions about reasons for wanting to join the staff, extracurricular activities, and background for the position sought. His ability can be appraised by asking him to write two or three shorts, the facts for which are given him, and by giving him a standard test in usage and mechanics. His work can then be evaluated for style, clarity, mechanics, and the other important phases of journalistic writing.

Once admitted to the staff, the member should retain his position or be promoted according to a clearly explained merit system. This system should be constructed to reward the staff person according to his over-all merit and to aid the paper by placing the best students in the various positions. A merit system should also be constructed with a view to keeping any chances of favoritism at a minimum. Further, merit systems should take cognizance of such important qualities as punctuality in handling assignments, thoroughness in work, and reliability in executing major and minor details.

Personality Problems. In dealing with the student staff, the adviser must be aware of the immaturity that naturally accompanies youth. He must be on guard for the indiscretions, the rash judgments, and the radical ideas that longer life softens. There will be the student who wants to blast editorially the entire administration of the school or college; the student who wants to discuss some taboo or delicate subject in an open or brazen manner; the student who wants to use the paper as a sounding board for his pet ideas; and the student who wants to print the hopelessly dull material which he thinks is screamingly funny. These students must be suppressed painlessly, if possible, and any talent of theirs diverted into the proper channel. The adviser must also stress the concept of responsibility. All too many students seem to think that deadlines are elastic things to be stretched at will, and any mistake in copy is a minor matter.

Financial Situation

Before even the first issue, the adviser and his staff should know the financial pattern for the entire school year. Signed contracts with printer and advertisers should be on file, firm income figures should be on hand, and every last expense should be anticipated. When a paper fails financially, advertisers are difficult to procure after publication resumes, and numerous other embarrassing events are likely to occur.

The matter of contracts has recently become especially important because of the rising costs of printing. As the price of paper, labor, and other services has risen, printers have raised their charges overnight, thereby creating real difficulty for staffs without long-range contracts. A further thought on printing contracts is this: most printers are refusing to contract for a constant price. Instead, they are inserting cost-escalation clauses into the contract to protect themselves against rising costs of paper and labor. Thus the printing of the last issue of a paper is likely to cost more than the printing of the first issue.

When considering the financial situation of the school paper, certain fundamentals should be recognized. The first is that the larger the school, the less financial strain there should be; the larger the enrollment, obviously, the larger the potential circulation and the higher the prospective advertising revenue.

Second, every effort should be made to sell the paper by subscription or by some other plan that guarantees circulation revenue for the entire year or semester, free from issue-to-issue fluctuations in sales.

Third, if the paper must be sold one copy at a time, it should appear simultaneously throughout the campus on the day of publication, preferably under conditions which hinder students' sharing a copy. Once a student has given a paper even a cursory glance, he will rarely buy it.

Fourth, the opportunity to advertise in the paper should be made as appealing as possible. Much of this appeal is achieved by attractive placing of ads and by presenting a good sales talk to the potential advertiser. A situation to be avoided is the proliferation of "Compliments of" ads. This kind of ad weakens the businesslike atmosphere by reducing the advertising to a patronage level; advertisers then have little expectation of return from their expenditure for ads.

Fifth, and most important, the stronger the paper journalistically, the greater the chances for wide circulation. In other words, the best way to increase revenue is to turn out a good paper.

School newspaper staffs should also avoid, if possible, complete dependence on revenue from sales and advertising to balance their budgets. In fact, few school newspapers can survive without secondary help. Sometimes the revenue from a school play is given to the newspaper; sometimes it is the profit from a sale; sometimes it is the income from a special athletic event. Then, too, in some schools the students pay a flat sum known as the "activity fee" at the beginning of the year. This payment entitles the student to admission to athletic events and social affairs and to copies of various publications. In this way, definite revenue is guaranteed to the paper.[8]

What to Print

When the staff and the adviser face the question of what is to be printed, they meet a surprising amount of difficulty. On the one hand, they have the student readers with all their likes and dislikes, their desires for everything from a joke book to a literary magazine. On the other hand, the paper has its responsibilities to the school and to good journalism in general. Accompanying these situations are the all-too-frequent forces that have axes to grind. A faculty adviser wants a big play for a story that concerns his sphere of activity, even though the story may be dull; the school administration wants the paper to

---

[8] This type of flat fee is very common in private secondary schools and small colleges.

preach long sermons and administer sound warnings; a small segment of the student body would like to see more chatter and much more scandal—provided, of course, that they are not the object of the ridicule. In short, everyone's idea is sharply different from everyone else's.

Amid such conditions, the paper should construct a policy based on good journalism and service. Thereafter, it should strive to convince all concerned of the basic concept that many situations in journalism must be handled as judgment calls. Only one small group can make the decision, and it must function independently—without benefit of mass advice. Faculty, administrators, and others may want to dictate, but in the last analysis, the staff must be restricted only by established editorial policy.

What Not to Print

As editors ponder the question of what not to print, they should remember above all the canon on which high-minded newspapers pride themselves: that no material should be used which takes unfair advantage or sets out to injure. This caution is especially important because the student writer, realizing his power over other students who cannot strike back in print, is often tempted to use this advantage. Another important caution concerns gossip. If the editor wants to use gossip, he should confine it to one clearly labeled column; it should never be spread throughout the paper, and a definite attempt should be made to keep it nonmalicious. In the hands of a clever writer, gossip can be entertaining and amusing, but too often it becomes dull and inane.

A type of writing which some advisers (but by no means all) think should be handled with reserve is the material wherein the student expounds on subjects treated by the daily papers—for example, the political column. On many occasions the student writer may attempt to theorize authoritatively about the international situation, recent legislation on monetary problems, or presidential appointments.

Although the advisers and staffs who disparage this kind of writing concede that the student himself may profit by doing such a piece, they argue that the subject has probably been covered more authoritatively by a journalist of national stature. In fact, they argue, herein lies the danger: the student frequently rehashes knowingly or otherwise the opinions of these well-known writers. And in the end, the paper suffers because readers tend to take the student writer of such material lightly—and hence tend to think less of the paper.

Those endorsing this view also see a questionable value in student-written book reviews, criticisms of motion pictures and plays, and editorials on subjects unrelated to the school or college.[9] They contend that the reviews and the criticisms are of little value because they have probably been done better by the

---

[9] Many college newspaper staffs would register a sharp disagreement with this statement. They would argue that as "adult" citizens of a democracy, they have not only a right but an obligation to criticize editorially any action that touches their lives. Hence they subscribe to the idea of editorials that lambaste Congress, the President, the courts, or any person or institution.

metropolitan papers or the leading magazines; the editorials fail because there is a question of the editor's grasp of the subject and of the appropriateness of the editorial in a school paper.

Considering further the subject of material to be questioned, one comes upon humorous writing. This material must be examined closely because more persons have failed in this field than in any other. Few students, the adviser soon learns, can write humorously, despite the fact that many think they are so gifted. The fact that few students can write humorously is not surprising, for skill in humor is extremely rare, even in the best of the large newspapers. Indeed, American newspapers are always ready to employ a writer with an appealing sense of humor. If there is a scarcity in the professional field, there is little likelihood that many humorous writers are to be found for the school paper.

If there is a shortage of humorous writers, however, there is no shortage of an opposite type of writer—the student looking for a quarrel. In this all-too-numerous group are found the individual with a grudge against someone, the radical who wants to make ill-considered changes, and the person who enjoys disagreeing for the joy of a heated argument. The writings of this group must be checked carefully because they can undermine seriously the paper's explicit or implied claim to publish carefully prepared, thoroughly documented, and objectively written material.

The question of what not to print is steadily growing more troublesome because of the many "revolutions" in use of language, sexual relations, and general behavior. Student writers submit material which would once have been flatly rejected everywhere. Advisers and editors find themselves in a quandary about printing the so-called "four-letter" words, stories of sexual behavior, and material in questionable taste (such as an explanation of how to throw toilet-paper rolls into the air after the important touchdown).

Further, the question is becoming more complex because people outside the paper are asking legitimate questions about editorial policy. Students, faculty, administrators, and members of society at large (media commentators, elected officials, and similar figures) are asking: Whom does the paper speak for? The entire student body? The staff? The individual writer? And more troublesome: Should any staff have the right to damage the reputation of its school and expose the paper to possible litigation simply because it regards the paper as its property—as a vehicle for printing whatever it may select in whatever manner it may choose?

Only a reckless or superficial thinker would offer quick and final answers in these areas. Yet the fact is clear that staffs must seek some guidelines.

Among the best-informed people, the belief holds that the staff should think of its paper as a person; then it should model its paper accordingly. Does it want a paper that resembles the loud and noisy drunk in the bar room? Does it want a paper like the man who discusses offensive topics at the dinner table? Does it want a paper like the refined, thoughtful, but perhaps too stuffy individual? Or precisely what does it want?

As it settles this question, it will have created for itself, at the least, the foundation upon which to construct its guidelines.

Instruction

One of the most time-consuming tasks of the adviser is that of teaching the newer members of the staff. They must be taught to write in the appropriate style, to follow the established practices of the paper, and to hunt for and recognize stories.

The ideal answer to this problem is a class in journalism. In this way, students can be prepared for their work on the paper and given valuable academic material. Failing such a class, the adviser should have a period of formal instruction for newcomers and a procedure for improving the work of the older members of the staff.

At all events, the adviser should never blandly assume that the students eventually will learn to write well. Nor should he refer his students to the files of the old issues for instruction. When he does, every issue soon comes to look like a former one.

Schedules

Making students recognize schedules and deadlines is one of the real problems in handling the school paper. Many staff members, seemingly unaware of the importance of schedules, hand in copy late, miss stories, or in some similar manner upset the routine of the paper. This condition is especially prevalent at examination time, immediately before and after vacations, and at the end of the school year. Other than maintaining a staff of reliable students, there is no set pattern for making students respect the calendar and the clock. The adviser, however, must take care that every key man understands his responsibilities. These key men, in turn, must take care that their subordinates act accordingly.

Of vast importance in this regard is smoothly run editorial office. Schedules must be posted and checked regularly; files must be kept absolutely up-to-date; and every tool and device used by the staff must be operated efficiently.

THE SCHOOL PAPER AND THE UNDERGROUND PRESS

Anyone attempting to understand the school paper of the present must also understand the phrase, the "underground press." This expression refers to certain publications which, impelled by the organized social protest that welled up in the 1960s and the accompanying unsettled atmosphere of secondary-school and college campuses, have emerged to serve specific readerships among the general citizenry and student populations.

As to the publications aimed at the general reader, the term "underground press" designates, essentially, a kind of muckraking newspaper that castigates the "establishment" with varying degrees of scorn and journalistic abilities; as to school and college papers, the term signifies, in the main, publications not officially sanctioned—circulated free or for a varying charge—that carry material not normally found in official school papers or in traditional newspapers.

The bulk of the material in the underground press, both off and on campus, lies squarely in the tradition of the exposé. It recounts intrigue in high places, attempts at deception of the public, and sham in general—all, of course, as evaluated and interpreted by the editors of the particular paper. Although news of a traditional nature is sometimes carried, it is used selectively according to its value in supporting the editorial policies of the publication.

Any detailed examination of the underground-press publications, however, reveals that they have little in common other than their aggressive tone and their unorthodox material. Underground publications extend from the mere political tract to the bona fide newspaper; they range from crudely mimeographed sheets to genuinely finished eight-column newspapers; and they appear irregularly or on a firm schedule. They may have a life span of one or two issues; or they may continue for years.

Significantly, the term "underground press" has been challenged on grounds of appropriateness. Many persons in the field prefer "alternate press" because few of the publications are "underground." Most operate in the manner of *Ramparts,* the Berkeley *Barb,* and *The Phoenix;* that is, they carry mastheads with pertinent information, and they regard themselves as news publications in every sense of the term.

The underground or alternate press appears, as this is written, to have reached its peak and to be sharply on the decline. In fact, most competent observers agree that 1969 was the peak year and that an ebb tide began in the early 1970s. These same observers also agree on a probable figure of 6,000 of these publications in 1969. No circulation figures are available because of the lack of standard compilation procedures. Hence estimates vary widely. *The Wall Street Journal,* for example, sets the figure at approximately one-third of a million—the magazine *Newsweek* places the figure at two million. Meanwhile the Underground Press Syndicate claims a whopping 30 million.[10]

For operating expenses, the noncampus underground publications have had to rely almost entirely on sales and advertisements. With some on-campus publications, however, the situation has been different. They have received financial support, in varying degrees, from "outside" organizations.

Although the underground paper has been statistically insignificant, it has influenced strongly the editorial policy of the official school paper. By virtue of its emphasis on "all the news," "news behind the news," and an approach highly critical of school and college adminstrations, the alternate press has forced the official paper to discuss matters heretofore ignored and to move sharply toward a completely free press. It has also helped to reduce the number

---

[10] See John Tebbel, *Saturday Review,* November 13, 1971, p. 89.

of college papers under strong administration control and to encourage secondary-school papers to move in the same direction.

RECENT CHANGES IN COVERAGE

Because of speaking more openly, official papers are now more likely to offend. When they handled only "safe" news in a circumspect manner, they were like the well-mannered, discreet elderly lady discussing the weather: they rankled no one. However, by extending their coverage to stories formerly considered outside their realm—and presenting these stories with a forthrightness and sometimes a recklessness or a belligerence—they are now generating a variety of sparks, fires, and explosions. The result has been, increasingly often, that the newspaper has drawn the wrath of the school administrations, as well as angering the subjects of a story to the point of suing for libel.

The common pattern of conflict between paper and administration has begun with the paper carrying a statement or a story disturbing to the administration. The administration then announces that the policies of the paper—which the administration quickly points out is an "official" school publication—must be "reviewed" and "appropriate action" taken. Thereafter, a round of conflicts ensues, ending eventually in a broadly worded compromise statement to serve as an uneasy truce. Although the newspaper sometimes appears to be the loser, in the majority of instances, it strengthens its right to speak freely.

The pattern of legal conflict can be elucidated by citing representative situations. In February 1970, a United States District Court judge in Boston, Massachusetts, declared that the President of the Fitchburg State College lacked the authority to set arbitrary restrictions on material to be used in the college's newspaper. Thus the judge set a guideline for the independence of the newspaper from administration control.

In March 1971, the Supreme Court of the United States ruled that the Board of Regents of the University of Texas could not restrict the distribution of underground newspapers on the campus. Thus the highest court, in effect, established the right of non-official papers to circulate on college campuses.[11]

On April 14, 1975, the Fourth Circuit Court of Appeals, Baltimore, Maryland, declared unconstitutional the regulations invoked by the Woodlawn (Md.) Senior High School against an alternate-press paper. The Court scored the regulations as "broad and vague." It also noted that this was the third case in which it was called upon to guarantee the "free speech aspect of secondary

---

[11] Similar rulings have been made throughout the nation in instances of secondary-school papers. For example, on July 8, 1970, Judge Robert C. Zampano, United States District Court, New Haven, Conn., ruled that students at the Rippowam High School, Stamford, had a right to distribute their "independent" mimeographed newspaper so long as such distribution did not disrupt the orderly function of the school. In his ruling, Judge Zampano stated that "student newspapers are to be encouraged, not suppressed," and he scored heavily the idea of any "prior restraint" by Stamford or other school officials.

public school regulations.'' (The case involved the paper's reference to the school's cheerleaders as "sex symbols." The school administration considered the reference "obscene and demeaning to the school.")

Since the late 1960s, a rash of libel suits has been instituted against secondary-school and college publications. In fact, the number is so high that final figures are not obtainable. These suits, instituted largely by faculty members and students, charge injury in every respect from loss of position (obviously a faculty member) to irreparable personal damage. All this litigation has forced many student publications, especially college newspapers, to have lawyers check stories for potential libel.

ADVISER'S PROBLEMS AND RESPONSIBILITIES

Most secondary school papers and many college papers are published with some degree of faculty participation. In the instance of the secondary school paper, the faculty member is termed an "adviser." On the college paper, he is an "adviser" or a "consultant."

Although the adviser's role, as was stated earlier, may vary from absolute censor to occasional consultant, he should be well-informed in every department of the paper. This section discusses the opinions and advice of more than 50 advisers regarding the adviser's function. The discussion, therefore, will cast light on the adviser's problems and responsibilities.

Financial Situation. The adviser is expected to help the paper avoid financial troubles. Because he understands the intricacies of day-to-day dealings with the printer, advertisers, suppliers of equipment, and subscribers, he can lead the staff around the traps of money matters. The competent adviser points the staff toward sound business procedures in everything from the largest expenditure—the printing of the paper—to such small details as obtaining and filing sales slips for miscellaneous purchases.

Because schools and colleges are part of the public domain, the adviser must be especially careful of the manner in which the paper spends its money. All contracts should be let as a result of open bids, and all expeditures should be listed carefully in accounts open for public examination. The expenditure of funds by the paper of the tax-supported school is especially important because occasionally some "public-spirited" citizen may be watching very closely. The adviser should also try to have the budget approved in advance by the principal, the headmaster, or other proper administrative official of his institution. This protects him against repercussions.

Finally, he must help the staff make necessary allowance for expenditures that vary. Among such items are the cost of photos, of travel, and of other expenses of staff members. When the allotment is not apportioned evenly, the staff may find that it has overdrawn its account early in the year.

Merit System. Adviser and staff must devise a merit system satisfactory to students and faculty alike for selections to staff positions. The usual procedure is to give points on the basis of ability, length of service, and background for the position sought. This tends to put the best persons in the jobs and to remove the protests of favoritism that frequently accompany direct appointments.

In the absence of a merit system, direct appointment by the adviser is the next best course.[12] The least desirable system is that of allowing the total student body to elect the top officers of the publication. Such a course is unwise because personal popularity, rather than ability, often becomes the chief criterion.

However, in some secondary schools (especially private schools) and in almost every college and university, the faculty adviser has no control whatever over choices for staff leadership positions. His only role is to check the academic eligibility of the students; thereafter, he takes a back seat.

Recruiting and Prestige. Adviser and staff should establish a policy designed to enhance the reputation of the paper so that many people want to serve on its staff. They should pursue an active staff-recruiting policy (even if low in key). A large staff provides numerous candidates for the higher positions and consequently a wider choice in filling them.

The best way to gain prestige is to publish a good paper, for students always like to be a part of a thriving activity. Another way is to award some sort of insigne, such as a pin, for service on the staff. The caution in this regard is that the insigne must not be earned too easily. A third way is to award points toward membership in the senior honor society, the number of points being awarded in proportion to length and value of service to the newspaper.

Staff Meetings. The adviser should encourage the staff to hold regularly scheduled staff meetings presided over by the editor. All concerned should try to make every member of the staff feel that he is part of the policy making of the paper. They should try to have the staff think of itself as a unit with a major responsibility to discharge.

Attendance at staff meetings should be compulsory, with only the best of excuses accepted for absence. By making attendance compulsory, the student with lackluster interest is frequently eliminated. This practice also eliminates the overloaded student—the student who spreads his energies thinly over many activities.

In planning staff meetings, an impressive agenda is essential. This agenda will offset the common complaint that meetings are often held routinely, despite the lack of important business.

Instruction. Because student writers must know certain principles of journalism, the adviser should strive to have a journalism course in his school. Where such a course is not feasible, he should try to have a journalism unit within one of the writing courses. The time spent in instructing students properly will save much time and effort later, and it will result in a better paper.

Faculty Responsibility. Faculty responsibility for the paper should be

---

[12] This statement presupposes that the faculty adviser uses a set of clearly visible, objective, reliable criteria.

divided into at least two departments, editorial and business. If possible, the adviser should not attempt to assume responsibility for both phases. In large schools, he should try for a further division so that no adviser has so much work that he cannot give his staff adequate individual attention.

The adviser should have a clear-cut agreement with other faculty advisers and students about responsibilities and authority. Such an understanding is absolutely necessary for harmony and efficiency.

Variety. Adviser and staff should try to get into each issue some feature that does not appear regularly. It may be a poll of student opinion, it may be an unusual picture, or it may be an exclusive interview. Whatever else is done, they should avoid making the paper routine.

An effective device in avoiding routine is that of gaining control of the source of important announcements. When a paper can make exclusive announcements in every issue, it is certain to have variety. A pleasing variety can be gained also by the use of features such as cartoons and puzzles, striking feature stories, and timely letters to the editor. A final way to gain variety, one that must be used cautiously, is that of varying make-up. This end can be achieved by using catchy ears, changing the position of the masthead, and varying the over-all mechanical composition.

Co-operation. Adviser and staff must have the co-operation of other students, faculty, and administration. The best approach for gaining such co-operation, aside from presenting a co-operative attitude, is to establish the prestige of the paper. If the school paper is well written, inclusive, and readable, others are bound to respect it, and as a result will be glad to co-operate with the staff when the need arises.

Time. The adviser should make certain that he has time enough to do his work. Without adequate time for guidance, especially in editing and proofreading, there can be little chance of achieving a finished publication. He must be prepared to convince his superiors of this necessity, for few persons outside the field realize the time involved in handling a paper.

Scrapbook. Every staff and adviser should keep a scrapbook of stories that are models of good journalism. Although the stories should be chiefly from their own paper, others should not be excluded. Such a book is valuable to the learner.

The caution to be sounded respecting a scrapbook, however, is that it is to be used as a guide—not as a collection of models to be imitated.

Exchanges. Every paper should maintain a good supply of exchange publications, especially of outstanding ones, to see what other papers are doing. There is always an excellent chance that any paper can learn something valuable from the other papers. Also, an exchange column, if well planned, constitutes an interesting item for the paper.

Press Association Conferences. The adviser should encourage the paper to join a press association with a view to attending conferences. Thus, the staff can gain the benefit of others' experiences and keep abreast of developments in the field. It can also have the opportunity to present its questions to persons who should know the answers.

Pictures. Too many school papers are weak in their art (pictures). The adviser must constantly warn the staff against the mistake of using pictures taken by unskilled photographers. He must also caution the staff against the use of pictures that are either too light or too dark, and against using a blurred picture simply because someone thinks that a photograph of some sort is necessary.

The adviser must also guide the staff away from the use of "assorted" photography in the total layout. If, for example, the paper has one fine action shot made with a first-quality speed camera, plus a rather dull studio portrait, plus a Polaroid shot or two, the whole paper may easily generate a distressing effect. Therefore, the layout person should place pictures side by side to see the total impact beforehand.

Editor and adviser must be especially careful of would-be photographers who want to learn photography at the expense of the school newspaper. These students can spend the paper's money faster and more wastefully than any other staff members.

Literary Efforts. The paper should encourage students to attempt the usual literary forms—short stories, poems, and essays—and when they are good, it should publish them. This should be done especially in schools where there are no literary magazines.

However, the use of this material should be kept proportionate to the space available and to the quality of the particular work; that is, the paper should not become a literary magazine. Second- or third-rate material should be rejected.

Commendation. The staff and adviser often get less commendation than they deserve. They cannot expect everyone to appreciate the fact that they are turning out a good paper. They must remember that the number of persons who appreciate high-quality journalism is surprisingly small. Therefore, they must strive to produce a paper that is journalistically sound rather than attempt the impossible feat of pleasing everybody.

SOURCES OF NEWS

As with the professional newspaper, the amount and the quality of news available for the school paper vary with the seeker. The good student reporter, like the good professional reporter, is able to find excellent stories where a less able person finds none. In fact, the good student reporter often finds a story where even the faculty adviser never thought of looking. Consequently, the most important statement to be made of source of news is that made earlier: the amount and the quality of news depend most heavily on the ability of the reporter seeking it.

Proceeding further, one finds more difficulty in saying what is *not* news than what *is* news because the source of news for the school publication is almost limitless. Just as the outside world always has a good story hidden somewhere for the able reporter, so does the world of the school. Highly interesting stories have been written about such apparently routine doings as the window cleaner at work, the janitor emptying the waste baskets, and the pigeons nesting under the eaves. Because so much about the school interests so many in the school, the searching reporter can find news everywhere.

The big difference between the source of news for the regular newspaper and that for the school publication is that the school furnishes very little spot news.[13] The regular newspaper has reporters visiting police stations, hospitals, and other such places where spot news is likely to break at any moment, but the school paper has almost no opportunity for such news. Instead, it must rely for its stories on events that occur with regularity and foreknowledge. To offset the deficiency in spot news stories, the school paper uses many feature and part-news-part-feature stories. Hence no detailed attempt will be made to treat separately the source of news for the feature story and the news story.

There are several broad classifications of sources of news, a discussion of which follows. The reader should remember, however, that many of these stories can be used as straight news or feature material, depending on the effect desired.

Events to Come. The most plentiful source of news for the school paper is to be found in events to come. Usually, the most prominent spot in the paper is given to the big event of the forthcoming week. Whether it be the senior play, the spring dance, or the award assembly, the event is generally the most newsworthy item of the moment. The student likes to read of the event in advance so as to anticipate all details, and the wise paper plays upon this interest to the maximum.

There are several significant points to be noted concerning the writing of events to come. First, the story should be written as interestingly and as attractively as possible because it is an important news item and because the event may need the publicity. A dance, for instance, relies heavily on a favorable preview, as do all other events that depend on student revenue or attendance. Second, the story should not be overplayed; that is, the story should not be padded out to fill several columns, thus squeezing out smaller items. Also, it should not deal in superlatives. The paper that overpraises every event soon loses its impact. Third, the newspaper should contain as many advance notices of newsworthy events as possible. These serve to keep the reader informed, to cater to a wider group of readers, and to make the paper an important source of information. Fourth, small routine events do not merit a story in every issue; they should be confined to the calendar box. Fifth, the writer must work hard to avoid dullness in the less significant stories of events to come. Never should the story of events to come read like filler.

The following list of story subjects covers the events to come common to most schools. Therefore, it can serve as a broad guide to show possible sources of news.

[13] The school paper must frequently compete with the commercially owned local newspaper in the use of campus spot news because the local paper often assigns top priority to such news. This is especially true in small communities where the local paper has to scratch hard to fill its columns. If the local paper comes out on a daily schedule, it can generally scoop the school paper without mercy. If it does, the school paper needs, nevertheless, to present the news, but slant it to the student-school viewpoint.

a. *Sports:*
   1. Candidates to report for tryouts.
   2. Scheduled games and meets, varsity and intramural.
   3. Individual tournaments and contests (tennis, golf, fencing, foul shooting, and the like).
   4. Exhibitions and sports carnivals.
b. *Dramatics:*
   1. Class plays—tryouts, rehearsals, and ticket sales, and a build-up story for the actual performance.
   2. Assembly plays—any of the above stories that may pertain.
   3. Dramatic Club productions—any of the above stories that may pertain.
c. *Assembly:*
   1. Outside speakers, entertainers, performers, or other personalities.
   2. Award and other special assemblies, such as pep rallies, school group performances.
d. *Clubs:*
   1. Announcement of formation—purpose, requirements for eligibility, general plans, and similar information.
   2. Candidates for offices.
   3. Meetings.
   4. Any special event or program.
e. *Class News:*
   1. Meetings.
   2. Any regular or special event to come (election of officers, trips, programs).
   3. Build-up story for any activity.
f. *Unusual Activity of Any Group:*
   1. Field trips.
   2. Class trips.
   3. Interclass contests.
g. *Grounds and Buildings:*
   1. Changes to be made—new construction, repairs, painting, etc.
h. *Social News:*
   1. Parties, dances, fetes, bazaars, or similar events.
i. *Exchanges:*
   1. Any especially interesting event to come in another school.
j. *Musical Organizations:*
   1. Tryouts.
   2. Calendar for each group.
   3. Build-up story for each event.
   4. Any previously unscheduled event—interschool contests, trips to other schools, broadcast performances, or the like.
k. *Debating and Other Nonathletic Teams:*
   1. Tryouts.
   2. Contests.
   3. Any previously unscheduled event (special programs, visitations).
l. *Contests:*
   1. All contests open to students (essay, poetry, short story, etc.), whether sponsored by school or by outside group.
m. *Yearbook and Other Publications:*

1. Tryouts.
2. Any information pertaining to publication itself—date on which pictures are to be taken, dates of issues, contracts to be let, subscriptions to be solicited, or the like.
3. Build-up story for appearance.

n. *Faculty:*
1. Any group activity—play, picnic, outing, professional gathering, or other.
2. Any newsworthy story—teacher to address group, to take interesting trip, to engage in unusual project, or the like.

o. *Administration:*
1. Standard announcements—important dates, curriculum changes, new regulations, and similar items.
2. Open letter to student body—greetings at opening of year, Christmas, Easter, special programs or opportunities, and the like.
3. Scholastic record summaries.
4. Board of trustees' proposals and plans.

p. *Miscellaneous:*
1. Charity drives, donations for worthy causes, outside organization events given on campus, parent-teacher events, alumni events, or the like.

Past Events. Another large source of news lies in describing past events. In this category are the stories of dances, parties, celebrations, and other extracurricular activities. The most important pitfall to avoid in writing of the past event is the tendency to overplay. The spring dance, for instance, attended by three-fourths of the school and now almost a week old, certainly does not merit a spread on page 1. Yet the student reporter who had a highly pleasant time at the dance is ready to write several columns. A further caution concerning past events is to use warily the device of writing of an event before it takes place. When the paper appears, only the most naive of students is deceived, and the publication frequently loses face. Then, too, a long history of embarrassments could be written about papers that have used this device to their sorrow. One such paper belonged to a mid-West high school where a glowing account of a play was written for an issue to appear the day after the performance. The article was to be displayed prominently on page 1, and as the editor looked at the final proof six hours before the curtain was to rise, he congratulated himself on his cleverness. However, an hour before curtain time, the heating system in the building failed and the play had to be postponed. The paper was now in print, so the staff was faced with the unpleasant choices of retiring a whole issue (in which case they would have to make refunds to advertisers and lose revenue from sales); postponing the issue until the printer could make the correction, thus necessitating many other changes and great expense; or distributing the paper as it was. Since they were limited financially, they could only distribute the paper. There is no need to detail their embarrassment and loss of prestige.

By examining the list of events to come, the staff of the school paper can select those stories which will have a follow—that is to say, the events which will merit another story when they have occurred. Frequently, however, there are other newsworthy events which have not been pre-announced. Some examples are the unannounced visit of a world-renowned alumnus to the school, the unexpected return to school of a seriously injured student, and the appearance of the Governor of the state who "just dropped in."

The Classroom. The most common use of the classroom as a news source is the column that recounts unusual occurrences (a bird flies about the classroom), humorous student mistakes, student comments on courses, startling remarks by instructors, and similar light commentary. Strange to say, however, this type of material is very difficult to make appealing. Hence only the best of student writers can find and use it. In lesser hands, it becomes dry, meaningless, trite, or trivial.

An easier kind of classroom news to handle is the stories that tell of tangible objects—such as the unusual experiment in science class or the unusual construction made in metal shop. These stories present less difficulty to the writer because they center on physical objects. The writer can describe the experiment more easily than he can point up the humor in a political-science discussion.

Another common type of story of the classroom concerns new courses being offered (such as computer operations and seminars on contemporary problems); changes in old courses (like the use of television in laboratory courses, or of field work in sociology); and changes in graduation or degree requirements.

Recently the classroom has become the rostrum for some of the most interesting speakers to visit the school. On the secondary level, these speakers are usually termed "community-resource personnel"; on the college level they are "guest lecturers."

Among the community-resource personnel appearing at a representative high school during the past year were: a local psychiatrist to speak about emotional difficulties and the use of drugs; the chief of police to explain the police officer's role in law enforcement; an alumnus who was a prisoner of war in Vietnam; an old-fashioned pottery maker with samples of his craft; a specialist in prisoner rehabilitation; and a member of Alcoholics Anonymous.

Among the lecturers at a representative college were: a medical missionary just returned from a 20-year stay in India; a quadruple amputee; a Seminole chief; a black militant leader; a reformed professional gambler; a publicist for the gay-liberation movement; and a spokesman for the Jewish Defense League.

Naturally, such speakers provide material for often fascinating stories.

Sports. Across the years, the extracurricular activity that has generated the most concerted interest among students is sports: most schools' sports contests draw the largest crowds and represent the topic most likely to recur in most out-of-class discussions of the school's activities. Clearly the school paper must react to this interest by giving a competent and exciting coverage of the athletic program.

Naturally, the varsity team contests receive the biggest emphasis, but intramural and similar programs can provide excellent stories as well. In addition, an occasional story crops up about a student engaged in a nonschool contest like a boxing tournament or a bicycle or motor-vehicle contest.

The sports editor should capitalize especially on student interest in statistics—boxes that show wins and losses, total team points scored to date, and individual scorings. The reader of the sports page, it seems, is one of the country's most statistics-minded citizens. Equally important, the first-class sports page always needs a well-written, authoritative column and an appealing feature story or two.

Overhanging the sports page, however, stands an important caution: in most instances, the school paper should concentrate on background stories of an interpretive nature rather than running accounts of actual contests. This caution is especially pertinent where local papers also cover the school's athletic contests. If the local paper details the action of the contest, it thereby, in effect, scoops the school paper. Hence if the school paper, appearing at a later date, also gives a running account of the action, it courts the danger of loss of impact. Meanwhile, it sacrifices space that could be used for a more appealing background story.

Feature Stories. The feature story demands more ingenuity of the reporter than any other. Like the professional newspaperman, the student reporter must be able to locate and handle feature story material. The feature story, when presented properly, represents for most house organs the most interesting kind of material. Therefore, the school paper should use it heavily.

Because of the nature of the feature story, there can be no stock list of sources. Indeed, the minute a story becomes stock, it loses much of its appeal. However, there are some broadly outlined fields to be cited as rich sources. The best is that of the unusual student activity. One student may have a singular hobby, such as collecting automobile license plates from every country in the world; another may have a highly interesting collection of autographs; another may be a special student of some sort (greatly over age, extremely handicapped physically, from some distant country, or otherwise unusual). Such students represent feature material ready-made.

Another abundant source of feature material is the faculty. Contrary to popular belief, many faculty members do live interesting lives. They may have fascinating hobbies, they may have extraordinary accomplishments, they may have entertaining observations to pass along. Where these stories exist, they should be unearthed and used.

Appealing feature stories can also be gathered about colorful employees (janitors, cafeteria workers, groundkeepers, to suggest a few), renovations in the school buildings or on the campus, history of buildings and departments, and changes over the years as shown in old publications and records.

The important fact to be remembered concerning the feature is the one already cited—the feature story, like all creative work, depends most heavily on individual ability and enterprise.

The following is a partial list of the feature stories found in 10 representative school papers for a one-year period. It should serve merely as a guide to show the kind of story used by most school papers.

a. *Unusual Student Activities:*
1. Student is professional radio announcer.
2. Student meets President of the United States.
3. Student wins $1400 on television quiz program.
4. Student tells of being lost in severe snowstorm.
5. Forty-one-year-old man becomes college freshman.
6. Triplets (all boys) enter college.
7. Father and son graduate from college together.
8. Ten of school's 12 faculty children take courses under fathers.
9. Student commutes to college by helicopter.
10. Youngest of eight brothers enters school from which other brothers have been graduated.
11. Students challenge faculty to barbershop quartet contest.
12. Student acquires suit of medieval armor.
13. High-school senior wins amateur boxing championship of entire state.
14. Student has returned from round-the-world trip.
15. Student exhibits amazing collection of autographs.

b. *Scheduled Activities:*
1. Students receive photographer's proofs for yearbook.
2. Ridiculous answers to examination questions.
3. Seniors visit Washington, D.C.
4. Lecturer on snakes loses blacksnake backstage—snake still at large.
5. Reactions to forthcoming graduation.
6. Color story on visiting football team.
7. Student confusion regarding new regulations covering dining room, library, and student social room (humorous treatment).
8. Dramatic Club tries center-stage performance of famous play in gymnasium.
9. Blind gymnasts to perform in assembly.
10. Student club corresponding with students in foreign land.

c. *Faculty:*
1. Professor makes unusual mountain-climbing trip.
2. Shop teacher and wife build eight-room house for themselves.
3. Latin professor retires after 50 years of teaching.
4. Teacher buys 1914 Ford to drive in antique automobile parade.
5. Story on unusual faculty hobbies.
6. Story on faculty men who were former athletes.
7. Physics professor invents device for automatic home laundry.
8. English teacher publishes volume of poetry.
9. Color story on new headmaster.
10. Exchange teacher returns from abroad.

d. *Miscellaneous:*
1. Squirrels found nesting in old attic storeroom.
2. Forty-five-year-old newspaper found under floor of headmaster's office.
3. Popular janitor celebrates twenty-fifth anniversary in service of school.
4. School bus driver (man) defeats all other contestants (women) in cake-baking contest.
5. College librarian tells of many love notes and other articles, left in books returned by students.
6. Faculty member explains architecture on campus.
7. Little-known facts of feeding students in college dining room explained.

8. New equipment in science laboratory explained.
9. Professor of ornithology explains mysterious appearance of snowy owl in eastern Pennsylvania town.
10. Stories in 50-year-old issue of college paper printed with comments.

Polls. A never-failing source of news to the school newspaper is the poll of student opinion. If conducted properly, this type of news is always interesting because students like to know how others feel about leading questions. Straw votes on presidential and other important elections, surveys of opinion concerning a recent or proposed change, and even tabulation of answers to such trifling questions as "The Actress or Actor I Should Most Like to Date" provide a highly interesting source of news.

There are five cautions to be exercised concerning polls. First, the poll should be as exhaustive as possible. As many students as possible should be consulted if the poll is a sampling; sometimes all students should be approached. Second, the issue should be stated clearly and simply. There should be no ambiguity or evasiveness in the manner of asking the question. Unless the question is stated clearly, the answers are likely to be of little value. The question, for example, "Do you favor our student government?" does little to bring into focus the idea which the maker of the question has in mind. It is so broad that it can elicit nothing more than a broad, loose, vague answer. Third, the poll should be taken on an interesting subject. "The Classics I Most Admire" is a fine subject for the bookish student, but for the great mass, it may be less than a fascinating topic. Fourth, if the poll is of the interview type, the paper should generally concentrate on newsworthy students. Fifth, in the poll of opinions, the dull answers should not be printed or the interest of the reader will be lessened.

Interviews. A source of news which is very interesting, if used properly, is the interview with students, faculty, or other personalities known to the readers of the paper.

Students are interviewed because they are newsworthy (they are top figures in some school activity or they have interesting material to give), or they are interviewed at random to express their views on some pertinent topic of the moment. Faculty are interviewed because they are instrumental in guiding some school activity or because of some specially attractive concern or hobby.

The chief caution concerning the interview is to do it capably. The interviewer must try hard to avoid routine approach and treatment. Questions must be so phrased as to elicit interesting answers, and all newsworthy elements must be gathered.

THE COLUMN AND THE EDITORIAL

The procedure for writing the school column can be much the same as that for the regular newspaper. The same methods of gathering information, the same styles, and the same sources of appeal can be observed. Generally speaking, the most successful school columns are written on sports, observations on school life, and patter.

There are, however, several other kinds of columns which can be quite interesting. Capable writers turn out good columns on stamps, hobbies, exchange material, and little-known information about the school. The column in the school paper, like so many other features, varies in proportion to the ability of the person writing it.

Like the column, the editorial for the school paper is handled in much the same manner as that in the professional newspaper. However, in addition to keeping in mind what was said in Chapter 10, the student editorial writer should note some other important facts. Above all else, the tone of the school paper's editorial should always be high, and the message should always have a definitely constructive note about it. The editorial should not sound as though it has been released through the president's or the headmaster's office, but neither should it sound like a recording from a local gathering place for students. The editorial writer should have fairly mature judgment and broad vision so as not to be caught off base in his opinions.

Usually the person best qualified to write editorials is the editor himself, but he should not be forced to shoulder the entire responsibility. Assistant editors and even good reporters can be drafted into this work.

FOR FURTHER READING

College Press Review. Iowa City, Iowa: National Council of College Publications Advisors. A semiannual work which aims primarily to serve the faculty adviser of college publications.

Columbia Journalism Review. New York: Columbia University. A bimonthly journal containing discussions of the most recent issues in the world of journalism.

Johnson, Michael L. *New Journalism: the Underground Press, the Artists of Non-Fiction and Changes in the Established Media*. Lawrence: University Press of Kansas, 1971.

Journalism Quarterly. Grand Forks, Iowa: American Association of Teachers of Journalism and American Association of Schools and Departments of Journalism. A publication devoted to discussions and investigations of the main questions in journalism.

Kobre, Sidney. *Successful Public Relations: For Colleges and Universities*. New York: Hastings House, Publishers, 1974.

Quill & Scroll. Iowa City: State University of Iowa Press. A publication for secondary-school staffs, issued four times during the school year.

Scholastic Editor. Minneapolis: University of Minnesota Press. A publication for the secondary-school staff. Published monthly except for July and August.

School Press Review. New York: Columbia University. A newspaper serving secondary
    school publications staffs that are members of the Columbia Scholastic Press Asso-
    ciation.

Ward, William G. *The Student Journalist and Creative Writing.* New York: Richard
    Rosen Press, 1967.

Williamson, Daniel R. *Feature Writing for Newspapers.* New York: Hastings House,
    Publishers, 1975.

★ **13** ★

Radio: the Background
Television: the Background
Basic Principles of Writing
News
    Recognizing News
    Preparing the News
    Determining Audience
    Demands
Specialized Newscasts
Difference between Radio and
   Television Newscasts
Editorials
Program Continuities
The Commentary
    Writing the Commentary
Sustaining Announcements
Miscellaneous Writing

Writing for Radio and Television

The special character of the electronic media creates needs for special kinds of writing. Writing for radio differs from writing for television in several important respects, and both kinds of writing differ sharply from writing for the newspaper or the magazine. Whoever seeks to comprehend the nature of writing for the broadcast media, therefore, should understand their backgrounds at least broadly.

RADIO: THE BACKGROUND

Radio, from its sudden and dramatic appearance in the American home in the earliest years of the decade 1920–1930, has influenced every phase of the American consciousness. It has provided news, entertainment, eyewitness accounts, speeches of worldwide import, and numerous other kinds of listening—all with a directness and an immediacy of appeal that have revolutionized American life in many respects. Its great significance can be demonstrated in a single statement: until the advent of radio, there existed no way by which one person could address millions of people dispersed across vast geographic regions. Also, there was no way by which those millions could receive news during its actual occurrence (as of a Presidential inauguration) or within moments thereafter (as of a train wreck); and there was no way by which they could be given the same entertainment simultaneously as they sat in their homes.

Radio, naturally, has been a changing institution. From the small local stations, broadcasting to a relatively small number of homes where listeners sat straining to hear first from "crystal sets" and later from "loudspeaker sets," vast networks soon developed.[1] These networks, in turn, often linked with foreign sources to broadcast news and newsworthy events (e.g., the funeral of a king) from every corner of the world.

Meanwhile, mechanical advances have made radio a more pleasing medium. The physical imperfections (static and fading in particular) of early broadcasting have been largely corrected; and improved mixers (the devices that control pitch, volume, and other voice qualities) and other equipment have brought radio nearer to the situation of hearing someone in an adjoining room.

Radio, however, has changed in other ways. With the coming of television in the late 1940s, radio was forced to change its whole approach in order to prosper. No longer could it hold family audiences in the evening hours with the kind of entertainment so popular in the 1930s—the serial, the orchestra featuring popular music, the song and joke routine. In consequence, many of the entertainers and other performers on radio had to switch to television or fall by the wayside.

Although this change brought gloomy predictions at the time regarding the future of radio, the medium has not only survived; it has even become, in one sense, the most pervasive of all the media of mass communication. Currently, radios are found in most automobiles, in waiting rooms, in business houses, in homes, and in numerous other places where listeners can hear them comfortably while engaged in some other activity. In addition, the blare of the pocket transistor radio is heard in innumerable places—the high-school student carries it to and from school, the spectator at the football game presses it to his ear as he listens to the progress of another football game, it entertains the workers in the shipping department as they address packages, and it broadcasts news, entertainment, and advertising to the patron of the bus-station washroom.

The significance of radio is demonstrated in a common finding of researchers in the field of mass communications: the average radio listening time in the United States is approximately 2½ hours daily per person. This figure is accepted by the numerous agencies throughout the nation which handle advertising accounts.

In the 1970s, radio possesses a rather special kind of maturity. It has great appeal for the person who wants "all the news in a hurry"—without fanfare or

---

[1] Since the advent of television, network radio programming has decreased in favor of local programming.

numerous interruptions; for the person who enjoys "talk shows"—especially interviews, panel discussions, and listener telephone conversations with people in the studio; for the person who likes specialized music programs—such as classical music and country music; and for the person who desires a relaxing, entertaining, informative medium that permits a listener to exert whatever effort he may choose.

TELEVISION: THE BACKGROUND

Comprehending the role of radio in American life makes understanding the place of television easier.

Of all the media of mass communications, television reaches the largest audience for the longest periods. Research findings set the average viewing time of television in our nation at three to four hours daily per person—a surprisingly high figure in view of the many activities which compete for everyone's free time.

To state that television exerts a vast and powerful influence on American life and thought is to state the minimum. Its impact, in fact, extends beyond any detailed analysis. The television camera takes the householder, the student in his dormitory room, and the viewer in countless other places to the foreign nation to see the military coup in action; it takes him to the disaster area, to the arrest of the bank robber, to numerous other newsworthy events—all with the force of the actual visitation.[2] Thus it exhibits an immediacy of appeal and a power not found in the other media. In addition, it supplements many programs, especially news programs, with maps, charts, graphs, models, and other visual aids—presented by a speaker with the ability of the master teacher—thereby further increasing an already strong thrust.

Of television's many ways of influencing American life and thought, one of the most striking is its ability to bring presidents, congressional leaders, and other high ranking figures into the viewer's home for critical examination. There, in the full glare of the camera, the subject must stand like a defendant before a jury; he must, as it were, come before the voters to explain and to defend. Thereafter, directly or by implication, he faces pointed questions while the viewer passes a judgment upon his answers.

The power of this exposure is demonstrated by the reaction of political leaders to the President's use of television in appealing to the nation. Senate and House leaders argue that the President enjoys an almost insurmountable advantage over Congress by virtue of his access to television: he can present his case to the public without immediate concern for contesting arguments, simply by pre-empting prime time to address the country at large. Hence he is often

---

[2] An especially pointed example of this situation occurred in November 1963, when millions of Americans witnessed via television the actual murder of Lee Harvey Oswald, accused assassin of President John F. Kennedy, by Jack Ruby.

able to persuade citizens to pressure their congressional representatives into supporting Presidential legislation.

On the other hand, a President's immediate assistants often see the significance of television in another light. They argue that immediately after the Chief Executive addresses the nation, television commentators can seize the audience attracted by the President and try to discredit him—thereby capturing the advantage of the last word.

Whatever view anyone may take on this controversy, one fact stands indisputably: all concerned see television as a potent influence on the opinions established and held by society.

The foregoing discussion has dealt with the power that television possesses. Something must also be said about the problems which it has created.

The emergence of TV as a strong force in molding public opinion raises a need for editorial policy guidelines on both the local and the network level. This need, however, has not been met to the satisfaction of many knowledgeable people. Among competent observers, for example, a troublesome question mark hangs over the role of television in reporting the Vietnam war.[3] Did the networks present every aspect objectively, or did they sometimes sacrifice the important but undramatic event for the less significant but more interesting incident—thereby offering an unbalanced or distorted portrayal?

Similarly, debate still flourishes over coverage of important events on the home front. An example is the still widely discussed confrontation of young political activists and police at the 1968 Democratic Convention in Chicago. In this instance, the cameras were concentrating, many well informed persons charge, on scenes of violent action in order to provide "entertainment" for the viewer in his living room. Meanwhile, these same accusers contend, the camera crews ignored the many more numerous scenes where police calmly controlled student protesters and the protesters politely obeyed police orders. Hence a distorted coverage led to distorted conclusions in the minds of viewers and other citizens.

A more subtle phase of this problem lies in the ability of television coverage to shape movements within society. For instance, if the television networks emphasize their coverage of a civil disturbance (as, a racial clash or a student uprising), does it tend to foment similar situations in other areas by giving other people ideas?

Even more immediate is the situation of national elections. Because of the time-zone difference between the Atlantic and Pacific coasts, election projections telecast from the East can deter citizens in the West from voting in national elections by convincing them that the major offices (especially the Presidency) have already been decided. As a result, local offices and issues on the West coast suffer from low voter turnout. (Obviously, any curb in this instance would have to extend to radio.)

Another major problem that has arisen with television is the charge of

---

[3] Several excellent documentaries on Vietnam represent an exception to this statement.

presenting undesirable or negative fare to its viewers. On occasions, television has been accused from the pulpit, the lecture platform, the halls of Congress, the editorial column, and many other places of lowering moral values, propagating unsound ideas, cheating the public through fraudulent advertising, impairing the health of children by holding them enthralled for hours on end, and helping to create a nation of cultural cripples by presenting low-level viewing.

In some instances, these charges have had rather serious repercussions— even forcing networks to drop certain entertainers and advertisers and making some participants alter their material and approaches.

However, for the most part, the defenders of television have answered the accusers with valid arguments. They have cited the generally high tone of their material, their many public-service programs, and their over-all success in keeping their audiences entertained and informed. Meanwhile, they have emphasized that they are in a competitive market where they must provide, within limits, the programs which the public demands. They are also the victims, they have argued, of the brand of criticism hurled at any kind of entertainment placed before the general public; that is, they are likely to be criticized adversely as the theater, the motion pictures, the novels, and all similar productions have been.

Underneath all this criticism, however, runs a very disturbing thought— the ever-present threat of Federal government intervention. As is well known, the electronic airways are squarely under Federal control. More specifically, they are governed by the rulings of the Federal Communications Commission. Hence every time a serious or semiserious criticism arises, some congressman or senator proposes that "perhaps the FCC should be looking into this."

Although this type of latent threat may be discounted in some quarters, it is not taken lightly by persons knowledgeable in the maneuverings and horse-trading ways of official Washington. They are well aware that the FCC, an agency acutely sensitive to political pressure, has reacted to politically inspired actions in granting licenses and in denying applications for renewals of existing licenses.

BASIC PRINCIPLES OF WRITING

With the technical advances and the developments in program content of radio and television, simultaneous changes in the writing done for each medium have occurred. Where the composing of introductory material, station breaks, commercials, and other writings were once rather simple undertakings, they now require a greater command of skills and a far greater capacity for originality. Therefore, those who would learn to write for these media face a more challenging task than existed even a decade ago.

The initial step, naturally, in learning to write for radio and television is to study the basic principles that must be respected in any type of writing for these media. This chapter, therefore, will treat first these broad, general principles;

then it will consider specifically the writing of news, program continuities, commentaries, sustaining announcements, and miscellaneous types. Only the "workday" types of writing—the kinds done by regularly employed station writers—will be discussed. The full-length play, the short story, and other highly creative types of writing cannot be discussed because they are, in themselves, extensive subjects.

The first basic principle is that the *radio and television writer prepares material for listeners rather than for readers.* Accordingly, his whole approach is affected. Where the newspaper reader, for example, has banner lines, banks, and above all the printed word to rely on, the radio audience is limited to the spoken word and the television audience is limited to the spoken word and any visual aids (signs, drawings, on-screen captions, or others) employed by the producer. The newspaper reader may peruse stories as he wishes, reading and rereading according to his desires and his abilities, but the listener must follow a pattern prepared for him. Therefore, this first principle requires that all writing for radio and television must make "good listening"—that is to say, it must be material that listeners of varied backgrounds can follow easily, enjoyably, and intelligently.

The second principle, closely related to the first, is that *the writing must make "good speaking."* Hence, the material has to be cast in the style of the speaker rather than in the style of the writer. In fact, the test of the effective broadcast is that it never sounds like writing or reading; it sounds, rather, like a fluent conversationalist addressing a small group in a clear, interesting manner.

To see the nature of writing prepared for a speaker as opposed to that for a reader, a simple test is helpful. Take a well-written radio script and read it aloud.[4] Then do the same with a page from a science textbook. This exercise will demonstrate immediately the difficulty encountered in attempting to read to listeners material not designed for oral delivery.

Third, because material is to be prepared for listeners and speakers, *certain considerations of vocabulary must be observed,* the most important of which are listed:

1. Short, crisp words are preferable to longer, "difficult to pronounce" ones. Compare "The players stood around the injured halfback" with "The competitors circumscribed the fallen gladiator." Note the difference in both clarity and ease of delivery.
2. Simple, immediately meaningful words are preferable to less used, less well-known words—even though the latter words may be more precise. "The rushing waters flooded the field" is preferable to "The turbid tributary inundated the pasture." The first sentence is preferable because of the clarity and ease of delivery gained.
3. Highly technical terms, if they must be used, should be explained as tactfully as possible. Such terms as "minister without portfolio," "multiple sclerosis," and "escrow," which often must be used in newscasts and

---

[4] Also see the illustrative material in this chapter.

similar writing, need definition for many persons. In such instances, definitions should be given unobtrusively by such constructions as: "The funds held in escrow—that is, the money kept by the bank until the work was finished—were delivered as directed." . . . "The judge objected to the word 'anent,' which, as crossword-puzzle fans will tell you, means 'about'." . . . The separator, a tank 15 feet wide and 10 feet deep, was examined for blood stains."

4. Euphony must take precedence over cacophony wherever possible. The "s" sound, for example, should be avoided, as also should any combination of words that makes a harsh or unpleasant sound. Note the undesirable quality of the following: "The soldiers slipped surreptitiously past the shops." . . . "The gelatinous globules made a glub-glub sound in the gluey mixture." . . . "To two twosomes, at least, the music was too tiresome."

5. Doubtful words must be examined carefully. Doubtful words include many found in common use ("dope," "craps," "bum," etc.); slang, especially that which is known to have a vulgar or obscene meaning; and localisms and other words likely to present difficulty or ambiguity in meaning.

The fourth consideration in writing for radio and television is that *certain stylistic practices must be observed*. The purpose of these stylistic devices is to gain a maximum of intelligibility, interest, and pleasure for the listener. The most important stylistic considerations follow:

1. Strive for short, immediately meaningful sentences because long involved ones are difficult to follow. Be especially wary of lengthy dependent clauses, involved structure, and parenthetical elements. Note the differences between the following two versions of the same incident: "The arrested man was angry. He protested; he stormed; and he berated the officer. But he was still helped into the police van and delivered to the city jail." . . . "The arrested man was, to say the least, angry. Although he was eventually helped into the police van, this action did not become a reality until after he had protested and stormed, followed by a berating of the arresting officer."

2. Use the active, rather than the passive voice. The active voice is usually more direct, while the passive voice frequently creates delayed reference. Compare the following: "The shortstop misjudged the ball." . . . "The ball was misjudged by the shortstop."

3. Use the most effective device obtainable for impressing essential data. If, for example, a name is important, it must be repeated or even spelled out as effectively as possible. If an unusual term must be used, it can be spelled, syllabized, or spoken slowly in order to be made impressive.

4. The positive approach is generally stronger than the negative. Unless negatives are emphasized strongly, they are often lost. Compare the following versions: "The driver was proceeding at a lawful speed."—"The driver was not exceeding the speed limit." . . . "Now is the time to

act."—"This is not the time to delay action." . . . "Rely on a tested remedy."—"Do not rely on an untested remedy."

5. Strive for originality whenever possible. Although certainly no formula can be given, the good writer can recognize originality at sight. An unusual phrase, a catchy rhetorical device, or a pleasantly humorous line can be very effective. The following instances of originality were once striking. Now, of course, many have been used to the point of triteness. "The right time is 6 o'clock. The right time to have your car checked is now. The right place to take it is Smythe's Garage, Main Street and Sixth Avenue, Worcester." . . . "Look at your shoes. Everybody else does. Do they need Griffith's Polish! Easy to find in the handy tin at your neighborhood store." . . . "Safety is no accident. Be safe—not sorry."

NEWS

The clearest proof of the importance of news to radio and television stations is the distinct emphasis accorded it. Station directors have long known the newscast to be a strong source of attraction to many listeners, and they have planned their broadcast day accordingly. Seldom does a broadcast hour pass without a newscast of some kind, and many stations attempt to hold listeners with the reminder that a newscast will follow the program being aired. The appeal of news is further established by statistical investigation which reveals that 10 to 25 percent of adult listening time is devoted to newscasts. An even stronger proof, perhaps, is the fact that many cities have at least one radio station which gives its entire program day to the broadcast of news. How stations gather, edit, and prepare news naturally varies with the size of the station. In the small station, a staff announcer may have as one of his duties the entire handling of news. He gathers, prepares, and delivers all news. In the larger station, however, there is usually a full-time news director with staff assistants. When one announcer handles all the details, he generally works in a small room with a wire-service teletype. State, national, and world news he obtains from the wire service [5]; local news he gets by telephone (from police stations, hospitals, and similar sources), as tips from friends, as publicity releases, and as letters requesting announcements (banquets, plays, dances, meetings, or the like). Also, he seldom feels any compunction in appropriating from local newspapers any item he desires. When a station has a news director with a staff, the process more nearly resembles the procedure of the newspaper. The news gatherer functions as a district man or reporter; writers and editors in the office prepare both local and wire news for broadcast; and the news director supervises the entire staff.

Whether the handling of news is to be the function of one person or of a staff, certain competencies must be present. They are, in order of importance,

[5] This practice has given rise to the disparaging phrase, "rip and read journalism."

(1) the ability to recognize news, (2) the ability to prepare news, and (3) the ability to determine audience demands at every hour of the broadcast day.

Recognizing News

The ability to recognize news is fundamental because the newscast succeeds in direct proportion to the appeal of the material aired. Hence the person selecting the items must have the journalist's know-how in appraising stories.[6]

To develop the ability to recognize news for radio and television, the writer should first re-examine the qualities that constitute "news" for the paper; then he should examine the newscasts of representative stations for a given day. This latter step will give him an insight into general trends. For purposes of examination, stations can be classified as (1) large metropolitan, (2) smaller metropolitan, and (3) small-town.

The newscasts of the large metropolitan station usually emphasize foreign and national news. Although local news is broadcast, it is only the most significant brand (major changes in municipal policy, serious accidents, new laws, municipal elections, and the like). The reason is that the large metropolitan station serves an area well beyond its immediate city. Consequently, local news interests only a portion of its audience. The large metropolitan station generally has at least one newscast an hour, even though it may be limited to headlines and quick summaries.

The smaller metropolitan station, because of competition, often aims to capture a specific audience. It may seek, for instance, to attract the high-school population in the late afternoon and the young adults in the evening by a heavy emphasis on popular music. The smaller metropolitan station may even seek to capture national-origin groups by using music from specific foreign lands in full-length programs ("The Italian Hour," "The Irish Program"). In such instances, the newscasts are written with the particular audience in mind. The newscast of the smaller metropolitan station naturally includes world and national news, but generally it emphasizes local news more than the large station does.

The small-town station airs a newscast entirely different from that of the large stations. Because its signal power is usually weak, the small-town station is heard only in its own area and therefore makes its pitch to that area. Thus it often has an overbalance of local news. In fact, the small-town station frequently has a half dozen or more newscasts daily—even though it may have nothing more significant to report than minor automobile accidents, births at the local hospital, and grass fires.

[6] The magnitude of the task of selecting news can be appreciated by citing two common statistics. For nationwide telecasts, the central personality and his staff (usually six assistant editors) spend approximately five hours in preparation for a half-hour program. For large metropolitan stations, the figure is decreased by less than an hour. Even the small local radio station has a problem in selecting news because of the abundance of wire copy.

Preparing The News

In preparing news, the writer should first observe the broad principles of writing for radio and televison already discussed. Then he should focus on the specific guidelines for handling news.

The primary guideline is this: the appeal of electronic-media news is the appeal of print-media news—the forces that draw the listener to the newscast are the forces that draw the reader to his newspaper. The listener and the reader want to be *interested, informed,* and *entertained.* The writer, therefore, must respect these key words as he selects and prepares his material.

However, the newscast writer faces a special problem in achieving appeal. He must present all his material as an attractive totality rather than as a string of unrelated items. Therefore, he must know how to arrange his items, blend them into each other, and give the whole program a continuity of interest.

Another guideline concerns length. While the newspaper writer varies story length according to play, the newscast writer must keep every story brief. Naturally, some treatments may be longer than others, but every item must be in capsule form. The persisting reason is that the typical newscast is pressed severely for time. Somehow, every newsworthy story since the last newscast must be included—along with additional data for stories already aired.

Finally, the writer of the newscast must observe certain qualities of (1) structure, (2) style, (3) vocabulary, and (4) objectivity.

Structure. The most important fact concerning structure is that the listener must never be aware of structure. He must feel that someone is giving the data of a story in a friendly, conversational manner. In essence, the question of structure turns on the familiar guideline: the story must make good listening.

As a result, the story cannot have the tightly packed quality of the newspaper lead nor any structural device that detracts from a fluent, narrative-like flow. To see this quality, compare the following story as it appeared in a prominent newspaper and as it was broadcast by a leading station.

State gets NOAA funds

The U.S. Commerce Department's National Oceanic and Atmosphere Administration has awarded the State of Alabama a $120,000 grant to continue efforts to assure preservation, enhancement and development of coastal areas.

It is the second of three anticipated planning grants necessary for the state to develop a coastal zone management program meeting the requirements of the Coastal Zone Management Act of 1972, designed to achieve wise use of the nation's coastal areas.

Last year's grant was $10,000, according to R. W. Knecht, NOAA assistant administrator for coastal zone management. Under terms of the act, the state must provide an amount equal to at least 50 per cent of the federal funding.

—*The Mobil* (Ala.) *Register*

ALABAMA IS TO RECEIVE A GRANT OF $120,000 TO HELP FINANCE ITS EFFORTS TO PRESERVE, ENHANCE, AND DEVELOP ITS COASTAL AREAS. THE MONEY WILL COME FROM THE NATIONAL OCEANIC AND ATMOSPHERE ADMINISTRATION OF THE U.S. DEPARTMENT OF COMMERCE.

THIS IS THE SECOND OF THREE ANTICIPATED GRANTS TO ALABAMA TO AID IN DEVELOPING THE COASTAL ZONE MANAGEMENT PLAN REQUIRED BY THE FEDERAL COASTAL ZONE MANAGEMENT ACT OF 1972. THE ACT AIMS AT MAKING THE WISEST POSSIBLE USE OF THE NATION'S COASTAL AREAS.

UNDER THIS ACT, THE STATE MUST MATCH THE AMOUNT PROVIDED BY THE FEDERAL GOVERNMENT.

- <u>WABB</u>, MOBILE, ALABAMA

Style. The important considerations concerning style are all part of a major point already stressed—the newscast is for listeners, not readers. Therefore, the newscast must depend on short, clear sentences; it must have an easy, flowing style; and everything must fit smoothly into a whole generally referred to as the "news picture of the moment." Because of these considerations, the writer often uses standard transitional phrases such as "From the Nation's capital comes . . .", "In the world of show business today . . .", "On the labor front . . ." These transitional phrases serve the double purpose of blending one item into the next and creating a pattern for the listener. This pattern, incidentally, has been found to be exceedingly important. The listener, it seems, is pleased by the grouping effected; he prefers it to the jumbled arrangement of the unorganized newscast.

Also to be recognized is the frequency of expressions found in spoken rather than in written language. The device of asking a question in a conversational tone, for example, is often quite effective. ("What is the feeling of the plain people, you and me, about this question? Here's the answer.") Other oral-language expressions, such as the colloquialism, may also be used within limits. Thus, such expressions as "put up with," "gag (practical joke)," and "odds-on favorite" can be used when certain of comprehension.

Examine the following newscast, noting especially the stylistic devices employed:

BRUNHILDA---THE HEROINE OF WAGNER'S FAMED OPERA "SIEG-
FRIED"---PROBABLY NEVER THOUGHT SHE'D END UP IN WASHINGTON'S
SMITHSONIAN INSTITUTION. BUT THERE SHE IS---THE STAR OF THE
SMITHSONIAN'S NEW HALL OF HEALTH SCHEDULED TO OPEN NEXT SUN-
DAY.

BRUNHILDA---A LIFE-SIZE "PLEXIGLAS" MODEL GIVEN HER NAME
UNOFFICIALLY BY MUSEUM WORKERS---IS TRANSPARENT. SHE IS A
ONE-GIRL LESSON IN ANATOMY---WITH ORGANS THAT LIGHT UP AND
VEINS THAT GLOW IN THE DARK. THE MODEL IS ONE OF THE MOST
COMPLICATED OF ITS KIND IN THE WORLD. ONE BY ONE ... 25 OF
HER ORGANS LIGHT UP ... AND A VOICE DESCRIBES THEM TO MUSIC.

- <u>UNITED PRESS INTERNATIONAL</u>

Vocabulary. As the writer of the straight newscast prepares his material, he finds that a knowledge of the qualities of vocabulary already discussed is sufficient fror his purpose. However, as he turns to the specialized newscast (sports or theater, for instance) he must also possess the ability to use the appropriate terminology precisely and authoritatively. This ability is necessary in order to gain the all-important attribute—note of authority.

To grasp the importance of this point, one need only consider any of the specialized newscasts. Suppose, for example, that the writer of the sportscast were to make errors in the nomenclature of baseball, or that the writer of the women's program were to confuse the terminology of cooking, sewing, or any other such activity. The fate of any such program is obvious.

Objectivity. Throughout all newscast writing, the keynote must be objectivity. Stories must be written with a detachment that clearly demonstrates impartiality, thus making the newscast usable without hesitation by any major station in the land. For this reason, coloring, slanting, or any other device that leans toward the biased or the partial must be removed. Radio and television stations, unlike the newspaper, rarely take a stand on political questions or controversial issues.[7] True, the local station is likely to favor the activities of its

[7] While the editorials of radio and television stations, as is pointed out later in this chapter, are much more vigorous than they were a short time ago, stations still refrain from taking a stand on such questions as public abortion clinics because of the heat of the issue and the sharply drawn sides among the general populace. Also, radio and television personalities who take firm stands on controversial issues represent personal rather than official viewpoints.

area (as by playing up farm interests in a rural area), but essentially the station is calm and impartial.

To appreciate the role of impartiality in newscasting, a competent observer need only examine a story as it is aired in a widely accepted program as compared with its treatment in a program sponsored by a special-interest group like a labor union or a political party. The difference in selection and arrangement of facts, the choice of vocabulary, and the implications make the versions barely recognizable as the same basic story.

The two types of stories demanding the most care in insuring objectivity are crime and politics. Crime stories present difficulty because of the writer's natural tendency to score wrongdoing and to dramatize. A kidnaping story, for example, occasions a strong tendency to express resentment and to overpaint the picture. Politics presents a problem because the news writer, like most others, often has a settled opinion that approaches the passion of the crusader. Therefore, he is certain to reflect his bias unless he is exceptionally careful.

Determining Audience Demands

Anyone making decisions regarding newscasts must have a knowledge of audience demands for the obvious reason that stations, like other businesses, must satisfy their customers. Therefore, the station operators must know the programs that attract and the programs that lose listeners.

Although analyzing listener demands is an enigmatic problem, some strong influences are discernible. They are (1) sex of probable audience, (2) age of probable audience, and (3) background of probable audience.

Sex of probable audience is important because men and women often display sharply different interests. Consequently, program offerings must be arranged accordingly. Newscasts, for example, are more likely to be composed of straight news and sports in the early morning and evening because of the probability of many men listeners. Women's news (fashions, shopping tips, etc.) are best suited to mid-morning and afternoon because of the probability of many women listeners. Thus, sex is a distinct influence.

Age of probable audience is important because many programs are pointed toward children, teen-agers, young adults, or other such groups. The child's program, for example, is broadcast in the late afternoon, early evening, or on Saturday morning because those are the times children are most likely to be listening.[8] Age of probable audience usually can be determined easily by the process of elimination; e.g., children cannot be reached in the morning because they are in school, elderly persons seldom listen after 10 o'clock in the evening.

Background of probable audience is the most difficult of the influences to evaluate. It is difficult because it involves an attempt to "weigh and consider"

---

[8] An interesting sidelight on the subject of children as an audience is this: many advertisements for products used by adults are promoted in children's programs on the theory that children pressure adults into certain purchases.

such baffling conditions as educational background, religious affiliation, national origin, and common interests. Naturally, such facts as these are not easily appraised. Therefore most stations must rely on conjecture.

A further difficulty encountered in learning listener demands arises with the off-day and the off-hour cross-section. What, for example, is the nature of the Saturday and the holiday audience? What is the nature and the extent of the audience that listens in automobiles, restaurants, and waiting rooms? Does this audience remain numerically consistent from day to day, or does it fluctuate sharply? If the answers to these questions were available, they would be helpful indeed.

The program director should always check two sources in ascertaining listener demands. First, he should check the programs of competing stations because they reflect the opinions of someone faced with the same problem; if the competing station has been at all successful, it has demonstrated sound judgment in choosing programs. Second, the director should check the scientific studies made by professional organizations, which usually are discussed in the trade magazines. Most stations, however, prefer a third procedure. They prefer to make their own analyses of listener interest in their area, followed by a trial-and-error process. Programs which they find successful they retain. Those which do not draw are dropped. Continuing success of a station they believe, is possible only if the station develops a thorough knowledge of its area and its listeners.

A final thought concerning audience demands is this: many radio stations are now relying on professional agencies to determine the nature and emphasis (time of airing, length of program) of their programs. The three chief agencies in the United States are Pulse, Hooper, and Arbitron (ARB).

The most important finding of these agencies is that the MOR stations (middle of the road) draw the largest audiences for the longest periods. MOR offerings rely on soft music, time-tested dialogues, and conventional approaches—all mixed with a little of the popular music styles that seem to have more than a passing appeal. This last procedure creates an atmosphere of being up-to-date but not offensively avant-garde.

SPECIALIZED NEWSCASTS

In addition to the facts concerning the general newscast, there are specific points pertaining to the special types of newscasts. Besides the general newscasts, most stations usually have programs concerning women's news, sports, and special activities.

Women's news programs most often concern home activities, shopping, fashions, and stories of well-known women.[9] Although the wire services pro-

---

[9] According to the trade magazines, the women's-liberation movement has not—as late as 1975—affected seriously the content of either the specialized women's programs or the general program for all listeners and viewers. However, the movement has aided in placing more women in radio and television station personnel.

vide some women's newscasts, stations sometimes have to gather additional material to fit the local situation. For those who do so, the most important caution is to recognize the woman's viewpoint. Consequently, stations often employ a woman to gather, prepare, and deliver the material. A second important consideration is novelty. For very clear reasons, the woman is a specialist in fashions, foods, and other items concerning the home and her sex in general, and so she does not want to hear facts she already knows—she wants something new and interesting. Hence, the writer must strive to meet her demands.

The newscast of sports, more often termed a "sportscast," must be as much specialized for the men as the women's newscast is for its audience. The sports devotee is a species unto himself. He demands accuracy, an enthusiastic but impartial treatment, and an extensive knowledge of all kinds of background information. Throughout all, he demands news that is recent, pertinent, and factual—the kind of news that will give him background material for discussion and argument with other sports enthusiasts.

Below is an Associated Press specialized newscast. AP terms this type of newscast a "Spotlight Extra."

A MAIN REASON YOU CAN STAY ALIVE AND HEALTHY IS EXPRESSED IN ONE WORD: ANTIBODIES.

ANTIBODIES ARE TINY PROTEIN MOLECULES THAT SEEK OUT AND ATTACK THE (B) BILLIONS OF GERMS AND VIRUSES OR ANY OTHER "FOREIGN" SUBSTANCES THAT MAY ON ANY DAY THREATEN YOU WITH HARM.

ANTIBODIES CAN HELP COMBAT CANCER. INDEED, ONE SCIENTIFIC SUSPICION IS THAT CANCERS OFTEN MAY START UP BUT THE ANTIBODY OR IMMUNOLOGICAL RESPONSE KILLS OFF THE TINY CANCERS BEFORE THEY BECOME DANGEROUS. MUCH CANCER RESEARCH IS DEVOTED TO BEEFING UP THE BODY'S NATURAL IMMUNE RESPONSE.

BUT IF YOU NEED A NEW HEART OR KIDNEY, IT IS ALSO ANTIBODIES THAT BECOME INVOLVED IN TRYING TO PROMOTE REJECTION OF THE BORROWED ORGAN.

DR. GERALD EDELMAN SAYS BY SOME MIRACULOUS PROCESS YOU WERE BORN WITH A WHOLE GREAT LIBRARY OF ANTIBODIES, AND THE CO-WINNER OF A NOBEL PRIZE FOR PHYSIOLOGY AND MEDICINE SAYS THESE ARE ABLE TO RECOGNIZE ANYTHING FOREIGN IN YOUR SYSTEM. DR. EDELMAN'S AWARD WAS FOR BASIC DISCOVERIES ABOUT THE CHEMICAL STRUCTURE AND BEHAVIOR OF ANTIBODIES.

THE 43-YEAR-OLD SCIENTIST TOLD A NEWS CONFERENCE IN NEW YORK

(THURSDAY) THAT THE RECOGNITION FACTOR STILL IS ONE OF THE PRIME MYSTERIES ABOUT ANTIBODIES.

THREE YEARS AGO, DR. EDELMAN AND A TEAM OF SCIENTISTS WORKING WITH HIM AT ROCKEFELLER UNIVERSITY ANNOUNCED SUCCESS IN SPELLING OUT THE EXACT CHEMICAL STRUCTURE OF AN ANTIBODY KNOWN AS GAMMA GLOBULIN.

THEY ESTABLISHED THAT AN ANTIBODY DOES TWO THINGS. PART OF IT ACTS LIKE A SEEING-EYE DOG, IN THE DARK RECESSES OF THE BODY, TO TRACK DOWN AND SEIZE THE OFFENDING FOREIGN MOLECULE. ANYTHING FOREIGN TO YOU IS CALLED AN ANTIGEN, WHICH ELICITS THE ANTIBODY RESPONSE.

ANOTHER PART OF THE ANTIBODY ACTS TO NEUTRALIZE THE OFFENDER.

THE PORTION OF THE ANTIBODY KNOWN AS A VARIABLE REGION PERMITS AN ENORMOUS NUMBER OF COMBINATIONS WITH FOREIGN MATERIALS SO THAT THE ANTIBODY CAN RECOGNIZE AND LATCH ONTO AN "ENEMY". ONCE THE ANTIBODY FITS WITH AN ANTIGEN, IN A KIND OF LOCK-AND-KEY FASHION, THE OTHER PORTION GOES TO WORK TO DESTROY IT.

THE ANTIBODY FIRST ANALYZED BY THE EDELMAN TEAM CONTAINED 1,320 AMINO ACIDS, THE CHEMICAL LINKS THAT CONSTITUTE PROTEINS. IT CONTAINED 19,996 ATOMS, AND WEIGHED 150,000 TIMES AS MUCH AS A SINGLE HYDROGEN ATOM.

A COUPLE OF TIMES AT HIS NEWS CONFERENCE, DR. EDELMAN REFERRED TO THE FACT THAT "A NEWBORN BABY HAS ALL THE ANTIBODIES HE NEEDS BEFORE HE EVER MEETS AN ANTIGEN."

HE SAID HOW THE HUMAN BODY MANAGES TO GENERATE SO MANY ANTI-BODIES, AND HOW GENES SPECIFY THEIR PRODUCTION, ARE GREAT CONTINUING QUESTIONS.

DIFFERENCES BETWEEN RADIO AND TELEVISION NEWSCASTS

The requirements for writing in radio and television newscasts have much in common but they also have two important differences. The first difference is the obvious fact that the radio newscaster is unseen while the television newscaster is on view. The second difference is that the radio newscaster is held to the spoken word while the television newscaster often uses films, videotape and other devices.

The fact that the television newscaster is on view makes some differences in his written material. Unlike the radio newscaster, he cannot simply sit back and read. Instead, he must bring something of the lecturer and something of the actor to his performance. He must point, gesture, smile, and be generally appealing to his public. The script, therefore, must contain appropriate openings or even instructions for physical action. The fact that the television newscaster uses films and other aids divides his script into two kinds of writing—"on-camera" and "off-camera" writing. On-camera writing is that which is read while the speaker is on view; off-camera writing is that which serves as a running commentary for the material (films, objects, etc.) on view.

Because the television newscaster has a more involved performance, he must plan his program as an actor rehearses. The radio newscaster need only be certain that he is going to read correctly and appealingly.

EDITORIALS

Of all the program items aired by television stations, one of those which contribute most significantly to the total impact of the medium itself is the editorial.

Television editorials first appeared in sizable numbers in 1958. At that time, however, they were not so much editorials as pleasant little essays on safe subjects. They urged respect for local historic shrines, concerted response to education week, generous support of the local animal-shelter drive, or appropriate attitudes toward some similarly noncontroversial cause. Editorials of that time invited no replies because no replies were necessary. At best, they merely elicited a pleasantly affirmative nod.

Yet before another decade passed, the television editorial matured into the thought-provoking item of the present. In its new form, it is often a call for strong action on an important question. A respected personality on the station's staff appears, usually at the close of a news program, as spokesman for the editorial staff of the station. He then presents an argument on concerns like the enactment of tighter laws to control gambling, condemnation of a police raid, or increased protection of consumers against the ill effects of household detergents.

Because the editorials are controversial, many stations now invite challenges and disagreements. In some cases, they ask a person holding an opposing viewpoint to express his thoughts, but in most instances, they conclude their presentation with a statement such as: "This station welcomes dissenting opinions from responsible persons, and it promises to present those opinions fairly and fully." Then, true to its commitment, the station airs such opinions when submitted. The over-all result is that television often gives citizens an important question to reflect upon—as well as the major arguments for adopting a given conclusion.

The radio editorial is quite similar to the television editorial, although it naturally lacks the visual impact of an impressive personality on a screen. Furthermore, unless presented at the close of a newscast or other program which the listener is following closely, it often loses its power because the listener is only "half listening."

Like the television editorial, the radio editorial in general was rather innocuous for many years. Then, paralleling the trend in television, it suddenly began to develop a punch in the late 1960s.

Currently, radio editorials are most likely to be heard on the stations which devote much or all of their day to news—the "all-news-all-the-time" stations. Editorial opinions are often presented also on "talk" shows and "news roundup" programs. Further, many large metropolitan stations air the conventional editorial; that is, the editorial which is similar in every detail to the television editorial except visual presentation. And in many cases, especially when well prepared and competently delivered, radio editorials of this kind are impressive and influential.

The writing of the editorial for television and radio is similar to the writing of the newspaper editorial in every major respect except one: television and radio editorials must be prepared for listeners rather than for readers. Hence, like every other form of electronic media writing, the editorial must be cast in the style of the speaker, and it must make comfortable listening.

In addition, some small differences between the television editorial and the radio editorial are woth citing. The spokesman for the television station can naturally use such visual aids as maps and charts; the radio editorialist must rely totally or oral delivery. This, in turn, makes some minor stylistic differences: for instance, the television editorial may have a sentence that refers to a prop. Also, the delivery of the television spokesman (gestures, facial expression, manner) can aid in conveying the message, but the radio personality is limited to the use of his voice. Therefore, the writer of the editorial constructs his material in the light of this difference.

PROGRAM CONTINUITIES

The program continuity, as the name suggests, is the running dialogue for shows. Music programs, for instance, need introductions, observations, and other writing to carry them along; and therefore, a writer must assemble appealing material beforehand if the show is to move smoothly.

Most often, the continuity contains an introduction to the program itself, introductions for specific phases of the program, commercials, observations, humor (if appropriate), and a sign-off announcement.

The following are typical program continuities:

MUSIC UNLIMITED...PART ONE

DATE: JULY 21

TIME: 7:05 - 7:30 PM

JOHN: WGN PRESENTS...MUSIC UNLIMITED for July Twenty-One!

MUSIC: <u>THEME</u>

JOHN: Good Evening.   John Mallow inviting you to join us each

week night at this time and Sunday mornings at 9:05 - for

a journey to the World of Music.

This evening, Music takes us traveling to an island in the

sun - the place where Napoleon tarried and, according to

legend, the spot Jason loved so much that he momentarily

forgot his search for the Golden Fleece.

It's recalling some good advice from Abraham Lincoln -

The Waltz -

And a Summertime Song.

A look to the Land of Milk and Honey -

The Sound of the Marimbas -

And Arthur Fiedler conducting the Boston Pops Orchestra -

a Vincent Youmans' movie tune dating back to 1933 and the

film "Flying Down to Rio" ... THE CARIOCA.

Of Make Believe -

and Fantasy.

Of Memories, Travels, and Songs to Sing.

This is the Way of our World

in Music...MUSIC UNLIMITED.

MUSIC: <u>THE CARIOCA (1:54)</u>

MUSIC: <u>IF THIS IS GOODBYE (2:15)</u>

JOHN: Rachmaninoff came up with the melody.   Some years ago, Robert

Wright and George Forrest borrowed the tune, re-arranged it,

and gave it a new title - IF THIS IS GOODBYE.   Margaret Whiting.

MUSIC: <u>BLUE TWILIGHT (3:45) UP, FADE FOR</u>

JOHN: It's good to know that there are still a few places in this
          world of ours where the weary traveler can get away from it all
          if he wishes. And one of them is a famous island in the sun
          a little less than four hours from Rome. The Island of Elba.
          Here according to legend, Jason and his Argonauts stopped for
          what they thought would be only a short time. But the sea, the
          white beaches, the blue sky above and the beauty of the place
          were a heady temptation to remain longer. And so they
          tarried - day after day - nearly forgetting their search
          for the Golden Fleece. Here, in a house on a hill,
          Napoleon lived from May of eighteen-fourteen until February
          of eighteen-fifteen. This was after his defeat in Russia
          and before his escape to Waterloo. His desk is still in the
          house and in his reception room one can still see the
          Nile River frescoes recalling his success in Egypt. Napoleon,
          however, was the only visitor who really wanted to leave,
          and he would stand on the small terrace of his house, watching
          the British warships that kept him prisoner. At his desk and
          on the terrace he plotted his escape.
          Today the island of Elba is a tranquil place where man is
          proud to go backward in order to go forward. "What is so
          wonderful about concrete and asphalt?" a native asks. "The
          way to make progress here -- perhaps anywhere" -- he explains
          - "is to go backward." And so - on the island of Elba, during
          the last twenty years - an immense reforestation project has
          been carried out. Trees that the Etruscans cut down some
          twenty-five centuries ago have been replaced, and the island
          is becoming increasingly rural - and greener than it has been
          for hundreds of years. It's Elba's approach to tourism -
          and it's one of the few places left in our world where a man
          can look to the stars, get away from it all, and dream his
          dream.
          Just a few thoughts on a place you might like to visit some
          time in the future - maybe this summertime - the Island of Elba.

MUSIC: BLUE TWILIGHT...TO FINISH

MUSIC: THE SUMMER KNOWS (2:45)

JOHN: Roger Williams with chorus, the theme from "Summer of '42." -
             THE SUMMER KNOWS.

MUSIC: MILK AND HONEY (2:28)

JOHN: He gave us Dolly and he gave us Mame, but his first on-
             Broadway score was that for MILK AND HONEY. It, too, will
             be remembered. The music of Jerry Herman - the orchestra of
             Melachrino.

MUSIC: NON DIMENTICAR (2:12)

JOHN: Singing the days away in Italy where music is a passport to
             Happiness - Robert Goulet - NON DIMENTICAR.

MUSIC: I SAY A LITTLE PRAYER...(2:18) UP, FADE FOR

JOHN: The Sound of Marimbas for a melody by Burt Bacharach - I SAY A
             LITTLE PRAYER.

MUSIC: I SAY A LITTLE PRAYER...TO FINISH

MUSIC: THEME

JOHN: A pause now in our journey to the World of Music. This is
             John Mallow, inviting you to stay tuned for PART TWO of
             MUSIC UNLIMITED at 7:32 -
             Carry a rabbit's foot for good luck if you want. Many people
             do.
             The Movie Theme -
             Humperdinck and the waltz -
             And recalling some good advice from Abraham Lincoln.
             7:32 - PART TWO - MUSIC UNLIMITED.

MUSIC: THEME

MUSIC UNLIMITED...PART TWO

DATE: JULY 21

TIME: 7:32 - 7:50 PM

MUSIC: THEME

JOHN: A Journey to the World of Music. PART TWO - MUSIC UNLIMITED
for July Twenty-One! This is John Mallow and during
the last part of our program this evening, Music brings to
mind some good advice from Abraham Lincoln - his Key to
Success.
It's a Movie Theme recalled -
The Waltz -
And the Love Song.
Some thoughts concerning Good Luck and the rabbit's foot -
And the Les Reed Sound for - THERE'S A KIND OF HUSH.
Evening Comes -
Another day draws to a close -
And Music helps
Take us out of ourselves
MUSIC UNLIMITED!

MUSIC: THERE'S A KIND OF HUSH (2:35)

MUSIC: IT MUST BE HIM (2:42)

JOHN: He's a man who moves with the musical times, Enoch Light
and his singers - IT MUST BE HIM.

MUSIC: THE CHILD DAVID (2:37) UP, FADE FOR

JOHN: Long, long ago when our land was much younger, a lad named
Isham Reavis wrote a letter to Abraham Lincoln asking him how
best to succeed. The Great Emancipator was in Springfield,
Illinois. He had yet to be elected the sixteenth President
of the United States, and he called his letter in reply,
"Advice to a young boy who aspires to become a
lawyer."
"My dear Sir:
I have just reached home and found your letter. If you are

(CONTINUED)

JOHN: resolutely determined to make a lawyer of yourself, the thing
is more than half done already. It is but a small matter
whether you read WITH anybody or not. I did not read with
anyone. Get the books and read and study them 'til you
understand them in their principal features, and that is the
main thing. It is of no consequence to be in a large town while
you are reading. I read at New Salem, which never had three
hundred people living in it. The books and your CAPACITY for
understanding them, are just the same in all places.
Always bear in mind that your own resolution to succeed is
more important than any other one thing ... Abraham Lincoln."
...And so it is with anything any of us want to do in life
...it is our own resolution to succeed that is more important
than any other one thing.

MUSIC: <u>THE CHILD DAVID...TO FINISH</u>

MUSIC: <u>THE LAST WALTZ...(2:58)</u>

JOHN: Engelbert Humperdinck - THE LAST WALTZ.

MUSIC: <u>THEME FROM FELLINI'S "EIGHT AND A HALF" (2:22) UP, FADE FOR</u>

JOHN: Should you happen to carry a rabbit's foot for good luck -
don't let anybody make fun of you. About ten million people
in our country carry a rabbit's foot for luck - and most of
them seriously believe in the superstition. Most of them,
of course, have been waiting a long, long time, for luck
to come, but they still believe it will. While waiting - a
movie theme remembered - the orchestra of Riz Ortolani - the
THEME FROM FELLINI'S "EIGHT AND A HALF".

MUSIC: <u>THEME FROM FELLINI'S "EIGHT AND A HALF"...TO FINISH</u>

MUSIC: <u>THEME</u>

JOHN: And then we have the quizmaster who suggested to a contestant
who was obviously hard of hearing that perhaps he needed a
hearing aid. "Couldn't use it, son," said the man. "Hear
more now than I can understand."

(CONTINUED)

JOHN: This is John Mallow and this has been MUSIC UNLIMITED for

          July Twenty-One! Join us again tomorrow evening at this

          same time for another Journey to the World of Music.

          Bright and Exciting -

          Vivid and Descriptive -

          MUSIC UNLIMITED!

MUSIC: THEME

The program continuities shown above are examples of a widely employed type, a type that is especially suitable for competing against television. The relaxed atmosphere, the reliance upon established musical favorites, and the lack of commercials create a strong appeal for the many persons who like to read or work while listening—activities that are not possible if one must look at a television screen.

There is, however, another kind of program continuity which is used extensively but unobtrusively; it is the continuity for the radio or television program wherein an eyewitness account is to be given. Examples are: the state funeral of a President of the United States; the famous Mardi Gras parade in New Orleans; the arrival of a foreign dignitary at the airport; and the aftermath of a Mississippi River flood.

For this type of continuity, the writer must first learn the agenda or probable course of events involved and then collect background material. From this material, he prepares descriptive sentences, running commentary, and factual observations which he arranges in a chronological sequence—that is to say, in the order in which they are most helpful to the speaker's description. The speaker then uses the prepared script as he sees fit, employing some passages as written, editing others, and omitting others.

Below is the general broad outline used by CBS, Washington, for its commentary on arrivals of heads of state in Washington and the official welcoming ceremonies at the airport.

   I   Arrival of plane carrying dignitary

  II   Simultaneous appearance of Presidential car

 III   Meeting of President's party and dignitary's
       party at the ramp

 IV   Identity of every major figure in both parties

  V   Statement about security precautions

 VI   Cameras on President and dignitary for official
       greetings

```
        VII    President escorts dignitary to car

        VIII   Departure
```

```
        Before using this general outline, the writer must

naturally supply appropriate specific subheadings.  He must also

make allowances for any such last-minute changes as the presence

of the Under Secretary of State in the absence of the Secretary.
```

Before using this general outline, the writer must naturally supply appropriate specific subheadings. He must also make allowances for any such last-minute changes as the presence of the Under Secretary of State in the absence of the Secretary.

THE COMMENTARY

A type of radio and television program that can be highly successful in careful, talented hands is the commentary. The commentary, as the name implies, is a series of observations on a given subject. Although the most popular commentary is that which treats the day's news, many other fields are also covered. Sports, the theater, women's fashions, local feature stories, and a host of other material are the bases for successful commentaries.

The commentary can best be understood by thinking of the commentator as a newspaper columnist broadcasting his material. In fact, many commentators have used the expression ''columnist of the air'' to name their programs. The role of the commentator is to observe, to interpret, to provide background information, and hence to inform. He is expected to examine his subject authoritatively and tell his listener in a pleasant, unassuming, yet capable manner facts that the listener does not know.

Aside from respecting the general considerations of writing for radio and television, the writer of the commentary must exercise care as he decides on the tone of his program. Tone is important because the appeal of the commentary, like the appeal of the newspaper column, is essentially that of a personality. The listener must react favorably to the commentator; or, to state the matter negatively, he must not be repelled by an atmosphere of conceit, condescension, or other offensive quality. As a result, the writer of the commentary must work constantly for a tone that attracts readers day after day.

The tone of the commentary, however, naturally varies with the type of material. The commentary on the news, for example, must be dignified and generally serious; the commentary on popular music may be light, even breezy. The commentary on the week's religious news must reflect scholarly impartiality; the commentary on the theater may be heavily flavored with personal opinion. The commentary on the world situation must treat up-to-the-minute facts; the commentary on sports can reminisce about events months or years old.

Writing the Commentary

Despite differences of subject and tone in commentaries, certain fundamental points are common to all types.

Above all else, the writer *must always remember the power of his medium of expression.* Radio and television, like the newspaper, exert a tremendous force in molding public conclusions—as has already been mentioned. Therefore, the writer must be aware of the impact of his material and conduct himself accordingly. In short, his keynote must be a sense of responsibility.

When the commentator forgets his responsibility, he injures his standing and his profession by providing ammunition for those influential people (well-known clergymen, educators, political figures, and others) who are forever flaying the broadcast media for irresponsibility.

If the writer of the commentary accepts his responsibility, he knows that he *must clearly separate fact from conjecture and opinion.* His writing must leave no doubt in the mind of the listener concerning the line between established and nonestablished fact. Even though the station and the sponsor may protect themselves by such statements as "the opinions of the commentator are his own," the writer should not feel free to offer nonfact as fact. The writer must be especially careful of such statements as "Public opinion is clearly in favor of this proposal" and "There can be no doubt as to the outcome of this issue." Such statements are often easy to make but without basis in reality.

To make certain that his facts are sound, the writer of the commentary *must check and recheck.* Although he can generally rely on facts from the wire services for accuracy, he must learn how to verify statements from other sources (like police, labor organizations, or plain citizens); that is, he must develop the newspaper reporter's ability to get the truth.

As the writer casts the material in its final form he must *make sure that it does not sound like the Ultimate Uncontestable Utterance.* Although the commentator is expected to be authoritative, he must not issue his material as final, unquestioned pronouncements; and he must not let his writing develop a patronizing or condescending ring. Some little devices can be recognized immediately as objectionable. Easily seen examples are the objectionable aspects of the overuse of the first person pronoun; of an excessive overemphasis on personal experience; and of a too-obvious attempt to aggrandize one's role in life or as a commentator. Essentially, the writer gains a note of authority without being overbearing by striving throughout for a semblance—and the reality—of humility.

Finally, the writer *must not let his commentaries become narrow or one-sided.* The writer of the commentary, like most persons, has favorite subjects which reflect his interests. Unless he is careful, these subjects are likely to dominate his program to the exclusion of equally important ones. Therefore, he must attempt to treat every aspect of his subject, to give both sides of every controversial question, and to convey a general atmosphere of breadth. Prejudice, slanting, and coloring are conditions to be shunned.

SUSTAINING ANNOUNCEMENTS

A type of writing that closely resembles the radio or TV commercial is the sustaining announcement. This writing covers the announcement made as a public service, the announcement to advertise one of the station's programs, and the announcement made in the public interest.

The announcement made as a public service includes a wide field. Such announcements include "plugs" for the sale of government savings bonds, charity drives, clean-up campaigns, medical research, and similar causes. The organizations behind these drives generally have their own publicity staffs who supply releases with instructions for timing and delivery. The station, however, may have its own writers phrase the announcement. Sometimes the releases must be recast to fit station editorial policy; sometimes the release consists only of bare facts, not in form to be aired.

The announcement to advertise a program is often a short statement between programs. For established programs, it usually consists of a brief announcement such as "Start the day right by listening to . . . on the Breakfast Hour, every weekday morning beginning at seven o'clock over this station." For new programs, it usually contains some kind of "come on" element.

The announcement made in the public interest is generally prompted by some condition of the moment. Examples cover the following situations: urging citizens to vote, reminding listeners of the deadline for tax returns, urging cautions for driving, stressing accident prevention in the home, reminding listeners of the advent of daylight-saving time. This type of announcement is always brief, with an attempt at a slogan or emphasis of a striking fact. Here is a typical announcement: "Voting is a privilege and a duty in a democracy. Exercise your privilege and do your duty!"

MISCELLANEOUS WRITING

Writing for radio and television involves several other types not readily classifiable. One of the most common of such types is the *station-break announcement*.

The station-break announcement may be a simple statement to identify the station, a slogan to advertise the station, or a commercial. The simple announcement to identify the station usually follows this pattern: "This is station WOR, New York." . . . "You are listening to station WCE, Cleveland." . . . "This is station WXZ in the Nation's Capital."

The slogan to advertise the station generally follows this pattern: "This is station WFIL, where the news watch never stops." . . . "You are tuned to station KDKA, where you get news every hour on the hour." . . . "This is station WRVA, the station with programs for all the family."

The station-break announcement used as a commercial follows this pattern: "Station WLMA, where Kahn's, the home of good used cars, brings you the day's news every evening at six." . . . "This is station WTBC, through whose facilities you can hear the Wiley music hour tonight at 9 o'clock." . . . "You are listening to station WBAL, which will broadcast the Burns-Tulsa game tomorrow afternoon at 2 o'clock."

The requirements for the writing of the station-break announcement are clearly apparent. The writer must have a well-developed sense of originality to gain the novelty needed; he must be able to write a clear, crisp sentence; and he must be able to vary the language to suit the message.

Another type of miscellaneous writing is the *announcement and blend-out* for the program staged by an outside agency. If, for example, a church, a civic organization, or a college group is to present a program, the station naturally supplies the announcer to introduce and sign off the program. He, of course, needs prepared material. Here is a typical announcement, followed by the close-out and transitional sentences: "At this time, station WCOJ presents the Choir of the West Chester State College in a 15-minute program of Christmas carols. The Choir will sing 'O Little Town of Bethlehem,' 'O Holy Night,' 'Silent Night,' and the 'Hallelujah Chorus.' The Choir will perform under the direction of Professor Roy D. Sweet. We take you now to the Phillips Memorial Auditorium on the college campus." . . .

"You have been listening to a 15-minute program of Christmas carols, sung for you by the Choir of the West Chester State College, under the direction of Professor Roy D. Sweet. The program came to you from the Phillips Memorial Auditorium on the college campus. We take you now to our studios in Coatesville."

This program differs from the ordinary continuity in that the station merely broadcasts the program. It presents the program without interruption from the station, thus placing the outside agency or group "on its own" from the time it is given the air until the station retakes the air.

A third type of miscellaneous writing is the *"extemporaneous" remark*— which obviously is not extemporaneous. The extemporaneous remark covers such situations as the casual remark of the disc jockey in mid-program that the next record reminds him to complete his Christmas shopping; the observation that summer is drawing closer; the little humorous story; and the reminiscence. The "extemporaneous" writing is often done by the announcer who uses it, but such is not necessarily the case. Examples of effective extemporaneous remarks are usually found in the network broadcasts where professional gag writers are employed. However, regardless of how small a station may be, someone should prepare extemporaneous remarks, for they are an essential of many programs. They should always be done well in advance because when the announcer is permitted to ad-lib, the program often becomes dull.

Below are examples of the "extemporaneous" remark, selected at random, from radio and television programs.

```
Brr.  This is the kind of day that brings
the color to your face ... purple.

I'm sure glad this ain't television, folks.
Every time I play this record, I blush like
a school girl at her first party.

As I tell my wife.  She's only a printer's
daughter, but I like her type.

Stay tuned for Bill Conner ... the answer to
a maiden's prayer, a sales girl's dream, and
a big game hunter's cry for somebody to hold
down a rhinoceros by sitting on it.

Here he is, our genial newscaster, Jim Turner.
The man I would like to see condemned to wear
forever the ten most unwanted Christmas ties.

And now, ladies and gentlemen, Hal Nelson ...
a real dog fancier.  If he fancies a record, you
can be sure it's a real dog.
```

EXERCISES

1. Write a continuity for a 15-minute program of popular music on either radio or television.
2. Select the national television newscaster who in your judgment exerts the

greatest impact on the largest number of viewers, and evaluate the personality which he projects.

3. Compose sustaining announcements for any five worthy causes.

4. Write five good station-break announcements.

5. Compose a three-minute off-camera writing to describe a film of a raging department-store fire.

6. After watching a television program wherein a nationally important personage answers the questions of one or more newsmen (as on "Face the Nation" or "Meet the Press"), write a careful answer to the question, "Who emerged victorious?"

7. Write a commentary for the radio station "hit parade" of popular songs of the past year. The program is to be aired on the year's last Sunday night.

8. Write a newscast, either radio or television, for a 10-minute program of local news.

9. Can you envision a woman achieving the status of the most popular telecaster of general news in the nation? Support your answer with a reasoned explanation.

10. Evaluate any five sustaining announcements currently used on a national network, either radio or television.

11. Discuss the work of a television personality who, in your opinion, overcomes a rather serious handicap (such as extreme shortness of stature or unappealing oral movement) to achieve great success.

12. Write the announcement and the blend-out for a church service.

13. From the sports pages of a large metropolitan daily, prepare a five-minute sportscast to be aired at either the breakfast hour or the five o'clock "going home" show.

14. Write a set of detailed instructions for the chief of the camera crew which is to cover the performance of a well-known singer on a stage where he is backed up by a chorus of six—three girls and three men.

15. Evaluate the performance of any well-known television personality who handles a specialized program (the weatherman, the garden expert, or some other).

16. Examine the front-page stories of your local newspaper and choose the stories you would use on a large metropolitan station's news telecast.

17. Compose a station announcement for a "wake-up" program that is to be aired every morning from six until nine, beginning next week.

18. Select three brief stories from your local newspaper and rewrite them for radio or television broadcast.

FOR FURTHER READING

Barnouw, Erik. *A History of Broadcasting in the United States.* 3 volumes. New York: Oxford University Press, 1966, 1968, 1970.

DeForest, Lee. *Father of Radio: The Autobiography of Lee DeForest.* Chicago: Wilcox and Follett, 1950.

Fang, Irving E. *Television News.* Revised and enlarged edition. New York: Hastings House, Publishers, 1972.

———. *Television/Radio News Workbook.* New York: Hastings House, Publishers, 1974.

Friendly, Fred W. *Due to Circumstances Beyond our Control . . . .* New York: McGraw-Hill, 1962.

Hall, Mark W. *Broadcast Journalism: An Introduction to News Writing.* New York: Hastings House, Publishers, 1971.

Hilliard, Robert L. (ed.). *Radio Broadcasting: An Introduction to the Sound Medium.* 2nd edition. New York: Hastings House, Publishers, 1976.

———. *Writing for Television and Radio.* 3rd edition. New York: Hastings House, Publishers, 1976.

Johnson, Nicholas. *How to Talk Back to Your Television Set.* New York: Bantam Books, 1970.

Lichty, Lawrence W., and Malachi C. Topping. *American Broadcasting: A Source Book on the History of Radio and Television.* New York: Hastings House, Publishers, 1975.

National and International Systems of Broadcasting: Their History, Operation, and Control. East Lansing: Michigan State University Press, 1969.

Rubin, Bernard. *Political Television.* Belmont, Cal.: Wadsworth, 1967.

Sarnoff, David. *Looking Ahead—The Papers of David Sarnoff.* New York: McGraw-Hill, 1968.

Small, William. *To Kill a Messenger: Television News and the Real World.* New York: Hastings House, Publishers, 1970.

★ 14 ★

What "Magazine" Means
Who Writes What Magazines
    Publish?
Changes in the Magazine Field
Qualities Affecting Salability of
    Material
Literary Forms in Magazine
    Writing
    The Short Story
    The Essay
    The Personality Sketch
    The Personal-Experience
    Account
    Popularizing Facts
    The Utility Article
    Poetry
The Writing Process
    The Market
    Planning the Magazine
    Article

Rough Draft and Finished
    Copy
Selling Material
    Literary Agents
    Do's and Don'ts of
        Submitting Manuscripts
        to Magazines
Kinds of Magazines
    Quality Magazines
    Professional Magazines
    Business Magazines
    Technical Magazines
    Farm Magazines
    Company Magazines
    Special-Interest Magazines
    Popular Magazines
    Women's Magazines
    Men's Magazines
    Children's and Adolescents'
        Magazines
    Sunday-Supplement
        Magazines
    Giveaways, Throwaways, Free
        Magazines

Writing for Magazines

The mass-medium which attracts the greatest number of writing aspirants, both amateur and professional, is the magazine. Every year vast hordes of writers—motivated by the desire for remuneration, fame, or personal satisfaction—submit literally thousands of manuscripts to the nation's magazines; and even though many individuals realize that any chance of acceptance is quite limited, they continue in the effort, buoyed up by an unusual brand of enthusiasm. What is this attraction?

WHAT "MAGAZINE" MEANS

The expression "magazine" covers a wide area. The term is so broad that it cannot be defined concisely. There are in the United States over 7,000 publications classified as "magazines," but the label designating them is their only similarity.

At the one extreme of editorial quality are the excellently done publications such as *Harper's,* a collection of high-level short stories, essays, poems, and reviews. At the other are the so-called "pulps," usually collections of love stories, westerns, and bizarre tales, printed on the cheapest of paper. At the one extreme of readership appeal is the publication leveled at a wide audience—the family magazine, the popular weekly, the free magazine sent through the mails by the home-appliance manufacturer. At the other is the publication leveled at a narrow audience—the professional magazine, the trade journal, the union magazine. At the one extreme of physical form is the publication resembling a well-printed book in every detail except the cover. At the other is the "magazine" such as the Sunday supplement which is nothing more than a section of the newspaper. Between the extremes cited lies every conceivable variation. Indeed, a collection of "magazines" can be a strange assortment.

Accompanying these sharp differences in content and purpose among publications termed "magazines" is an equally wide difference in writing patterns. Some magazines reflect a highly formal approach with a definitely finished quality of writing. Such a publication is the scholarly journal or the university quarterly, which carries detail-laden articles often cast in a heavy, ponderous style. Other magazines have an informal approach with a light, bouncy style. Such a magazine is the little television publication that comes stuffed in the Sunday paper. Some magazines, such as the trade journal, are cast in a specific technical language; others, such as the neighborhood magazine, use the language of the newspaper. Some magazines restrict language to conservative usage; others permit colloquialisms, slang, and even vulgar expressions. Each magazine develops its own different pattern of writing.

WHO WRITES WHAT MAGAZINES PUBLISH?

Some magazines carry only work written by their own staffs; some carry only work by outside writers; and some carry work by both their own staff and outside writers.

A common example of the publication written exclusively by the staff is the "company" magazine—the publication maintained by an industrial or business organization. This magazine is the province of an editor, with a full-time staff, who assigns articles, edits copy, and acts as general supervisor. Although the magazine may have a "Letters to the Editor" or "Contributor's Column," it is basically a staff product from cover to cover.

An example of the publication containing only material by outside writers is the scholarly journal. This magazine makes all its selections from manuscripts submitted by scholar-writers within the professional discipline itself. Because of an abundance of manuscripts, the same author rarely has more than one article per year in the magazine.

An example of the publication that carries work by both its own staff and outside writers is the *Saturday Review*. This magazine obtains a pleasing assortment of articles and viewpoints by assigning articles to its own writers and by soliciting and accepting stories, poems, essays, and articles from unaffiliated people.

Because the great majority of magazines fall within this last category (articles by both staff and outside writers), the opportunity for aspiring writers is greatest in this field. Among the most common writers are: the authority in a given field (such as medicine, law, education) who explains an important or complex point in his field; the newspaperman who does an extensive feature story (such as, crime in Chicago, an interesting housing development in New York, a political problem in San Francisco); the free-lance writer who does an article of general interest; the individual who recounts an interesting personal experience.

CHANGES IN THE MAGAZINE FIELD

Anyone who observes magazines at all closely finds that, like most other institutions, they are always in a process of change. Editorial policies shift, new trends become discernible, and magazines seem constantly to appear and disappear. As a result, the entire field often veers under our very gaze.

An example of an editorial-policy change is quite clear in the instance of the *Atlantic Monthly*. This widely read publication has returned over the past three years to an editorial policy that more nearly approaches its pronouncement of "A Magazine of Literature, Art, and Politics." (The statement on the title page of its bound volumes on library shelves.) From about 1965 until 1972, *The Atlantic* was likely to carry such articles as "How I made $193.85 selling cars" (January 1970), a rather earthy description of the cheating involved in used-car sales, and "It's Only A Game: The Beasts of Baltimore" (January 1972), a bluntly written account of the savagery and animalism of professional football. Now, once again, *Atlantic* articles concentrate almost exclusively on topics of great import for the nation and the world. Examples of the appearance and disappearance of magazines are obvious and numerous—the number of new publications which suddenly emerge, then die after a few issues, the sudden closings of publications that have been standbys for decades.

Changes such as these have occurred despite the efforts of editors and publishers to solve the many enigmas that characterize the magazine field. The best of seers and prophets, for example, have been discredited by the meteoric rise of magazines like the *Reader's Digest* and *TV Guide;* they have been baffled in the attempts to save magazines like *Collier's* and the *Saturday Evening Post* [1]; and they have been caught off-guard by the sudden death of magazines like *Life* and *Look*.

---

[1] A famous weekly for more than a century, which collapsed, then was revived as a quarterly, then stepped up to nine issues per year at the time of this writing.

QUALITIES AFFECTING SALABILITY OF MATERIAL

Before a careful thinker considers writing a magazine article, he asks himself over and over, "What qualities will make this manuscript salable?" Naturally, the answer to this question will determine the whole nature of his approach; it will shape the structure upon which he will build all his procedures. Although no all-inclusive formula can be given for making a manuscript salable, certain basic considerations can be cited. The relative strength of these considerations varies, of course, from situation to situation.

The primary yardstick used by all magazines in evaluating material is the *appeal* of a given article for its readers. As already stated, every magazine aims to capture a specific audience; consequently, it chooses its material accordingly. Therefore, the manuscript editor constantly asks himself as he considers material, "Would this interest the readers of our magazine?" If he thinks the material has such appeal, he then proceeds to the other considerations. If not, he rejects the manuscript immediately. The manuscript editor holds his important position because, among other reasons, he is believed to possess a sensitivity to the demands of the magazine's readers.

Closely associated with appeal in determining salability is the consideration of *pertinency*. When an article deals effectively with a timely topic, it stands a good chance of acceptance by a magazine interested in that field. An article, for example, that deals authoritatively with the benefits of and the ill effects from sunburn certainly will be considered by a health magazine for its June issue. An informative treatment of winter care for boats certainly will be examined carefully by the editor of a boating magazine. Pertinency is an important consideration for the self-evident reason that readers want to read about the subjects which interest them most at the moment.

If the manuscript editor concludes that an article has both the necessary appeal and pertinency, he next looks for a note of *originality*.

An article that possesses a striking view, new information, or some other novel quality has a strong count in its favor. A national magazine, for instance, recently carried a highly successful article on juvenile delinquency—a topic worn thin by innumerable treatments. The article was widely read and quoted because of its originality. The approach was new; the information was new; the treatment was new. Originality, in short, was the essence of its success.

Granted that an article has the three qualities discussed above, *effectiveness of expression* now becomes a consideration. For an article to be publishable, it must be written clearly, forcefully, and correctly; it must reflect, at every turn, the competence of the seasoned writer.

Lacking this quality, manuscripts otherwise salable are often returned—the editor likes the article but is repelled by the badly wrought expression. In some instances, the magazine may purchase the article with the thought of recasting it completely. This procedure, however, is quite rare. In fact, it is done only when the basic material is unusually good.

Hovering over all other considerations, however, is the *identity of the au-*

thor. (Who is he? What importance has he? Is he somebody? Is he anybody? Is he competent? Is he trustworthy? How can we check up on him?) Obviously, some articles will be accepted immediately because of the identity of the writer. A piece by a just-resigned member of the President's cabinet, for example, will certainly reach print. The same is true of writings by highly respected authors, established figures in the entertainment world, well-known personalities, and the obscure individual suddenly caught in the spotlight (for instance, the janitor who discovered the Watergate break-in). In fact, when these people do not take the initiative, they are usually approached for articles.[2]

For the fledgling writer, the matter of identity of the author can sometimes present an insurmountable barrier—as for instance, when he submits an opinion piece to a prestigious magazine. Therefore, before he can see his material in some magazines, he must first establish a reputation in an outside field.

LITERARY FORMS IN MAGAZINE WRITING

The most common forms published in magazines are the short story, the essay, the personality sketch, the article popularizing facts, the utility article, and poetry.[3] These terms, of course, are broad and several subdivisions exist for each. This fact is significant because many magazines are interested only in highly specialized forms within the major form. For instance, some magazines are interested only in the short expository essay rather than in essays in general. Some magazines will consider the traditional short story but not the other common forms. Other magazines emphasize the utility article at the expense of all other forms. The writer, therefore, must be aware of specialized-form demands before he prepares his material.

Each form is associated with an appropriate style. The traditional short story, for example, is generally cast in the "literary" style—the style that one associates with the literary masters. The utility article, on the other hand, is often cast in the style employed in the newspaper feature story. Thus, as the writer thinks of form, he should also think of style.

The following discussion treats the major literary forms and the most common subdivisions within each.

The Short Story

The short story is the form most often attempted by aspiring writers. This form is popular among writers because it is popular among readers. Manuscript editors of the quality magazines estimate that attempts at short stories out-

---

[2] When these people lack the educational background or the ability to write the article desired, the publication may suggest or provide a "ghost writer." He then either writes the story for the person—giving the person full credit for the writing—or he uses the standard "as told to" approach.

[3] This listing is not based on any specific kind of order of importance.

number all other forms by a ratio of three to one. Naturally, only a small fraction of those attempting the short story ever see their material in print.

What are the qualities necessary for writing the short story? The writer must have three attributes: (1) inspiration, (2) the ability to perceive, and (3) the ability to portray. *Inspiration* actually means desire. Unless the writer burns with the desire to compose, he can hope for little success. He must want so earnestly to write short stories that he is willing to undergo all sorts of discipline, study, and arduous effort. He must not be one who is discouraged easily. Rather, he must be prepared to practice and re-practice, to write and re-write, to strive and re-strive. His desire must be so strong that he can withstand the most barbed criticism. As for discouragement, he must remember the time-worn advice of the professional, "Don't feel discouraged about rejection slips until you have enough to paper every room in the house."

Ability to perceive means being able to recognize short-story material. The writer must be able first to recognize the story itself, and then to recognize the subtleties, the intricacies, and the little qualities that give depth and appeal. How to develop the ability to perceive can scarcely be reduced to a set of rules—in fact, many writers and teachers of writing believe that this ability is almost completely congenital. Others, however, feel that it can be developed. In either case, there are certainly exercises that will help. The simple practice, for example, of jotting down all the observations of a given week that might be incorporated into a projected novel sharpens one's ability to perceive. So do little discussions among aspiring writers about the dominant qualities in atmospheres they know (hometown places, football stadia, shopping crowds—everyday ordinary things). The importance of the ability to perceive can be realized in an analysis of the truly great short stories, for these works invariably reflect an unusual insight into common events and experiences. The short stories, for instance, of Nathaniel Hawthorne, Charles Dickens, and Robert Louis Stevenson illustrate the importance of this ability. Note, for example, how Hawthorne has looked hard at the scene in order to perceive all the important detail in the situation described below. Note also how he really understands each detail. This selection is from "The Ambitious Guest":

One September night a family had gathered round their hearth, and piled it high with the driftwood of mountain streams, the dry cones of the pine, and the splintered ruins of great trees that had come crashing down the precipice. Up the chimney roared the fire, and brightened the room with its broad blaze. The faces of the father and mother had a sober gladness; the children laughed; the eldest daughter was the image of Happiness at seventeen; and the aged grandmother, who sat knitting in the warmest place, was the image of Happiness grown old. They had found the "herb, heart's-ease," in the bleakest spot of all New England. This family were situated in the Notch of the White Hills, where the wind was sharp throughout the year, and pitilessly cold in the winter—giving their cottage all its fresh inclemency before it descended on the valley of the Saco. They dwelt in a cold spot and a dangerous one; for a mountain towered above their heads, so steep that the stones would often rumble down its sides and startle them at midnight.

Ability to portray is the attribute which receives most attention in courses in short-story writing. This phrase means the ability to find the most effective words, stylistic devices, and structural patterns for relating the story—or, in simpler words, the best way to tell the story. Once again, there can be no set of rules for developing this ability. The writer simply must learn to recognize the most effective manner of telling his story.

The initial step toward developing this ability is to acquire a sound sense of criticism of short stories in general. The writer must have this sense of criticism in order to pass judgment capably upon his own efforts.

He can proceed by reading a specific story and asking such questions as: What are the qualities that make this writer successful? What are the strengths and the weaknesses of this story? What makes this work unusual, routine, or whatever else it may be? When the writer can answer these questions satisfactorily, he is on the road to developing his sense of criticism.

In acquiring a sense of criticism, however, the aspiring writer must avoid a common pitfall: he must beware the all-too-common tendency to imitate the subject matter and style of a well-known master. The works of writers like Ernest Hemingway, William Faulkner, and James Baldwin, for instance, have become traps for numerous young writers. The material and approach appear to be simple matters. In actuality, their selection and execution demand unusual talent. Yet the novice, unable to recognize the true situation, concludes that he, too, can work in the fields made popular by these masters. The most serious result is, of course, that the imitator may destroy his most precious asset—his own originality.

The next step is to work with words, phrases, sentences, and paragraphs to obtain the most effective expression possible. Only when the writer is satisfied that his expression cannot be improved should he think of submitting his manuscript to a publisher. The ability to portray is undoubtedly the most difficult of the three attributes to develop. Hence many persons can say truthfully, "I could be a great writer, if I could only write!" These are the persons who genuinely want to write, who see many experiences and events to write of, but who are unable to find the words and the general expression.

Types of Short Stories. After recognizing the qualities necessary for writing the short story, the writer should know the three types of short stories for which there is the best market. They are (1) the traditional, (2) the detective, and (3) the slice of life.

The *traditional short story* is the kind most persons know. It is the story which has a structural pattern consisting of five parts—the situation, the generating circumstance, the rising action, the climax, and the denouement. Such a story is Sherwood Anderson's "I'm a Fool." The situation is the backdrop for the action; the generating circumstance is the action or event which starts the action rising; the rising action is the series of acts or thoughts which heighten the basic question or the suspense; the climax is the point at which the action is resolved into a single, inescapable conclusion; and the denouement is the final unraveling of the plot. The traditional has always been the most popular of the short story forms, and hence the kind most often published.

The *detective story* is characterized by what is often termed the "reversed-plot" structure. It is the story wherein the author presents an apparently unanswerable question (such as the identity of the person who has stolen a huge sum of money from within a locked bank vault) and then proceeds to unravel it. The detective story makes heavy demands on the writer. He must have great powers of reasoning; he must have a very logical mind; and he must have an extraordinary ability to invent. With these attributes, there must be an ability to present details with clarity and vigor. As an example, a common brand of detective story can be analyzed.

The body of a man murdered under baffling circumstances has been discovered. The author presents all the facts, and if the story is sound the reader is completely puzzled. The author then proceeds, as does A. Conan Doyle in his famous Sherlock Holmes stories, to heighten the situation with details that seem irrelevant or meaningless. Next he begins to weave his skein of facts together skillfully until suddenly, as the story closes, he solves this baffling murder in a manner that elicits admiration and wonder.

The author of the successful detective story must always demonstrate a clear superiority over the reader. The superiority must be based on imagination, logic, and reasoning; it can never be founded on cheap deception or withholding of facts. Hence, the sound detective story resembles the complicated puzzle to be solved only by a superior mind—one that leaves lesser minds standing by to admire or to envy.

There can be many variations of structure and plot in the detective story, and for this reason, the writer must point his work toward the magazine to which he plans to send his story. Some magazines want only the standard puzzlers, the "whodunits." They are not interested in the more complex, more finely wrought works. Others want a more delicately executed type; they want a story in the tradition of the literary master. The most important statement to be made of this market, however, is that there is always a sale to be found for a good detective story. Success, therefore, often lies in finding the right magazine.

The *slice-of-life short story* is characterized by an absence of structural pattern. It is based on the principle that in life there are many little scenes which, in themselves, are intensely interesting. It, therefore, depicts these scenes only, without thought of beginning, ending, or other structural consideration. The slice-of-life author is comparable to the operator of a moving-picture camera who looks at a mass of people and shoots any scene that appeals to him. He has no special interest in what has preceded or what follows; he is interested purely in the appeal of a given scene. In fact, the appeal is heightened by not knowing what has preceded or what has followed. The slice-of-life technique has been handled admirably by such famous writers as James Stephens, Katherine Mansfield, and Thomas Wolfe. It is also a popular form with magazines like the *New Yorker, Esquire,* and many Sunday supplements.

The specific market for the various kinds of stories can be determined only by analyzing magazines. Although the discussion on kinds of magazines presented in this chapter is helpful, the writer still can learn his market only through analysis. Therefore, many writers keep a card file of such analyses to guide them in preparing and submitting manuscripts.

The Essay.

Because the essay is the most common type of article found in magazines, special consideration must be given it. The essay is either formal or informal in approach and treatment. Each type, the author soon learns, lends itself to specific materials and approaches better than the other.

The *formal essay,* as the name implies, follows a formal pattern. It is characterized by seriousness, authoritativeness, and a sharply delineated approach. Thus, the formal essay is employed to write of important topics in a serious manner. It is used, for example, by the statesman writing of the international situation, by the educator explaining the school system, and by the general writer expressing a serious viewpoint on a matter of general interest.

The formal essay follows a basic structure of three parts—introduction, body, conclusion. The *introduction,* obviously the first part, has three functions; it sets the over-all structural pattern of the essay, it establishes the atmosphere to characterize the writing, and it attempts to lure the reader to continue reading the work. Notice how the following introduction to a well-known essay [4] by Alexander Hamilton performs this function:

> Assuming it as an established truth that in case of disunion the several states, or such combinations of them as might happen to be formed out of the wreck of the general confederacy, would be subject to those vicissitudes of peace and war, of friendship and enmity with each other, which have fallen to the lot of all neighboring nations not united under one government, let us enter into a concise detail of some of the consequences that would attend such a situation.

The *body* of the formal essay is the part containing the actual message. In the instance of the formal argument, it advances the reason for the stand. In the instance of the expository writing, it carries the actual explanation. In the instance of the descriptive writing, it presents the details. Thus, it is truly the "body" of the essay.

The *conclusion* serves to draw the entire writing together in the form of a summary and to leave a dominant thought with the reader. Notice, for example, the conclusion to Hamilton's essay:

> This is an idea not superficial nor futile, but solid and weighty. It deserves the most serious and mature consideration of every prudent and honest man, of whatever party. If such men will make a firm and solemn pause, and meditate dispassionately on its vast

---

[4] *On War Between the States of the Union.*

importance; if they will contemplate it in all its attitudes, and trace it to all its consequences, they will not hesitate to part with trivial objections to a constitution, the rejection of which would, in all probability, put a final period to the Union. The airy phantoms that now flit before the distempered imaginations of some of its adversaries would then quickly give place to the more substantial prospects of dangers, real, certain, and extremely formidable.

The *informal essay,* in contrast to the formal, does not have a pronounced structural pattern; it is often light and humorous in tone; and it has a genuinely subjective quality. The informal essay lends itself especially well to casual observations, humor, and trivia. However, this type of essay, popular from the time of Charles Lamb, is far more demanding than is popularly realized. In fact, it is very much like the performance of the diving champion: its inherent challenge can be appreciated only by attempting it.

Furthermore, paradoxical though it may seem, the informal essay is often the strongest way to support a serious or important point. E. B. White, for instance, has dealt effectively with ecological considerations; Wallace Stegner has made some penetrating observations on contemporary life; and Archibald MacLeish has sounded the dangers of forsaking the values of traditional education. And all have relied on the informal essay as their vehicle of expresion. They have simply approached their topics as concerned people, speaking their innermost thoughts in a straightforward manner. The result has been strong, convincing and above all, appealing writing.

The *reflective essay* expresses a viewpoint upon a condition, an event, or a problem—for instance, the thoughts of a college-president on today's youth or the thoughts of a student on college administrators. It may be formal or informal, according to the author's aproach and treatment. Also, it is much like the reflective newspaper column adjusted to fit the magazine environment. There is usually a good market for appealing reflective essays, sometimes a very good market.

The qualities necessary for handling the reflective essay are writing ability, note of authority, originality, and general appeal. The need for the ability to write clearly, forcefully, and correctly is self-evident. The second quality, note of authority, is especially significant; it means that the writer must demonstrate clearly-that he has a sweep and a grasp of his field. The reflective article that does not reveal keen thinking coupled with wide knowledge rarely impresses many readers. There can be no errors in facts and certainly no flaws in reasoning. The third quality, originality, is important because the reader wants information or viewpoint that he has not met before. He wants something new, something that no other writer has given. Hence, the writer must have originality of thought and approach. The final quality, general appeal, is the most difficult to explain and to attain. It is the general charm that the essay of reminiscences possesses; it is the note of respect that the essay of the revered figure commands as it appears in print; it is the intangible quality of the appealing columnist.

Because of the necessity of the last three qualities, the writer of the reflective essay is usually someone who has demonstrated clearly his right to speak. The well-established figure in politics, professional life, journalism, or similar activities is most often the one to write the reflective essay because of his claim to authority. Consequently, the novice writer can rarely hope to sell a reflective essay unless the appeal of his work offsets his lack of reputation.

The market for the general reflective essay lies chiefly in the quality magazines; the market for the specialized reflective essay lies chiefly in magazines that concentrate on the special fields. But even special-field magazines sometimes print essays on subjects outside their fields and, because of the broad editorial policies of many magazines, specialized reflective essays often appear where least expected. Hence, as always, the writer should analyze the magazines to determine the potential market at the time of his writing.

The Personality Sketch

Because "interesting personalities are interesting," the personality sketch has always been highly popular. Almost any newsworthy figure is automatically a possibility for a personality sketch, and the degree of interest involved is the best index of his value as a subject.

The writer faces several difficulties in the field of the personality sketch, the greatest being that the best subjects have nearly always been covered. No one rises to a high position in sports, politics, entertainment, or similar area without becoming the subject of an article of this kind. Therefore, the writer either must be the first to sketch a subject or else use a new approach if he is to be successful.

Another difficulty arises because most sketches demand the writer have personal contact with his subject. This situation presents a problem for the unknown writer in gaining an interview. Well-known personalities are reluctant to deal with unknown writers because there is no guarantee that the material will be printed and because there is no foreknowledge of the writer's basic integrity in presenting facts accurately and sympathetically. Why, for example, should a screen star give an interview to an unknown writer when he or she does not know where, if at all, the article will appear in print and with what unfavorable statements, distortions, or outright untruths?

A final difficulty to be noted is that the interviewing involved is often a genuine problem. The subject of the sketch may be excessively modest, too demanding, or otherwise "hard to handle." Aside from remembering the attributes of the successful interview discussed in Chapter 4, the interviewer can do little to handle this problem.

The success of the personality sketch stems from the author's ability to depict an interesting three-dimensional character. The personality revealed should be one that gives the reader a new insight; an understanding of the subject not otherwise possible; a picture from another angle. Because this result is often difficult to achieve, good personality sketches are not numerous.

Finding a market for the personality sketch is troublesome because many magazines employ their own or established writers to do this work. *Time*, for instance, uses a staff member to do its cover-story personality sketch, while *Sports Illustrated* uses staff members or established writers for its sketches. The reason: to make sure of factually sound stories. Magazines, one soon learns, must be careful of accuracy of facts for the same reasons—potential libel suits and loss of prestige—that newspapers must exercise care. Hence the best approach is to use the writers upon whom there is some check or whose accuracy has been demonstrated.

The unknown writer is most likely to sell a personality sketch in the following instances: (1) he has material that has some quality of the scoop; (2) he has found an interesting subject, usually an obscure but important personality, not yet treated; (3) his writing has a distinctly appealing quality (an insight, a charm, an attractive ring).

The Personal-Experience Account

Because normal people can be fascinated by the unusual activities of others, the personal-experience account has become very popular.

Most informed citizens throughout the world, for instance, are excited about space exploration—especially about man's attempts to land on other planets. As a consequence, they follow avidly the print and electronic media accounts of space travel. Yet however fascinating these presentations may be, people are even more interested in the first-person accounts of the participants. What, specifically, crosses the astronaut's mind as he sits in the space capsule waiting for blast-off? What is his reaction as the capsule leaves the pad? How did it feel to step on the surface of the moon? Was he frightened as he splashed down in mid-Pacific? The general public wants these answers directly from the astronaut rather than strained, filtered, or interpreted by a second person.

Even the day-to-day activity of less well-known or even obscure people can be the source of a personal-experience account. We all seem to be interested in learning of the work of the tea taster, the motion-picture stand-in, the window washer at the tallest building, the captain of the fishing trawler in the North Atlantic, the control-tower supervisor at the international airport. Hence such material possesses a genuine appeal.

Popularizing Facts

The field of popularizing facts represents a rich source of material for magazine writers in general. The natural reason is that most readers find great appeal in little-known data about familiar subjects. As a consequence, a well written and properly documented article in this area, submitted to the right magazine, will always get a favorable reception.

A cursory examination of magazines of all kinds over the past decades shows popularizing facts articles on the following: the making of golf balls, the relative cost of automobile license plates from state to state, changes in women's clothing styles, the reaction of theatergoers to certain plays, taxpayers' gripes, the conditions behind the do-it-yourself trend, women *vs.* men in various occupations, the origin of some common words, the meaning of common surnames, the cost of maintaining the White House, the art of glassmaking.

In doing a popularizing facts article, the writer often follows a simple procedure. He first selects an interesting but relatively unpublicized field. Then he examines the field thoroughly enough to become something of an authority. Next he compiles the facts that will interest the readers of a magazine likely to accept his article, and finally he begins to write.

Another common practice is to search through textbooks, scholarly journals, and similar publications for interesting material that can be recast into everyday language for the nonspecialist reader.

To illustrate the above procedure, a common situation can be described. Each year, university-based archaeologists make discoveries that have genuine interest for a wide segment of the general populace. Usually, under professional tradition, they record their findings first in formal reports couched in a technical language unintelligible to anyone outside the particular field. Then, some alert writer discovers the information and re-casts it in popular diction for a publication such as the *National Geographic Magazine*. This, in turn, causes feature writers everywhere to compose pieces for daily newspapers and Sunday supplement magazines.

In instances such as the above, the original writer had accomplished the task of researching and reporting the material. If, however, he had wanted to sell his material to a nontechnical magazine, he would have had to recast the technical nomenclature, state his findings in a simple, easy-to-follow style, and supply the underlying information that the scientist could assume was known to scientific readers. In the described situation, this adaptation was done by the later writers.

An important caution to be exercised in this procedure concerns literary property. It involves certain subtle distinctions turning on ownership of the original material.

Some facts and information are common property; that is, they are in the "public domain." Examples are the common facts of history and nature (names of constellations, habits of birds). But the intellectual organization and the approach followed in a particular writing may not be common property. For example, a historian may take the facts of the Pearl Harbor debacle (December 7, 1941) and refine them into a new thesis. This thesis belongs to the historian until sufficient time has elapsed for it to enter the public domain. Obviously, the word "sufficient" creates a problem in definition.

If the writer appropriating material is not careful, he may easily find himself and his publisher in expensive litigation. It is good business, therefore, as well as good manners, to obtain the owner's permission before selling adapted material of the kind described. And when any doubt whatever arises, the writer should consult a lawyer who specializes in copyright law.

The Utility Article

Among the feature-story types mentioned in Chapter 5 is the utility article. In the magazine as in the newspaper, the utility article explains "how to"—how to develop a skill (play golf, for example), how to perform some piece of work (build a house, for an extreme), or how to proceed in any other complex or unfamiliar activity. The difference between the utility article as it appears in the newspaper and in the magazine is usually simply a difference in length. The newspaper article is generally briefer, hence more superficial.

The market for the utility article is a wide one, indeed. Many magazines carry utility articles; therefore, many manuscript editors are receptive to good ones. The probable success of the utility article can be determined by (1) novelty of material and approach, (2) note of authority, and (3) general effectiveness of expression. Because these qualities are discussed in Chapter 5, there is no need to explain them again.

The secret of the successful utility article lies in finding a source of interesting information. Such sources are likely to be unique. An obscure newspaperman, for example, recently sold an article on faking antiques to a national magazine. He obtained his information from an elderly cabinetmaker who explained how unscrupulous persons can create highly deceptive replicas of originals. His article sold because of its authoritative ring, its timeliness, and its general appeal.

The unknown writer is handicapped in his search for utility-article material in one field—that involving the well-known person. He is handicapped because the well-known person, as has been shown, is generally reluctant to deal with unknown writers. The reason, once again, is the question of the writer's basic integrity and the lack of assurance that the material will achieve publication.

Poetry

Before anyone can speak of the writing of poetry for magazines, a definition is necessary because the term itself is too all-inclusive. It may mean anything from the highly serious, complex poems of the magazines devoted to the advancement of poetry to the light, humorous quatrains appearing in the popular magazines. Therefore, two terms should be employed. The term "poetry" should be used as it is in college literature classes—to denote the lofty expression of great literary masters. The term "verse," on the other hand, can mean simply light rhymed material.

The market for poetry is both extremely competitive and highly limited. It is competitive because probably nine out of every ten persons who genuinely appreciate poetry attempt to write it. Naturally, many of this group submit their work for publication, thus creating a supply far beyond the demand of the magazines that print poetry. The market is limited because it is confined largely to quality magazines, scholarly periodicals, and the subsidized magazines that devote themselves to the cause of poetry and the publication of poems.

And what of remuneration? The sad fact is that payment is the exception rather than the rule. The quality magazines pay, but even their fees are relatively small. Scholarly periodicals may also pay. The subsidized magazines can seldom pay anything; they reward the poet with the satisfaction of publication.

The market for verse is both wider and more remunerative than the market for poetry. Genuinely humorous verse always merits a reading by the editor of the popular magazines. Some magazines devote a full page to this kind of writing, and many close out the blank space after articles with little verses. The aspiring writer should note, however, that the market is keenly competitive, the returns are definitely limited, and the opportunity for fame is quite restricted. Such writers as Franklin P. Adams and Ogden Nash attained reputations through verse, but theirs are exceptional instances.

THE WRITING PROCESS

When a writer believes he has material worthy of publication, he should first think of the literary form to be employed. He should settle upon the short story, the essay, the feature article, or whatever other form best suits his material and his abilities. A writer, for example, may have had the experience of narrowly escaping death in a small fishing craft during a heavy storm. In this instance one of at least three forms can be used—the short story, the reflective essay, or the personal-experience story. This writer, like all writers, must make this basic decision at the outset. Later planning may alter this first decision, but nonetheless it represents the initial step in writing.

The Market

The second step in the writing process is to consider the probable market, or to state the matter more bluntly, the specific magazines to which the manuscript can be sent with some hope of sale.[5] All magazines do not carry the same kind of material, and the writer, therefore, should not waste time and postage in sending his manuscript to unreceptive editors.

The question of market is so important that some authorities on magazine writing believe it should precede all other considerations. Consequently, they place the decision about market as the first step in the writing process. They argue that before a writer begins, he should determine the specific magazine to which to submit his work. Then he should "slant" his entire planning and writing toward that publication. Selling a manuscript, they argue, demands such slanting. However, whether determining potential market is the first step or the second, it must be considered carefully.

The initial procedure in considering potential market is to try to visualize one's material in various magazines. An article on junior-high-school sports,

---

[5] Kinds of magazines are discussed later in this chapter.

for example, would hardly appear in *Field & Stream,* but it would be appropriate to several other sports magazines. An article on cooking might be visualized in *Harper's Magazine,* but it would be more suitable to a women's magazine. If the article seems "at home" in a given publication, the writer should make a more detailed analysis of the magazine before deciding to submit his manuscript. This analysis involves five steps: (1) analyzing the articles; (2) examining the entire contents; (3) analyzing the style of the contributors; (4) examining the advertisements; and (5) determining the editorial policy.

Analyzing the article in a given magazine reveals the floor plan of the magazine's interests. A currently popular quality magazine, for example, generally carries 12 to 14 essays, two short stories, and two or three poems. The essays are nearly always by authorities of a sort; one of the stories is by an established author while the other is the work of an obscure or unknown author. Further analysis reveals that the essays deal with currently important questions such as politics and education; the short stories are generally of the character-delineation type; and the poems are upon conventionally "safe" subjects. This analysis, therefore, shows important aspects of this magazine as a potential market.

Examining the contents of a magazine is revealing as an indication of the areas whereon the emphases are placed. The publication referred to above, for example, emphasizes essays on current questions, good-quality fiction, and serious poetry. The reason for these emphases is that this magazine, like all magazines, has a specific type of reader in mind. It aims to capture the intellectually inclined segment of society—those persons interested in topics and literature well above the popular level. Hence, it chooses its material accordingly. Naturally, the writer gains an insight into potential market from studying such emphases.

Analyzing the style of contributors is helpful as an indication of editorial policy regarding general approach. A magazine exclusively for men, for example, is likely to permit considerable latitude in style. The conversational tone, the informality, and the air of relaxation of the men's club are likely to be present. In such a magazine, the highly formal approach of the excessively discreet literary magazine would be inappropriate. Thus, style analysis reveals an important facet of the magazine.

An analysis of advertisements shows much about the age, cultural, and social group at which the magazine is pointed. The magazine for adolescents, for example, can be recognized by its advertisements for young people's clothing, popular records and tapes, current fads, and other products likely to interest this age group. An analysis of advertisements, therefore, serves further to reveal a magazine's policy.

Determining editorial policy (largely a matter of considering the foregoing analyses) tells the writer whether his article harmonizes with the tone of the magazine. This tone, as with the newspaper, is established by the magazine in its first issue, and it is changed or retained over the years primarily through selection of material. The article that is consistent with desired tone is likely to be considered sympathetically. Conversely, the article that clashes with this tone stands little chance of even slight consideration.

Planning the Magazine Article

The third step in the writing process is the actual planning. Although planning naturally varies with the form (short story, essay, feature article, etc.), certain common truths must be observed. The first is that planning must be all-inclusive—that is to say, it must treat every facet of the subject thoughtfully and thoroughly. The writer must turn his subject over and over in his mind in order to see every aspect. This first deliberation, many authors believe, is the most important.

After the writer has considered his material exhaustively, he should list all pertinent thoughts, without regard to final outline. *Any* thought, however small, should be listed at random, for when this list is eventually complete it becomes the basis for the final outline. Note, for example, the listing of thoughts, followed by the final outline, for an article on "The Need to Control Noise in Our Environment."

LIST OF THOUGHTS

—With growth in population, incidence of noise is increasing.

—Freedom from noise (i.e., quiet) is necessary for emotional health.

—Growth of aviation creates noise in places where it did not exist before.

—Some seriously disturbing noises (e.g., fire sirens and danger whistles) are necessary.

—Some noises (e.g., industrial noises and building-construction noises) are impossible to eliminate entirely.

—Any loud noise tends to impair the operation of some activities (e.g., schools and hospitals).

—Some noises (e.g., automobile body shops) can be controlled by restricting hours of operation and requiring soundproofing equipment.

—Noise-making agencies (factories, etc.) can be zoned out of residential areas.

—Some noises (e.g., aircraft breaking the sound barrier) can be genuinely dangerous to mental health of many people.

—Legislation is the most effective course toward correcting dangerous conditions in noise environment.

—Public education concerning the problem can insure necessary legislation.

—Definition of "noise" is needed: What distinction can be made between the shouting of children on the playground as opposed to the shouting of patrons in the bar room?

—Noise can be defined in the scientific terms of the physicist or in the more subjective terms of the psychologist.

—People can be conditioned to withstand some noises (e.g., normal automobile traffic) but only rarely some other noises (e.g., low-flying planes).

—Some laws controlling noise (e.g., loud parties) are already in effect.

—Some noises (e.g., loud singing and playing musical instruments) are difficult to delineate and hence to control because they involve the delicate question of individual liberty versus the common good.

—Entire problem is severe.

—Corrective action is certain to meet some opposition.

FINAL OUTLINE

I. Introduction

A. Noise control is one of the most severe phases of the total problem of control of the environment.

B. The problem of noise control will intensify with the continuing increase in population.

C. Before detailed examination of the problem, the term "noise" must be defined.

1. Noise must be defined in the subjective terms of the psychologist rather than the scientific terms of the physicist.

2. Any legal definition will be fraught with semantic difficulties—e.g., the shouting of children on a playground as opposed to the shouting of the patrons in a bar room.

II. Body

A. Current situation:

1. New noises—e.g., new airports and new industries—are increasing each year while retreat areas are decreasing.

2. Some noises (fire alarms, police sirens, etc.) are necessary.

3. Some noises (building constructions, some industries, etc.) are impossible to eliminate entirely.

4. Some noises (inordinately loud parties, gunning motorcycle engines, etc.) result from selfishness.

5. Some noises (e.g., sounds from automobile-body repair shops) are being controlled through restricting hours of operation and by zoning some areas as purely residential.

6. People are conditioned to withstand some noises (e.g., normal automobile traffic) but not others (e.g., low-flying airplanes).

B. Dangers involved:

1. Freedom from noise (i.e., periods of relative quiet) is necessary for emotional and physical health.

2. Some noises (e.g., a plane breaking the sound barrier) can induce severe mental shock.
3. Some agencies (e.g., schools and hospitals) cannot operate if loud noise prevails.

III. Conclusion

A. Achieving successful controls will be hampered by selfish interests (e.g., industry will oppose some programs).
B. Legislation will have to strike a delicate distinction between individual liberty (the right of a person to practice a musical instrument whenever he pleases) and the common good (e.g., the right of his neighbors to "quiet").
C. Severity of the problem demands immediate consideration and action.

Rough Draft and Finished Copy

After constructing the final outline, the writer is ready to compose his first draft or "rough copy" as it is often termed. This draft should be prepared thoughtfully and painstakingly, taking whatever time is needed. Especially important is the truism that no writer, amateur or professional, works with equal facility at all times. Writers, being artists, experience times when they write easily, naturally, and effectively. Conversely, they also experience times when they have the greatest of difficulty in composing simple material. The right word cannot be found; the sentences come haltingly; and the entire article when written seems like the work of somebody better suited to accounting, plumbing, bricklaying, tree pruning, or any other occupation distantly removed from writing. Obviously, the writer should take advantage of the situation wherein he is "in the mood," "on the right track," "in the groove," or whatever else he may term the condition. This caution is especially important because writers are always reluctant to discard completely any product of their efforts. Thus they often waste time attempting to improve a poor paragraph when actually they would gain by beginning anew.

When the rough copy has been completed, the writer should put it aside for a few days, if possible, and then return to improve it. The intervening time gives a perspective which is invaluable. The writer can now come to his work with a calmness, a detachment, and an energy that enable him to rework his thoughts and his sentences more easily. The freshness of vewpoint thus gained leads many writers to make several successive drafts in order to benefit from these "rests" between them.

When the author is thoroughly satisfied with his work, he is ready to make his final copy. This is the last step in the actual writing for some authors. For others, however, there is still another state—that of seeking the critical judgment of other persons. The usual procedures are to ask a competent friend to evaluate the work, to read it to a small group, or to engage a writer or a teacher of writing to criticize it. If one of these procedures is followed, the writer obviously must expect to make still another copy.

Of especial value in seeking the criticism of others is that they may detect factual errors. The effective article or story, the author should never forget, must "hold water." Thus, great care must always be exercised. Factual errors, incidentally, are sometimes found in soundly established authors. Two examples of such errors are evident in O. Henry's story, "Gift of the Magi," and in Willa Cather's story, "Paul's Case." O. Henry opens his story with these sentences:

One dollar and eighty-seven cents. That was all. And sixty cents of it was in pennies.

But O. Henry's character could not have assembled $1.87 in United States coins with sixty cents in pennies. When three-cent coins were circulating, he might have done so (these were minted from 1851 to 1889). But "The Gift of the Magi" was published years later. So the facts of the opening sentence were inaccurate or at best implausible.

In "Paul's Case," which is an otherwise excellent story, Miss Cather has the central characters sipping lemonade on their front porch in Pittsburgh, Pennsylvania, on the last Sunday in November. Because this time of year usually finds winter weather in Pittsburgh, a grave question of accuracy arises.

Another value in seeking critical judgment is that "miscellaneous" pitfalls may be avoided. A second person can often detect unconscious plagiarism, triteness, grammatical errors, misspellings, and misuse of words. Naturally, no explanation of the importance of avoiding these pitfalls is necessary.

SELLING MATERIAL

Literary Agents

Beginning writers with manuscripts for sale often ask the question, "Should I work through a literary agent?" To reach the answer, one should know the three types of literary agencies.

The first is the prominent agency, the one which handles the work of established writers. These writers employ the agencies because of the time saved in contacting magazines directly and because the agencies can often effect a more advantageous agreement. Such agencies generally pride themselves on the quality of their services and the reputation of their clients. Hence the aspiring writer experiences great difficulty in gaining acceptance by one of these agencies; but if he does, he has definite advantages, the strongest being that the agency has an entree into the offices of leading magazines. By virtue of the agency's endorsement, the manuscript often gains a careful reading not obtainable otherwise.

Another advantage of working through this type of agency is that it generally has an acute sense of potential market for every kind of manuscript. Where the writer may lose much time in sending his manuscript to dozens of magazines, the agency can send it immediately to the editors likely to give serious consideration.

The second type is the less known agency, the relatively new agency which has not yet gained a business foothold. It has few well-known writers as clients and hence is striving to establish itself. This agency generally accepts as clients anyone whose work it believes has merit. Consequently, a capable writer can often effect an agreement with such an agency. The advantages are once again that the agency has an entree into editorial offices, and it is likely to have a good sense of potential market. The caution to be sounded is that the agency is often overanxious to sell material. Therefore, the talented writer may find his material sold to relatively unknown magazines for a small fee, thus sacrificing good material to the agency's financial gain. Also, the contract with this kind of agency is generally clearly favorable to the agency. Legally, it may hold the manuscript indefinitely, as it often does, in the hope of eventual sale. Thus the writer may well see his material go out of date.

Yet against the discussion in the above paragraph an important point must be cited: many of the less-known agencies make a fetish of being ethical. They believe that ethical procedures must underlie their every move. Only by ethical conduct, they reason, can they hope for success. Hence any writer whose work they accept is certain of a concerted, honest effort to place the manuscript and a fair treatment in every respect.

The third type of agency is to be avoided at all costs; it is the one which is clearly dishonest. Usually it follows this pattern. Advertisements are placed in the cheap magazines and newspapers to lure aspiring writers. The reader is told that the agency accepts manuscripts, if they are "good," from unknown writers. The reader, full of high hope, sends his manuscript. Shortly thereafter he receives a letter telling him that his work "shows real promise," but that it needs a critical review. The letter explains that for a "fee" the critical review will be provided. The fee is sent, a critical review is returned with the manuscript, and the writer then revises and returns his work to the agency. After several months, the manuscript is again returned to the writer with the suggestion that perhaps it should be rewritten for another market. Once again a suggestion for a critical review is given—for a "fee," of course. This process naturally can go on indefinitely. In short, the agency exists for the primary purpose of capitalizing on the aspirations of naive persons.

Do's and Don't's of Submitting Manuscripts to Magazines

Whether the writer works through an agency or independently, there are certain do's and don't's of preparing and submitting manuscripts that will bear consideration. A listing of the most common follows.

1. Manuscripts should be typed neatly, on one side of the paper only, with each page properly numbered. All material should be double spaced. Ample margins should be left at top, bottom, and sides.
2. Manuscripts should be accompanied by a self-addressed, stamped envelope for their return.
3. Although a letter attempting to "sell" the manuscript is sometimes helpful, most editors prefer to judge the manuscript on its merits. Therefore, a letter should be included only when the author is certain that it will help.
4. If an article, such as a startling personal experience writing, contains material likely to be challenged, it should be accompanied by proof of accuracy or a statement that such proof will be submitted upon demand.
5. If consideration of the manuscript will be increased by the author's identity, he should make certain that his identity is made clear. Sometimes a mere footnote on the title page of the manuscript is sufficient. Other times a letter to the editor may be needed.
6. Authors should always keep a carbon or photo copy of their work against the possibility of loss in transit. If the author wants to know that a manuscript has been received, he may send it by registered mail, "return receipt requested." This procedure, however, may irk an editor or his staff, especially in the instance of the unsolicited manuscript.
7. If a magazine states flatly that it does not consider unsolicited manuscripts, the editor should be queried before the manuscript is sent. This step removes prejudice against the article, and when a magazine holds fast to its policy, it prevents a waste of postage.
8. Editors dislike correspondence about manuscripts, especially unsolicited ones. A delay in receiving word of acceptance or rejection may well indicate favorable consideration. Consequently, a letter of inquiry may do harm rather than good.
9. The writer should keep a card catalog or some other record of his experiences in submitting manuscripts. Such a record frequently becomes a valuable guide in attempting to place additional articles.
10. The writer should note any special instructions contained in the magazine involved for submitting manuscripts. These instructions often give important details concerning address, responsibility assumed, and general advice for preparation.

KINDS OF MAGAZINES

If a writer is to be successful, he must know the various kinds of magazines. He must have this knowledge as part of his sense of market. Magazines may be classified in several ways, but the simplest, most logical procedure is to group them according to their basic purpose; that is to say, according to the readers they seek, the material they publish, and the general editorial policy they pursue.

The attempt to classify magazines, however, is not so easy as it may appear. Some magazines, naturally, can be classified readily because their nature and purpose are immediately clear. Professional magazines in particular are aimed at specific groups. Business magazines and children's magazines aim at broader but nevertheless specific reader groups. Other magazines aim at groups less limited and less readily identifiable, a situation that makes classification difficult. Aims change, moreover. What follows is meant to clarify the trends in aim and character of magazines.

First in significance is the fact that no magazine has any assured monopoly over any kind of reading matter, or is excluded from publishing any kind of material. And this trend toward diversity is increasing steadily. Within the past several years, for instance, the following apparent incongruities have appeared: *The Atlantic Monthly* carried a "confessions" article replete with very earthy language; *Harper's* carried an article on the sex life of men past 70; the *New Yorker* carried a highly serious article blasting a well-known digest; *Bazaar,* ostensibly a women's fashion magazine, carried an article on the legal implications of all types of sex acts; and a company magazine distributed by a public utility carried an article on Christmas cards. A picture of the wide field presently covered by magazines can be seen by examining the articles condensed for *Reader's Digest*. In a representative sampling are articles and stories on every conceivable subject, directed toward readers of almost all types.

A second significant fact is that magazines continue to become more and more visual. Readers still fairly young can remember when a simple illustration or two was the normal expectation; magazines, even the same magazines, have changed to the free use of numerous large pictures and other illustrative material. More and more frequently they devise new make-ups to gain attractive layouts. This fact is especially true of the popular weekly. Thus, the author can sometimes make the difference between acceptance and rejection of his article by including interesting illustrative material or a pertinent suggestion for a layout.

A third significant fact is that the hurry, the hustle, and the general emphasis upon speed of twentieth-century life have influenced magazine writing. The fast tempo of modern life has placed an emphasis on brevity, sharpness, and incisiveness not known heretofore. As a result, the leisurely approach of earlier times has given way to a more condensed, more pointed treatment. It has affected especially the writing of the popular weeklies, many of which are read in snatches in the bus, the subway train, the dentist's waiting room, and the club lounge. The present-day reader often cannot study a magazine at length; he needs to read quickly and easily. This situation has given rise to the popularity of the digests and the pocket-size magazine of capsules and brief articles.

A fourth significant fact is that magazines are coming more and more to deal with the problems of the day. Instead of leaning in the direction of the literary undertaking—as did the magazine of a relatively short time ago—the present-day publication is approaching more and more the role of "newspaper of the nation." Now it tends to present and interpret significant topics of the moment rather than merely to reflect on familiar matters. Consequently, articles of general interest now outnumber the short story and other forms of creative writing.

A fifth significant fact is that magazines, like newspapers, are definitely big business. The capital investment necessary to launch a magazine is higher than ever; so is the cash flow needed to keep it running. Circulations, of necessity, are larger; and the whole field has become increasingly competitive. For the writer, this situation means that many magazines pay substantial fees for material, but it also means that competition to sell articles has increased.

The following is a discussion of the prominent types of magazines. The purpose is to give the aspiring writer some idea of the peculiar nature of each type, especially as it concerns opportunities for publication. The writer should never forget, however, that the magazine field is always changing, and that with the many changes, opportunities for writers alter favorably and unfavorably.

Quality Magazines

"Quality magazines" is a rather loose category that embraces the magazines which deal with the arts, current questions, and intellectual topics in a restrained, fairly exhaustive manner. The quality magazine is pointed squarely at the person interested in the loftier, more complex, and more significant aspects of life. Examples are the *Atlantic Monthly, Harper's Magazine,* and the *Saturday Review.* [6]

The quality magazines, with some few exceptions, have traveled a rough road; many have risen and attracted a large following, only to die a slow death. *Scribner's* is an example of a genuinely excellent quality magazine that suffered such an eclipse.

The quality magazines are a strong lure for the aspiring writer because of the fame derived. The writer, for example, who places an article in the *Atlantic Monthly* joins a famous fraternity—that of the great figures who have written for that publication since its founding in Boston in 1857. In that fraternity are some of the most famous names in American literature—Emerson, Whittier, Lowell, Holmes, Thoreau, Perry—and such highly important personalities in American political history as Woodrow Wilson, Al Smith, Wendell Willkie, Dean Acheson, and innumerable senators and congressmen.

The quality magazines represent a potential market for the essay, the short story, the general feature story, and poetry. Also, some quality magazines use squibs, vignettes, shorts, and similar writings.

No general statement concerning the fee paid by the quality magazine can be given. As stated elsewhere, the larger the circulation, the higher the fee is

---

[6] As is mentioned elsewhere, these magazines are making changes in their editorial policies.

likely to be. Moreover, the quality magazine frequently adjusts the fee according to the prestige of the author.

Professional Magazines

The professional magazine, as the name implies, is a publication aimed squarely at the members of a given profession. Examples of professional magazines are the *American Medical Journal,* the *National Education Association Journal,* and the many "law reviews" published throughout the nation. Because the magazine is designed for a specific professional group, its material must bear directly on the activity of that group. For this reason, most articles are written by members of the profession.

The only opportunity for the nonprofessional writer to publish in this magazine lies in one of three situations: he writes of a professional matter from a layman's viewpoint; he writes of an "outside" subject of interest to the professional group; or he ghost-writes an article for a professional person.

An example of a layman writing of a professional matter is to be seen in a landmark article in a county medical magazine entitled "The Layman Looks at His Doctor." This article was based on a layman's assembling, evaluation, and presentation of local opinion about the physician and his role in society.

An example of an "outside" subject of interest to a professional group is an article on compulsory automobile insurance in a legal journal. In this article an insurance executive cites some obscure ramifications of this type of coverage.

Examples of ghost-writing are, of course, numerous. Often a professional man merely lacks the ability or perhaps merely the time to express himself effectively. Therefore, he tells his story to a writer who outlines the material, writes the article, and then submits it for the approval of the "author."

The professional magazine offers highly limited opportunities for the aspiring general writer for two reasons: (1) as shown above, there is a distinctly limited field for the nonprofessional writer, and (2) the professional magazine frequently pays only a token fee or no fee whatever. This latter fact is true because professional men, interested in fame within their profession, are generally more than willing to forgo remuneration to reach print. Hence, the magazine does not have to pay to obtain acceptable manuscripts.

Business Magazines

Because business in its many forms is the basis of the American economic system, business magazines have become a necessity. Every major field has at least one magazine, and many have magazines for their subdivisions. Consequently, one can find a magazine for literally every product used between cradle and grave.

The fundamental aim of the business magazine is to present helpful information, interesting news, and continuing orientation regarding the particular field involved. It accomplishes this aim by presenting articles on innovations in materials, latest developments in equipment, hints for improving operational procedures, the economic environment, new laws, and any other information that will assist the people with a stake in the business.

Business magazines pointed toward special areas nonetheless treat related topics. Many of them tell of general economic conditions, offer or examine stock market predictions, report general sales indexes, or almost any other major phase of business-world activity. They also carry articles and features concerning narrow phases of business life. Some business magazines, such as *Nation's Business,* contain articles of clearly popular appeal. Hence they make easy, entertaining reading for persons outside the subject treated.

Opportunities for writing for the business magazine, as for similar publications, vary. The large magazines employing a full staff present a clearly limited opportunity for the outside writer. His lone chance lies in selling an unusual article on a free-lance basis. The smaller magazines, however, frequently buy articles from outside writers. The writer, therefore, should query the editor when he has material.

The most important attributes for success in writing for the business magazine are significance of material, note of authority, and general effectiveness of expression.

Technical Magazines

The technical magazine combines aspects of the professional and business magazines. It presents material for the highly trained person—the engineer, the technician, the scientist—and it presents material concerning the general condition of a particular business field. The latter might be aerodynamics, rubber, building construction, or some other field of application.

The opportunities for writing for the technical magazine are essentially similar to those for the professional journal. The magazine, being pointed at a specific group, is successful in proportion to its ability to interest and inform that group. Hence, a writer with material of sufficient value can hope for a favorable reaction to his manuscript. He should note, however, that many technical magazines are written wholly or chiefly by staff, thereby precluding, in many instances, any chance for an outside writer to place material.

Anyone wishing to write for the technical magazines should remember above all else that because the fields are technical they are scientific. Therefore, the material and the presentation must be characterized by scientific accuracy, scientific approach, and scientific evaluation.

Farm Magazines

A publication almost unknown to the city dweller but very much of a reality in the rural area is the farm magazine, a long-popular institution. The first of such publications was the *Genessee Farmer,* founded in 1831, and from that time to this, farm magazines have flourished. At present, there are an estimated 140 farm magazines in the United States, the largest of which, *Farm Journal,* boasts a circulation of approximately three million.

There are two major types of farm magazines, neither of which should be imagined as a wholly specialized kind of publication. The first is the "general" as opposed to the "specialized" farm magazine. The general farm magazine contains news and material for every member of the family. Thus it resembles the popular weekly, with an emphasis on farm news. For the farmer, there are columns of farm news, prices, and general information; for the women, articles on fashions and the home; for children, little stories and puzzles; for readers of all classes, a host of varied and interesting items. The specialized farm magazine, on the other hand, is aimed at a special farming interest such as dairy, cotton, or grain. Thus, it usually contains specialized news, as do the trade journals and the professional magazines.

Some farm magazines are written for a definite geographical area only. The *Southern Planter,* the *New England Homestead,* and the *Ohio Farmer* are instances of "section" publications. Also to be noted, however, is that the larger general farm magazines have section editions. *Farm Journal,* for example, appears in three section editions—East Central, Western, and Southern. As a consequence, the larger magazines are actually not completely "general."

There are also certain common tenets in the editorial policy of the farm magazines. Above all else, they recognize the importance of farming and everything related to it. The idea of bygone days that the farmer was a "hick," distantly removed from the main questions, thoughts, styles, and other facets of life, has long since disappeared. Instead, the farmer is to be respected for the great contribution he makes, for the detailed knowledge that he must possess, and for the general business acumen that must be his. Another tenet is that the interests of the farmer must be safeguarded. He must receive his share of favorable legislation, and his rights and privileges must be maintained.[7] Still another tenet is that the farm family is a closely knit unit representing one of the mainstays of the American way of life—an anchor amid the upheavals that arise with urban living.

The opportunities for writing for the farm publication are essentially similar to those of the other magazines; that is to say, opportunities vary according to the nature of the specific magazine. The larger general magazines naturally present a wider chance. Almost any article of interest to the farm family is likely to receive favorable consideration. For the specialized farm magazine, the opportunity is naturally limited to the particular field involved.

The person wishing to write specialized articles for the farm magazine should observe, however, one special caution: his material must always reflect a thorough knowledge of his subject. The farmer is traditionally suspicious of anyone holding forth authoritatively on farming. Consequently, he looks with a

---

[7] Two major concerns of the farmer at present are: (1) the small farmer is being squeezed out of business by the large farm operation with its specialized and expensive equipment, and (2) the farmer is often unjustly blamed for the sharply increasing food costs.

questioning eye on the writings in the farm magazines; he wants to know that the author knows whereof he writes. As a result, anyone submitting specialized material should be very careful of accuracy of detail, for certain rejection faces articles displaying factual errors, fallacious reasoning, or "lunatic fringe" ideas.

Company Magazines

Most large business and industrial organizations have a company newspaper, a company magazine, or both. The company publication exists primarily to build a sound relationship between employer and employee. Therefore, it chooses its material with a view to publishing an interesting magazine wherein to "sell" the company to the employee.[8]

As stated previously, this publication is nearly always handled by a company-employed editor and staff. Outside writers, however, are sometimes able to place articles when their material has general interest to employees. A random examination of company publications revealed the following articles by outside writers: a social-security official had an article in an automobile-manufacturing magazine on a recent change in benefits; a sportsman had an article on fly casting in a steel-company magazine; a building engineer had an article in a tire-company magazine on hints for home construction; a physician had an article in a large business-house magazine on protecting one's self against summer heat; a well-known sports writer had an article in a chain-store magazine on predictions for the coming baseball season.

Some company magazines are almost entirely staff-written except for employee contributions. Some, however, pay for outside-written articles if they are of strong interest.

Special-Interest Magazines

The special-interest or specialty magazines comprise those written in a popular vein about such specialized fields as the theater, sports, coin collecting, travel, radio, television, and similar subjects. Some of these magazines, such as *TV Guide,* have circulations that are phenomenal.[9]

Specialty magazines frequently change editorial policy to include other material. *TV Guide,* for instance, contains much material that could be used elsewhere, and such a magazine as *Theatre Arts* includes many feature stories usable in popular weeklies and other publications.

No general statement can be offered regarding placing articles in the specialty magazines because of the many differences in policy. Some have few or no restrictions. They accept any appealing article, whether by amateur or pro-

---

[8] But many company magazines have recently altered their editorial policy to include material for family reading and for the general reader. Also significant: the company magazine has proved to be, in many cases, a sound public-relations device.

[9] *TV Guide's* circulation for the six months ending on June 30, 1975, was 19,684,429.

fessional. Others, such as *Sports Illustrated,* carry only articles by their own staff and by others whom they know to be qualified. Neither can any general statement be given regarding remuneration. The larger the circulation, the larger is likely to be the remuneration. Also, once again, the prestige of the author often affects the fee to be paid.

Popular Magazines

The publications known as "popular magazines" in the decades—almost the century—preceding World War II had practically dropped from sight by the early 1970s. Although they are not yet extinct, they are decidedly an endangered species. But the brand of reading matter they published is still read widely in other kinds of publications. Therefore, some discussion of these magazines is useful—especially since efforts are under way to restore them to the American scene.

The "popular magazines" in prosperous days were aimed at the general readership in the middle intellectual class—the biggest class of American citizens. One of them, the *Saturday Evening Post,* seemed almost as solid as the national Constitution and was nearly as old. Its content was typical of the whole category—fiction, essays, feature stories, puzzles, poems, cartoons, letters to the editor, and any other matter believed capable of increasing circulation.

Of the once-solid popular magazines, *Liberty* and *Collier's* are now scarcely remembered. The *Saturday Evening Post* has been revived but is no longer a giant.

Many reasons have been suggested for the weakening of the popular magazines. Television has been blamed; so have rising postal rates, increased costs of publication and distribution, and public apathy. The more commonly accepted explanation is that other magazines have taken over their function and their readers. The quality magazines, the women's magazines, farm magazines, Sunday supplements, and many others now contain material once conceded to the province of the popular magazine. All these magazines are thus in some degree "popular," and in a sense therefore the popular magazine lives on.

But a writer should not think of writing "for the popular magazines"; instead, he should think of writing popular material. Such writing can be submitted to the surviving popular magazines but can also be submitted to many others. Examination of any issue of a current "popular" magazine will show that much of its material would be "at home" in many other publications.

However, some general characteristics can be cited as guides for writing for popular magazines. The short stories are of the lighter, more rapidly moving type; serious poetry is almost nonexistent; articles are of the superficial, easy-to-follow variety; and feature stories are definitely in the newspaper tradition.

Women's Magazines

The field of the women's magazine has been important from its beginning in the last century, primarily because of the great circulation possibilities. Women, it seems, have always been greater readers of magazines than men—especially when the material is for the general rather than the specialist reader.

The appeal of the women's magazine has not changed greatly over the years. When L. A. Godey founded *Godey's Lady's Book* in 1830, that famous publication catered to two of women's primary interests, fashions and the home. The ensuing years have seen this key emphasis continued in women's magazines, but an interest in topics of a wider nature has become descernible as women have become "emancipated." Thus, today the primary appeal of this kind of publication centers about fashions, furniture, decorations, house plans, decorum, and subjects discussed in women's clubs and similar places. But also, because so many women are now directly involved or interested in careers, business, job, and professional topics are now handled in women's magazines. Therefore, an interesting treatment of any of the topics cited will be read carefully by the manuscript editors of magazines like *The Ladies' Home Journal, Redbook, Harper's Bazaar,* and even a publication like *Good Housekeeping.*[10]

Besides the above topics, women's magazines look for good short stories and appealing poetry. Although the short stories vary from one magazine to another, basically they are stories that appeal to women. This statement, of course, is a broad one because women read many types of stories. The poetry, generally speaking, should be on the light or humorous side. The poetry of the modern impressionistic school stands little chance of acceptance by the women's magazines

Men's Magazines

For many years, the magazines designed for either an all-male or largely male readership have concerned themselves mostly with handicraft, sports, hunting, fishing, and the outdoors generally. These publications, essentially, have been leveled at the hobbies and the physical interests of men.

However, in December 1953, a magazine with another kind of emphasis made publishing history. It was *Playboy,* the creation of Hugh Hefner, a young man only a few years out of the University of Illinois. Hefner, operating from an extremely thin financial base, sought the audience once held by *Esquire.*

---

[10] Surprising though it may seem, the contents of the women's magazines have not changed seriously with the women's liberation movement. Although the women's publications carry articles on the liberation movement and its interest, they remain relatively unchanged. However, as a result of the recent emphasis on equal rights, some rather specialized women's magazines like *Ms.* have arisen. These magazines follow a variety of approaches and sometimes have distinctly unusual editorial interests. To place material with these magazines, therefore, the writer must analyze the particular magazine carefully—as is suggested under the heading "The Market" in this chapter. Then he can know if his article will be rejected without a reading or given a fairly openminded reception.

Hefner's editorial slant, set forth in a letter to a friend, was to publish an "entertainment magazine for the city-bred guy—breezy and sophisticated." Hefner felt that the publication, at first, should rely principally on the "girlie feature . . . but . . . would have quality, too." After its first year, *Playboy* was selling 175,000 copies. A decade later (1963), it had reached 1,310,000 to become one of the circulation champions of all time.[11]

As sales increased, Hefner de-emphasized the girlie feature somewhat and incorporated top-flight fiction and essays. Meanwhile, *Playboy* encouraged a host of imitators, none of which even approached its great circulations. Yet a new brand of magazine was now on the market.

Playboy and similar magazines—now known by the rather vague designation of "men's magazines"—rely on material that is urbane, witty, sophisticated, and generally speaking, thought-provoking. Although these magazines have full-time staff writers, they turn to established writers for articles, and they are receptive to unsolicited manuscripts—if, of course, these meet the usual standards of quality of content and effectiveness of expression.

Children's and Adolescents' Magazines

With the so-called "modern" school, there has come an added emphasis on the magazines for children and adolescents. These magazines may be distributed through the schools, as are *Jack and Jill, Children's Digest,* and *Scholastic,* or they are handled directly by publishing houses as are *Boy's Life* and the *American Girl.*

The essence of successful writing for children's and adolescent's magazines lies in finding appealing material. Although this statement is a self-evident truth, it actually encompasses a wide area, for understanding these age groups is not easy. The interests of small children, for example, have changed drastically with the advent of television. Where heretofore the small child was greatly interested in fairy and animal stories, librarians now report that children are more interested in the material seen on television—western stories, space travelers, comic characters, and travelogues. Understanding the interests of adolescents is even more enigmatic. The area of interests for the teen-ager is so wide, so complex, and so changing that one must constantly seek reliable evidence of the true situation. Currently, there are some magazines leveled squarely at the adolescent (*Young Athlete, Seventeen, 'Teen, Youth*), but this age group leans more toward magazines that center around fields in which they hope eventually to participate (*Cycle, Dirt Track, Hot Rod Magazine, Hounds and Hunting, Rod & Reel*) or in adult magazines that treat crafts, hobbies, and skills (*Popular Mechanics, Scuba, Mademoiselle, Fashion*).

The actual writing for children's and adolescents' magazines can be han-

---

[11] *Playboy* now has five editions with the following circulation rate bases: national edition, 6,000,000 per month; northern California, 290,000; southern California, 410,000; New York, 475,000; Chicago, 220,000.

dled fairly easily by knowing the average mental and intellectual levels of the group involved. The style of the small child's magazine, for instance, is nothing more than the recorded speech of the primary school teacher. The sentences are short; the vocabulary is simple; and the style is distinctly conversational. The adolescent's magazine is naturally more mature in content, approach, and style.

Just as the first three grades of elementary school are generally best handled by women teachers, so are the best articles for this age group usually done by women writers. However, with children from nine years of age upward, successful material is written by both men and women.

Because the small child is so keenly interested in narrative writings, these magazines place a heavy emphasis on little stories. However, they do contain very brief essays and poems, also. The essays are usually about interesting activities, children in other lands, and similar topics of interest to small children. The poems are generally brief and humorous. The magazine for the adolescents usually contains a fairly even balance of stories and articles of general interest. It also places a fairly heavy emphasis on puzzles, contests, quizzes, and other challenging features.

Magazines for children and adolescents, generally speaking, are always receptive to effectively written, interesting material. Therefore, the writer can be quite certain of a favorable reception for his article.

Sunday-Supplement Magazines

The Sunday-supplement magazine in most cases is essentially an illustrated collection of extended newspaper feature stories. As such, it can be understood best in terms of the material discussed in Chapter 5. Articles in Sunday-supplement magazines come from three sources: (1) staff writers, (2) syndicates, (3) outside (free-lance) writers. Generally, editors strive for a wide variety of material in order to attract as great a readership as possible.

Material for the Sunday supplement may be sold either to the syndicate or, sometimes, directly to the newspaper. If the local newspaper buys material directly, the writer should try to make contact with the proper editorial office to convince editors of his reliability. Articles offered by known and trusted writers are generally considered on their merits, although naturally other conditions may influence the editor's decision to accept or reject. A personal association, an established reputation in some field related to the writing, or a record of successful writing naturally is helpful.

To sell material to a syndicate, the writer can either send his material directly or work through an agency. Unknown writers often face difficulty in selling their material to syndicates because of the question of trust. Some syndicates are reluctant to deal with persons not known to them. Acceptance, however, is by no means impossible, for most syndicates are always receptive to acceptable manuscripts.

Giveaways, Throwaways, Free Magazines

Almost every day most Americans meet one or more magazines termed "giveaways," "throwaways," or "free magazines." These publications cannot be considered a class because they cover too wide a field. They range from the little pamphlet mailed to "Resident" or "Occupant" to beautifully printed controlled-circulation business magazines. They extend from neighborhood advertising tabloids on cheap newsprint to expensive public-relations slicks distributed to the customers and clients of very large corporations.

They also reach their readers by varying methods. They may come through the mail—the addressee's name having been taken from a carefully compiled mailing list. They may be stuffed inside the daily newspaper. They may be piled prominently at the end of the checkout counter at the supermarket. Or they may be placed in home mailboxes by a professional circular-delivery service.

Furthermore, the three names given these publications are imprecise. The term "giveaway" is imprecise because it is likely to be confused with one or more of the vague expressions found in common parlance—as for example, a genuine bargain, a gift presented with the purchase of a specific item, a condition such as a buffed spot on an automobile fender that "gives away" the fact that the car has been in an accident. The term "throwaway" is inexact because these publications are not discarded any more than many other magazines are thrown in the trash can after reading. The expression "free magazine" is inappropriate because it also designates the publication of the rebellious underground press.

No blanket statement can be made regarding opportunity for publication or remuneration in the instance of these magazines. Some are closed to outside writers; some are not. Some pay for articles; others run only donated or borrowed material. Some have a definitely limited scope; others range so widely that editorial policy is scarcely discernible. Therefore, the best procedure for the aspiring writer is to query the editor when he has material suitable to a given magazine.

An interesting point in the history of the free magazine is that some have become so successful that they have progressed to the stage of regular magazines. *Woman's Day,* for instance, was once distributed without cost by the Great Atlantic and Pacific Tea Company. However, the demand for the magazine became so great that publishing costs necessitated some financial return. As a result, a price of five cents was established. Later it became seven cents, and from there it increased to its present almost unbelievable price, 35 cents for regular issues and 95 cents for special issues—and with inflation, it may rise still higher. Also, its owners were forced through legal action to permit its sales in places other than A & P stores. Today it continues to prosper with a circulation of over three million, and on some occasions, almost five million.

EXERCISES

1. Analyze the contents of the following magazines: a quality, a popular weekly, a Sunday supplement.
2. Diagram the structural pattern of any three magazine stories.
3. Discuss analytically the poetry in any five issues of any quality magazine.
4. Discuss the layout of any magazine that uses illustrative material profusely.
5. Analyze the contents of a company magazine in the light of editorial policy.
6. Select five general magazines from a library reading room and explain the type of reader each is pointed toward.
7. Analyze the advertisements in any three magazines intended for the general public. Try to find instances of advertisements which you consider to be in "poor taste."
8. Select five instances of appealing verse, explaining the reasons for your choices.
9. Assume that you are about to establish a magazine for the general public. What material would you include? Give your reasons.
10. Select and compare the following: a personality sketch in a newspaper and one in a magazine; a utility article in a newspaper and one in a magazine; a newspaper column on politics and a magazine essay on politics.
11. Assume that you have just written the following: Nathaniel Hawthorne's short story, "The Minister's Black Veil"; Matthew Arnold's essay, "Culture and Anarchy"; and Charles Lamb's essay, "Old China." In what magazines would you attempt to place them? If you prefer, select three short stories or essays from current magazines and suggest other magazines to which they might have been sold. Explain your suggestions for the placing.
12. What are your three favorite magazines? Why?

FOR FURTHER READING

Dickson, Frank A. *Writer's Digest Handbook of Article Writing.* New York: Holt, 1968.

Filler, Louis. *Crusaders for American Liberalism.* New York: Harcourt, 1939. An account of the muckraking magazine writers.

Gunther, Max. *Writing the Modern Magazine Article*. Boston: The Writer, 1973.

Kramer, Dale. *Ross and the New Yorker*. Garden City, N.Y.: Doubleday, 1951. An account of the guiding force behind an important magazine.

Mott, Frank Luther. *A History of American Magazines*. Cambridge, Mass.: Harvard University Press, 1957.

Peterson, Theodore. *Magazines in the Twentieth Century*. Urbana: University of Illinois Press, 1964. This author has also done several articles on phases of the magazine industry. See any index to periodical literature.

Publisher's Weekly. 1180 Avenue of Americas, New York, N.Y. 10036.

Wood, James P. *Magazines in the United States*. New York: Ronald, 1956. Revised, 1971.

Writer. 8 Arlington Street, Boston, Mass. 02116.

Writer's Digest. 22 E. 12th Street, Cincinnati, Ohio 45210.

Appendices

The Stylebook

A stylebook is a newspaper's set of instructions for writing and editing copy. The reporter must know his paper's stylebook so that he can do his work well; the copy editor must know the stylebook verbatim for he cannot work without it. The following material has been extracted from the stylebooks of leading newspapers throughout the nation. It is, therefore, a typical stylebook that could be used in handling copy in a typical newspaper office.

1. GENERAL INSTRUCTIONS

a. PREPARING COPY—All material must be typed; longhand articles are not acceptable. Typing must be done clearly, without strike-overs or blurred erasures. Only regulation copy paper should be used. Typing must be on one side only. Typing must be double spaced in order to leave room for corrections. Ample space should be left at top and bottom and margins should be wide.

b. MAKING CHANGES—All changes should be made clearly and positively. The reporter should not make changes in long-hand. The copyreader should use a standard copy pencil and standard symbols in making changes. When corrections have been made in longhand, the letter "n" should be overscored and the letter "u" should be underscored.

c. PAGE MARKINGS—The slug (name of the story) should be written or typed in the upper left-hand corner of the first page and on every succeeding page. The reporter's name should follow the slug. Every page should be numbered when a story has more than one. The slug, usually given by the editor, should be short and expressive.

When there is to be more than one page, the reporter should write and encircle the word "more" at the bottom of all pages except the last. The end of the last page should bear the mark ⌐30 or # or ⟨///⟩ .

If the copyreader plans to write the head for the story after finishing the last page, he should mark the first page "hed to cum" so that the composing room will know the situation.

d. STYLE—All writing should be in accepted journalistic style. It should not be bombastic, trivial, overenthusiastic, or gushy.

The reporter should not place important details in the last paragraph because this section is usually the first affected by trimming. Where the reporter has done this, the copyreader must be careful as he trims.

e. ACCURACY—The writer must be accurate at all times. When in doubt, he should check. The standard sources for checking are the dictionary, the *World Almanac, Who's Who,* the telephone directories, and the numerous catalogs and publications of such places as universities and churches. Newspapermen must remember that most persons are extremely sensitive about the spelling of names, correct titles, and many other details that seem trvial to the person not concerned.

f. OFFENSIVE EXPRESSIONS—The reporter should not use and the copyreader should delete expressions and nicknames that are likely to give offense. Some examples are: *dago, Polack, shanty Irish, ward heeler, small fry, schoolmarm, high-pressure salesman, yes man.* The offending expression is most likely to appear in a quotation, but, nonetheless, it is certain to offend some readers. The reporter and the copyreader also must be careful of words or innuendoes that are indecent, either directly or by implication.

PUNCTUATION MARKS

a. THE PERIOD:

The period is used AT THE END OF A SENTENCE as it is in ordinary writing. Where the reporter has struck the typewriter key lightly, the copy reader should make the period heavier. Where the copyreader inserts a period, he should encircle it or use one of the standard devices—either ⊙ or ⊗.

The period should be omitted after headlines, captions, figures, the names of radio stations, and letters standing for well-known agencies.

The period is used WITH ABBREVIATIONS, as, for instance, the following: the *Rev. Dr.* Robert L. Peters, *Capt.* John K. Rossen, *Supt.* Earl P. Thomas, Chrysler Motors *Inc.*, Smith *Mfg. Inc.*

A series of periods is used TO INDICATE OMISSION, as, for instance, "Many a flower is born *to . . . waste* its sweetness on the desert air."

b. THE COMMA:

The comma is used IN A SERIES. *Ex.:* He chose *toys, baskets, ties, and vases.* (The last comma is optional.)

The comma is used TO SEPARATE UNRELATED ADJECTIVES; *Ex.:* It was a *long, difficult* pull.

The comma is used TO SET OFF THE NONRESTRICTIVE CLAUSE. *Ex.:* Senator Davis, *who leaves office next year,* predicts a hard fight.

The comma is used TO SET OFF THE APPOSITIVE. *Ex.:* Representative Connally, *the chairman of the committee,* spoke to his group.

The comma is used TO SET OFF THE DIRECT QUOTATION. *Ex.: "The time,"* said he, *"is now at hand."*

The comman is used TO SET OFF THE INTRODUCTORY ELEMENT. *Ex.: Therefore,* the disaster was forestalled.

The comma is used TO SET OFF THE PARENTHETICAL ELEMENT. *Ex.:* Algebra, *how I hate that subject,* gives me a great deal of trouble.

The comma is used TO SET OFF THE NOUN OR THE PRONOUN USED IN DIRECT ADDRESS. *Ex.:* That course, *John,* is very important.

The comma is used IN THE COMPOUND SENTENCE. *Ex.: Jones spoke for a long time, but he did not disclose his final plans.*

The comma is used IN THE COMPLEX SENTENCE if the dependent clause precedes the independent clause. *Ex.: If Thompson is to be re-elected,* he must work now.

The comma is used TO SEPARATE THE ELEMENTS IN DATES AND PLACES. *Ex.:* The candidate was born on *August 1, 1910, in Bay View, Potter County, Maine.*

The comma is used TO SET OFF CONTRASTED EXPRESSIONS. *Ex.:* The president, *not the advisory board,* is responsible.

Generally speaking, the comma should be used also IN ANY SITUATION WHERE: (1) the meaning is doubtful without one and (2) the presence of one makes for easier reading.

c. THE COLON:

A colon is used AFTER A STATEMENT INTRODUCING A DIRECT QUOTATION. *Ex.: He made his point tersely: I am not going to accede.*

A colon is used TO INTRODUCE A LONG SERIES. *Ex.:* Those present included: *Katherine Thompson, secretary; Mary Williams, treasurer; etc.*

A colon is used TO INTRODUCE A FORMAL RESOLUTION. *Ex.: "Resolved: That this assembly . . ."*

A colon is used TO INTRODUCE A SPORTS RESULT. *Ex.: Score:* Whitney, 20; Harrow, 12.

A colon is used TO SEPARATE CHAPTER AND VERSE in scriptural references. *Ex.:* I Corinthians *13:1.*

d. THE SEMICOLON:

A semicolon is used TO SEPARATE TWO CLOSELY CONNECTED CO-ORDINATE CLAUSES. *Ex.: The Trojans were outclassed; they were beaten from the start.*

A semicolon is used IN A SERIES that would not be clear by the use of commas. *Ex.:* The president spoke to *Johnny Kirk, our captain; Pete Smythe, our manager; and Mr. William Meyer, our coach.*

The semicolon is used, generally speaking, as THE NEXT PUNCTUATION MARK AFTER THE COLON. *Ex.:* The apparatus is used thus: *to combat, if necessary, any unexpected disaster; to aid in the regular work; and to supplement the equipment already on hand.*

e. THE DASH:

The dash is used TO REPLACE THE PREPOSITION "TO" IN SCORES. *Ex.:* The final score was *2—1.*

The dash is used, without a period, FOR THE UNFINISHED STATEMENT. *Ex.: "Why, if I had known ——"*

The dash is used TO DENOTE THE OMISSION OF OFFENSIVE WORDS. *Ex.:* The senator said, *"You can go to ——."* (Note—Some newspapers either use the offensive word or avoid this construction.)

The dash is used FOR AN EMPHATIC PAUSE. *Ex.: John got his answer—fired.*

The dash is used occasionally FOR THE LONG APPOSITIVE. *Ex.:* Pete Jeffers—*a winner, a runner-up, and an also-ran in previous tournaments*—never had a chance this year.

The dash is used FOR THE LONG, INVOLVED, PARENTHETICAL ELEMENT. *Ex.:* The team captain—*and in my calm, considered judgment I say I have never seen a better one, on this field, at least*—fought from start to finish.

The dash is used FOR EMPHASIS IN DIRECT ADDRESS. *Ex.: John*—I think you are right! (Quotation marks are not needed with this form.)

The dash is used AFTER QUESTION AND ANSWER in verbatim testimony. *Ex.: Q.—Where do you live? A.—Chicago.*

The dash is used in such instances as these: *First*—, *Second*—, *Table 4—Continued, Note*—.

f. THE HYPHEN:

The hyphen is used TO COMBINE TWO OR MORE WORDS INTO ONE WORD. *Ex.: a Truman-like* gesture, a *through-the-house* chase, a *bent-on-murder* move.

Use the hyphen in writing such SPELLED-OUT NUMBERS as *forty-six, eight-one*. Use no hyphen in *two hundred, five thousand, $6 million*. Use the hyphen in fractions thus: *one-third, three-fifths*, but *six twenty-thirds*.

Write as one word: *baseball, football, today, tonight, tomorrow, homecoming, textbook, bookcase, downstate, upstate, snowstorm, lineup, newsman, writeup, makeup*.

Use the hyphen WITH PREFIXES USED WITH PROPER NAMES. *Ex.: post-Roosevelt, un-American, anti-Wallace*.

Words compounded of the following prefixes and suffixes are not hyphenated: *a, after, ante, auto, bi, demi, ever, grand, holder, in, inter, intra, less, mid, mis, non, off, on, over, post, re, some, sub, super, trans, tri, un, under, up, ward, wise, with. Ex.: ever present, grand march, mid afternoon*.

Words compounded WITH THE FOLLOWING PREFIXES AND SUFFIXES are hyphenated: *able-, anti-, brother-, by-, cross-, -elect, ex-, father-, great-, half-, -hand, mother-, open-, public-, quarter-, -rate, self-, semi-. Ex.; semi-monthly, anti-Democrat, president-elect*.

However, if the word if used widely, it may be written as a single word, or without the hyphen, as usage dictates. *Ex.: antitoxin, byway, quarter final exam*.

g. THE APOSTROPHE:

The apostrophe is used TO DENOTE THE POSSESSIVE CASE OF NOUNS. *Ex.: John's* book; *Mr. Smith's* house; *Mrs. Roberts's* daughter.

The apostrophe is used TO DENOTE A CONTRACTION OR AN OMISSION. (Strictly speaking, this mark, although the same as an apostrophe, is an omission mark.) *Ex.: He'd* put his house in pawn! He aims *t'* please.

The apostrophe is used TO MAKE LETTERS PLURAL. *Ex.:* The student earned two *A's*.

The apostrophe is omitted where general usage has already done so. *Ex.:* State *Teachers* College, the *Engineers* Club, the *Lawyers* Guide.

IN THE CASE OF PARTNERS, the second name is apostrophized. *Ex.:* Dun and *Bradstreet's* index.

h. FIGURES:

Numbers from one to ten are spelled out; numbers from 11 on may be written in their Arabic numeral form.

There are, however, several exceptions. Time should be written as *8:15 a.m.* yesterday; *11 p.m.* Thursday; *1:35 p.m.* next Tuesday afternoon.

Sums of money should be written as $12 (not $12.00); $5,000; $15.80.

Street numbers are always figures: 2158 N. 14 St.; 821 Roosevelt Blvd.; 61 Barton Pl. Figures are also used for scores, degrees of temperature, automobile license plate numbers, telephone numbers, distances, numbers in election returns, prices, dimensions, and all similar situations.

A sentence should never begin with Arabic numerals if any other course is possible. If the first word in a sentence is a number, it should be spelled out. *Ex.: Twelve* members were present.

If a sentence contains a number below ten and one above ten, use Arabic numerals for both. *Ex.:* The ages varied from *6 to 20 years, 2 months.*

Phrases should be spelled out. *Ex.:* One man in a *thousand.*

i. PARENTHESES:

Avoid parentheses as much as possible.

Parentheses may be used sparingly FOR EXPLANATION. *Ex.:* John spoke last *(the first time this year),* but he was effective nonetheless.

Parentheses may be used sparingly FOR THE PARENTHETICAL ELEMENT. *Ex.:* Harold said the answer was five. *(Boy, was he wrong!)*

A caution to be noted is this: Brackets, not parentheses, must be used for any words interpolated by the editor into a direct quote. *Ex.:* Said the President, ''We *[Americans]* . . . must be ready for the battle.''

j. THE QUESTION MARK:

The question mark is used, in general, as THE END PUNCTUATION IN A QUESTION. *Ex.:* Is that *all?* Are you *ready?*

The question mark is used TO CREATE DOUBT FOR THE SAKE OF HUMOR. *Ex.:* The actress will be a *raving (?) success.*

k. QUOTATION MARKS:

Quotation marks are used FOR A DIRECT QUOTATION. *Ex.: ''Here,''* he said, *''is the table.''*

No quotation marks are necessary for a quotation when it is set in smaller or different type to indicate the fact that it is a quotation.

Single quotation marks are used FOR A QUOTATION WITHIN A QUOTATION.

Place ''weak'' punctuation marks—periods and commas—inside quotation marks. Place the ''strong'' marks—question marks, exclamation points, colons, and semicolons—outside.

Use quotation marks FOR TESTIMONY, CONVERSATION, AND STATEMENTS GIVEN IN DIRECT FORM. The one exception is the quotation which employs the dash.

Use quotation marks TO SET OFF A WORD OF UNUSUAL MEANING or an unfamiliar or coined word used for the first time. *Ex.:* The ''tagee'' then becomes ''it.''

Use quotation marks FOR THE NAMES OF BOOKS, PLAYS, PAINTINGS, SONGS, MAGAZINE ARTICLES, etc. (Note that this is newspaper style. Some publications use *italic* for the names of books, plays, and paintings.)

Use quotation marks AT THE BEGINNING OF EACH PARAGRAPH OF A QUOTATION extending to two or more paragraphs. Place marks at the end of the last paragraph only.

Use no quotation marks for names of newspapers or periodicals, as *New York Times,* or for common nicknames, as *Sad Sam* (except when they are used with the full name, as *Samuel "Sad Sam" Smith*).

1. INDIVIDUAL PUNCTUATION MARKS:

The copyreader should consult the slot man before approving any distinctly individual punctuation marks (stars, asterisks, arrows, etc.).

ABBREVIATIONS

Abbreviate the following TITLES WHEN THEY PRECEDE: *Dr., Mr., Messrs., Mrs., Mme., Mlle., Prof., Rev., and all military titles except Chaplain.*

Abbreviate NAMES OF STATES and of DISTRICT OF COLUMBIA when they are preceded by the names of cities. *Ex.: St. Louis, Mo.* (The following State names are not abbreviated: Alaska, Hawaii, Idaho, Iowa, Ohio, Utah.) The generally accepted abbreviations are:

Ala.	Fla.	Md.	Nev.	Ore.	Tex.
Ariz.	Ga.	Me.	N.C.	Pa.	Va.
Ark.	Ill.	Mich.	N.D.	P.I.	Vt.
Calif.	Ind.	Minn.	N.H.	P.R.	Wash.
Colo.	Kan.	Miss.	N.J.	R.I.	W.Va.
Conn.	Ky.	Mo.	N.M.	S.C.	Wis.
D.C.	La.	Mont.	N.Y.	S.D.	Wyo.
Del.	Mass.	Neb.	Okla.	Tenn.	

(These are preferred rather than the postoffice abbreviations like Ak., Al., Ar., Az.)

Abbreviate the NAME OF MONTHS having five or more letters when used in dates and datelines. *Ex.: Dec. 24.*

Abbreviate the word NUMBER before figures. *Ex.: No.* 16.

Abbreviate UNITS OF MEASURE when preceded by numerals. *Ex.: 21 ft.* 6 *in.*

Abbreviate common designations of WEIGHTS AND MEASURES in the singular only. *Ex.:lb., in.* Exceptions: *Figs.* 1 and 2, *Vols.* 1 and 2, *Nos.* 1 and 2.

Abbreviate COLLEGE DEGREES. *Ex.: A.B., S.T.D., V.M.D..*

Abbreviate avenue, street, alley, drive, boulevard, road, and place when used in an ADDRESS. *Ex.:* 28 Firth *Ave.,* 29 Warden *Dr.*

Abbreviate MORNING to a.m. and AFTERNOON to p.m.

Abbreviate NAMES OF COMMON ORGANIZATIONS. *Ex.: R.O.T.C., G.A.R., D.A.R., W.C.T.U.* (Note—Omit period in names of radio stations and very common abbreviations. *Ex.: KNBR, PX*)

Do not abbreviate *Christmas* to *Xmas,* first names (*J. W. Smith* but not *Jno. Wm. Smith*), or such titles as senator, congressman, bishop, president, secretary, and chairman when used with a last name.

TITLES

Men's initials or first names should be used when the name appears for the first time. Thereafter, use simply the last name except in the case of high-ranking people. Where only initials appear, the reader assumes that the name is that of a man.

First names of unmarried women should always be given. Thereafter, the title *Miss* and the last name are to be used. If no title is given before the name of a woman, the reader assumes that she is unmarried.

Divorced women and widows are given the title *Mrs.* and their original first names unless they wish otherwise. The title *Ms.* should be used in situations where the person named is known to prefer that form.

Men in religious orders should always be given their proper titles. A clergyman is *the* Rev. Mr. Jones.

The following are approved forms for foreign titles:

ENGLISH

King	Queen
the Duke of	the Duchess of
the Marquis of	the Marchioness of
Earl (or the Earl of)	Countess
Viscount	Viscountess
Baron (*more commonly* Lord)	Baroness (*more commonly* Lady)
Sir Paul Barry	Lady Barry
(*thereafter* Sir Paul)	

Baronet is a hereditary title. Baronets are distinguished from *knights* by the abbreviation *Bart.* or *Bt. Ex:* Sir John Turner, *Bart.*

Use the *Right Honorable* rarely. Say *Captain Sir Clarence Peters;* thereafter in a story it is *Sir Clarence* or *Captain Peters.* The Lord Mayor's wife may be called the *Lady Mayoress.*

FRENCH

Prince	Princesse
Marquis	Marquise
Vicomte	Vicomtesse
Comte	Comtesse
Baron	Baronne
Monsieur (M., *plural* MM.)	Madam, Mademoiselle
	(Mme., Mmes.; Mlle., Mlles.)

GERMAN

Herr   Frau, Fräulein

INDIAN

Maharaja   Maharani (*or* ee)
Raja   Rani (*or* ee)

ITALIAN

Principe   Principessa
Duca   Duchessa
Marchese   Marchessa
Conte   Contessa (*sometimes* Contesina)
Barone   Baronessa
Signore   Signora, Signorina

Use the last name with the Signore, Signora.

RUSSIAN

Most Russian titles of eminence or offices are translated into corresponding English words: *Chairman* or *President Kosygin, Secretary Brezhnev*.

Titles of respect may remain in Russian:

Tovarishch Petrov, Tovarishcha Petrova (Comrade Petrov, *masculine* or *feminine*)

Gospodin Shchukin, Gospozha Shchukina (Mr. Shchukin, *Mrs.* or *Miss* Shchukin)

Grashdanin Borodin, Grashdanka Borodina (Citizen Borodin, *masculine* or *feminine*)

It is not usual to feminize Russian surnames when they are used with English titles of respect. Thus: *Chairman Khrushchev, Mrs. Khrushchev.*

Russian names are often used with patronymics, formed by adding a suffix to the personal name of the father. Thus: Boris Vladimirovich Romanov, Nikita Sergeyevich Khrushchev, Mariya Aleksandrovna Romanova, Varvara Alexeyevna Pushkina. The patronymic always follows the personal name and is never used without it.

SPANISH

Principe   Princesa
Duque   Duquesa
Marques   Marquesa
Conde   Condesa
Baron   Baronesa
Señor   Señora, Señorita (Miss)

SWISS

The Swiss use French, German, and Italian forms.

CAPITALIZATION

Do not capitalize:
Names of national, state, and city bodies, boards, etc.
Ex.: assembly, council, legislature, house, senate, department of welfare, highway commission, tax office, city hall, capitol.

The words "street," "avenue," etc. *Ex.:* 10 Downing *st.,* 241 Maple *ave.* However, it should be: 241 *Boulevard of the Allies,* 833 *Avenue of the Pacific.*

Seasons of the year: *spring, summer, autumn, winter.*

Points of the compass: *north, east, south, west, northeast, southwest.*

The subject of debate. The standard style is: *"Resolved: That the minimum age requirement for voting in national elections should be lowered to 18 in all states."*

These prefixes: *von, de, di, la, le,* except where they begin the sentence. *Ex.:* Hermann *von Bülow,* Henri *de la Rouge.*

Time: *a.m.* and *p.m.* Write *12 o'clock noon* or *midnight.*

Names of school departments and all studies except names of languages and subjects containing a proper noun. *Ex.: mathematics department, philosophy, Latin, American history.*

Titles when the name precedes. *Ex.: Howard Thomas, professor of chemistry.*

Names of classes: *freshman, sophomore, junior, senior.*

College degrees written out. *Ex.: bachelor of arts, master of arts, doctor of philosophy.* However, it is *A.B., A.M., Ph.D.*

Titles in lists of officers: *Ex.:* The newly elected officers are: Peter Johnson, *commander;* George Harris, *vice-commander.*

Widely used common nouns or adjectives derived from proper nouns. *Ex.: phoenician alphabet, russian dressing, macadamize, german measles, swiss cheese.*

SOME REALISM ABOUT STYLEBOOKS

It is not easy to keep in line with a stylebook. However, a newspaper may look and read like a slapdash creation unless its reporters and copy editors maintain a continuing effort to respect an agreed style, to be consistent, and to be careful. Readers sense this kind of care, sometimes without full awareness of the fact, and it gives them confidence in the paper. Reporters and copy editors can hold themselves to high standards despite knowing that styles are at leastly partly matters of fashion—indeed sometimes of whim—and that stylebooks differ. The book in which this is printed, for instance, does fully not conform to the stylebook rules given above—its author and editors worked with other rules in mind.

Stylebooks, though they prescribe details, are also concerned with attitudes toward writing and even with philosophies of writing. In fact, some stylebooks have extensive sections devoted to direct advice and guidelines for the newspaper writer. These sections often read like college manuals on writing; that is, they counsel the writer on how to conduct himself as he prepares his material.

On the following pages, a section from the stylebook of the *Detroit News* is reprinted. Note how this material deals with the writer's attitude rather than with mechanical detail to be used in the preparation of copy.

Quotes Must Ring True

Direct quotations liven a story, but they must sound authentic. For instance, a News reporter once quoted a three-year-old as saying "Mother was morose and spoke of shooting father."

Actually, of course, direct quotes usually will be paraphrases. For one thing, few reporters use shorthand. For another, we ordinarily correct barbarisms in diction. (But don't make a person say "It is I" if he obviously would have said "That's me.")

Above all, don't toss in identifications and addresses to produce such improbable quotations as:

"So I went into a drugstore at 5804 Hamilton and called my buddy, Peter J. Maginnis, 26, operator of a handbook at 21046 Riopelle, to tell him the police were on the way."

Avoid Overworked Words

No word in current general use is barred in The News except for reasons of decency or good taste.

Discretion should be used, however, to avoid overworking any word or phrase. For instance, since many newspaper stories deal with investigations, there can easily be a ludicrous number of **probes**, **sifts** and **quizzes**. When feasible, use the longer but less trite **investigation** or **inquiry**. Among other possibilities are these: examination, review, query, check, scrutiny, study and interrogation.

> **Note that, despite some newspaper stylebooks, Webster's recognizes the use of "probe" in the investigative sense. It is approved both as a verb (to investigate thoroughly) and as a noun (an inquiry directed to the discovery of evidence of wrongdoing). The intent here is not to bar its use but to caution against its overuse.**

Adjectives, as well as nouns and verbs, easily become hackneyed. Among such chestnuts are "full dress" meetings, "full dress" conferences and "full dress" inquiries; "wide," "searching" and "sweeping" investigations; and "brutal" murders.

Dozens of other words and phrases are similarly trite. Every year hundreds of feature stories begin with the words, "This is the story of . . ." Prosecutors are invariably quoted as saying, "We have barely scratched the surface." Mayors, councilmen and legislators are forever "whetting an ax" or "sharpening a knife" for a budget. Congressmen "dump bills into the legislative hopper."

Nomination on the Democratic ticket in a Southern state is repeatedly "tantamount to election." Pay increases are generally "pay hikes." Ships damaged by storms "limp into port."

Every adult who encourages a child to steal is a "Fagin." Popular products "sell like hot cakes" and their vendors "do a land-office business." Bad weather slows traffic to a "crawl" or a "snail's pace."

Some other cliches may be less obvious. What, for instance, are "modest" homes and "fashionable" homes? The terms are virtually meaningless.

Express It in Plain English

In court stories avoid legalistic language such as "certiorari" or "quo warranto" or "subpena duces tecum." The meaning of "subpena duces tecum," for instance, is a subpena requiring a person to appear in court, or to produce records in court. Why not write it in English?

If a legal term seems essential to a story, be sure that its meaning is made clear. Example: He pleaded nolo contendere (no contest) to the tax evasion charge.

Avoid such awkward words as "gubernatorial," even if they are technically correct. Why write "gubernatorial mansion" when it's just as easy to write "governor's mansion"? Similarly "the Republican nomination for governor" is better than "the Republican gubernatorial nomination." And either "the governorship race" or "the race for governor" is preferable to "the gubernatorial race."

Be Wary of 'Pointed Out'

Only rarely is it correct to use such expressions as "pointed out," "noted," "stressed," "justified," etc. Example: "The governor pointed out that all the ills of his administration were the fault of the Legislature." This use of "pointed out" makes The News say that the governor's statement is an unchallenged fact.

Avoid unnecessary use of "according to" and "it was announced today by . . ." Often such phrases are used by lazy writers to get someone's name in the paper. Example: "The 1962 general election fell on Nov. 6, according to John A. Smith, Elections Commission record keeper." If there is some reason for using Smith's name, use it some other way. Do not qualify the undisputed fact, or attribute the obvious.

Write What You Mean

● Distinguish between **bring** and **take. Bring** indicates motion toward the story's point of origin; **take** refers to motion in any other direction. Examples:

The liner America **brought** 3,000 passengers to New York; it **took** 3,200 back to Europe.

One courier **brought** the message to Detroit; others **took** copies to New York and Cleveland.

● The word **eager** indicates ardor or enthusiasm, or sometimes impatience; **anxious** emphasizes deep desire mixed with worry or fear. Example:

The mother was **anxious** for her daughter's safety; the girl was **eager** to be an actress.

● A writer or speaker **implies** something in his words or manner;

APPENDIX
II

Reading Proofs

The copy editor should know how to check proof because he is expected, when time permits, to read the proofs of stories he has handled, even though the composing-room proofreaders check all printed matter routinely. The copy editor must also know how to check proofs because there are times when he needs to change something already in type. Obviously, these changes must be made on the proof.

The following chart shows the principal marks used by proofreaders in the United States and Canada. Although these marks are somewhat similar to those used by copy editors, there are several differences necessitated by the closeness of type as compared to the openness of copy.

Journalists in the 1980s will need these proofreaders' marks but soon will also need others. The marks now in use were developed to deal with the kinds of correction needed in movable metal type—invented in the Renaissance and adapted continuously over the five centuries since. New typesetting methods are supplanting metal type and will require new proofreaders' marks—which journalists will have a share in devising.

SYMBOL	MEANING	EXAMPLE
⌣ ⌐ *tr*	Transpose	He (ready is) for the trip. *tr* /
ʺ ʺ	Quote marks	He said, Come. ⌃ ʺ/ʺ /
ᵛ ᵛ	Single quotes	He said; "I am touchy now." ᵛ/ᵛ
ᵛ	Apostrophe	He had his brothers book. ᵛ/
⌃,	Comma	He was a short stocky man. ⌃/
?/	Question mark	Is that all ⌃ ?/
⊙	Period	The firm is Smith Bros, Inc. ⌃ ⊙/
ital	Italics	He never denied his guilt. *ital*
bf	Boldface	Now is the time. *bf*
/-²⁄ₘ-/	Two-em dash	That was all ⌃ he was finished /-²⁄ₘ-/
w.f.	Wrong font	BANᴋER INDICTED *w.f.*
ꝯ	Turn over letter	The mat ron spoke to the woman ꝯ
rom	Use roman type	She spoke in Act 3. ⌃ *rom*/
!/	Exclamation mark	The day was lost ⌃ !/
/ *l.c.*	Make lowercase	Soper and his ꞙrother Now HE lives in New York. *l.c.* ⌃
ᵟ ℯ	Delete	Mr. Joines was president. ᵟ Mr. Joines was president. ℯ
⋯ *stet*	Leave as was	He ~~never~~ denied his guilt. *stet*
⌃	Insert	He was leader. *the*/
¶	Paragraph	That was all he did. ¶ Rugby ended the inning as Adler struck out all the heavy hitters.
no ¶	No paragraph	Clark finished the first inning. *no* ¶ Then he went to the showers.

SYMBOL	MEANING	EXAMPLE
⌐	Move left	Clark finished the first inning. ⌐ Then he went to the showers.
⌐ (reversed)	Move right	Smith plans ⌐ to talk with Rickey early.
‿	Less space	Smith plans ⌐ to talk with Rickey early.
#	More space	Smith plans ⌐ to talk with Rickey early.So he **#/**
⌒	Close up	When h e is ready, he will begin.
≡	Make a capital	Harper and peters stood guard.
=	Make small caps	Chicago, Illinois
see copy	See copy	Just then the man entered the room and‿to the woman sharply. *see copy*
▢	Indent one em	he left the town early. But ▢— for all his care — he made a mistake.
═	Straighten line	The story was a very exciting one. The main character was a man who never thought of any
⌐⌐	Move up	There was never a really dull moment from the time that he entered the room until the time **⌐⌐**
⌊⌋	Move down	The storm kept lashing the coast from the early hours of the morn- ing. By noon the entire populace **⌊⌋**
(?)	Is this correct?	Back and forth. Forth and back. Back and forth. Back and forth. **(?)**
✗	Bad letter	The defendant never wavered in his testimony. He averred that **✗**
/=/	Hyphen	In the post‿war era the council **/=/**
⌒	Spell out	The firm is Smith Bros Inc.

APPENDIX
III

A Glossary

The following list represents the basic newspaper terminology in use today. The student of journalism should view this list as a "must" to be learned if he is to move about freely and successfully in the newspaper world.

Ad. Shortened form of "advertisement." Although the term usually denotes classified ads, it is used to cover any advertisement in the paper.

Ad copy. Copy for an advertisement. It consists of all matter to be printed, with appropriate directions for setting and arranging.

Add. Additional parts of a story. When the first page of a story is sent to the composing room, it is marked "number 1" or "page 1." The next page is marked "add 1" or "page 2," according to the system used by the particular newspaper. The term "add" is employed similarly by the wire services to identify the consecutive parts of the stories filed.

Advance. Story not to be released until a specified time or until a definite order has been issued. In this category are wire service stories released in advance and advance copies of speeches.

Agate. 5½-point type. This is the smallest type used by most newspapers usually for classified ads. Hence also *agate line*.

Alley.   Aisle in the composing room. Hence, there are the ad alley, the lino-type alley, the proofreader alley, etc.

All in hand.   Denoting the fact that all copy has been given to the composi-tors.

All up.   Term used as a synonym for the sentence, "The copy has all been set in type." It is also used by the various departments of the newspaper to in-dicate that their work has been completed.

Angle.   Viewpoint or premise from which a story is to be written or the slant taken. Hence, the angle may be humorous, serious, etc.

AP   Associated Press.

Art.   Pictures used in a newspaper.

Assignment.   News-gathering task assigned to a reporter or a picture-taking task assigned to a photographer.

Assignment book.   Editor's record of assignments. The record usually bears the name of the story and the reporter to whom it has been assigned.

Astonisher.   (1) Name applied by some newspapers to a banner line; (2) name applied by some newspapers to a startling lead; (3) newspaper slang for an exclamation point.

Axe-grinder.   (1) Editorial that purports to be news; (2) person who has a per-sonal motive (usually publicity for a cause) in supplying news to a paper.

Bad break.   Term used to denote any situation wherein the type causes an un-pleasant appearance; as, for instance, a short line at the opening of a sec-ond column.

Bank.   (1) Lines under the headline that enlarge upon or add to the ideas in the headline; (2) table on which type is kept in the composing room.

Banner.   Line that crosses the entire page or the greater part of the page. Also known variously as a "streamer," a "banner line," and a "screamer."

Bastard type.   Type that does not conform to the standard system of "one point equals $1/72$ inch.

Beat.   (1) Story printed by one newspaper before its rivals have been able to obtain it; (2) story that is the exclusive property of one newspaper; (3) dis-trict or special news source (courts, city hall, etc.) assigned to a reporter. In the first two uses listed, the term "beat" is synonymous with the terms "scoop" or "exclusive."

Bleeding cut.   Cut that touches the outside edges of either of the outside col-umns. Once viewed as a serious error, the bleeding (or bleed) cut is now used widely in the newspaper and book world.

Blind interview.   One wherein the person interviewed is quoted but not named. Examples are "a White House spokesman," "a high government authority," "an unimpeachable source."

Body type.   Type used in the body of the story.

Break.   (1) Actual occurrence of events that are newsworthy (thus, a story "breaks" when it happens); (2) release of facts for a story (thus, a story is given reporters with the understanding that they will "break" it at a specified time); (3) point at which printed matter "breaks" to be continued in another column.

Break page or **split page.** When a paper is split into separate sections, the first page of the second, third, or other section is a "break" or "split" page.

Bromide. Overused expression such as "hall of fame," "quick as a deer," "fleecy clouds," etc. Also termed a "cliché," a "trite expression," a "stereotype."

Bug. Ornament used in a headline or as special-purpose punctuation.

Bulldog. (1) Name given to the first edition of a newspaper; (2) name sometimes given to a specially printed edition.

Bullpup. First mail edition of a Sunday newspaper.

By-line. Reporter's name placed over the story. Thus we read, "By Joseph K. Preston."

Cablese. Abbreviated or coded language used for copy sent by cable.

Canned copy. Copy provided by publicity agents and others desiring publicity.

Caps. Abbreviation for "capital letters."

Caption. (1) Heading; (2) heading over a picture.

Case. (1) Cabinet at which the printer works; (2) terminology used for capital and small letters. Thus, a printer speaks of "upper case" and "lower case" letters.

Catchline. Guideline or slugline used to identify a story before the type is set in page form. Thus, a story slugged "flood" will bear that catchline at the top of the type until the type is set in the page.

Challenge. Term used to denote a situation wherein the copyreader reports his doubts of a story's authenticity to the slotman.

Chase. Frame in which all the metal (type, cuts, etc.) for a given page is placed. In large print shops, the stereotype mat is molded from type, etc., locked in the chase; in small print shops, the chase is used on the press with the type, etc.

Cheesecake. Slang used within and without the newspaper world to denote pictures of shapely women, especially emphasizing their legs.

C.l.c. Abbreviation used for capital and lower case letters.

Clear. Term used to indicate completed action. Thus, a story "clears" the copy desk when it leaves for the composing room. When a department completes its work, it is said to be "all clear." Thus, the city room is "all clear" when all stories for an edition have been written and sent to the copy desk.

Circus make-up. Make-up wherein many headlines of various kinds and sizes are used. The idea is to have each story act as a circus barker to attract attention.

City editor. Editor in charge of local news. On very large papers, this editor may have so many reporters and rewrite men working for him that a separate room is required. This room is appropriately termed the *city room*.

Clean. Term used to denote copy or proof which needs few corrections.

Clipsheet. Sheet of stories supplied by a publicity agent or agency. Because the sheet has printing on only one side, it may be clipped as desired.

Col. Abbreviation for "column."

Condensed type. Narrow, hence "condensed," type.

Copy. (1) Material to be set in type, as news copy, ad copy, etc.; (2) person about whom a story is to be written. Colorful public figures, for instance, sometimes are referred to as "good copy."

Copyboy, copygirl. Person who carries copy from one department or person to another, does errands, and performs other minor duties in the news room. Frequently termed an *office boy, office girl.*

Copycutter. Composing-room employee who assigns copy to compositors. His name arises from the fact that he frequently cuts copy apart, especially on long stories, to speed the copy into print.

Copy editor, copyreader. The man or woman responsible for getting copy ready to go to the composing room.

Correspondent. (1) Person who submits news from his home town or area, usually on a space basis, to a newspaper; (2) reporter assigned by his newspaper to a distant news source. Most large newspapers in the United States, for instance, maintain correspondents in their own state capitals and in Washington, D.C.

Cover. To handle an assignment. Hence, a reporter "covers" a story by getting the facts and a photographer "covers" the story by getting the pictures.

Credit line. Line that credits a source. Examples of the credit line are the wire-service credits at the opening of the story and the line beneath a photograph crediting a photographer or an agency.

Crossline. Single-line headline.

Cub. Beginning reporter.

Cut. (1) Metal plate bearing a picture or illistrative material; loosely, a picture. (2) copyreader's term for eliminating material from a story.

Cut line. Term used synonymously with "caption for a cut." Sometimes called "underline." The term "cut lines" usually means the lines under the cut, but it may also include the lines over a cut.

Cutoff. Rule placed across one or more columns in order to make a solid line.

Dagger. Reference mark.

Dateline. (1) Line at the beginning of a story giving the point and/or the date of origin; (2) lines across the top of the page giving the date and the name of the newspaper.

Dead. (1) Said of part of the newspaper already in type in which no further changes will be made (the classified ad section, for instance, is "dead" several hours before the presses begin); (2) said of type or plates already used that will not be used again. Generally, a pressroom employee defaces it to prevent accidental reuse. (*Note*—the terms "killed" and "dead" must not be confused.)

Deadline. Time at which all the work of a given department must be completed. Thus, there are deadlines for the news department, the copy desk, and the various departments of the composing room and the pressroom.

Deck. Part of a head that adds to or enlarges upon the main lines. Also termed a "bank."

Desk. (1) Copy desk; (2) place of authority. Hence, a reporter calls the "desk" (the city editor or his assistant).

Devil. Term used to denote a printer's apprentice.

District man. Reporter assigned to cover a definite section of the city. He maintains a vigilance over hospitals, police stations, morgues, and other places likely to be news sources. He is known also as a "legman." "He" is often a woman.

Dog watch. The period after the regular issues of the paper have gone to press but before the next full day begins, during which some editorial and shop personnel stay on duty to deal with replates or emergencies—or, in the past, to get work started on extra editions. Sometimes called "lobster trick."

Dope. Slang term for advance news story material, background material for a story, actual facts of a story.

Double leading. Placing of two, rather than just one, metal strips between lines of type to fill out space as the page is set in metal form.

Double struck or **double truck.** A two-page layout made up as a single unit, in which reading matter or pictures may fill the gutter between facing pages. It is often used for department-store and supermarket advertisement.

Doublet. Word or material set twice by mistake and repeated in the same issue. A synonymous term is "dupe."

Down style. Style of writing wherein the use of capitals is reduced to a minimum. Its opposite is, of course, the "up" style.

Drop lines. Second and subsequent lines of a slanted headline.

Dummy. Diagram showing the position of stories, features, cuts, ads, etc., that are to appear on a given page.

Dupe. Same as "doublet."

Ears. Little boxes placed on either side of the nameplate on the first page of the various sections of the paper. The ears usually give circulation figures, a slogan, the name of the edition, or some similar statement.

Editor. Name given loosely to an editorial department employee who is in charge of a department. Thus, one finds the sports editor, the city editor, the radio editor, etc. The simple title, "editor," is usually given the highest-ranking person on the newspaper, excepting the publisher. A copyreader or copy editor is not quite an editor in these senses.

Editorialize. Expression of opinion in a news story or a headline that supposedly is nonopinionated.

Em. (1) A unit of type measure, equal in width to the size of the type; thus, an eight-point em is 8 points wide, and a twelve-point em is 12 points wide. The width is about that of the letter *M* in most typefaces. (2) Loosely, a pica—12 points; used to give the size of a space, rule, or other element, as "a 12-em column."

En. One half of an em.

Exclusive. Story that is the property of one newspaper exclusively.

Fake. Falsified story.

Fat head. Headline too crowded for the space it occupies. Thus, it is difficult to read.

Feature. (1) Act of giving prominence to a story; (2) feature story; (3) one of the comics, cartoons, drawings, and similar material used in the paper.

File. (1) Sending of a story, usually by telegraph; (2) filing of material, as in the business world.

Filler. Material that can be placed almost anywhere in the paper to fill out blank space. Filler is most often very short stories or simple statements that are almost dateless.

Fingernails. Printer's term for "parentheses."

Five W's. "Who, what, when, where, why." With the interrogative "how," they represent the questions to be answered in the conventional lead.

Flag. (1) Piece of lead place in a projecting position in a column of type to warn the printer that a change is to be made; (2) name plate of the newspaper; (3) editorial heading.

Flag waver. Newspaper that emphasizes patriotism excessively.

Flash. Wire-service term for the first capsule statement of an important news break. This term has come to cover similar statements printed or broadcast.

Flimsy. Carbon copy on onionskin or similarly thin paper.

Flush head. Headline with all lines beginning flush at the left side of the column but leaving uneven blank spaces at the far right.

Folio. (1) Page; (2) page number.

Follow. (1) Further developments in a story that has already been in print (hence, big stories almost always have a "follow"); (2) smaller story accompanying a bigger story. This latter story is frequently termed a "supplementary story."

Font. Complete set of type of one size and family.

Form. Metal square (chase) into which the type to be used on a particular page is placed.

Foto. Newspaper photograph.

Future. Notation placed in the "futures" file to remind the particular editor that a story will develop on that day.

Galley. Metal tray on which is kept type that has been set.

Glossy. Photograph with a shiny finish. The glossy is preferred because it provides better detail when used for a cut.

Goodnight. Expression used to denote that one's work is finished and he may leave.

Green proof. First proof pulled after type has been set. Consequently, this proof must be read carefully for typographical errors.

Guideline. Name given to a story to identify it. This term is synonymous with "catchline" or "slug." Thus, a story slugged "theft" would bear that guideline above it for purposes of identification. Guidelines are removed before the page is printed.

Hairline. Border rule that prints a very fine line. Used for fine cutoff work.

Half stick. Material set in half-column measure.

Handout. "Canned" copy distributed by a press agent or a publicity office.

Hanging indent. Headline having the top line flush to the left and the lower line or lines indented.

Head. Term used synonymously with "headline."

Headlines. Main lines over a story.

Hellbox. Box in the composing room wherein discarded type and other metal to be remelted may be thrown.

High lines. Lines cast unevenly by the linotype machine so that, when printed, they appear unusually black.

Hold for release. Line appearing as titular matter on copy not to be printed until a given date (stated on copy) or until a release order has been given.

H. T. C. Abbreviation for the expression "hed to cum." This expression is used by the copyreader or the editor to state that the story is to be set before the head is decided on.

Human interest angle. Appeal of the personal element, apart from the straight facts, of a given story.

INS International News Service.

Insert. Term used to cover material to be placed in the body of type already set.

Ital. Abbreviation for "italics."

Jump. Part of a story continued on another page. The lines telling where the jump is located are called the "jump lines" (e.g., "Continued on page 7, column 5"); and the headline over the continued part is called the "jump head."

Kill. (1) To decide not to use (hence to kill) a given story; (2) to discard type already in galley or page form; (3) to deface by striking with a hammer a type page so that it may not be used. The last situation occurs in the pressroom as pages are taken from the presses after a printing.

Label head.   Head that lacks life or originality. So called because it presents the appearance of having been seen, like a label, many times before.

Layout.   Same as "spread."

L.C.   Abbreviation for "lower case" letters.

Lead.   (1) (Rhymes with *feed*.) The introductory sentences of a story. (2) Rhymes with *bread*.) Space between lines—once provided by inserting pieces of metal between the lines of type.

Leaders.   Dots or other marks that lead the reader's attention across a column, as from a table entry to the number column in the table.

Legman.   See *District man*.

Library.   Newspaper repository for cuts, clippings, editions, reference material, etc., commonly needed. Also known as the "morgue."

Lobster trick.   See *Dog watch*.

Local.   (1) Sometimes a synonymn for "city," as "local room"; (2) a local story.

Localize.   To emphasize the local angle of a story.

Make-up.   The arrangement of material on a given page. The representative of the editorial departments in the composing room is the "make-up editor"; the composing-room employee who assembles and arranges the type is the "make-up man."

Masthead.   Information in every issue of every paper listing the place of publication, the top officials, and other pertinent facts about the newspaper. Usually on the editorial page.

Mat.   Abbreviation for "matrix."

Matrix.   (1) Brass mold used for type casting; (2) papier-mâché of fiber impression of a photoengraving or a page used in casting a stereotype plate.

M. E.   Abbreviation for "managing editor."

Mill-line rate.   Advertising rate per agate line per million copies circulated.

More.   Term written and encircled at the bottom of news sheets when copy extends over two or more pages. At the bottom of the last sheet, the writer uses one of the conventional signs (30, etc.) to indicate that copy has been completed.

Morgue.   See *Library*.

Must.   (1) Story which an executive decrees must be used; (2) employee whose rise is assured.

Name plate.   Large heading on page 1 which gives the paper's name.

News summary.   (1) Index or summary of the day's news; (2) wire-service round-up of the day's or the week's news.

Night side.   Term used to cover employees working the night shift.

Nonpareil.   (1) Old name for 6-point type (2) A unit of measurement equal to 6 points or one-half pica type; (2) a unit.

Obituary. Biography of a dead person, usually run at the time of the death. Also known as an "obit." Obituaries of well-known people are generally written in advance so that, in case of sudden death, they are ready for use.

Overline. Term used to denote "caption over a cut."

Overmatter. Synonymous with "overset."

Overset. Material set in type that cannot be used because the alotted space is already full. Synonymous terms are "overmatter" and "overs."

Pad. To make a story longer by padding it out.

Page proof. Proof of the entire page. Such a proof is rarely taken of news pages but is frequently pulled on feature material pages of the Sunday edition.

Photojournalism. Emphasis on pictures as a means of relating news.

Pi. Term used to denote type so badly jumbled as to be beyond use. Also spelled "pie."

Pic. Picture.

Pica. (1) Old name for 12-point type. (2) A unit of measurement equal to 12 points, about one-sixth of an inch.

Pick-up. Self-explanatory term used at close of newly set material to indicate that such material is to precede material already set. Thus, a new lead may read: "Pick up 'At the time the judge, etc.' " Abbreviated, P.U.

Pictorial journalism. Relating a story through a sequence of pictures.

Picture editor. The editor in charge of pictures. His duty may be simply to write the lines for all pictures used in the paper, or he may have further duties extending to being in charge of a corps of photographers.

Pig iron. (1) Heavy, serious material; (2) material that allows no opportunity for light treatment.

Pix. Pictures.

Plane. Wooden block used by the printer to make certain that the type surface of the page is smooth. The printer slides the block over the type, tapping the block lightly with a mallet.

Plate. Metal page made by the stereotype department to be placed on the presses. Thin aluminum sheet used in offset printing.

Play up. To emphasize an angle of a story or to emphasize any material that is being placed in print.

P. M. Paper that appears in the afternoon.

Point. Unit of type measurement, approximately one seventy-second of an inch.

Police blotter. Record kept in police station of arrests. The district man checks the police blotter for information.

Pork. (1) Material that can be saved from one edition to another; (2) material that can be prepared and saved for use at almost any time.

Precede. Material that precedes a story. Examples of precedes are late bulletins placed before stories already set in type, editors' notes, and explanations.

Q-A. Question and answer material. This kind of material is used in stories telling of extensive questioning. Examples are court proceedings, congressional investigation hearings, and lengthy interviews.

Quad. A space equal to 1 en, 1 em, or to 2 or more ems. See *Em, En.* Usually "em quad."

Query. (1) Question telephoned or teletyped to a newspaper by a correspondent asking whether a given story is wanted and the desired length; (2) question sent to a newspaper by one of its regular reporters about a story; (3) question received by mail from a reader and answered in print.

Quotes. (1) Synonym for "quotation marks"; (2) synonym for "direct quotations."

Rack. Cabinet used for the storage of type.

Read-in. Printed material, two or more columns wide, that reads into one column to the right.

Read-out. Printed material, two or more columns wide, that reads into one column to the left.

Release copy. Copy received by the newspaper to be held until a specified date. Examples of release copy are speeches of well-known people, wire-service feature stories, and important statements. The purpose of release copy is to enable the newspaper to have the material in type at the time of release.

Replate. Page of type that has been recast. The page is usually replated because a very important story or new development has been received after the page has been cast.

Revise. (1) To change a written account; (2) a second proof to check changes necessitated by errors shown in the first proof.

Rewrite. See Chapter 3 for a complete discussion.

Rim. Copy desk. See Chapter 7.

Ring. Synonymn for "encircle."

Ring machine. Linotype machine used for making corrections.

Ring man. Linotype operator or cold-type setter who makes corrections.

Roto. Abbreviation for "rotogravure."

Run. Synonymn for "use." Hence, to "run" a story is to use a story.

Run flat. Synonym for "use as is." Therefore, copy that is to be "run flat" is copy which is not to be changed.

Running story. Story sent to the composing room in parts. Hence, the story is "running" until all parts have been received.

Rush copy. Copy that is to take precedence in being set.

Sacred cows. Persons, groups, or institutions given special favorable treatment by a newspaper.

Schedule. List of stories. Every editor keeps a schedule for his department, and the slot man keeps a schedule for the copy desk.

Scoop. Story that is exclusively the property of one paper. This term is synonymous with "beat" and "exclusive."

Screamer. Large, bold headline covering all or nearly all of a page. This term is synonymous with "streamer" and "banner."

See copy. Self-explanatory direction placed on proof when an error is detected.

Sheet. Slang for "newspaper."

Short. Very brief story.

Shout. Printer's slang for "exclamation point."

Sked. Abbreviation for "schedule."

Skeletonize. To omit from wire copy words not necessary for understanding. Wire copy is skeletonized to save time and expense in transmission.

Slant. Angle or perspective taken on a story. Also, the practice of preparing magazine articles or other material with the purpose of submitting it to a specific publication. Hence, the material is slanted toward the particuular publication.

Slot. Section cut inward on the copy desk in which the head copy editor or "slot man" sits.

Slug. (1) Guideline or catchline name by which a story is known; (2) strip of metal used between lines of type to space it out.

Soc. Abbreviation for material for the "society" page.

Spike. To decide not to use a story. This term arises from the fact that usually the story is placed on the editor's spindle file.

Split page. Same as "break page."

Spot news. News which gives little or no forewarning of its occurrence. Examples of spot news are accidents, fires, and altercations.

Spread. Arrangement of material over two or more columns. Hence, a picture and a story over three columns are said to be a "three-column spread." This term frequently is used synonymously with "layout."

Squib. Very short news item; frequently used a a filler.

Standard type. Type of standard width; not condensed or extended.

Standing. Material kept in type because it is used frequently. Boxes are kept standing for such material as baseball statistics; some heads, such as the box head over the columnist's writings, are kept standing because they are used daily; many ads are kept standing because there is frequently little or no change.

Step lines. See *Drop lines*.

Stereotype. (1) Metal plate, usually semicylindrical, from which printing is done; it is cast from a *matrix* made from type or cuts assembled in a *chase*. (2) See *Bromide*.

Stet. Editor's or copyreader's order to the printer to "let it stand." If a correction is made and the editor or the copyreader decides to let the original material stand, he simply writes "stet" in the appropriate place.

Stick. Unit of measurement denoting about 2 inches of type.

Stone. Flat surface upon which the printer makes up the page.

Streamer. Same as "screamer" or "banner."

Stringer. A part-time employee who supplies news and other stories to the newspaper. He is usually paid on a per-story basis, but sometimes he works for a flat salary.

Stylebook. Principles, practices, and guidelines for preparing material for print. See Appendix I.

Supplementary story. Same as "follow."

Syndicate. Organization that sells feature material to the newspaper. Syndicates generally handle comics, columns, and other features.

Table. Term covering any tabular material printed.

Take. Small part of any story. Hence, a small part of the news story sent to the composing room is referred to as a "take."

Telephoto. Photograph sent by wire.

Thirty. The end. This term is often written "30" or "xxx" in a circle.

Tie-back. Part of a story that ties the story back to something already printed.

Tight. Having more news than is needed for a particular issue. Hence, on days when newsworthy events are plentiful, a paper is said to be "tight."

Time copy. Copy set in type to be held for future use. Hence, time copy is not limited severely by time.

Tombstone. Term used to cover a situation when identical heads appear side by side. The heads are said to "tombstone" each other.

Tr. Abbreviation used in proofreading for "transpose."

Trim. To reduce the length of a given story.

Turn. A story "turns" when it runs from the bottom of one column to a logical place in the next; or when it runs from the bottom of the last column on one page to the top of the first column on the next.

Type book. Book showing all the variations of type used by a given newspaper.

Underlines. Lines used beneath a cut. Synonymous with "cut lines."

UPI United Press International.

Up style. Style in which numerous words are capitalized. Its opposite, the "down" style, holds the use of capitals to a minimum.

Verse style. Style wherein copy is set in the manner of poetry.

Wooden head. Dull, lifeless head.

Wrong face, wrong font. Type used is not of the kind (family, size, etc.) specified.

Yellow journalism. Journalism which emphasizes the obscene, the risqué, the gory, the sensational.

APPENDIX
IV

The Basic Professional Library for the Journalist

REFERENCE BOOKS

The journalist, no matter how well informed, needs access to almost innumerable publications for general reference. There are too many of these for all to be listed in this appendix; many valuable collections of data must be omitted. Furthermore, few newspapers (and far fewer individuals) can own all of the publications listed below. Yet the person who works for any prolonged period in the world of journalism will use all of these publications at one time or another. Therefore, he must be thoroughly familiar with them.

In addition to the titles listed, the journalist should also have available those reference works that pertain to his local situation—city directories, local almanacs, school and college catalogs, and the like. The active and competent journalist will also expand his reference library by keeping abreast of authoritative new publications.

Atlases

American Guide Series
Rand, McNally Commercial Atlas and Marketing Guide
Rand, McNally Standard World Atlas

Biographical Sources

Authors Today and Yesterday
Current Biography
Dictionary of American Biography
Dictionary of National Biography (English)
Living Authors
Who's Who
Who Was Who
Who's Who in America (and its regional and special-category publications)
World Biography

Dictionaries

Many newspapers adopt a specific dictionary as part of their standard resources for style and spelling. Every writer or copy editor should have this dictionary at hand; usually the "college" version is best, being of handy size and adequate coverage. The newspaper should also have one or more full-scale ("unabridged") general dictionaries.

There are numerous good dictionaries. Among them are:

The American College Dictionary (Harper)
The American Heritage Dictionary
Collins' Authors' & Printers' Dictionary (Oxford)
The Oxford English Dictionary
The Random House Dictionary
The Thorndike-Barnhart Dictionaries
Webster's New World Dictionary (World Publishing Company) and its abridged editions
Webster's Third New International Dictionary (G. & C. Merriam Company) and its abridged editions

It is pertinent to mention that the Merriam Webster's Dictionaries specifically disclaim the function of giving authoritative guidance to usage.

The Oxford English Dictionary is one of the most magnificent dictionaries ever published but may be too strongly inclined toward British usage and toward high-level scholarly needs to serve routine journalistic functions. But for some uses it has no substitute.

Old dictionaries remain valuable, even when superseded by updated editions. However, they are probably better kept in the library than at the desk of the working journalist.

Directories and Indexes

Agricultural Index
Annual Magazine Subject Index
Broadcasting Yearbook
Editor & Publisher Yearbook
Engineering Index
Industrial Arts Index
New York Times Index
Ayer Directory of Publications
Reader's Guide to Periodical Literature

Encyclopedias

Columbia Encyclopedia
Encyclopædia Britannica
Encyclopedia Americana
New International Encyclopedia

English Usage and Vocabulary

American Dialect Dictionary
Dictionary of American English Usage
Dictionary of Modern English Usage
Thesaurus of English Words and Phrases

In addition, there are numerous acceptable handbooks of usage, frequently revised.

Facts

Associated Press Almanac
Facts on File
National Association of Broadcasters—Radio and Television Codes
Standard Dictionary of Facts
The World Almanac and Book of Facts

Proverbs and Quotations

Bartlett's Familiar Quotations
Benet's Readers' Encyclopedia
Everyman's Dictionary of Quotations and Proverbs
Stevenson's Home Book of Proverbs

Yearbooks

American Yearbook
Americana Annual
Economic Almanac
New International Year Book
Statistical Abstract

GENERAL RESOURCES

In addition to the suggested readings listed at the close of each chapter, the journalist should know certain publications of a general character which are not readily classifiable under any single heading. They are publications which treat so many phases of the world of mass communications that they cannot be placed easily into specific categories. Below is a list of this kind of publications.

Ayer Directory of Publications. Philadelphia, Pa.: Ayer Press. An annual directory containing extensive statistical treatments.

Editor & Publisher International Year Book. New York: Editor & Publisher. An annual work containing current information regarding many journalistic publications throughout the world.

Editor & Publisher—The Fourth Estate. New York: Editor & Publisher. A weekly publication concentrating on subjects within the fields of journalism and advertising.

Professional Periodicals. Most of the large universities offering a journalism major program (e.g., Missouri, Wisconsin) and several of the large organizations devoted to journalism education publish professional periodicals (e.g., *Journalism Quarterly*). These publications often carry valuable articles on many phases of the communications field.

Publisher's Weekly. New York: R. R. Bowker Co. A magazine containing articles of interest to writers and others in the communications field.

Standard Rate & Data Service Publications. Skokie, Ill.: Standard Rate & Data Service, Inc. Monthly figures and analyses in separate volumes for the newspaper, the magazine, radio, and television.

Ulrich's International Periodicals Directory. New York and London: R. R. Bowker Co. A bi-annual classified guide to current foreign and domestic periodicals.

Working Press of the Nation. Burlington, Iowa: National Research Bureau, Inc. Four directories published annually: newspaper and allied services directory; magazine and editorial directory; radio and television directory; feature writer and syndicate directory.

Index

Abbreviations, use of (stylebook), 345
Activists, in journalism, 57-58
Adams, Franklin P., 235, 236
Adams, Gibbs, 13⁻
Adolescents' magazines, 332, 333
Advertising, 16-17; in magazines, 17; in newspapers, 5, 200; on television, 5, 283 and *n*.
Advertising agencies, photographs supplied by, 129
Agate, 162, 163
Agnew, Spiro T., 10
Airbrushing of photographs, 121
American Bar Association, 8
American Civil Liberties Union, 13
American Medical Journal, 326
American Newspaper Publishers Association, 9
American Newspaper Publishers Research Institute, 133

American Opinion, 22
American Society of Newspaper Editors, 18*n*.
Anderson, Sherwood, 308
Announcement: and blend-out, 298; stationbreak, 297-98; sustaining, 297
Anti-Defamation League, 202
Arbitron (ARB), 284
Article(s) for magazines, 318-21; errors in, detection of, 321; finished copy for, 320-21; list of thoughts for, 318-19; markets for 315, 316-18; outline for, final, 319-20; personal-experience, 313; personality-sketch, 312-13; planning, 318-20; popularizing-facts, 313-14; rough draft and finished copy for, 320-21; utility, 315
Associated Press, 39, 128, 285
Astonisher lead, in newspaper feature story, 93

371

Atlantic Monthly, 304, 324, 325
Audience, mass, 15-17
Aware, Inc., 20 and *n.*

Baker, Bobby, 52
Baldwin, James, 308
Baltimore *Sun,* 197
Banner line, 147
Bay of Pigs invasion, 196
Berkeley *Barb,* 256
Berrigan, Philip, 137
Birch Society, John, 22
Black Panther Party, 13
Body: in editorial, 213, 214; in formal
    essay, 310; in magazine article, 319-20;
    in news story, 41-43
Boston Globe, 11, 183, 185, 243
Boston Herald American, 242
Breslin, Jimmy, 58
Brisbane, Arthur, 233
Bromides, avoidance of, 48
Broun, Heywood, 235
Buchwald, Art, 233, 235
Buckley, William F., 206, 233
"Bumping," among mass media, 4
Butts, Wally, 20
Byrne, W. M., Jr., 11*n.*

Cable television, 2, 23
Caen, Herb, 240
Caldwell, Earl, 13
Capitalization, instructions for (style-
    book), 348
Capsule (cartridge) lead, in newspaper
    feature story, 94
Cather, Willa, 321
Central Intelligence Agency, 196
Chicago Sun, 192
Chicago Tribune, 39, 200
Children's magazines, 332, 333
China, 10
Christian Science Monitor, 28, 220
Chronological method, for writing body of
    news story, 42
Cobb, Irvin S., 235
College paper, *see* School paper
Collier's magazine, 304, 330

Colored news, 51, 52, 57*n.*
Columbia Broadcasting System, 12, 19
    and *n.*
Columbia Journalism Review, 59*n.*
Column, 206-07, 232-45; anecdotal style
    in, 239-40; attracting readers to,
    235-37; authority in, note of, 236-37;
    departmental style in, 240-41; examples
    of, 237-44 *passim;* gossip, 207, 234;
    humorous, 235, 236; nonsyndicated,
    232; originality in, 235; and personality,
    attractive, 236; philosophic, 234-35;
    question-and-answer style in, 243-44;
    readers attracted to, 235-37; reflective,
    234, 237; scoop by, 236; sources of
    material for, 234-35; specialized, 234
    and *n.*; style of, 237-44; syndicated, 232,
    234, 236, 237; unified style in, 237-39;
    unrelated-facts style in, 241-42
Commentary, on radio and television,
    295-97
Communications, mass, *see* Mass com-
    munications
Compound-sentence lead, in newspaper
    feature story, 95
Continuities, program, 288-95
Contrast lead, in newspaper feature story,
    93
Copy editor, 133, 134-59 *passim;* accu-
    racy checked by, 137; brevity sought
    by, 136; functions of, 135-38; headlines
    written by, *see* Headline(s); and libel,
    guarding against, 136-37; readability
    sought by, 135; and style of newspaper,
    137-38; symbols used by, 138-46; and
    tone of story, keeping high, 138
Copy pencil, 139
Copyright law, 314
Cousins, Norman, 225*n.*
Cropping of photographs, 121, 123
CRT (cathode ray tube), 133
Crume, Paul, 239
Culture, mass, and mass communications,
    2-3
Cut lines, 53-56

Daley, Richard, 45*n.*
Dallas *News,* 197

Death notices, 38
Decker, Bernard M., 22
Defamation, defined, 20
Defense Department, U.S., 12
Definition lead, in newspaper feature story, 94
Dependent-clause lead, in newspaper feature story, 95
Detective story, 309
Dialogue lead, in newspaper feature story, 94
Dickens, Charles, 307
Dickinson, Larry, 13
Direct address lead, in newspaper feature story, 94-95
District reporter, 35
Doyle, A. Conan, 309
Dulles, John Foster, 10

Editor: copy, *see* Copy editor; picture, 113, 114; telegraph, 159; whims of, and editorial policy, 203
Editorial(s), 212-31; aggressiveness of, 227, 228; authority in, note of, 227, 229; body in, 213, 214; to call attention to a wrong, 222; classification of, 220-27; to comment lightly on news, 226-27; conclusion of, 213; to congratulate or praise, 224; consistency in, 220, 227, 228; defined, 212-13; dignity in, 227, 229; editorial essay presented in, 225-26; and editorial policy, effect of, 206; to enlighten readers, 223; examples of, 213-27 *passim;* guiding points for writing, 227-29; to help a cause, 223-24; to influence opinion, 221-22; language of, 217-20; lead of, 213, 214, 215, 216; to praise or congratulate, 224; and thinking issue through, 227, 228; tone of, 217, 219; writing, 213-20, 227-29; *see also* Editorial policy
Editorial policy, 190-211; business considerations in, 200, 204; columnist's relationship to, 206-07; conditions affecting, 191-92; crusades affecting, 205-06; and editorial, effect on, 206; ethnic and social considerations in, 201-02; finances affecting, 192-93;

group and personal considerations in, 203; patriotic considerations in, 202-03; personal and group considerations in, 203; and political outlook, 199-200; publisher's influence on, 205; readers' demands affecting, 198-99; religious considerations in, 201; and responsibilities of press, *see* Responsibilities of press; and sectionalism, 203-04; social and ethnic considerations in, 201-02; and taboos, 205; and tone of newspaper, 197-98; and whims of editor, 203; *see also* Editorial(s)
Eisenhower, Dwight D., 10
Electronic media: *see* Radio; Television
Ellsberg, Daniel, 11 and *n.*
Epigram lead, in newspaper feature story, 93
Ervin, Sam, Jr., 52
Espionage Act (1917), 8
Esquire magazine, 309, 331
Essay, 310-12
Euphemisms, avoidance of, 49

Fairness Doctrine, 24
Farm Journal, 328
Fashion magazine, 332
Faulk, John Henry, 20
Faulkner, William, 308
Feature story, newspaper, *see* Newspaper feature story
Federal Communications Commission, 19, 275
Field & Stream, 317
Figurative lead, in newspaper feature story, 93
First Amendment, 8, 9, 12, 13
Formal essay, 310-11
Freedom of expression, in mass media, 8-14
Futures file, 36

Gallup poll, 199
Genessee Farmer, 327
Gertz, Elmer, 22
Gertz v. Welch, 22
Ghost writer, 306*n.,* 326

Godey, L. A., 331
Godey's Lady's Book, 331
Golden, Harry, 235
Good Housekeeping magazine, 331
Government: and mass media, 3, 8-13 *passim,* 273-74; responsibility to, of press, 195-97

Hamilton, Alexander, quoted, 310, 311
Handouts, 37
Harper's Bazaar, 331
Harper's Magazine, 302-03, 317, 324, 325
Harper's Weekly, 206
Harris Poll, 17, 196*n.*, 199
Hawthorne, Nathaniel, 307
Headline(s), 138, 147-59, 160-61; abbreviations used in, 148-49; attractive, 147-48; axis, 156; with banks, 157-58, 159; copy for, 158, 159; counting process for, 153-55; crossline, 157; dropline, 155; examples of, 150-51, 152-53, 155, 156, 157, 158; exceptional, 151-53; for feature stories, 149; flush left, 156; full-line, 155; functions of, 147-48; with hanging indent, 156; and hed sked, 147, 158-59, 160-61; importance of story indicated by, 147; inverted pyramid, 155-56; jump, 157; keyline, 157; kinds of, 155-58; letter or number codes for, 147; and make-up, 181; number or letter codes for, 147; and overline, 157; pyramid, inverted, 155-56; readability of, 149, 150; reader attracted by, 147-48; stepped-line, 155; and subheads, 158; for summarizing story, 147, 149; and synonyms, command of, 148; and vocabulary, command of, 149; writing, 148-51
Hearst newspapers, 197
Hed sked, 147, 158-59, 160-61
Hefner, Hugh, 331, 332
Hemingway, Ernest, 308
Henry, O., 321
Highlight method, for writing body of news story, 41-42
Hooper agency, 284
House organ, 248 and *n.*

Humorous lead, in newspaper feature story, 94
Humphrey, Hubert H., 18

Infinitive lead, in newspaper feature story, 95
Informal essay, 311
Interpretative reporting, 28*n.*, 56-59
Interview(s), 70-82; and favorable impression upon interviewee, 71; for feature story, 74-75, 78-82; kinds of, 74-76; and knowledge of subject, reporter's, 73; note taking during, 76-77; preinterview contact before, 73; preparation for, 73; reader's questions asked during, 72; recorder used during, 77-78; requisites for successful, 71-73; and routine, avoidance of, 72-73; for society page, 76; of sports figures, 75; for straight-news story, 74; technique for, appropriate, 71-72; of theater-connected persons, 75-76
Investigative reporting, 32, 205

John Birch Society, 22
Johnson, Lyndon B., 10, 52
Journalism: activist, 57-58; defined within context of mass communications, 1-2; electronic-media and print, 2; as "fourth branch of government," 13; and freedom of expression, 8-14; and library for journalist, basic professional, 367-70; new, 58, 59 and *n.*; pictorial: *see* Photographs; Press photographer(s); print and electronic-media, 2; professionalism in, 5; recent developments in, 4-5; visual: *see* Photographs; Press photographer(s); yellow, 197; *see also* Magazines; Mass communications; Newspapers
"Journalistic style," 56
Justice Department, U.S., 9

Kansas City Star, 206
Kastenmeier, Robert, 14
Kennedy, John F., 10, 52, 273*n.*

Kissinger, Henry, 196
Kraft, Joseph, 18

Ladies' Home Journal, 331
Lamb, Charles, 311
Lead(s): in editorial, 213, 214, 215, 216; in feature story, 92-95; grammatical structures in, 95; literary devices in, 92-95; in news story, 39-41
Lerner, Max, 206
Letterpress, defined, 132
Libel, 20 and *n.*, 21, 22, 30, 313; copy editor's duty to guard against, 136-37; defined, 20, 21; in photography, 109-10, 112
Liberty magazine, 330
Library, basic professional, for journalist, 367-70
Life magazine, 304
Lippmann, Walter, 233, 235
Literary agents, 321-22
Look magazine, 304
Los Angeles Times, 39

MacArthur, Douglas, 137
MacLeish, Archibald, 311
Mademoiselle magazine, 332
Magazines, 3, 4, 5, 23, 302-03; adolescents' and children's, 332-33; advertising in, 17; article(s) for, *see* Article(s) for magazines; business, 326-27; changes in, 304, 324-25; children's and adolescents', 332-33; company, 303, 329; do's and don'ts of submitting manuscripts to, 322-23; essays in, 310-12; farm, 327-29; free, 334; giveaway, 334; kinds of, 302-03, 323-34; libel suits against, 313; and literary agents, 321-22; literary forms in writing for, 306-16; as markets for manuscripts, 305-06, 316-18; men's, 331-32; number of, 2; personal-experience accounts for, 313; personality sketches for, 312-13; poetry for, 315-16; popular, 330; popularizing-facts articles for, 313-14; professional, 326; pulp, 303; quality, 316, 325-26; salability of manuscript for, 305-06, 316-18; scholarly, 303, 316; short stories for, *see* Short Stories; special-interest, 329-30; Sunday-supplement, 333; technical, 327; throwaway, 334; utility articles for, 315; verse for, 315, 316; women's, 331; writing for, 302-36 *passim*
Mailer, Norman, 58
Make-up, 168-89; and accentuation, 181-82; as art, 168-69; attractiveness of, 169-70; balanced, 169, 171, 172; broken-column, 175-77, 181; and clarity, 182; examples of, 183-88; and headlines, 181; horizontal, 175, 176; individuality of, 183; inside-page, 182; inverted pyramid, 171, 173; and news value, 182; panel, 175, 178-79; patterns of, using, 179-80; and position, 181; poster, 179, 180; principles of, 169-71; pyramid, inverted, 171, 173; readability of, 169, 170-71; section, 182-83; for tabloids, 179; unbalanced, 175-79; weighted, 172-74
"Managed news," 10
Mansfield, Katherine, 309
Mass audience, 15-17
Mass communications: adverse criticism of, 3-4, 17-19; audience for, mass, 15-17; competition among, 4-5, 14-15; and culture, mass, 2-3; defined, 1-2; and freedom of expression, 8-14; and government, 3, 8-13 *passim,* 273-74; influence and role of, 2; issues in, recent, 7-25; mass audience for, 15-17; and mass culture, 2-3; and prestige, 17-20; professionalism in, 5; recent developments in, 4-5; recent issues in, 7-25; role and influence of, 2; value of, 3-4; *see also* Magazines; Newspapers; Radio; Television
Mass culture, and mass communications, 2-3
Mass media, *see* Mass communications
Media: electronic: *see* Radio; Television; mass, *see* Mass communications
Mencken, H. L., 236
Miller, D. Thomas, 19*n.*; quoted, 19
Milwaukee Sentinel, 200
Monahan, D. Leo, 242
Montazzoli, John, 204

MOR radio stations, 284
Ms. magazine, 331*n.*

NAACP, 202
Nasby, Petroleum Vesuvius, 233*n.*
National Education Association Journal, 326
National Geographic Magazine, 314
National Recovery Act (1933), 9
National security, and news sources, 10, 11, 12
Nation's Business, 327
New England Homestead, 328
New journalism, 58, 59 and *n.*
New York *Daily News,* 28
New York *Herald-Tribune,* 192
New York Times, 11, 13, 18, 39, 58, 179, 187, 188, 196, 197, 200, 206, 220
New York Times Company v. Sullivan, 21-22
New York World, 8, 206
New Yorker magazine, 309, 324
News services, 38-39, 159, 162, 284
News story, newspaper, *see* Newspaper news story
Newscasts, 278-86; and audience demands, determining, 283-84; objectivity in, 282-83; preparation of, 280-83; recognizing news for, 279; specialized, 284-86; of sports, 285; structure of, 280-81; style of, 281-82; vocabulary in, 282; women's, 284-85
Newscasts on radio, 4, 14, 278*ff.*; and television newscasts, differences between, 286-87
Newscasts on television, 15, 22, 278*ff.*; and radio newscasts, differences between, 286-87
Newspaper copy editing, *see* Copy editor
Newspaper feature story, 83-105; abilities needed for writing, 86-90; on arts and crafts, 92; defined, 83-85; about dramatic situation, 91; examples of, 95-102; facts popularized in, 92; as guidance story, 91; headline for, 149; interviewing techniques for, 74-75, 78-82; leads in, 92-95; personal experience related in, 91-92; popularization of facts in, 92;

seasonal, 91; sources of, 90-92; and straight news, 84-85, 90; as supplementary story, 91; unusual type of, 90; as utility article, 92
Newspaper news story, 26-69; accuracy of, 28, 30, 34, 47-48; body in, 41-43; choice of words in, 45-46, 51; clarity of, 31, 44; coherence of, 45, 46; coloring, 51, 52, 57*n.*; conciseness of, 43-44; and controversy, 28-29, 57-58; and cut lines, 53-56; dictional don'ts for, 48-49; examples of, 59-64; finding, 29-39; forceful expression in, 45-47; handling of, 31; lead in, 39-41; names in, importance of, 34; from other newspapers and newscasts, 38; reader interest in, 27; recency of, 28; recognition of, reporter's, 30-31; rewriting, 49-51; slanting, 51, 52, 57*n.*; sources of, 32, 35-39; structure and writing of, 39-43; style of, 43-49; and unsolicited calls, 38; unusualness in, 28; writing and structure of, 39-43; *see also* Interpretative reporting; Investigative reporting; Journalism; Reporter
Newspapers, 3, 4, 5, 7, 14, 15, 17; advertising in, 5, 200; circulation of, combined, 2, 23; and controversial aspects of news, 29; copy editing of, *see* Copy editor; crusades by, 205-06; distrust of, 17, 19; editorial policy of, *see* Editorial policy; feature story in, *see* Newspaper feature story; finances of, 192-93; and freedom of expression, 8-12 *passim;* future of, 22-24; headlines in, see Headline(s); and libel, *see* Libel; make-up for, *see* Make-up; mergers of, 23; news story in, *see* Newspaper news story; number of, 2; photography in: *see* Photographs; Press photographer(s); and prestige, 17, 18*n.*; radio and television stations owned by, 23-24; readers' demands on, 198-99; responsibilities of, *see* Responsibilities of press; school, *see* School paper; stylebooks of, 137, 147, 158, 191, 339-51; and taboos, 205; television and radio stations owned by, 23-24; tone of, 197-98; *see also* Journalism

Newsweek, 45*n.,* 256
Nixon, Richard M., 10, 18 and *n.,* 52, 137, 194
Nonpareil type, 163

OCR (optical character recognition), 133
Offset, defined, 132-33
Ohio Farmer, 328
Oswald, Lee Harvey, 273*n.*
Overstatements, avoidance of, 48-49

Panama Canal, 8
Parody lead, in newspaper feature story, 93
Participial lead, in newspaper feature story, 95
Pentagon Papers, 11, 12, 13, 196, 215
Personality sketch, 312-13
Personification, overworked, avoidance of, 49
Philadelphia *Evening Bulletin,* 19-20, 220
Phoenix, The, 256
Photocomposition, 133-34
Photographer(s): amateur, 128, 129; commercial, 128, 129; free-lance, 129; press, *see* Press photographer(s)
Photographs: accuracy in, 117-18; of activities interesting to readers, 118, 119; airbrushing, 121; attractive, importance of, 118, 119; clarity of detail in, 117; color and tone contrasts in, 117; composition of, 116, 117; cropping, 121, 123; emphasis in, 116-17; of events witnessed by readers, 118, 119; of familiar persons and sights, appeal of, 118-19; feature-story appeal of, 118; functions of, 114-15; improvement techniques applied to, 119-23; information disseminated by, 118, 119; in newspaper operation, 113-15; and picture editor, 113, 114; qualities of effective, 116-19; representative, 123-28; retouching, 121, 123; sources of, 128-29; and "thirds" for effective placement, 116, 117 and *n.*; tone and color contrasts in, 117; *see also* Press photographer(s)

Pica, 163
Pictorial journalism: *see* Photographs; Press photographer(s)
Pittsburgh Press, 183, 186
Playboy magazine, 331, 332 and *n.*
Poetry, for magazines, 315-16
Points, type size measured in, 162-63
Police, and reporter, 33
Polish National Alliance, 202
Popular Mechanics magazine, 332
Post Office Department, U.S., 9
Prepositional lead, in newspaper feature story, 95
Press: *see* Journalism; Magazines; Mass communications; Newspapers
Press photographer(s), 106-13; in courtroom, 108; and feeling for pictures, 107; and handling people, ability for, 107; as journalist, 112; and libel, knowledge of, 109-10, 112; originality of, 109; qualities needed by, 107, 109, 112; specialties of, 113; technical ability of, 107; women, 113; *see also* Photographs
Privacy, invasion of, 21, 22, 78
Program continuities, 288-95
Proofreading, 352-54
Proxmire, William, 24
Public domain, 314
Public-relations agencies, photographs supplied by, 128, 129
Publicity releases, 37-38
Pulitzer, Joseph, 8
Pulse agency, 284
Pun lead, in newspaper feature story, 94
Punctuation marks, instructions for (stylebook), 340-45
Pyle, Ernie, 236
Pyramid method, for writing body of news story, 42-43

Question lead, in newspaper feature story, 93
Quotation lead, in newspaper feature story, 94

Radio, 3, 4, 14, 15, 17, 23; announcement on, *see* Announcement; back-

Radio (*continued*)
  ground of, 271-73; commentary on,
  295, 296; editorials on, 288; extemporaneous remarks on, 298-99; and listening time, average, 272; music programs on, 273; newscasts on: *see* Newscasts; Newscasts on radio; and number
  of stations, 2; talk shows on, 273; writing for, 275, 276, 277, 278, 296,
  297-99; *see also* Program continuities
Ramparts, 256
Rand Corporation, 11
Rather, Dan, 18*n*.
Reader's Digest, 304, 324
Reasoner, Harry, 18
Redbook, 331
Reflective essay, 311-12
Religion, and editorial policy, 201
Reporter, 29-36; accuracy of, 28, 30, 34,
  47-48; and adjusting approach, 31-32;
  and area, knowledge of, 33-34; clarity
  of expression by, 31, 44; contacts built
  by, 33; district, 35; editorializing by,
  avoidance of, 34, 49; general-
  assignment, 36; handling of story by,
  31; improvement of, constant effort toward, 34; ingenuity of, 32; names
  checked by, 32-33; and names in story,
  importance of, 34; and news sources,
  knowledge of, 32; personality of, pleasing, 31; and police, retaining favor of,
  33; promises respected by, 33; and quotations, accuracy in handling, 34; and
  recognition of news story, 30-31; respect of, for journalism, 34; and rivals,
  working agreement with, 34; roving,
  36; special-assignment, 35-36; speed
  of, 32; *See also* Interpretative reporting;
  Investigative reporting; Journalism;
  Newspaper news story
Reporter as Artist, The (Weber, ed.), 58*n*.
Responsibilities of press: to government,
  195-97; to individuals, 194-95; to society, 193-94
Reston, James, 18, 233
Retouching of photographs, 121, 123
Rewriting, 49-51
Rim men, 134
Rogers, Will, 233, 235

Roosevelt, Franklin D., 9
Roosevelt, Theodore, 8
Roving reporter, 36
Ruby, Jack, 273*n*.
Russo, A. J., 11*n*.

St. Louis Post-Dispatch, 28, 39, 158, 179
SALT (Strategic Arms Limitation Treaty),
  196
San Francisco Chronicle, 179, 240
Saturday Evening Post, 20, 304 and *n*.,
  330
Saturday Review, 225*n*., 256*n*., 303-04,
  325
School paper, 246-70; and administration,
  conflict between, 257, 258; advertising
  in, 252; and adviser's problems and
  responsibilities, 258-61; basics for,
  246-48; business manager of, 250; censorship of, 247 and *n*., 248; and
  changes, recent, in coverage by,
  257-58; classroom as news source for,
  265; column in, 268-69; coming events
  covered by, 262-64; and co-operation,
  how to gain, 260; editor of, 250; editorial in, 269; and exchange publications,
  260; faculty responsibility for, 259-60;
  feature stories in, 266-68; financial situation of, 251-52, 258; instruction in
  writing for, 255, 259; interviews published in, 268; libel suits against, 257,
  258; literary forms in, usual, 261; merit
  system for selections to staff positions
  on, 258-59; news for, sources of,
  261-68; operation of, 248-49; past
  events covered by, 264-65; personnel
  and staff of, 249-51, 258-59; pictures
  in, 261; polls of student opinion published in, 268; and press association
  conferences, 260; prestige of, 259, 260;
  problems of, 249-55; schedules for,
  255; and scrapbook, keeping of, 260;
  sources of news for, 261-68; sports covered by, 263, 265-66; staff and personnel of, 249-51, 258-59; subscriptions to, 252; time, adequate, for adviser of, 260; and underground press,
  255-57; variety in, ways to gain, 260;

what and what not to print in, 252-55; writing for, instruction in, 255, 259

Schrank, Jeffrey, 19*n*.; quoted, 19

Schweiker, Richard, 18

Scott, Hugh, 137

Scribner's magazine, 325

Scuba magazine, 332

Sedition Act (1918), 8

"Selling of the Pentagon," 12, 13

Shield laws, 13-14

Short stories, 306-10; markets for, 310; types of, 308-10

Siegel, Albert E., 19

Simons, Howard, 18

Slander, defined, 20

Slanted news, 51, 52, 57*n*.

Slice-of-life short story, 309

Slot man, 134, 135, 138

Smith, Red, 233

Sons of Italy, 202

Southern Planter, 328

Soviet Union, 196

Space writer, 38

Sports Illustrated, 313, 330

Sportscast, 285

Staggers, Harley O., 12

Standard Rate and Data Service, 23

Stanton, Frank, 12

State Department, U.S., 10, 196

Station-break announcement, 297-98

Stegner, Wallace, 311

Stephens, James, 309

Stevenson, Robert Louis, 307

Streamer, 147

Stringer, 37, 38

Stylebook, newspaper, 137, 147, 158, 191, 339-51

Sullivan, L. B., 21, 22

Sunday-supplement magazines, 333

Supreme Court, U.S., 8, 9, 11, 13, 21, 22, 78, 257

Suspended-interest lead, in newspaper feature story, 93

Symbols, copy editor's, 138-46

Tabloids, 26, 27, 28, 191, 197, 198, 220; make-up for, 179

Talese, Gay, 58

Taylor, Bert Leston, 237*n*.

Tebbel, John, 256*n*.

Telegraph editor, 159

Teletype machine, 23

Television, 3, 4, 7, 14, 15, 17, 22, 23; advertising on, 5, 283 and *n*.; announcement on, *see* Announcement; background of, 273-75; cable, 2, 23; commentary on, 295, 296; criticism of, 274-75; editorials on, 287-88; extemporaneous remarks on, 298-99; impact of, on American Life and thought, 273; newscasts on: *see* Newscasts; Newscasts on television; and number of network-affiliated stations, 2; and President, U.S., 273-74; and prestige, 17, 18-19; violence on, 18, 19; writing for, 275, 276, 277, 278, 296, 297-99; *see also* Program continuities

Theatre Arts magazine, 329

Time magazine, 18, 313

Tipster, 36-37

Titles, instructions for use of (stylebook), 346-48

Trading with the Enemy Act (1917), 8

Traditional short story, 308-09

Truman, Harry S., 137

TV Guide, 304, 329 and *n*.

Tweed, Boss, and Tammany, 206

Type: families of, 162, 163; heaviness of, 162, 164; size of, 162-63

Underground press, 255-57, 334

United Press International, 39, 128

Utility article: for magazine, 315; as newspaper feature story, 92

U-2 flights, over Soviet Union, 196

Verse, for magazines, 315, 316

Vietnam War, 11, 194, 233, 274 and *n*.

Visual journalism: *see* Photographs; Press photographer(s)

Wall Street Journal, 256

Ward, Artemus, 233*n*.

Washington Post, 11, 17, 18, 179, 196

Watergate story, 17, 18, 137, 194
Weber, Ronald, 58*n.*
West, E. Gordon, 13
White, E. B., 311
White, William Allen, 205, 235
White House staff, handouts by, 37
Wilmington (Delaware) *Evening Journal,*
    183, 184, 200
Wilmington (Delaware) *Morning News,*
    200
Wire editor, 159
Wire services, 38-39, 159, 162, 284

Wolfe, Thomas C., 309
Wolfe, Tom, 58
Woman's Day magazine, 334
Women's-liberation movement, 284*n.,*
    331*n.*
World War II, 236

Yellow journalism, 197

Zampano, Robert C., 257*n.*